T0326385

Integrating Business Management Processes

Integrating Business Management Processes

Volume 1: Management and Core Processes

Dr. Titus De Silva, PhD

Consultant, Pharmacy Practice, Quality Management, Food Safety

BSc (Chemistry), BSc (Pharmacy) Hons. Post-graduate Dipl (Computer Sci), MBA, PhD, CChem, FRSC, MRPharms, MPS

Routledge
Taylor & Francis Group

A PRODUCTIVITY PRESS BOOK

First published 2021
by Routledge
52 Vanderbilt Avenue, New York, NY 10017

and by Routledge
2 Park Square, Milton Park, Abingdon, Oxon, OX14 4RN

Routledge is an imprint of the Taylor & Francis Group, an informa business

Library of Congress Cataloging-in-Publication Data
A catalog record for this title has been requested

ISBN: 978-0-367-48549-8 (hbk)
ISBN: 978-0-367-52954-3 (pbk)
ISBN: 978-1-003-04282-2 (ebk)

Typeset in Garamond
by codeMantra

This book is dedicated to my two loving grandchildren, Stella Maya De Silva (7) and Leonardo Enzo De Silva (4) in Oxford (UK) who lighted my life in my twilight years.

Contents

List of Figures xxi
List of Tables xxiii
List of Forms...xxvii
Disclaimer xxix
Foreword..xxxi
Review of Integrating Business Management Processes, Volumes 1, 2 and 3....................xxxiii
Preface xxxv
Acknowledgements xxxvii
Review..xxxix
Author.. xli

SECTION I   MANAGEMENT PROCESSES

1 History of Management Systems...3
  1.1   Quality Management 3
  1.2   Food Safety 7
         1.2.1   Pre-refrigeration Era... 7
         1.2.2   Refrigeration Era... 8
         1.2.3   HACCP Era... 8
  1.3   Environmental Management 10
         1.3.1   Montreal Protocol..13
         1.3.2   Kyoto Protocol 13
         1.3.3   Carbon Footprint...13
  References 14

2 Impact of Management Systems on Business Performance.....................17
  2.1   Introduction 17
  2.2   Impact of Quality Management Systems..17
         2.2.1   Case Study – Motorola...20
         2.2.2   Case Study – Xerox.. 22
  2.3   Impact of Food Safety Management Systems 23
         2.3.1   Impact of Food Safety System on the Environment 27
         2.3.2   Barriers to Implementation 27
         2.3.3   Case Study – Implementation of HACCP System in an Airline
                    Catering Company 27
                    2.3.3.1   Plan Development.. 28
                    2.3.3.2   Plan Implementation... 29

     2.3.3.3 Certification..29

   2.3.4 Case Study – Implementation of HACCP System in a Pasteurised
     Milk Plant..29

 2.4 Impact of Environmental Management Systems.....................................30

   2.4.1 Case Study – Implementation of EMS on Gastonia
     Water Treatment Division..32

     2.4.1.1 Planning and Implementation...................................32

     2.4.1.2 Continual Improvement Programme 33

   2.4.2 Case Study – Implementation of EMS in Novozymes
     North America Inc...34

     2.4.2.1 Background..34

     2.4.2.2 Planning and Implementation...................................34

     2.4.2.3 Continual Improvement..36

 References 36

3 Strategic Planning...39

 3.1 Introduction 39

 3.2 Definition 39

 3.3 Aims of Strategic Planning 39

 3.4 Benefits of Strategic Planning 40

   3.4.1 Improvement of Focus 40

   3.4.2 Improvement of Teamwork to Achieve Goals................................40

 3.5 Progressive Evolution of Strategic Planning 40

 3.6 Strategic Planning Process 40

   3.6.1 Initiate and Agree on a Strategic Planning Process.......................42

   3.6.2 Identify Organisational Mandates 42

   3.6.3 Clarify Organisation's Mission and Values...................................42

     3.6.3.1 Create a Mission...42

   3.6.4 Assess External and Internal Environment...................................43

     3.6.4.1 External Analysis 43

     3.6.4.2 Internal Analysis 43

   3.6.5 Identify the Strategic Issues...43

   3.6.6 Formulate Strategies..44

     3.6.6.1 Development of Strategies...44

     3.6.6.2 Three Aspects of the Strategy 45

   3.6.7 Review and Audit the Plan..47

   3.6.8 Establish a Vision..47

     3.6.8.1 Vision Statement 48

   3.6.9 Develop an Implementation Plan...48

   3.6.10 Strategy-Focused Organisation: Balanced Score Card...................49

     3.6.10.1 Principle 1..49

     3.6.10.2 Principle 2..49

     3.6.10.3 Principle 3..49

     3.6.10.4 Principle 4..49

     3.6.10.5 Principle 5..50

   3.6.11 Final Assessment...52

     3.6.11.1 Frequency of Monitoring and Evaluation.................52

     3.6.11.2 Monitoring Reports 52
     3.6.11.3 Deviations from the Plan 52
     3.6.11.4 Changing the Plan 52
 3.7 Failure of Strategy Implementation 53
 References 54

4 Risk Management 57
 4.1 Introduction 57
 4.2 The Evolution of Risk Management 58
 4.3 Terminology 59
 4.4 Benefits of Risk Management 59
 4.5 Nature of Risk 60
   4.5.1 Business Risks 61
   4.5.2 Environmental Risks.. 62
   4.5.3 Food Safety Risks 63
 4.6 Principles of Risk Management 63
 4.7 Categories of Risk..65
   4.7.1 Preventable Risks 65
   4.7.2 Strategy Risks 66
   4.7.3 External Risks.. 66
   4.7.4 Pure versus Speculative Risk Exposures 66
 4.8 Components of Enterprise Risk Management 66
 4.9 Planning for Risk Management 67
 4.10 Risk Management Plan 68
 4.11 Identifying Risks 69
   4.11.1 Techniques for Identifying Risks 69
 4.12 Assessment of Risk 70
   4.12.1 Risk Tolerance 70
   4.12.2 Assessment of Likelihood and Impact 70
   4.12.3 Risk Descriptors... 70
 4.13 Control and Treatment of Risks 72
   4.13.1 Evaluation of Controls 73
   4.13.2 Evaluation of Treatments 73
   4.13.3 Risk Treatment Options 73
 4.14 Planning for Business Continuity 74
 4.15 Measure, Monitor and Control..76
 4.16 Learning and Reporting Risk 77
 4.17 Implementation of Risk Management Plan 77
 4.18 Creating a Risk-Aware Culture.. 77
 4.19 Problems of Managing Risk Plans 78
 4.20 Guidelines for Successful Risk Management 80
 References 81

5 Good Manufacturing Practice 85
 5.1 Introduction 85
 5.2 GMP Activities..85
 5.3 GMP Philosophy 86
 5.4 Foundation of GMP 87

	5.4.1	Effective Manufacturing Operations	87
	5.4.2	Effective Food Control	87
	5.4.3	Management Controls	87
5.5	The Preliminary Process		88
5.6	GMP Requirements		88
	5.6.1	Organisation and Personnel	90
	5.6.2	Training and Personnel Hygiene	90
		5.6.2.1 Recruitment and Induction	90
		5.6.2.2 Competence and Training	90
		5.6.2.3 Food Hygiene Requirements	91
	5.6.3	Building and Facilities	91
	5.6.4	Cleaning and Sanitation	91
		5.6.4.1 Method of Sanitising	92
		5.6.4.2 Cleaning Methods	92
		5.6.4.3 Sanitisation Methods	92
	5.6.5	Equipment	93
	5.6.6	Production and Process Control	93
	5.6.7	Warehousing and Distribution	94
	5.6.8	Storage and Distribution	94
		5.6.8.1 Storage	95
		5.6.8.2 Distribution	95
	5.6.9	Defect Action Levels	95
5.7	Food Safety Requirements		95
5.8	ISO 22000 Standard, ISO 9001 Standard, GMP and HACCP System		96
5.9	Benefits of GMP		96
References			97

SECTION II   CORE PROCESSES

6	**Purchasing**		**101**
6.1	Historical Aspects		101
6.2	Definitions		102
6.3	Objectives of Purchasing		103
	6.3.1	Product	103
	6.3.2	Cost	103
	6.3.3	Supplier	104
	6.3.4	Others	104
6.4	Features of Purchasing and Supply Organisations		104
	6.4.1	Small Organisation Producing a Single Product, e.g. Fruit Picking and Packing	104
	6.4.2	Assembly Industry, e.g. Motor Car Industry	104
	6.4.3	Manufacturing Industry, e.g. Plastic Bottle Industry	105
	6.4.4	Processing Industry, e.g. Wine Industry	105
	6.4.5	Mining Industry, e.g. Gold, Coal, Oil Industries	105
	6.4.6	Wholesalers and Retailers, e.g. Pharmaceutical Wholesalers, Supermarkets	105
	6.4.7	Service Industry, e.g. Medical Service	105

	6.4.8	Public Sector, e.g. Departments, Health Authorities, Municipal Authorities	106
	6.4.9	Multifunctional Organisations, e.g. Ford Motor Company, Sony	106
6.5	Types of Purchases		106
	6.5.1	Raw Materials	106
	6.5.2	Semi-Finished Items and Components	106
	6.5.3	Finished Products	106
	6.5.4	Items for Maintenance and Repair	107
	6.5.5	Production Support Items	107
	6.5.6	Services	107
	6.5.7	Capital Equipment	107
	6.5.8	Transportation	107
	6.5.9	Outsourcing	107
6.6	Centralised Versus Decentralised Purchasing		108
6.7	Purchasing Strategy		108
6.8	Purchasing Process		110
6.9	Approval of Suppliers		110
	6.9.1	The Process	111
		6.9.1.1 Categorical Plan	113
		6.9.1.2 Weighted Point Plan	113
6.10	Contract		113
6.11	Green or Sustainable Procurement		115
	6.11.1 Green Products		115
	6.11.2 Checklist for Procurement		115
6.12	Procurement of Products for Food Processing		116
6.13	e-Procurement		116
	6.13.1 Objectives of e-Procurement		117
	6.13.2 Seven Categories of e-Procurement		118
	6.13.3 Benefits of e-Procurement		118
	6.13.4 Challenges of e-Procurement		119
References			120

7 Production and Provision of Services 123

7.1	Definitions		123
7.2	Concept of Production		123
7.3	Provision of Service		124
	7.3.1	Differences between Production and Service Operations	124
	7.3.2	Similarities between Production and Service Operations	125
7.4	Types of Production		127
	7.4.1	Job Shop Production	127
	7.4.2	Batch Production	127
	7.4.3	Flow Line or Mass Production	127
	7.4.4	Continuous Production	128
7.5	Effect of Processes on Production Management		128
7.6	Types of Service		128
	7.6.1	Classification of Services	128
7.7	Challenges for Service Providers		130

7.8 Production Planning..130
    7.8.1 Objectives of Production Planning (Dalal, 2011) 131
    7.8.2 Limitations of Production Planning (Dalal, 2011) 131
7.9 Scheduling...132
    7.9.1 Types of Scheduling...132
    7.9.2 The Process of Scheduling...132
    7.9.3 Limitations of Scheduling...132
7.10 Management of Processes 133
7.11 Maintenance Management 133
    7.11.1 Types of Maintenance 133
    7.11.2 Scientific Maintenance Management Programmes.........................135
7.12 Management of Specifications 135
    7.12.1 Standards..136
    7.12.2 Control of Specifications...136
7.13 Food Processing..138
7.14 Environmental Concerns...138
7.15 Risk Assessment during Production...138
7.16 Case Study: Bottling Operation of Sparkling Wine....................................139
    7.16.1 Monitoring the Quality of Raw Materials...................................140
    7.16.2 Monitoring the Food Safety Issues of Raw Materials 140
    7.16.3 Monitoring the Environmental Issues of Raw Materials 141
    7.16.4 The Process 141
    7.16.5 Control Operations...141
        7.16.5.1 Control Operations for Quality 141
        7.16.5.2 Control Operations for Food Safety...........................141
        7.16.5.3 Control Operations for Monitoring the Environmental
            Impact of Processing...141
    7.16.6 Assessment of Risk..144
    7.16.7 Records 144
References 144

8 New Product Development..145
8.1 Introduction 145
8.2 Definitions 145
    8.2.1 New Product Development...145
    8.2.2 Innovation 146
    8.2.3 Design 146
8.3 Reasons and Uses of New Products 146
8.4 Difference between Production and Product Development 147
8.5 New Product Categories 147
8.6 Case Study...148
8.7 Innovations and Risk..149
8.8 New Product Development Strategy...150
    8.8.1 New Product Development Strategy Plan 150
        8.8.1.1 Step 1 – Establish Goals and Objectives....................150
        8.8.1.2 Step 2 – Identify Arenas to Focus on and the R&D Effort........151
        8.8.1.3 Step 3 – Evaluate the Arenas 152

8.8.1.4 Step 4 – Develop Competitive and Entry Strategies 153
8.8.1.5 Step 5 – Implement Decisions, Allocate Funds, Establish
Priorities and Strategic Buckets 153
8.9 New Product Development Process 153
8.9.1 Linear NPD Model 154
8.9.1.1 Step 1 – Idea Generation 156
8.9.1.2 Step 2 – Idea Screening 156
8.9.1.3 Step 3 – Concept Development and Testing 157
8.9.1.4 Step 4 – Marketing Strategy Development 157
8.9.1.5 Step 5 – Business and Financial Analysis 157
8.9.1.6 Step 6 – Product Development 157
8.9.1.7 Step 7 – Product Testing 158
8.9.1.8 Step 8 – Commercialisation 158
8.9.2 Stage-Gate Process 158
8.9.2.1 Stages 158
8.9.2.2 The Gates 159
8.10 Product Service Model for NPD 160
8.10.1 Organisational Preparedness 160
8.10.2 Planning 160
8.10.3 Design 160
8.10.4 Post-processing 161
8.11 Design Mix and Characteristics of Good Design 161
8.12 Factors Influencing NPD 161
8.12.1 Organisational Structure 161
8.12.2 Leadership 162
8.12.3 Teamwork 162
8.13 Addressing Complexities in NPD Projects 162
8.14 Evaluation of NPD Projects 162
8.15 Failure of NPD Projects 163
8.16 Success Factors for NPD 163
8.17 Addressing Environmental Issues in NPD 163
8.17.1 Seven-Step Approach for Environmental Improvement 165
8.18 New Food Product Development 165
8.18.1 Product Testing 165
8.18.2 Product Formulation 167
References 168

9 Warehousing and Logistics **171**
9.1 Evolution of Warehousing 171
9.2 Definitions 172
9.2.1 Warehousing 172
9.2.2 Picking 172
9.2.3 Kitting 172
9.2.4 Cross-Docking 172
9.2.5 Logistics 173
9.2.6 Supply Chain 173
9.2.7 Supply Chain Management 173

9.3 The Need for Warehousing and Holding Inventory 173
    9.3.1 Reasons for Warehousing 173
    9.3.2 Reasons for Better Inventory Management 174
9.4 Types of Warehouses 175
    9.4.1 Based on Ownership 175
        9.4.1.1 Public Warehouses 175
        9.4.1.2 Private Warehouses 175
        9.4.1.3 Contract Warehouses 176
    9.4.2 Classification Based on Roles 176
        9.4.2.1 Raw Material and Component Warehouses 176
        9.4.2.2 WIP Warehouses 176
        9.4.2.3 Finished Goods Warehouses 176
        9.4.2.4 Distribution Warehouses..176
        9.4.2.5 Fulfilment Warehouses...177
        9.4.2.6 Local Warehouses 177
        9.4.2.7 Value-Added Service Warehouses...177
9.5 Warehouse Operations 177
    9.5.1 Receiving 177
    9.5.2 Storing..177
        9.5.2.1 Storage Policies..179
    9.5.3 Order Picking 179
    9.5.4 Sortation 180
    9.5.5 Consolidation 180
    9.5.6 Marshalling and Despatch 180
9.6 Logistics 180
9.7 Distribution 181
    9.7.1 Complexity of Organising the Distribution Department 182
    9.7.2 Training the Distribution Team...183
    9.7.3 Golden Rules 183
9.8 Transportation..183
    9.8.1 Modes of Transportation 184
9.9 Food Safety: Refrigerated Storage...184
9.10 Environmental Impact...186
9.11 Health and Safety Issues..186
9.12 Impact of Information Technology...187
    9.12.1 Applications of IT...187
9.13 Performance Assessment 188
References 188

10 Sales Management...191
10.1 Introduction 191
10.2 Definitions 191
10.3 Sales Management...192
    10.3.1 Sales Management Process 192
    10.3.2 Management Activities 192
        10.3.2.1 Strategic Level..192
        10.3.2.2 Tactical Level...193

    10.3.2.3 Operational Level 193
  10.3.3 Factors that Influence the Sales Management Process 194
    10.3.3.1 Behavioural Forces......................................194
    10.3.3.2 Technological Forces.....................................195
    10.3.3.3 Managerial Forces.......................................195
  10.3.4 Problems Related to the Study of Sales Management...........195
    10.3.4.1 Addressing the Problems..................................196
 10.4 Sales Strategy...196
  10.4.1 Sales Strategy Development 197
    10.4.1.1 Objectives 197
    10.4.1.2 Key Elements of a Sales Strategy..........................197
    10.4.1.3 Resources 199
    10.4.1.4 Training of Sales Force and Customer Support...............199
    10.4.1.5 Performance Measurement 199
 10.5 Common Mistakes Made by Sales Managers 199
 10.6 Sales Planning 200
  10.6.1 Sales Plan Elements....................................... 200
    10.6.1.1 Sales Goals, Targets, Challenges and Investments............ 200
    10.6.1.2 Revenue Model..201
    10.6.1.3 Fill the Funnel 201
    10.6.1.4 Selling Culture..201
    10.6.1.5 Execute and Measure 202
 10.7 Sales Process 203
 10.8 Sales Forecasting... 204
  10.8.1 Forecasting Process 205
  10.8.2 Forecasting Techniques.................................... 206
  10.8.3 Forecasting Sources....................................... 206
  10.8.4 Developing the Forecast................................... 207
  10.8.5 Measuring Success 207
 10.9 Sales Management Skills 208
 10.10 Impact of Sales Activities on the Environment 208
 10.11 Food Safety Issues .... ■ 208
 References 209

11 **Initial Environmental Review** **211**
 11.1 Introduction 211
 11.2 The Purpose..211
 11.3 Outcome of an IER 212
 11.4 Main Features of an IER 212
 11.5 Preparation 213
 11.6 The Process...213
  11.6.1 Selection of the Team......................................213
  11.6.2 Preparation 213
  11.6.3 Identification of Processes 214
  11.6.4 Site Review 214
 11.7 Communication 220
 References 221

12 Impact of Business and Industry on the Environment.................................223
    12.1 Introduction 223
    12.2 Environmental Movement.. 224
        12.2.1 Developments in the United States 225
        12.2.2 Global Concerns 225
        12.2.3 Kyoto Protocol 226
        12.2.4 Montreal Protocol 227
    12.3 Environmental Issues.. 227
    12.4 Resources.. 227
        12.4.1 Water Consumption 228
        12.4.2 Energy Use and Consumption 229
        12.4.3 Mineral Use and Depletion 230
            12.4.3.1 Environmental Damage.....................................231
            12.4.3.2 Impact 231
    12.5 Pollution...233
    12.6 Types of Pollution.. 234
        12.6.1 Air Pollution 234
            12.6.1.1 Particulate Matter.. 234
            12.6.1.2 Ozone Depletion 235
            12.6.1.3 Greenhouse Effect..235
        12.6.2 Water Pollution 236
        12.6.3 Soil Pollution 237
        12.6.4 Noise Pollution 238
        12.6.5 Marine and Coastal Pollution 238
        12.6.6 Solid Waste and Hazardous Material 239
        12.6.7 Radioactive Waste 240
            12.6.7.1 Chernobyl Nuclear Explosion 241
        12.6.8 Thermal Pollution 241
    12.7 Sustainable Development 242
        12.7.1 Objectives of Sustainable Development 242
        12.7.2 Factors Affecting Sustainable Development 243
        12.7.3 Carrying Capacity 243
    References 243

13 Environmental Aspects and Impacts...247
    13.1 Introduction 247
    13.2 Classification of Aspects 248
    13.3 Methods of Identifying Environmental Aspects 249
        13.3.1 Value Chain Method 249
        13.3.2 Materials Identification Method 249
        13.3.3 Regulatory Compliance Method...249
        13.3.4 Eco-Mapping...249
            13.3.4.1 Uses of Eco-Maps 249
            13.3.4.2 Eco-Map Checklist...249
            13.3.4.3 Eco-Maps..250
    13.4 Selected Techniques for Identifying and Evaluating Environmental
        Aspects and Impacts..250

13.4.1 Identification of Activities, Products and Services 250
13.4.2 Preliminary Information 252
13.4.3 Identification Process 252
13.4.3.1 Sub-Dividing the Facility...252
13.4.3.2 Developing Process Flow Diagrams 253
13.4.3.3 Environmental Aspects Outside the Organisation 256
13.4.3.4 Environmental Risk and Environmental Impact.................256
13.5 Environmental Impact of Food and Food Production 256
13.6 Evaluation of the Significance of Environmental Aspects 258
13.6.1 Qualitative Method 258
13.6.2 Quantitative Method 259
13.6.2.1 Assessment of Significance 261
13.6.3 Evaluation of Positive Environmental Aspects.............................. 262
13.6.4 Addressing the Significant Aspects: Issues to be Considered 262
13.7 Using the Information 268
13.8 Legal and Statutory Requirements.. 268
13.8.1 Legal Requirements 268
13.8.2 Resources Required.. 269
13.8.3 Process of Identifying Legal Requirements 269
13.9 Checklist for Identifying Legal Requirements 270
13.10 Ways to Ensure Legal Compliance.. 272
References 272

**14 Food Safety and Principles of Hazard Analysis and
Critical Control Points (HACCPs)** **275**
14.1 History of Food Safety 275
14.1.1 Protecting the Consumer 275
14.2 Foodborne Illnesses 276
14.2.1 Types of Foodborne Illnesses...276
14.3 Principles of Food Control...277
14.4 Food Safety Management System 277
14.5 Definitions 278
14.6 Development of HACCP.. 278
14.7 Costs and Benefits of HACCP.. 278
14.8 Management Commitment 280
14.9 Pre-requisite Programmes 280
14.10 Scope of the HACCP Programme 281
14.11 Seven Principles of HACCP 282
14.12 HACCP Development Plan 282
14.13 Assemble the HACCP Team 283
14.13.1 HACCP Training... 283
14.14 Description of the Product, Intended Use and the Process.................... 284
14.15 Types of Hazards 285
14.15.1 Biological Hazards.. 286
14.15.2 Chemical Hazards 287
14.15.3 Physical Hazards 287
14.16 Routes of Contamination 287

14.16.1 Raw Materials 288
14.16.2 Processing Steps 288
14.16.3 Machinery 288
14.16.4 Handling of Food 289
14.16.5 Environmental Conditions 289
14.17 Some Measures to Control Hazards 289
14.17.1 Raw Materials and Packaging 289
14.17.2 Processing Steps 290
14.17.3 Plant and Equipment 290
14.17.4 Storage and Distribution 290
14.17.5 Premises 291
14.17.6 Personnel 291
14.17.7 Measures at Post-processing and Packaging Stages 291
14.17.8 Consumer 292
14.18 Allergen Control 292
References 293

15 Application of HACCP 295
15.1 Introduction 295
15.2 Information Sources 296
15.3 Definitions 296
15.4 How to Conduct a Hazard Analysis 297
15.4.1 Some Questions to Be Considered When Conducting a
Hazard Analysis 297
15.4.1.1 Receiving Incoming Materials 297
15.4.1.2 Procedures Used for Processing 298
15.4.1.3 Observe Actual Operating Practices 298
15.4.1.4 Take Measurements 298
15.4.1.5 Analyse the Measurements 299
15.5 Assessing the Hazard Potential 299
15.5.1 Assessment of Raw Materials 299
15.5.2 Assessment of Processes 300
15.5.3 Assessment of the Product during Storage and Delivery 300
15.5.4 Assessment of End Use 301
15.6 Critical Control Points 301
15.6.1 Classification of CCPs 301
15.6.2 Location of CCPs 302
15.6.3 Identification of CCPs 303
15.6.3.1 Decision Tree 303
15.6.3.2 Risk Analysis 305
15.7 Risk Management 307
15.8 Risk Communication 307
15.9 Establishing Critical Limits for Each CCP 307
15.10 Establishing Operating Limits for Each CCP 308
15.11 Establishing Monitoring Systems for Each CCP 309
15.12 Taking Corrective Action 309
15.12.1 Adjusting the Process to Maintain Control and Prevent a Deviation ... 309

15.12.2 Action to Be Taken Following a Deviation at a Control Point 310
15.13 Verification 310
15.14 Documenting and Record-Keeping 310
15.15 Validation 311
15.16 Product Recall 311
15.16.1 Recall Classification 312
15.16.2 Media Release 313
15.17 HACCP and the Environment 313
15.18 Case Study: Hot Smoked Salmon 314
15.19 Role of GMPs and ISO 22000 322
References 326

Appendix: Abbreviations and Acronyms **329**

Index **331**

List of Figures

Figure 3.1   Strategy formulation. 45

Figure 3.2   Balanced score card. 51

Figure 3.3   Strategy map; alignment of strategies with balanced score card. 51

Figure 4.1   Overview of the risk management process. 68

Figure 4.2   Business continuity planning process. 75

Figure 5.1   GMP activities. 86

Figure 5.2   Core food business. 86

Figure 5.3   Preliminary process for GMP. 89

Figure 6.1   Evaluation and selection of suppliers. 111

Figure 6.2   Application of web-based tools in e-procurement. 119

Figure 7.1   Production process. 124

Figure 7.2   Production – Service interaction. 126

Figure 7.3   Effect of process variety and product mix on production management. 128

Figure 7.4   Sparkling wine production (packaging). 140

Figure 8.1   Product-Market matrix. 152

Figure 8.2   NPD process. 154

Figure 8.3   Stage-Gate process. 159

Figure 9.1   Common warehouse functions. 178

Figure 9.2   Physical flow of materials in a supply chain. 181

Figure 10.1   Selling process. 203

Figure 10.2   Total TV sets production in the United States. 205

Figure 10.3   Developing a sales forecast. 207

Figure 13.1   Input/output diagram of a generic organisation. 255

Figure 13.2   Input/output analysis of winery operations. 255

Figure 14.1 Production of pasteurised orange juice.. 286

Figure 15.1 Block diagram for the production of vacuum-packed hot smoked salmon. 316

Figure 15.2 Flow diagram for the production of vacuum-packed hot smoked salmon. 317

List of Tables

Table 1.1 Timeline of Quality Management 6

Table 1.2 Timeline of Food Safety Management 11

Table 1.3 Timeline of Environmental Management 14

Table 2.1 Impact of ISO 9000 Standard and EFQM Model on Performance 19

Table 2.2 Estimation of the Cost of the HACCP Programme.................................. 24

Table 2.3 Benefits of Food Safety Management Systems 25

Table 2.4 Barriers to Implementing the HACCP System 28

Table 2.5 Environmental Cost of Quality Framework (ECOQ) 32

Table 2.6 Significance of Environmental Aspects...35

Table 2.7 Business Practicability Score 35

Table 3.1 Four Phases of Strategic Planning...41

Table 4.1 Types of Business Risks 61

Table 4.2 Environmental Impact and Social Responsibilities of a Business 63

Table 4.3 Features of Food Safety Hazards 64

Table 4.4 Examples of Pure versus Speculative Risk Exposures 67

Table 4.5 Risk Impact and Likelihood Descriptors 71

Table 4.6 Risk Matrix 72

Table 4.7 Implementation of the Risk Management Plan.. 78

Table 4.8 Barriers to Embedding Enterprise Risk Management (ERM)................. 79

Table 5.1 Benefits of GMP 96

Table 6.1 Evolution of the Purchasing...101

Table 6.2 Advantages and Disadvantages of Centralised Purchasing....................108

Table 6.3 Advantages and Disadvantages of Decentralised Purchasing 109

Table 6.4 Categorical Method of Rating Suppliers...113

Table 6.5 Weighted Point Method of Rating Suppliers...114

Table 6.6 Checklist for Green Procurement 115

Table 6.7 Controls of Incoming Raw Materials to Ensure Food Safety 117

Table 7.1 Features of Production and Service 125

Table 7.2 Transformation Processes...126

Table 7.3 Types of Services and Management Challenges....................................129

Table 7.4 Advantages and Disadvantages of Maintenance
Management Programmes...134

Table 7.5 Example of In-process Controls for Sparkling Wine Production 142

Table 8.1 Profile of New Products 147

Table 8.2 New Product Development Approaches 151

Table 8.3 Criteria for Evaluating Strategic Arenas 153

Table 8.4 Models of NPD 155

Table 8.5 Milestone Process of New Food Product Development.........................166

Table 8.6 Product Testing 167

Table 9.1 Basic Warehouse Operations...178

Table 9.2 Modes of Transport 185

Table 10.1 Sales Management Process Model..193

Table 10.2 Environmental Impact of Sales Activities..209

Table 11.1 Legal and Other Requirements 215

Table 11.2 History of Accidents 216

Table 11.3 Raw Materials and Components 217

Table 11.4 Chemicals and Their Usage...217

Table 11.5 Energy Use...217

Table 11.6 Waste and Recycling...218

Table 11.7 Emissions to Air and Noise Levels 219

Table 11.8 Impact on Surroundings 219

Table 11.9 Transportation 220

Table 11.10 Company's Products 220

Table 11.11 Summary of Consumption and Emissions 221

Table 12.1 Major Environmental Disasters after World War II 223

Table 12.2 World Summits on Environmental Issues...226

Table 12.3 Environmental Impact of Business Activities of Citizen Group, Japan 228

Table 12.4 World Supply and Consumption of Energy Balance 230

Table 12.5 Source–Pathway–Receptor Model of Pollution 233

Table 12.6 Acute and Chronic Pollution Impacts 233

Table 12.7 Sources of Water Pollution 236

Table 12.8 Waste and Recycling in the United Kingdom 240

Table 13.1 Activity, Service, Aspect and Impact 247

Table 13.2 Examples of Categories of Aspects Associated with Operations, Services and Products 248

Table 13.3 Techniques for Identifying and Evaluating Environmental Aspects and Impacts 251

Table 13.4 List of Common Activities with Functional Areas 253

Table 13.5 Environmental Impact of Food and Food Production 257

Table 13.6 Qualitative Assessment of the Significance of Environmental Impact............... 260

Table 13.7 Quantitative Assessment of Environmental Impact 263

Table 13.8 Evaluation of Positive Environmental Aspects 267

Table 13.9 Checklist for Identifying Legal Requirements Applicable to Environmental Aspects 270

Table 14.1 Costs and Benefits of HACCP Implementation 279

Table 14.2 Pre-requisite Programmes 281

Table 14.3 HACCP Planning Stages and Steps 283

Table 14.4 Responsibilities of HACCP Team Members 284

Table 14.5 Product Description of Orange Juice 285

Table 14.6   List of Raw Materials Used in the Production of Pasteurised Orange Juice 285

Table 14.7 Factors that Affect the Growth of Microorganisms in Food............................. 287

Table 14.8 Hazards Associated with Some Raw Materials 288

Table 14.9 Processing Methods to Control Microorganisms in Raw Material and Packaging 289

Table 14.10   Quality Assurance Methods to Control Incoming Raw Materials 290

Table 15.1 Hazard Analysis Form 297

Table 15.2 Some Examples of Control Points... 302

Table 15.3 Severity and Likelihood of a Food Safety Risk... 306

Table 15.4 Matrix for the Assessment of the Significance of Risk and CCPs...................... 306

Table 15.5 Examples of Critical Control Limits 308

Table 15.6 Product Description of Vacuum-Packed Hot Smoked Salmon 314

Table 15.7 Symbols Used in HACCP Flow Diagrams 315

Table 15.8 Hazard Potential of Raw Materials 318

Table 15.9 Hazard Potential of Processes 319

Table 15.10 Hazards Potential of Packing Hot Smoked Salmon 321

Table 15.11 Hazard Potential of End Use 321

Table 15.12 Critical Control Points (CCPs) for Vacuum-Packed Hot Smoked Salmon 323

Table 15.13 Control Schedule for Vacuum-Packed Hot Smoked Salmon CCPs 324

List of Forms

Form 7.1 Packaging Specifications for Sparkling Wine 136

Form 7.2 Sample Specification Sheet for a Wine 138

Form 15.1 The Decision Tree 304

Disclaimer

While the author has used reasonable efforts to include accurate and up-to-date information for the content in the publication, he does not represent, warrant or promise (whether express or implied) that any information is or remains accurate, complete and up-to-date, or fit or suitable for any purpose. Any reliance a reader places on the information in this publication is at their own risk (including their use of the forms and procedures), and this publication is not intended as a substitute for ISO standards, including ISO 9001, ISO 22000 and ISO 14001. Reprinted material is quoted with permission, and sources are indicated. The authors and publishers apologise to copyright holders if permission to publish in this form has not being obtained. If any copyright material has not been acknowledged, please write and let us know so we may rectify in any future reprints.

These three books on *Integrating Business Management Processes* are designed to provide practical guidance and do not constitute technical, financial or legal advice or any other type of advice and should not be relied on for any purposes. It is not intended to guarantee certification of the integrated management system.

The procedures in Volume 3 of the series are based on the author's personal experience of developing, implementing and auditing management systems in pharmaceutical, cosmetic and food industries in an executive quality assurance role during a period of over 25 years as well as on contributions from numerous resources. The author does not claim them to be original and/or has been developed specifically for this publication. In particular, the author acknowledges the valuable contribution from the resources listed in the bibliography.

Foreword

The usual definition of a business management system is that it is a set of policies, processes and procedures used by an organisation to ensure that it can fulfil the tasks required to achieve its objectives, covering all the key aspects of the organisation's operations. But this definition doesn't really do justice to the importance and complexity of an effective business management system. It should be, but often isn't an integrated and dynamic system that links the organisation's key activities and provides guidance and motivation for staff at all levels. Not a set of stand-alone, isolated procedures and objectives, but something which drives the organisation to continuous improvement and ultimately, business success.

The integration of different activities into a cohesive and inter-linked system is key to this. Various books and articles have been written analysing different approaches in an attempt to provide guidance on how to derive effective integrated management systems, often based on satisfying the requirements of ISO standards. But this book takes the approach a step further, on the premise that it is more logical to integrate management processes, rather than management systems, and to focus on customer satisfaction and not just ISO standards.

It is aimed principally at manufacturing and consulting organisations where quality, food safety and environmental management are key but also cover the full gamut of management processes, which are integral to most businesses. Based on his own wide-ranging experience, Dr De Silva presents a series of three volumes on *Integrating Business Management Processes*, which sets out a rational and detailed approach to the development of a fully integrated business management system using process-based principles. Volume 1 gives a comprehensive coverage of the key management and core processes and also makes a case for the inclusion of good manufacturing, quality and food safety practices, which are often dealt with separately. Volume 2 sets out support and assurance processes in a business environment. This is followed by Volume 3 that describes the integration of quality, food safety and environmental processes, complete with procedures and flowcharts, based on Dr De Silva's own personal journey in developing successful integrated business management systems.

It is an account and an approach which I thoroughly recommend. The series of these three volumes is a valuable resource for any organisation, large, small or medium in the development, implementation, maintenance and improvement of an integrated management system.

Dr David C Taylor
BSc Pharmacy (Hons), PhD, Former Director of Product
Development, Analytical Development and Project
Management, AstraZeneca, United Kingdom.
December 2019

Review of Integrating Business Management Processes, Volumes 1, 2 and 3

Dr De Silva has written an excellent series of three books on *Integrating Business Management Processes* that provides a structure to manage four key elements of a modern business:

- Quality and food safety.
- Respect for the environment.
- Respect for employee wellbeing.
- Good business.

Dr De Silva demonstrates that these principles need not be at odds with each other. Rather, when applied with understanding and care, they work harmoniously for the good of the business, its employees, customers and community.

The process of integration adopts a novel approach, focusing on processes encountered in day-to-day business operations without the need for formalised third-party accreditations.

To write this series, encompassing quality, food safety and environmental activities requires a comprehensive knowledge of these disciplines. Dr De Silva's wide experience in developing management systems and auditing provides the essential competency to put together complex processes in a simple format.

I worked extensively with Titus to set up formalised quality and business management systems, so this work is no surprise. An added bonus is the historical and philosophical context Titus provides to frame our modern position.

These books, with their series of examples and procedures, show how organisations can benefit from satisfying customer requirements and the requirements of ISO standards to gain entry into lucrative markets.

The series is detailed enough to be comprehensive as a complete guide to systems development, or the reader may be selective in addressing specific issues that they may be encountering. Volumes 1 and 2 provide a broad knowledge base on management, core, support and assurance processes encountered in the business environment. In Volume 3, quality, food safety and environmental procedures are merged to form an integrated management system.

The aim of the series is to enable readers, at very little cost, to set up an effective and efficient integrated quality, food safety and environmental management system for themselves. The three books complement each other, and this series on *Integrating Business Management Processes* is a complete business management system capable of being adapted to suit a business without the need of a specialist to do it for them.

All three volumes are practical workbooks necessary for any organisation, small, medium or large, to develop, implement, maintain and improve an integrated quality, food safety and an environmental business management system and they are highly recommended.

Nick Rowe
Supply Chain Manager and Logistics Consultant
Marisco Wines, New Zealand
December 2019

Preface

The three books on *Integrating Business Management Processes* cover quality, food safety and environmental processes encountered in a business environment. This book (Volume 1) includes five chapters on management processes and ten chapters on core business processes. Good Manufacturing Practices (GMPs) and Hazard Analysis and Critical Control Points (HACCPs) are key chapters in this book. Volume 2 describes ten support processes and three assurance processes required to assure quality, food safety and good environmental practices. Volume 3 is about building an integrated management system (IMS) by merging quality, food safety and environmental processes.

Management systems form an integral part of any business. Business organisations have to satisfy not only the customers they serve but also statutory and regulatory requirements, industry standards and their own internal requirements, while keeping the environment clean. To meet these needs, organisations have developed a multitude of stand-alone management systems. Most organisations that design IMSs resort to satisfying the clauses of relevant ISO standards. These standards *per se* are not management systems but are minimum requirements and tools that can be used to evaluate the effectiveness of management systems. Organisations that design management systems merely to satisfy the clauses of ISO standards lose sight of the ultimate aim of implementing these systems. Books on IMSs that focus on procedures that are only relevant to ISO standards tend to ignore programmes such as marketing and finance, which are integral parts of any business organisation. Employees do not take ownership of such systems, which is an important consideration for the success of the programme. A management system should be designed to cover all business activities to satisfy its stakeholders, and certification should only be used to evaluate its effectiveness and promote continual improvement.

These three volumes on *Integrating Business Management Processes* include many disciplines encountered in the business environment. Numerous case studies are included in the chapters. The integration approach used in Volume 3 is unique: (a) Most books on integration deal with the integration of quality, environmental and occupational safety and hygiene standards with management systems or ISO standards. A rational approach is to integrate management processes rather than management systems or ISO standards; (b) quality, food safety and environmental processes are integrated, a rare combination not found in books on IMSs. It is a rational approach because food safety is closely linked to quality, GMPs and environmental issues; (c) business processes are described in sufficient detail in Volume 1 and Volume 2 to provide a comprehensive understanding; (d) business processes have been classified into management, core, support and assurance procedures and are described using the process-based approach. Procedures associated with these processes in Volume 3 can easily be tailored to suit the needs of any organisation; (e) the procedures are supplemented with numerous forms, tables and flowcharts; and (f) procedures specific to quality, food safety and the environment are also described.

Food safety is an integral part of quality and good manufacturing practices. Therefore, these three books take the lead in integrating closely related, but different, business processes. The management skills necessary for developing and implementing management systems are well described in my previous book, *Essential Management Skills for Pharmacy and Business Managers* (CRC Press, 2013).

In my corporate role as the head of quality assurance in the largest winery in New Zealand (Montana Wines Limited), the experience of developing and implementing management systems, auditing them, and exposure to several industry sectors (such as pharmaceutical, cosmetic, food and beverage, and retail pharmacy) provided me with the depth of knowledge and expertise required to write this series.

These books focus on business processes and not on ISO standards, and as such, it is not intended as a substitute for these standards. Those who intend to use this book for developing or integrating management systems should thoroughly understand the processes described in Volume 1 and Volume 2. Then, the necessary management, core, support and assurance processes required to satisfy the needs of the organisation and its customers should be identified. The final phase is to adopt the procedures presented in Volume 3 of the series to suit individual needs. *The Way Forward* in Volume 3 takes you through this process. The primary aim should be to satisfy the needs of stakeholders rather than the clauses of ISO standards. When the system has been implemented and found to meet expectations, the organisation can work towards certification, consulting the relevant ISO standards.

The journey is arduous. Staff development and team work are essential ingredients for success. It is a dynamic process, and continual improvement takes place when employees take ownership of the system.

Acknowledgements

During the five-year period of developing these three books on *Integrating Business Management Processes*, many individuals devoted their time and effort to make this project a success. Over the years, I have come to know many colleagues in management who shared their knowledge with me. I wish to thank Dr David Taylor, in the United Kingdom, Former Director of Product Development, Analytical Development and Project Management, AstraZeneca, for writing the foreword in this book in spite of his busy schedule. I am grateful to Mr Nick Rowe, Logistics Consultant in New Zealand, for reviewing the chapters on new product development, and warehouse management and writing a valuable review. I appreciate his comments and recommendations, which were incorporated in the chapters. I acknowledge with thanks the contribution made by Mr Chanaka De Silva, a Chartered Accountant in New Zealand, for reviewing the chapter on financial management and making worthy recommendations. I acknowledge with thanks the unwavering encouragement and enormous support given to me by son, Dr Samitha De Silva, in the United Kingdom, a Partner at C'M'S', the seventh largest law firm globally. Special thanks go to my son, Pradeepa De Silva, Head of Global Marketing Programs at Facebook based in Singapore, who supported me in numerous ways, including the review of the chapters on marketing and sales management. My wife, Anoma De Silva, a librarian and an archivist, presented me with many recommendations and challenges for which I am very grateful. These enabled me to achieve my objective of completing the manuscript on time. I wish to thank Helen McDonald in New Zealand for excellent proofreading. I also thank the organisations I worked for in senior management roles in New Zealand (Hoechst NZ Limited, Penfolds and Montana Wines Limited), Japan (National Institute of Hygienic Sciences), the United Kingdom (Eli Lilly Research, Boots and Lloyds Pharmacy Limited), Kuwait (Ministry of Health) and Sri Lanka (Ministry of Health). Finally, I acknowledge with thanks the professionalism of the editorial team of Taylor & Francis.

Review

At a personal level, I have found that, with advancing years, I need the support of organised systems to ensure that I complete the tasks that I need to do, rather than those that are unnecessary or unhelpful. Having undertaken research and development as an employee in the pharmaceutical industry, as an academic member of multi-task industrial project teams and a governmental regulatory authority, I am well aware of the benefits of organisational systems to achieve successful outcomes. I was therefore fascinated to see the extensive aspects of such systems as provided by Dr De Silva in the three volumes on "Integrating Business Management Processes". He has considered the wider, fundamental aspects of the range of systems and their organisation in a manner which supports the delivery of a successful product or project.

While examples are provided for particular industries, the principles provided in the 29 chapters can be applied to many systems. Thus, the content of each chapter may not be relevant to every management system or situation, but Dr De Silva has emphasised that, where relevant, integration of relevant chapters is beneficial. He has evidenced this from the development stage of these systems, through to their implementation and control. The dynamic nature of these systems is clearly demonstrated, as is the likelihood that they will change as new knowledge, materials, and processing and test methods emerge and the operational performance of these management processes is observed.

The lists of references at the end of each chapter provide the source of the information used to present the text and indicate that each chapter could probably be expanded into a book. This work, however, offers succinct and comprehensive information regarding the important issues involved for each system. The figures, flowcharts, forms, procedures and tables provide a valuable contribution to the understanding of this work on organisational systems.

Dr J.M. Newton
Emeritus Professor of the School of Pharmacy of London University,
Honorary Professor in the Department of Mechanical Engineering at
University College, London, Member of CPS (Chemistry, Pharmacy and
Standards), a subcommittee of the CSM (Committee on the Safety of Medicines:
1978–1995), and Member of the Medicines Commission: 1978–2000).
March 2020

Author

Titus De Silva, PhD, is a consultant in management skills development, pharmacy practice, quality management and food safety and has been an advisor to the newly established National Medicines Regulatory Authority in Sri Lanka.

Dr De Silva gained his pharmacy degree (with Honours) from the University of Manchester in the United Kingdom. In addition, he has a BSc degree in Chemistry, a post-graduate Diploma in Computer Science (New Zealand), and a MBA and PhD in Management Science (United States). He is a Chartered Chemist (CChem) and a Fellow of the Royal Society of Chemistry (FRSC), United Kingdom, a member of the Royal Pharmaceutical Society of Great Britain (MRPharmS) and a member of the Pharmaceutical Society of New Zealand (MPS).

For over 30 years, he held senior management positions in New Zealand, the United Kingdom and Sri Lanka. He has worked in the United Kingdom, New Zealand, Japan and Kuwait in many sectors including manufacturing, research, cosmetics, beverage, and hospital and community pharmacy. Before immigrating to New Zealand, he was the head of the National Drugs Quality Control Laboratory in Sri Lanka. During his time in Sri Lanka, he was a visiting lecturer and examiner at the Faculty of Medicine of the University of Colombo, School of Pharmacy. While in Kuwait, he served as a specialist in drug analysis and quality control in the Ministry of Health. In Japan, he was attached to the National Institute of Hygienic Science in Tokyo, where he worked with experts in pharmaceutical science. Other organisations he has worked for include the Southland Hospital Board (New Zealand), Hoechst Pharmaceuticals (New Zealand), Pernod-Ricard (New Zealand), Eli Lilly Research (United Kingdom), Ballinger's Pharmacy (New Zealand), Boots Chemists (United Kingdom) and Lloyds Pharmacy (United Kingdom).

Pernod-Ricard (previously Montana Wines Limited) owned the largest winery in New Zealand, with wineries in four regions. In his role as Corporate Quality Assurance Manager, he was responsible for developing and implementing management systems to comply with international standards. In this role, he coached and trained staff for management positions. He gained competency as a lead auditor and was a registered auditor in quality management and occupational safety and hygiene. He worked closely with suppliers, auditing their management systems and providing encouragement and support. His auditing experience enabled him to gain broad knowledge of many disciplines encountered in the business environment.

Dr De Silva's expertise has been sought by many professional organisations. He has presented numerous papers at international seminars and published a number of papers and articles on quality management, food safety, pharmacy practice and topics of general interest in management journals and magazines. He was the co-author of the chapter, "Hazard Analysis and Critical Control Point" in the book *Handbook of Food Preservation* published by Marcel Dekker, New York (1st Edition) (1999). In the second edition of the book, published by CRC Press, Boca Raton, Florida, in July 2007, he was the author of the revised "Hazard Analysis and Critical Control Point

(HACCP)" chapter and the "Good Manufacturing Practices" chapter. His book *Handbook of Good Pharmacy Practice* was published in 2011 in Sri Lanka. In 2013, his book *Essential Management Skills for Pharmacy and Business Managers* was published by CRC Press.

Dr De Silva was a member of the Review Board of the Joint Accreditation System of Australia and New Zealand (JAS-ANZ) and its Technical Advisory Council. JAS-ANZ is the sole body responsible for accrediting certifying bodies in Australia and New Zealand. He was enlisted as a consultant to the United Nations Industrial Development Organization (UNIDO).

In 2004, the New Zealand government conferred the Queen's Service Medal (QSM) for his services to the New Zealand community.

MANAGEMENT
PROCESSES

Chapter 1

History of Management Systems

1.1 Quality Management

Attempts to manage the quality of products and services can be traced back to medieval times. During this time in the latter part of the 13th century, craftsmen began to organise themselves into unions called guilds that formalised procedures for assuring product and service quality (American Society for Quality, n.d.). The focus was on regular inspection of goods and a decision was made to accept or reject them. Special symbols marked on the goods signified good quality. The creation of inspection roles in workplaces led to a series of issues (Department of Trade Industry, n.d.). For example:

- Technical problems which required specialised skills not possessed by workers.
- Allocation of untrained inspectors to perform tasks.
- The focus was on output, and inspectors were ordered to accept defective products.
- Promotion of skilled workers to other positions left a vacuum filled often by workers unskilled to perform operational jobs such as manufacturing.

Mass production following the Industrial Revolution in the early part of the 19th century required factory settings and systems where the role of craftsmen changed to factory workers. The work performed by these craftsmen was categorised into specialised tasks.

Further developments took place during the late 19th century through the work of Frederick W. Taylor (1856–1915) who developed management systems aimed at the improvement of productivity through scientific techniques. Taylor formulated four principles to increase efficiency (Taylor, 2012): (a) replace rule of thumb methods with those based on scientific study; (b) select, train and develop each worker; (c) cooperate with workers to ensure that adopted methods are being followed; and (d) divide work equally between management and workers.

In May 2001, the first international conference on the Bata System of Management was held in Zlin (Czech Republic) to discuss its impacts on management and entrepreneurship in the third millennium. The conference intended to communicate the contribution of management theory and practice developed by Tomas Bata and his associates. Bata introduced fundamental changes in management philosophy and techniques and his principles are embodied in the following:

- "Our customer – our master".
- Thinking to the people – labour to the machines.
- The best quality at the lowest prices.
- The best in the world is good enough for us.
- "Every employee a capitalist".

The western world adopted the approaches originated by Tomas Bata during 1905–1932, which are now recognised as quality management practices (Tribus, 2001).

Statistical quality control began to be applied to quality control in the 1920s, which was widely attributed to the work of Walter Shewhart at the US firm Western Electric. Before the introduction of statistical quality control, finished products were inspected to remove defective items (Shewhart, 1986; Fisher & Nair, 2009).

The actual development of statistical science into acceptance sampling took place following the formation of the Inspection Engineering Department of the Western Electric Bell Telephone Laboratory in 1924. H.F. Dodge, P.S. Romig, W. Shewhart and other associates applied the techniques to shop operations at the Western Electric plant in Chicago. The early developments of the group included the following:

1924 First control chart now popularly known as process control charts.
1925–1926 Terminology of acceptance sampling.
1927 Average Outgoing Quality Limit (AOQL) sampling tables.
1928 Demerit system.

In 1930, the application of acceptance sampling was further developed within Western Electric and elsewhere by the engineers of the American Society for Testing and Materials (ASTM) and engineers of other professional bodies (Schilling, 1993; Fisher & Nair, 2009). These developments created huge interest in England, and during the mid-1930s, Egon Pearson published the British Standard Institute standard No. 600 (Pike & Barnes, 1996). Dodge-Romig "Sampling Inspection Tables" were then published during the early 1940s. These tables consisted of (a) single sampling lot tolerance tables; (b) double sampling lot tolerance tables; (c) single sampling AOQL tables; and (d) double sampling AOQL tables (Dodge, 1969, 1970).

At the end of World War II, Japan's industrial sector was virtually destroyed. The workforce was unskilled, and the products were shoddy. In the early 1940s, General Douglas MacArthur, who embarked on post-war reconstruction, invited Homer Sarasohn, a radio engineer, to establish a communication industry in Japan. When he arrived the entire industry from Tokyo to Yokohama was destroyed. There was no equipment, no functioning companies, and all managers were either in jail or dead. Sarasohn started from scratch by constructing premises, installing equipment, getting supplies, and selecting managers and workers. Workers were instructed daily on how to carry out their tasks (Fisher & Nair, 2009).

In 1948, Charles Protzman arrived in Japan to rebuild the communication system. Management seminars were held at which top managers from companies such as Fujitsu, Furukawa, Hitachi, NEC and Toshiba participated (Sarasohn, 1997; Fisher & Nair, 2009).

It was at this time, Sarasohn invited Shewhart and Deming to Japan. Shewhart taught statistical process control, and Deming presented a course on "Elementary Principles of Statistical Control of Quality". During his visit, he had an informal dinner with a group of presidents and senior officials of leading Japanese industries to talk about quality. He did not have a background in engineering, had no experience in line management and had not created an operational system. Those who were inspired by his 14 principles had a similar background but continued to teach quality management practices (Fisher & Nair, 2009). This was followed by further visits by Deming during which he conducted courses for top management. In 1951, Joseph Juran published his *Quality Control Handbook*, which was brought to the attention of Japanese in 1952. Juran also conducted seminars to top and middle management to explain the role of promoting quality.

Sarasohn, Deming, Juran and others made it clear to the Japanese workforce that statistical process control is necessary, but not sufficient, to provide product and service quality to customers. They emphasised that statistical process control should be supported by a broad quality management culture and approach with total commitment from top management.

Also in the picture was Genichi Taguchi, who introduced parameter design, a framework for quality improvement in 1980. It was a cost-effective approach designed to reduce variation in products and processes, and introduce the design and development of new products and processes or improve the quality of existing ones (Phadke, 1989; Nair, 1992).

Following this period, the quality of Japanese goods dramatically improved. After the 1950s, the Japanese themselves developed quality tools such as quality circles, check sheets, control charts, histograms, the Ishikawa diagram and scatter plots. These attempts established a culture of continuous quality improvement in the Japanese industry (Box et al., 1988). By the late 1960s and early 1970s, Japanese goods appeared in the United States and European markets because of the low cost and higher quality of products compared to those produced in the western world.

The next development in quality improvement occurred in 1987 with the introduction of the Six Sigma concept by Motorola. Six Sigma is a disciplined quantitative approach to project selection and product improvement by removing defects from products, processes and transactions (Hahn et al., 1999).

In the western world, the progress was slow, and acute awareness of quality began in the early 1980s when companies introduced their own quality initiatives in response to Japanese success. Total Quality Management (TQM) became the buzz word. However, the principles of TQM were not fully understood and were often misinterpreted (Pike & Barnes, 1996). A public focus on quality management occurred in 1980 in response to an NBC news report, "If Japan can …Why can't we?" that featured prominent quality gurus at that time: Edward W. Deming, William Convey and the reporter Lloyd Dobyns (Crawford-Mason, 1980). During this period, quality professionals were actively promoting the concepts of quality: Juran conducted courses, lectures and consulting; Deming continued with consulting in a private capacity; Philip Crosby was promoting his concept "Quality is Free" through consulting without featuring statistical process control; and Armand Feigenbaum was consulting in quality control.

The British Standard (BS) 5750 was published in 1979, which was followed by a national quality campaign in 1993 because of the declining world trade share. Following the 1980 NBC report, American companies attempted to focus on quality management. Quality management consultants flourished, and companies started defining quality in terms of customers' needs for the first time. The introduction of the first ISO 9000 standard in 1987 played a significant role in recommending suppliers to improve their production and processes, document their practices and improve their measuring techniques.

The period of recognising achievements in quality commenced in the late 1980s, with the introduction of the Malcolm Baldrige Quality Award in the United States. The Australian Quality Awards emerged in 1989 as a result of initiatives by Australian businesses and the industry, and then Northern Ireland established the "Quality Price" following the Malcolm Baldrige criteria.

In the 1990s, the business environment became more competitive than ever before and companies recognised that simply meeting customers' needs was not sufficient. The new concept of Business Excellence Awards (BEAs) focused on business results, which were not considered in quality awards. The BEA framework included categories such as leadership and innovation, the strategy and planning process, data, information and knowledge, people, customer and market forces, and processes, products and services (Fisher & Nair, 2009).

The present outlook is not promising. Monthly board reports emphasise financial statements, which are often not accompanied by trend charts, graphics and other support material that can indicate business risk and its management. A good performance evaluation system for an enterprise should include sound critical outcomes.

A summary of the developments related to quality is shown in Table 1.1.

Table 1.1 Timeline of Quality Management

Year	Originator	Activity
13th century		Formation of Guilds
1865–1915	Taylor	Improvement of productivity through scientific techniques.
1905–1932	Tomas Bata	Bata system of management
1920s	Shewhart	Statistical process control
1924	Dodge, Romig, Shewhart	Acceptance sampling technique
1930s	Western Electric	Application of acceptance sampling
Mid 1930s	Pearson	British Standard No. 600
1940s	Dodge, Romig	Sampling inspection tables
Early 1940s	General Douglas McArthur	Invited Homer Sarasohn to Japan
1948	Sarasohn	Invited Charles Protzman to Japan to rebuild communication system Invited Deming and Shewhart to Japan
1951	Joseph Juran	Published *Quality Control Handbook*
After 1950		Japanese developed quality tools
1960–1970		Japanese goods appeared in the United States and Europe
1979		Produced the British Standard BS 5750

(Continued)

Table 1.1 (*Continued*)   Timeline of Quality Management

Year	Originator	Activity
1980s		West introduced quality initiatives Concept of TQM introduced NBC News Report, "If Japan can…Why can't we?" Philip Crosby introduced "Quality is Free"
1987	Motorola	Developed the Six Sigma concept. First ISO standard for quality management
Late 1980s		Quality Awards: Malcolm Baldrige Award Australian Quality Award Northern Ireland Quality Prize
1990s		Introduced the Business Excellence Award

1.2 Food Safety

The history of food safety can be considered in terms of three periods: (a) pre-refrigeration; (b) refrigeration; and (c) Hazard Analysis and Critical Control Point (HACCP).

1.2.1 Pre-refrigeration Era

Since the Middle Ages, food safety has been a concern to humankind, and regulatory measures have been enforced to prevent the sale of spoilt, adulterated or contaminated food. Religious and historical texts provide evidence of many rules and recommendations used to protect people from foodborne diseases and food contamination. Augsburg in 1276 assigned specially designated stands on Mondays for selling meat that had not been freshly slaughtered. Florentines too prohibited the sale of meat that had been on sale the previous day (Goetz & Sutton, 1983). Motarjemi et al. (1996) have discussed the concerns of food safety and emphasised the need for a food safety programme.

The laws of ancient Israel included advice on harmful foods and methods of preparation and food hygiene. According to the *Book of Leviticus*, in 2000 BC, Moses introduced laws to protect people from foodborne diseases resulting in the washing of clothes and bathing after the sacrificial slaughter of animals (Griffith, 2006).

Ancient Egyptians were pioneers in the development of silos, a storage tank designed to hold grain harvested from the fields, thereby keeping it cool and dry for long periods of non-harvesting months. The early Romans recognised the importance of freshness in fruits and other food. The rich would often have fresh food delivered to their homes where their cooks would prepare the meals. The art of preservation of food by salting was also practised by the Romans (Centre for Food Service Learning, 2011).

An important development in food preservation can be attributed to Napoleon Bonaparte and Nicolas Appert in the early 1800s. Napoleon offered a reward for anyone who could develop a method for keeping the food required by his soldiers from spoiling when they were fighting against their enemy. Appert put food into jars with secure lids and boiled it until he thought it was cooked. It was the first attempt at "canning", and Appert did not realise that cooking killed the germs (Centre for Food Service Learning, 2011).

Scientists in the 1600s isolated germs as a source of illness, although they did not realise what actually caused the illness. In the 1860s, Louis Pasteur's work on pasteurisation and fermentation made a huge impact on the medical field and food safety. In 1888, August Gartner isolated *Bacillus enteritidis*, which caused foodborne illness (Centre for Food Service Learning, 2011).

Robert Malthus (1766–1834), a British scholar who was influential in political economy and demographics, challenged world economists to address the food availability worldwide due to the ever-increasing world population. Advances in technological progress in food processing have created a greater awareness of problems associated with food preservation and preparation. International and national organisations have formulated and enforced laws and regulations to achieve quality and safety in food preparation and preservation in order to protect consumers from foodborne infections and toxicity (Rutherford, 2007).

1.2.2 Refrigeration Era

In basic terms, any means of keeping food cold is refrigeration. The application of scientific technology to refrigeration changed the concept of food safety significantly. Long before the invention of refrigerators, people stored their food, mainly milk and butter, in cellars, outdoor window boxes or even under water in nearby lakes, streams or wells. But these methods did not prevent the spoilage of food. Before 1830, food was preserved by salting, spicing, smoking, pickling and drying, and there was no need for refrigeration. Between 1830 and the Civil War, with the development of cities and the improvement of economy, there was a demand by the consumer for fresh food, mainly produce (Krasner-Khait, 2011).

The first home "refrigerators" were insulated boxes filled with ice and known as "ice boxes". The "ice man" delivered ice daily or once in two days to keep the ice box working. In 1879, following John Gorie's work, two scientists, John Standard and Thomas Elkins, improved the refrigeration apparatus and designed it to circulate compressed gas and absorb heat (Bellis, 2006). Refrigeration train cars developed in 1860 and transported food around the United States. However, refrigeration had its problems. Refrigerants like sulphur dioxide and methyl chloride were found to be toxic. Ammonia, if leaked, caused serious health issues. To circumvent the problem, synthetic refrigerants called halocarbons or chlorofluorocarbons (CFCs) were used in 1928. CFCs were replaced with "safe" refrigerant called Freon, which was later banned because of its contribution to the ozone layer.

The household refrigerator is one of the greatest inventions. Engineering technology perfected it and made it reliable and inexpensive enough for widespread use domestically. The refrigerator has no doubt made our food safe and enjoyable.

1.2.3 HACCP Era

From the early 1970s, the HACCP concept has continued to evolve. The HACCP system has contributed to the development of a complete, effective and efficient food safety management system (FSMS). Prior to 1970, even though scientists were aware of disease-causing bacteria, foodborne illnesses continued to occur throughout the world.

Howard E. Bauman had worked at the US firm Pillsbury since 1953 as head of the research laboratory in the bacteriological section. Later he assisted the National Aeronautics and Space Administration (NASA), the US Air Force Space Laboratory project group, and the US Army's Natick Laboratories to develop a safe food safety system for the human space flight programme. Initially, in 1959, Pillsbury developed cube-sized foods for the flight crews. NASA engineers clearly set out their specifications: (a) The food should not crumble to prevent particles from floating into instrument panels and contaminating the atmosphere and (b) it should be safe for astronauts to consume during their flights. The efforts of food technologists led to the creation of a compressed food bar with an edible coating that did not crumble during the flights (Ross-Nazzal, 2007).

The first attempts to conduct a scientific study of the dangers posed by food were due to Paul Lachance, NASA's flight food and nutrition coordinator at the manned spacecraft centre at Houston. He recognised the potential dangers caused by physical, chemical and microbiological contaminants. Further investigations revealed that the ingredients purchased by NASA were contaminated with viral and bacteriological pathogens. At this time, hazard analysis was unknown, and Bauman identified a programme known as "Models of Failure", which was adopted and applied for each food item. The study revealed the potential problems during the manufacturing process and the ingredients that were potentially dangerous. A list of hazards was then compiled (Ross-Nazzal, 2007).

Natick Laboratories established microbiological standards for foods that would be consumed during the flights. The standards were stringent and specified that the aerobic plate count should not exceed 10,000 per gram. Manufacturers had to comply with Natick Laboratories' standards and required them to conduct microbiological tests during the pre- and in-process phases and on finished products. Contractors were required to identify critical failure areas and Pillsbury started to determine Critical Control Points (CCPs) during the manufacture. NASA recognised 17 critical control stations that had acceptance standards. It was a mandatory requirement for contractors to keep records that documented the history of the product, the source of raw materials, whether they were processed and the location where they were processed, and the people who worked in their manufacture (Ross-Nazzal, 2007).

The concepts of the HACCP approach were first presented at the National Conference on Food Production in April 1971. The aim of the conference was "to develop a comprehensive, integrated attack on the problem of microbial contamination of foods". Although Bauman encouraged the food industry to adopt the HACCP concept, the principles were not embraced (Surak, 2009; Ross-Nazzal, 2007).

However, two serious incidents in the United States prompted the consumer movement to compel the industry and trade officials to implement a comprehensive food safety plan (Ross-Nazzal, 2007). The first incident occurred in the spring of 1971, a few days before the conference, when a woman from Connecticut detected a glass particle in her baby's creamy white cereal made by the Pillsbury plant, forcing them to recall the product. Robin J. Keith, the CEO, took prompt action and instructed Bauman at Pillsbury to develop and implement a secure product safety system to prevent a recurrence. In the summer of 1971, a second incident occurred when Samuel Cochran died of botulism poisoning after consuming cold potato soup. These incidents cast doubts over food safety in the United States and whether the Food and Drug Administration (FDA) could protect consumers from food poisoning. It was claimed that the FDA did not have the resources or motivation to protect consumers and lacked support from the Department of Health, Education, and Welfare (Ross-Nazzal, 2007). However, following recognition of the FDA's problems, in September 1972, 16 FDA inspectors were trained at Pillsbury, which included courses and fieldwork. The FDA was then able to establish low acid canned food regulations. From 1973 to 1977, the safety of the canning process improved. In 1974, Pillsbury achieved its objective of developing and implementing an effective and efficient food product safety programme at its facilities. The company's annual report recorded that the HACCP system was in use in the Pillsbury food plants and in its Burger King restaurants.

The concept employed three main principles, which are valid even today: (a) conduct a hazard analysis; (b) determine the CCPs; and (c) establish monitoring procedures. There had been 130 food safety-related recalls of food products from the marketplace and none were Pillsbury's products (Ross-Nazall, 2007).

In the 1980s, several publications were produced, which promoted HACCP as the predominant food safety system (Surak, 2009):

1. In 1985, the National Research Council of the National Academy of Sciences published the "Green Book", *An Evaluation of the Role of Microbiological Criteria for Foods and Food Ingredients*. HACCP was described as the most effective means to ensure the food safety of the US food supply and recommended its use in food processing industry and government agencies.
2. The National Advisory Committee on Microbiological Criteria for Food (NACMFC) published the first HACCP document in 1989, which included the seven principles of HACCP.
3. Microorganisms in foods: *Application of the Hazard Analysis Critical Control Point System to Ensure Microbiological Safety and Quality* was published in 1989 by the International Commission on Microbiological Specifications for Foods (ICMSF). The book defined the application of HACCP principles and the concepts of CCP1 and CCP2 to the entire food chain, from the farm through to food preparation in restaurants and homes, to eliminate or reduce the hazard to an acceptable level. For the first time, Pre-requisite Programmes (PRPs) were also defined.
4. During this period, the Codex Alimentarius Commission was actively involved with food safety issues and it published the first HACCP standard in 1990, providing the first international definition for HACCP. In the same year, the NACMCF reviewed its guidance standard, codifying the five preliminary steps and the seven principles of HACCP. The Codex and NACMCF standards were again revised in 1997, harmonising the US definition of HACCP with the Codex definition.

Recent developments include the development of the HACCP Auditor Certification by the American Society for Quality, designed to ensure that the principles of the HACCP standards are clearly understood by auditors. The British Standards Institution developed their food safety standard known as PAS 220:2008. Following the introduction of these standards, there were several private and national food safety standards developed. Third-party certification was a problem because of the significant differences among the various standards. Danish standards recommended that the International Organization for Standardization (ISO) develop an FSMS. The first version of the ISO 22000 standard was published in 2005. Further improvements will no doubt occur in the future, assuring food safety.

Table 1.2 shows the development of the concept of food safety.

1.3 Environmental Management

A major impact on the earth's resources occurred, and the balance of nature was disturbed in the 19th century in Europe during the Industrial Revolution. Factories started dumping industrial waste into nearby rivers. This period of mechanisation consumed a vast amount of non-renewable resources to support the industrialised society without due regard to the long-term effect on the

Table 1.2 Timeline of Food Safety Management

Year	Originator	Activity
Middle Ages		Salting, spicing, smoking, pickling
1810	Nicola Apart	First concept of "canning"
1888	August Gartner	Isolated *Bacillus enteritidis*
Early 19th century		Ice boxes
1860		Refrigeration trains transported food
1879	John Standard and Thomas Elkins	Improved Gorie's refrigeration apparatus
1919		Pillsbury produced cube-sized food
1971		National Conference
1972		FDA training
2005		Published the ISO 22000 standard

health of the population or on the environment. It was necessary for national governments to bring in legislation and impose severe penalties to control the worst excesses of industrial pollution (Whitelaw, 2004).

Environmental events and disasters occurring anywhere in the world have created public awareness of environmental damage, which, in turn, has pushed the authorities to enforce laws and systems to manage the environment.

The Seveso industrial disaster in July 1976 occurred in a small chemical manufacturing plant in the Lombardy region in Italy. An uncontrolled chemical reaction released large amounts of dioxin, which resulted in the highest known exposure to the chemical causing long-term health effects on humans. Within two years, 80,000 animals had been slaughtered (Homberger, Reggiani, Sambeth & Wipf, 1979).

In March 1978, *Amoco Cadiz*, a supertanker, broke in two and sank in Portsall Rocks in Britanny releasing its entire cargo of 1.6 million barrels of oil, the largest oil spill known at that time. It resulted in the largest loss of marine life ever recorded (Tony, 2007).

In 1969, the Bhopal plant which was built as a formulation plant by Union Carbide became operational in 1980. The plant commenced the manufacture of the pesticide, Sevin, using methyl isocyanate. In 1984, after four years of operation, 30 metric tons of methyl isocyanate gas escaped from the plant. According to the estimates, 20,000 people died and 200,000 were exposed to the toxic gas by varying degrees (Varma & Varma, 2005).

During the Vietnam War, from 1961 to 1971, the US Army sprayed Agent Orange all over the country. Among the herbicides manufactured at that time, Agent Orange proved to be the most lethal as it contained the toxic chemical dioxin. It defoliated the vegetation, and razed forests to the ground, revealing enemy hide-outs. In Danang, where it was stored before loading into planes, toxins leaked from the drums. After each trip, the tarmac was hosed down and the toxins from the drums and the residue from the planes seeped into the soil, finding its way into water and entering the food chain. Even after three generations, Agent Orange has caused severe birth defects among Vietnamese children (Olarte, 2012).

The history of environmental management includes its evolution of the problems in the 18th and 19th centuries followed by (a) industrial products and processes lacking in standards in the early 20th century; (b) the creation of environmental laws and regulations in the early 1970s; (c) the development of voluntary codes of corporate conduct and environmental management practices during the last 30 years; (d) international involvement in environmental management; and (e) recent developments in international environmental standards and guidelines. The "Environmental Movement" appeared in response to the smoke emerging from coal-burning factories and the expansion of the petroleum industry. A lack of standardisation had resulted in industry shortages and accidents, and in 1919, the petroleum and allied industries established the American Petroleum Institute (API) (Cully, 1998).

A number of factors contributed to the development of voluntary codes of environmental conduct and "eco-auditing" programmes for industries in the 1970s: (a) increasing regulatory pressure; (b) adverse publicity following industrial accidents; (c) expensive legal battles; and (d) increasing public concern over the environmental impact due to industrial processes (StudyMode, 2015). This led to the formalisation of approaches to prevent pollution and adopt co-auditing. The need for the development of standards and procedures was evident.

The term sustainable development was first used in 1987 in the report, *Our Common Future* published by the United Nations World Commission on Environment and Development (UNCED) (UN, 1987). Public support from more than 50 world leaders, and the pressure to discuss and act upon the report, prompted the UNCED to convene in 1992 the famous "Earth Summit" conference in Rio de Janeiro. Two documents emerged from the conference, a comprehensive policy guidance document and the *Rio Declaration*, which included 27 principles for achieving sustainable development (UN, 1992).

In the early 1990s, further developments took place in the international arena. BS 7750 was published in March 1992. At the same time, the French Standard AFNOR X30-200 appeared. The publication of these national standards promoted a variety of different groups to standardise environmental management systems (EMSs) to enable companies and institutions to share a common set of guidelines (de la Espina & Velasco, 2000).

The European Commission's initiatives commenced with the draft regulations on environmental management in 1990. The Eco-Management and Audit Regulations (1836/93/EC) were adopted in 1993, and they included the Eco-Management and Audit Scheme (EMAS). For business enterprises in the European Union, EMAS included specifications for voluntary EMSs. Other voluntary codes for environmental management include the *Business Charter for Sustainable Development and a Guide to Effective Environmental Auditing* developed in 1991 by the International Chamber of Commerce and the *Code for Corporate Environmental Conduct* developed by the Coalition of Environmentally Responsible Economies (CERES) (Pritwani, 2016; Cully, 1998).

These multiple standards and voluntary codes prompted the establishment of a Strategic Advisory Group on the Environment (SAGE) – consisting of the international standards organisations, the ISO and the Electrotechnical Commission – to develop recommendations on international standards for environmental management. On its recommendation, the ISO created Technical Committee 207 in 1993 to develop an international EMS standard. As a result of these efforts, the ISO 14001 EMS was published in 1996.

The US Environment Protection Agency (EPA) and the US Department of Justice (DOI) had not endorsed it formally because the ISO 14001 standard was not performance-based and did not ensure improved environmental performance. However, under the Clinton administration, the EPA established an EMS framework based on ISO 14001. Further initiatives included the Environmental Leadership Programme – the Common Sense Initiative, and Project XL (Scagnelli & Hollenbeck, 2009). Currently, the EPA is engaged in a number of initiatives (2017–2019 cycle) such as (EPA, 2018):

- Reducing air pollution from the largest sources.
- Reducing hazardous air pollutants.
- Ensuring energy extraction activities comply with regulations.
- Reducing risks of accidental emissions from industries.
- Reducing hazardous air emissions from waste facilities.
- Managing raw sewage and contaminated storm water.
- Preventing animal waste from polluting soil and water.
- Keeping industrial pollutants from natural waters.

Since the introduction of the ISO 14001, EMSs have helped companies, organisations and governments manage their potential environmental impacts and ultimately reduce them.

1.3.1 Montreal Protocol

The Montreal Protocol, which dealt with substances that deplete the ozone layer was signed on September 16, 1987, and took effect from January 1989. As of September 16, 2009, it has been signed and ratified by 196 countries (Environment and Climate Change Canada, 2010).

1.3.2 Kyoto Protocol

Following the ratification of the UN Framework Convention on Climate Change (UNFCC), three meetings of the Conference of the Parties (COP) were held. COP-3 was held in Kyoto, Japan, in December 1997. It was known as the Kyoto Protocol, and it specified targets and timelines to reduce greenhouse gas (GHG) emissions by at least 5% during the period 2008–2012 (UNFCC, 2014).

Table 1.3 shows the timeline of EMS development.

1.3.3 Carbon Footprint

The carbon footprint has historically been defined as the total set of GHG emissions caused by an organisation, event, product or person and is usually expressed in equivalent tons of carbon dioxide (CO_2). Carbon footprint is also applicable to nations, events, products and services. The word *carbon* is used because CO_2 is the predominant GHG emitted from human activities. Other gases such as methane (CH_4) and nitrous oxide (N_2O) also contribute towards global warming. When carbon footprint results are reported, these gases are normalised to the mass of CO_2.

Carbon footprint analysis refers to the measurement of GHG emitting processes, their origins and their composition and amounts and is accomplished through an audit or assessment process. Energy and carbon footprint reduction is achieved by reducing energy and GHG emissions through energy reduction, process/equipment changes and reallocation of resources (Franchetti & Apul, 2013).

Table 1.3 Timeline of Environmental Management

Year		Activity
1976		Seveso disaster
1978		Amoco Cadiz disaster
1980		Bhopal disaster
1961–1971		Vietnam war
1919		Established the American Petroleum Institute
1970s		Introduced voluntary codes of environmental conduct
1987		United Nations World Commission on Environment and Development (UNCED) published the report *Our Common Future*
1992		Earth Summit in Rio Published the British Standard BS 7750 Published the French standard AFNOR X30-200
1993		Adopted Eco-Management and Audit Scheme Published other voluntary codes ISO created Technical Committee 207 to develop the Environmental Management Standard
1996		Published the first Environmental Management Standard

References

American Society for Quality. (n.d.). *History of quality*. Retrieved March 12, 2018 from http://asq.org/learn-about-quality/history-of-quality/overview/overview.html

Bellis, M. (2006). *The history of refrigerator and freezers*. Retrieved March 26, 2018 from http://theinventors.org/library/inventors/blrefrigerator.htm

Box, G.E.P., Kacker, R.N., Nair, V., Phadke, M., Shoemaker, A. and Wu, C.F. J. (1988). Quality practices in Japan. *Quality Progress*, 21 (3), 37–41.

Centre for Food Service Learning. (2011). *History of food safety: A commentary*. Retrieved March 12, 2018 from http://www.food-safety-and-you.com/HistoryofFoodSafety.html

Crawford-Mason, C. (Producer). (June 24, 1980). If Japan can … Why can't we? *NBC White Paper* [Television series]. New York: NBC.

Cully, W.C. (1998). *Environment and Quality System Integration*. Florida: CRC Press.

de la Espina, E.Z.D. and Velasco, C.B. (2000). Environmental management in the industrial enterprises of the south of Spain. *Environmental Monitoring and Assessment*, 62 (2), 169–174.

Department of Trade and Industry. (n.d.). *The evolution of quality*. Retrieved March 12, 2018 from http://www.businessballs.com/dtiresources/quality_management_history.pdf.

Dodge, H.M. (1969). Notes on the evolution of sampling plans. *Journal of Quality Technology*, 77–88 (Part 1); 155–162 (Part 2); 225–232 (Part 3).

Dodge, H.M. (1970). Notes on the evolution of sampling plans. *Journal of Quality Technology*, 1–8 (Part 4).

Environment and Climate Change Canada. (2010). *International – Vienna convention and the Montreal protocol*. Retrieved March 12, 2018 from https://www.ec.gc.ca/ozone/default.asp?lang=En&n=D11D2440-1

EPA. (2018). *National enforcement initiatives*. Retrieved March 27, 2018 from https://www.epa.gov/enforcement/national-enforcement-initiatives

Fisher, N.I. and Nair, V.N. (2009). Quality management and quality practice: Perspectives on their history and their future. *Applied Stochastic Models in Business and Industry*, 25, 1–28.

Franchetti, M.J. and Apul, D. (2013). *Carbon Footprint Analysis: Concepts, Methods, Implementation, and Case Studies*. Florida: Taylor and Francis.

Goetz, P.W. and Sutton, M. (1983). Pre-food laws of Middle Ages. *The New Encyclopaedia Britannica*, 8, 695.

Griffith, C. (2006). Food safety: Where from and where to? *British Food Journal*, 108 (1), 6–15.

Hahn, G.I., Hill, W.J., Hoerl, R.W. and Zinkgraf, S.A. (1999). The impact of six sigma improvement: A glimpse into the future of statistics. *The American Statistician*, 53 (3), 208–215.

Homberger, E., Reggiani, G., Sambeth, J. and Wipf, H.K. (1979). The Seveso accident: Its nature, extent and consequences. *The Annals of Occupational Hygiene*, 22 (4), 327–370.

Krasner-Khait, B. (2011). The impact of refrigerators. *History Magazine*. Retrieved March 12, 2018 from http://www.history-magazine.com/refrig.html.

Motarjemi, Y., Kaferstein, F., Moy, G., Miyagawa, S. and Miyagishima, K. (1996). The importance of HACCP for public health and development: The role of the World Health Organisation. *Food Control*, 7, 77–85.

Nair, V.N. (1992). Taguchi's parameter design: A panel discussion. *Technometrics*, 34, 127–161.

Olarte, A. (2012, December 5). A toxic disaster. *The Island (Features)*, p. 7.

Phadke, M.S. (1989). *Quality Engineering Using Robust Design*. Englewood Cliffs: Prentice-Hall.

Pike, J. and Barnes, R. (1996). *TQM in Action: A Practical Approach to Continuous Process Improvement*. Norwich: Page Brothers.

Pritwani, K. (2016). *Sustainability of Business in the Context of Environmental Management*. India: The Energy and Resource Institute.

Ross-Nazzal, J. (2007). From farm to fork. In S.J. Dick, H. E. McCurdy and R.D. Launius (Eds.), *Chapter 12: Societal Impact of Spaceflight*, pp. 219–236. Washington, DC: NASA.

Rutherford, D. (2007) Les trois approches de Malthus pour résoudre le problème démographique. *Population*, 62, (2), 213–237.

Sarasohn, H. (1997, April). Progress through a commitment to quality. *Proceedings of the Australian Quality Council 12th National Quality Management Conference*, pp. 101–110. Sydney, Australia.

Scagnelli, J.M. and Hollenbeck, S. (2009). Pollution Prevention Act. In T.F.P. Sullivan (Ed.), *Environmental Law Handbook* (20th ed.), pp. 777–800. Maryland: Government Institutes.

Schilling, E.J. (1993). Acceptance sampling – past present and future. In M.J. Kowalewski and J.B. Tye (Eds.), *Statistical Sampling: Past, Present and Future Theoretical and Practical*, pp. 5–14. Philadelphia: ASTM.

Shewhart, W.A. (1986). *Statistical Methods from the Viewpoint of Quality Control*. E.W. Deming (Ed.). New York: Dover

StudyMode. (2015). *Sustainability in industry*. Retrieved February 17, 2018 from http://www.studymode.com/essays/Sustainability-In-Industry-68339437.html

Surak, J.G. (2009, February/March). The evolution of HACCP: A perspective on today's most effective food safety system. *Food Quality Magazine*. Retrieved March 12, 2018 from https://www.foodqualityand-safety.com/article/the-evolution-of-haccp/

Taylor, F.W. (2012). *Principles of Scientific Management*. Michigan: ReadaClassic.

Tony, A. (2007). *MV Amoco Cadiz* (+1978). Retrieved March 12, 2018 from http://www.wrecksite.eu/wreck.aspx?10339#10339.

Tribus, M. (2001, May). Tomas Bata's creative legacy and current entrepreneurial methods. *Proceedings of the First International Conference on Bata's System of Management*, Zlin, Czech Republic.

UN. (1987). *Report of the World Commission on Environment and Development: Our common future*. Retrieved December 15, 2012 from http://www.un-documents.net/wced-ocf.htm

UN. (1992, June). Earth Summit. *Proceeding of the UN Conference on Environment and Development (UNCED)*, Rio de Janeiro.

United Nations Framework Convention on Climate Change. (2014). *A summary of the Kyoto protocol*. Retrieved October 23, 2016 from http://unfccc.int/kyoto_protocol/background/items/2879.php

Varma, R. and Varma, D.R. (2005). The Bhopal disaster of 1984. *Bulletin of Science, Technology & Science*, 25 (1), 37–45.

Whitelaw, K. (2004). *ISO 14001: Environmental Handbook* (2nd ed.). Oxford: Elsevier.

Chapter 2

Impact of Management Systems on Business Performance

2.1 Introduction

Management systems enable organisations to plan and achieve their objectives. Numerous studies have been carried out to determine the impact of management systems on business performance. Often, certification standards such as ISO (International Organization for Standardization) standards have been considered as management systems. ISO standards are not management systems, as they are merely criteria against which the effectiveness of management systems is measured. A management system is as good as its design and implementation. It is an essential part of the culture of the organisation, and all elements of the system must fit together (Gordon, 2002). In this chapter, the impact of management systems (both certified and uncertified) on business performance is discussed.

2.2 Impact of Quality Management Systems

Organisations develop and implement various management systems, such as Total Quality Management (TQM), Six Sigma, Continuous Quality Improvement (CQI), with varying degrees of success to manage their operations. Both qualitative and quantitative studies have been conducted to evaluate their impact on business performance.

A study of the impact of certified Quality Management Systems (QMSs) in Portuguese companies has shown that those with higher financial performance are more likely to implement and certify their QMSs. Motivation emerged as a critical success factor for economic performance. However, some companies with non-certified QMSs have demonstrated higher financial performance (Sampaio et al., 2011).

The management staff of Malaysian small- and medium-sized enterprises specialising in electronic and electrical appliances participated in a 2009 study to assess the impact of a QMS on product quality and business performance (Samad, 2009). Two hundred questionnaires were used and the QMS was measured using eight dimensions:

1. Leadership.
2. Evaluation of activities.
3. Employee participation.
4. Recognition and reward.
5. Education and training.
6. Process control and improvement.
7. Quality system improvement.
8. Customer focus.

Financial performance was assessed in terms of annual sales, sales growth, profits, market share and export. Non-financial performance was evaluated using items that measure employee and customer satisfaction. All QMS dimensions had a significant positive effect on business performance and leadership emerged as the most important dimension. QMS dimensions other than recognition and reward had a positive effect on product quality, with evaluation activity being the most important dimension. QMS exerted a more important effect on business performance than on product quality.

The impact of quality improvement tools on the performance of firms using different QMSs has been studied using a personalised survey among 107 European Foundation for Quality Management (EFQM) assessors between February and April 2007 (Heras et al., 2011). The data on the degree of use of quality improvement tools and the impact on performance were collected and analysed using 17 quality improvement tools and 12 indicators of performance. Tools were classified into "hard tools" (quantitative) and "soft tools" (qualitative).

The impact on performance depended on the standard used for certification: ISO 9000 standard or the EFQM model. The survey revealed that hard tools have been used less frequently because their application required greater knowledge and experience. The use of hard tools in companies adopting the EFQM model demonstrated an improvement in performance. Companies employing the ISO 9000 standard used soft tools more often and showed a significant influence in improving commercial performance.

A study of the impact of quality management in European companies' performance has been conducted in Spain using the Delphi method, which is a method for structuring a group communication process so that the process allows a group of individuals as a whole to deal with a complex problem (Saizarbitoria et al., 2006). The method relies on (a) the assumption that collective knowledge is better than individual knowledge; (b) the ability to contrast knowledge; and (c) having more factors serving as objects of the study. However, its disadvantages are (a) a lack of quantitative basis; (b) an absence of scientific foundation; and (c) a reliance on opinions.

A panel of experts was formed to conduct the research project to assess the impact of the ISO 9000 standard and the EFQM model on business performance. The panel included 27 quality professionals, a specialist from the Basque Country in Spain company managers, consultants, certifiers, assessors, academic specialists and members of institutions such as Euskalit and the Knowledge Cluster. According to the opinion of the panel, the ISO 9000 standard is of limited importance because the standard specifies minimum requirements. Implementing the EFQM model can lead to a grade of excellence. Table 2.1 shows the impact of the ISO 9000 standard and EFQM model on business performance.

Table 2.1   Impact of ISO 9000 Standard and EFQM Model on Performance

Effect on	*ISO 9000 Standard*	*EFQM Model*
Operations	Positive effect: Greater control and follow up of processing orders, improvement of security of operations, minimising delivery times, errors and defects	Positive effect: Reduction of costs of errors, defects, and delivery times. Increase in safety of operations
Economic results	No significant effect on economic and financial results	Strengthens partnership between clients and suppliers improving profitability
Workers	No significant effect on workers. They feel more controlled	Greater employee involvement. Improvement of suggestions by workers, their safety at work, motivation and satisfaction
Clients	Positive effect: Reduction of complaints and increased repeat purchases	Greater client satisfaction, more repeat purchases and less complaints
Image	Improvement of image	Improvement of image, allowing companies to realise preferred status in the market
Quality of products and services	Better control over operations and materials. Reduction of defective products. Improvement of quality of final products and services	Achieve client's objectives. Improvement of quality of products and services

The effects of implementing an ISO 9000 standard compliant QMS on employees and employers has been studied in single plant firms in California by Levine and Toffel (2010). The study included 916 companies having a QMS certified to the ISO 9000 standard (ISO adopters) and 17,849 companies not certified to an international standard (non-adopters). According to the survey, sales and employment increased substantially more rapidly after certification of their QMSs. Compared with non-adopters, payroll and annual earnings per employee increased significantly after certification of ISO adopters. Some benefits of ISO certification were more evident in smaller firms than in larger firms. Adoption of the ISO 9000 standard had no influence on lowering the average injury costs.

An empirical survey of 353 companies with a management system certified to the ISO 9000 standard and 176 companies with management systems certified to both the ISO 9000 and ISO 14000 standards in the Spanish autonomous region of Catalonia was conducted to determine the benefits of certification (Casadesus et al., 2011). The survey studied the possible benefits of certification in terms of financial results, customer satisfaction, employee satisfaction and operational results. Companies with QMSs certified to multiple standards perceived more benefits in 15 out of 16 indicators. In addition, companies with integrated management systems demonstrated more benefits than those having separate standardised management systems.

In September to December 2002, 212 Slovenian companies were surveyed to evaluate the impact of QMSs certified to the ISO 9000 standard on customer satisfaction (Priskar, 2007). The survey indicated that the companies with certified management systems demonstrated a positive impact on customer satisfaction. Better results were shown by companies which gained QMS certification before 1997. It is possible that these companies have been successful in integrating the QMS into the culture of the organisation. However, the results showed that there is no direct impact of the QMS on an improvement in sales, profitability or gaining new customers.

Telrad Telecommunication Electronic Industries, Israel's largest communications equipment manufacturer, carried out a 1998 study among its 111 suppliers to determine the impact of ISO 9000 certification on product quality (Rabinovitz, et al., 1998). The following data was collected from the suppliers:

- Status of certification (42 out of 111 suppliers had ISO 9000 certified QMSs).
- Year of certification.
- Initiator of certification (supplier or Telrad).
- Type of supplier (manufacturer or sales organisation).
- Number of employees in each organisation.

Product quality was assessed on the basis of the percentage of rejected batches per year. The results of the study revealed the following:

1. Owing to the guidance and control by Telrad, the average product quality of suppliers whose QMS certification was initiated by them was higher than that of self-initiated suppliers. Although, in general, the product quality improved after certification, there was a greater variability.
2. The average product quality of products from small suppliers, irrespective of certification, was better than those from larger suppliers.
3. On average, product quality was better from manufacturers than from vendors.
4. Suppliers with ISO 9000 compliant suppliers offered higher-quality products than those without certified QMSs.

It is evident from the studies carried out that organisations reap some benefits after the implementation of QMSs. There is a great variation of benefits perceived among the organisations. However, in the absence of clear standards for measurement, it is difficult to assess the impact of QMSs on business performance. According to Dick (2000), the research clearly suggests that competitive advantage is achieved by effective process control, quality control and better conformance to quality standards. However, there is insufficient evidence to conclude that quality certification is consistently associated with business performance gains. A system is as good as the way it has been designed and implemented. QMSs designed and implemented with the sole intention of achieving certification with no input from the staff cannot be sustained long term.

2.2.1 Case Study – Motorola*

By the early 1970s, Motorola established itself as the world leader in wireless communication products with severe competition from Texas Instruments and Intel for the number one position in semiconductor sales. Owing to fierce competition in the consumer products market, Motorola sold its consumer electronic division to a Japanese company in 1973 and its future was at stake.

---

* Stoner, J.A.F., Freeman, R.E. and Gilbert Jr., D.R. (2005). *Management* (6th ed.). Delhi: Prentice Hall.

Senior management ignored the warning signs. Among the top eight semiconductor manufacturers in 1974 were five American and three European firms. By 1979, the Japanese were gaining ground and two of the top eight manufacturers were Japanese. Motorola's quality revolution commenced in May 1979 with the comments made by Arthur Sundry, Senior Sales Manager for the communications sector at the management meeting, that "Our quality stinks…". In 1980, Bob Galvin, the CEO, established a taskforce to review the quality of Motorola's products, with the aim of securing Motorola's global leadership (Six Sigma & Lean Resources, 2013). The review in the late 1980s revealed that their products have gained long-term reliability, while many new products often failed during the first three to nine months of service. There were also problems in manufacturing and delivery that damaged the reputation of the company.

In response to these failures, a new series of quality improvement initiatives commenced in 1981 with the object of achieving a 10-fold increase in quality improvement and customer satisfaction within five years. Employees were empowered to improve manufacturing processes throughout the company. Training programmes were initiated to improve the necessary skills, new human resources (HR) policies were written, a mission statement was developed, and over 4,000 teams were formed to reduce cycle times and defects, and improve customer satisfaction. As a result of these quality initiatives, Motorola was awarded the first Malcolm Baldrige Quality Award in 1988.

Although Motorola successfully completed the first phase of their quality improvement programme in 1988, Japanese companies were producing goods at quality levels far above than Motorola factories in the United States. When Japanese firms took over Matsushita factories in Chicago in 1974, the Motorola factory was producing TV sets with 150 defects for every 100 sets produced. After the takeover, Motorola's management initiated drastic changes in the operations, and by 1979, it was manufacturing TV sets with only four defects per 100 sets produced. These achievements were made with the same workforce, technology and designs, making it obvious that the problem was with the Motorola management.

In 1987, the CEO Bob Galvin embarked on another series of quality improvement initiatives. The goal was to achieve zero defects or 99.999% defect-free products by 1992. This programme was designated Six Sigma. It involved six steps: (a) identify products to be manufactured; (b) identify the customers; (c) select the suppliers; (d) empower employees to plan process changes; (e) evaluate and eliminate non-value added steps and sources of errors; and (f) determine the criteria for monitoring.

Motorola established the certified supplier programme and encouraged the suppliers to work towards the Malcolm Baldrige Quality Award. Six Sigma was a top-down approach with total commitment from the CEO. The programme was led by several categories of leaders:

■ Champions are high-level employees who understand the concepts of Six Sigma.
■ Sponsors are "owners" of the processes who initiate and coordinate Six Sigma improvement activities.
■ Master Black Belt is the highest level in the organisation with technical expertise.
■ Green Belts are Six Sigma project leaders who plan and facilitate Six Sigma projects from concept to completion.

With these quality improvement plans, Motorola was able to achieve a quality level of 5.7 Sigma in 1992. Sales per employee increased from $62,000 in 1986 to $111,000 in 1992. Defects per million decreased from 6,000 in 1981 to 40 in 1992. Net cash from operations, sales, capital expenditure and share price doubled during this period. Estimated savings as a result of quality improvement activities amounted to $1.5 million.

2.2.2 Case Study – Xerox

In 1938, Chester Carlson, a patent attorney and part-time inventor, made the first version of a xerographic image in the United States. However, there was no market for it until the Battelle Memorial Institute in Columbia, Ohio, requested Carlson to refine the product, which he called "electrophotography".

By 1976, the company's revenue increased to $ 4.4 billion with a profit of $407 million. The growth of Xerox was rapid. New controls and procedures were developed and implemented, and there was a need to increase the management layers, which created new problems in decision-making and product delivery. In addition, in the early 1980s, there was intense competition from both the US and Japanese competitors. Ricoh, Cannon and Sevin entered the new market. Several problems were emerging in Xerox, as its management failed to give strategic direction to meet the challenges of competitors. Its operating costs were high and products were of inferior quality in comparison to competitors' products. The decision-making process was highly centralised. Poor financial performance reflected the difficulties experienced by Xerox. For example, return on assets declined to less than 8%, market share decreased to 17% in 1984 from 68% in 1974, and between 1980 and 1984 profits decreased from $1.15 billion to $20 million.

When David T. Keans took over as the CEO in 1982, he realised that the cost of Japanese copiers was 40%–50% cheaper than Xerox products. To reduce manufacturing costs and improve quality, he embarked on the project called "Leadership Through Quality", part of which was the benchmarking programme.

Through these initiatives, it was possible to turn around the company in the years to come. Eventually, Xerox became the best example of successful implementation of the benchmarking programme.

Benchmarking involved the identification, understanding and adopting best practices and processes, both inside and outside the organisation, and implementing the results. The programme developed by Xerox compared the activities of this company, or part of it, with those of other companies (Hitt et al., 2005).

The "Leadership Through Quality" programme initiated by Keans revived the company. Benchmarking against Japanese companies revealed that Xerox took twice as long to bring a product to the market, employed five times the number of engineers, and made four times the number of design changes with three times the design cost. During this period Xerox had over 30,000 defective parts per million items produced (30 times more than its competitors). In addition, benchmarking also revealed that Xerox needed a massive growth rate for five consecutive years to meet the challenges of Japanese competitors.

Urgent action was necessary by Xerox to recover. It developed its own benchmarking model involving 10 steps classified under five stages:

■ Planning: Identifying the subject to be benchmarked, identifying appropriate best practice organisations and selecting/developing suitable data collection methods.
■ Analysis: Identifying the strengths of the competitors and comparing performance against them to determine the current competitor gap and expected competitor gap.
■ Integration: Establishing goals and integrating them into the planning process.
■ Action: Implementing and monitoring the action plan.
■ Maturity: Determining which goals have been achieved.

Xerox started collecting data on key processes which were analysed to identify and determine quality improvement opportunities. Its benchmarking model was implemented and reviewed. The model was applied to (a) the supplier management system; (b) the inventory management system; (c) manufacturing management system; (d) marketing; and (e) QMS. Soon results were evident:

- Highly satisfied customers for its copier/duplicator and printing systems increased by 38% and 39%, respectively.
- Customer complaints declined by more than 60%.
- Customer satisfaction with the sales process improved by 40%, service processes by 18% and manufacturing processes by 21%.
- Through the mid- and late-1980s financial performance improved considerably.

Many other benefits related to Xerox's products, sales and marketing were also realised.

The benchmarking programme was so successful that Xerox became the only company world-wide to win all three prestigious quality awards: the Deming Award (Japan) in 1980, the Malcolm Baldrige Quality Award in 1989, and the European Quality Award in 1992. Over the years, Xerox has won a series of quality awards in many countries (Dragolea & Cotirlea, 2009).

2.3 Impact of Food Safety Management Systems

Food quality has become an important issue in the food sector over the past decade. Consumers' demand for safer food is increasing as they become more affluent, live longer and become aware of the association between the diet and their health. Contaminated and unsafe food has a serious impact on consumers as well as on governments, food safety authorities, food producers and food serving institutions. According to the annual report of the Chief Scientist in the United Kingdom (Food Standards Agency, 2011), about one million people suffer from foodborne illnesses each year, about 20,000 people receive hospital treatment, about 500 people die, and it costs about £1.5 billion per annum. Each year in the United States, 31 pathogens cause 37.2 million illnesses and of these 9.4 million were foodborne. They cause 228,744 hospitalisations of which 55,961 were due to contaminated food. Thirty-one pathogens caused 2,612 deaths and of these 1,351 were caused by foodborne illnesses (Scallan et al., 2011). According to the basic cost of illnesses model (BCOI) and the enhanced cost of illnesses model (ECOI) in the study conducted by Scharff (2012), the annual aggregated cost was $77.7 billion and $51.06 billion for the BCOI model and ECOI model, respectively. The BCOI model includes economic estimates for medical costs, productivity losses and illness-related mortality, while the ECOI model replaces productivity with pain, suffering and functional disability measures based on monetised quality adjusted life-year estimates.

Several studies have identified the difficulties of estimating the costs associated with implementing and operating a Hazard Analysis and Critical Control Point (HACCP) programme. In most cases, food processing organisations do not formally estimate these costs prior to implementation. Lack of knowledge of HACCP principles and how the plan operates also make it difficult to identify and separate HACCP costs from production costs (Buchweitz & Salay, 2006; Donovan et al., 2001; Maldonado et al., 2005; Henson et al., 1999). Although it is important to evaluate the extent of costs before the HACCP system is established, only less than 15% of the organisations actually do estimate these costs at this stage (Henson et al., 1999).

The cost of implementing HACCP depends on several factors (Bata et al., 2006): Current hygienic conditions in the plant, size of the plant, complexity of the operations, number and experience of employees, extra resources needed for implementation, availability of technical support, and financial resources to improve the good hygiene practices (GHPs) requirements. However, the estimated costs are based on assumptions depending on the plant, the nature of the process and the country where the plant is located. Therefore, it is meaningless to present a generalised cost structure for the implementation of the HACCP programme.

Various cost structures have been used to estimate the total cost of the HACCP programme. According to Cusato, Tavolaro and de Oliveira (2012), the total cost can be broken down into three phases: initial, implementation and maintenance. Table 2.2 shows the cost items involved in each phase of the process. Bata et al. (2006), who examined the implementation costs in an airline catering company, divided the costs into (a) development; (b) installation; (c) certification; and (d) operational maintenance.

HACCP generally involves high fixed costs to establish the plan and carry out training of staff and the purchase of capital equipment, requiring an economy of scale. Variable costs include labour and/or material and are usually minor. However, at the farm level, variable costs could be more significant (Unnevehr & Roberts, 1997). According to McAloon (2005) and Suwanrangsi (2000), the relative costs incurred at all stages of implementing the programme, the technological level of the plant, and non-compliance with essential pre-requisite programmes (PRPs) led to higher costs in the implementation of the HACCP system.

The number of identified Critical Control Points (CCPs) and the PRPs in place in the plant has a direct impact on the resources necessary to implement, develop and maintain an HACCP programme. According to the study carried out by Roberto, Brandao and da Silva (2006), a reduction in the CCP numbers is associated with a corresponding decrease in cumulative cost after four months of implementation. Appropriate PRPs make it possible to reduce the number of CCPs, enabling easier adoption of the HACCP plan (Arvanitoyannis & Varzakas, 2008). The process has to be analysed carefully to determine the appropriate number of CCPs, and if a large number has been identified, the management of the process will be difficult and the audit process will be time-consuming (Wallace & Williams, 2001).

During the plan development stage, the main costs are related to consulting services and the use of staff on development activities, which are different from their routine work. In the implementation stage, the costs included the cost of improving the PRPs, administration and staff training, the cost of operational changes, and the procurement of equipment to fulfil HACCP requirements.

Table 2.2 Estimation of the Cost of the HACCP Programme

Initial Phase	Implementation Phase	Maintenance Phase
Employment of a consultant Appointment of staff to positions created by moving current employees to the HACCP Team	Staff training Improvement of PRP and HACCP tasks New equipment Laboratory costs Infrastructure changes Management changes	Record-keeping Monitoring Recruiting staff for monitoring Product testing Managerial/supervisory time

PRPs: pre-requisite programmes.

Costs associated with the routine activities necessary to maintain the HACCP programme, the time consumed in monitoring the CCPs, and the records required by the HACCP plan are identified as maintenance costs. According to Henson et al., (1999), major costs during the implementing and operation phases are related to staff time rather than investment in new equipment or upgrading the infrastructure (Bata et al., 2006). The time involved in monitoring and hiring people to monitor is associated with maintenance costs (Donovan et al., 2001).

The benefits of implementing an HACCP system result from the reduction of risk of illness due to the consumption of contaminated food. Many of the benefits are intangible in nature or difficult to quantify (Cusato et al., 2012). The main beneficiary is the consumer who is assured of better quality products because of the safety of the food. An HACCP system benefits the consumer, the industry, the government and regulatory bodies (Food Safety Programme, 1999). These benefits as reported in several studies are presented in Table 2.3

Table 2.3 Benefits of Food Safety Management Systems

| References | Benefits to | | |
	Internal (Industry)	External (Consumer)	Government
Unnevehr and Roberts (1997) Cost–benefit analysis	Longer shelf life for products Efficiency gains Ease of monitoring	Food safety Greater reliability to customers Access to distant markets Reduction of product liability	Reduction of public health service costs
Mutlu et al. (2003) Agro-food manufacturers and service firms in Turkey	Create a hygienic environment Better process control Better quality of raw materials New approach to quality management	Food safety Provide confidence to customer	
Henson et al. (1999) UK dairy industry	Improvement of product quality Improvement of efficiency and productivity Reduction of wastage	Ability to hold onto existing customers Ability to meet the increasing demand of the market place Access to overseas markets	Meet regulatory requirements
Bas et al. (2007) Food businesses in Turkey	Improvement of customer confidence Fewer customer complaints Useful business discipline	Food safety	Compliance with legislation

(Continued)

Table 2.3 (*Continued*) Benefits of Food Safety Management Systems

References	Benefits to		
	Internal (Industry)	*External (Consumer)*	*Government*
Semos and Kontogeorgos (2007) Food industry in northern Greece	Customers benefit Improvement of products and processes		
Wang et al. (2007) Food processing firms in China	Increase in turnover Better management Medium and large firms show positive profit	Customer confidence Higher market share	
Khatri and Collins (2007) HACCP implementation in Australian meat industry	Fewer customer complaints Improvement of product hygiene Fewer recalls and reworks Improvement of Staff morale	Access to overseas markets	
McAloon (2005) Implementation in the US firm Cargill	Safer food Better process control Reduction in cost and reworks Increase in commitment Longer shelf life of products		
Maldonando et al. (2005) Survey of Mexican meat industry	Increase in product sales Longer shelf life of products Enhanced ability to retain existing customers Reduction of product costs Reduction of microbial counts	Access to overseas market	

According to a survey of food processing firms in China carried out by the Certification and Accreditation Administration of the People's Republic of China (PRC), the cost/benefit of small-scale firms adopting the HACCP system showed a negative tax before profit (TBP), except for roasted food and the candy processing industry. This negative TBP has been attributed to the high cost of investments required. Medium-size and large-scale firms have shown a positive TBP (Wang et al., 2003).

2.3.1 Impact of Food Safety System on the Environment

There is an increasing demand for a more proactive approach from the food processing industry to manage organisations' activities, products and services that have or could have an adverse impact on the environment. A search for developments which meet current needs without compromising the ability to meet future generation's needs (sustainability) requires a review of traditional standards of waste management, production procedures and environmental management systems (EMSs), including the efficient use of non-renewal resources (Cusato et al., 2012).

The concept of "clean production" involves the use of technologies that ensure (Cusato et al., 2012):

a. Consumption of fewer natural resources (water, energy and raw materials).
b. Reduction of waste product.
c. Better operational practices.
d. Reduction of losses.
e. Better storage facilities.
f. Efficient disposal of residues.
g. Redesigning products and processes to use minimum amounts of raw materials and energy.

Although the HACCP system has been conceived as a means of assuring food safety, there are consequential benefits for the environment. Stringent control measures ensure more efficient procedures with a minimum amount of rework and rejects. Disposal or rework of products usually involves managing waste as well as product and packaging losses. In addition, disposal of products is minimised, which otherwise has to be subjected to retreatment (consuming energy, water and chemicals). There is a real possibility of chemical contaminants in raw materials from primacy producers and their efficient control through the HACCP programme minimises the risk. Therefore, the HACCP system, while assuring food safety, develops a sense of responsibility among the food processing industry to protect and sustain the environment.

2.3.2 Barriers to Implementation

Several barriers hinder the development of HACCP system, particularly in small and less developed businesses. These barriers vary from country to country and sector to sector. These are due to internal factors, such as a lack of knowledge or expertise and resources available to a business and/or external factors (e.g. a lack of support and guidance from governments and regulatory bodies) (Food Safety Programme, 1999). Table 2.4 summarises these barriers.

2.3.3 Case Study – Implementation of HACCP System in an Airline Catering Company*

The implementation of the HACCP system in an airline catering company supplying up to 10,000 meals per year has been studied by Bata et al. (2006). The following stages were involved in the establishment of the HACCP system:

1. Development of pre-requisite standard sanitation procedures and training of employees.
2. Changing the attitude and the organisational culture of the administration towards new management approaches.

---

* Details of the airline or catering company are not available.

Table 2.4 Barriers to Implementing the HACCP System

References	Internal Barriers	External Barriers

Food Safety Programme (1999)	Limited financial resources
	Human resource constraints
	Lack of expertise and technical
	  support
	Inadequate facilities and
	  infrastructure
	Inadequate communication
		Lack of government
		  commitment
		Lack of demands by customers
		  and businesses
		Absence of legal requirements

Bas et al. (2007)	Lack of pre-requisite programmes Lack of knowledge of HACCP and other food safety systems Time constraints High staff turnover Lack of staff motivation Complex terminology Inadequate training	
Semos and Konotogeorgos (2007)	Lack of trained staff Absence of staff motivation Inflexibility of production	

Ehiri et al. (1995)	Lack of understanding of HACCP
	  principles, implementation
	  process and related cost/benefits	

3. Adopting the HACCP philosophy and its requirements, conducting a hazard analysis of the products and services of the company, developing a documented HACCP plan and monitoring records.
4. Implementing the plan, and validation and verification of the HACCP system.
5. The company spent five years from the planning stage to the completion of training. A consulting company hired by the company developed the plan, trained the staff and followed up during the implementation phase. The development phase was spread out over nine months from March 1998 to December 1999.

2.3.3.1 Plan Development

Due to time constraints, rapid staff turnover, lack of expertise and trained personnel, the organisation adopted an existing and reliable HACCP system. The HACCP plan manager, the team members and the consulting company were all involved with the development of the plan. The cost of consulting services was estimated at €14,674.50. Personnel costs were also involved during this phase. A Quality Control (QC) Manager was appointed to manage the development of the system. Apart from his routine QC functions, he was responsible for auditing the record-keeping of controls and corrective actions. He regularly communicated with the consulting company. The QC Manager's contribution to the programme included: (a) participating in hazard analysis activities; (b) developing the HACCP plan and records of corrective actions, verification and documentation; (c) preparation of PRPs for sanitation and records; and (d) communicating with external coordinators and trainers. The QC Manager spent 975 hours on these activities. Team members also participated in the programme, and they spent a total of 360 hours during these activities at a total cost of €8,343.75.

2.3.3.2 Plan Implementation

The plan implementation phase included the improvement of PRPs, training of staff, operational changes and the purchase of new equipment as required by the HACCP plan. The total cost of implementation amounted to €108,673.41.

Operational and maintenance costs were (a) the cost of resources needed for routine requirements of the HACCP system (€4,420); (b) QC and hygiene laboratory costs (€55,500); (c) follow-up support provided by Lufthansa Service Geselleschaft (LSG) (€9,600); and (d) new equipment (€2,000). The total operational and maintenance costs were estimated at €71,520.

2.3.3.3 Certification

Certification of the HACCP programme included an initial cost of €6,000 for granting and maintaining certification, annual costs of inspection (€1,500) and audit costs, which included costs for preliminary assessment visits, assessment audits, surveillance audits, reassessment audits, and special audits conducted before and after certification (€1,500).

The company was capable of producing 25,000 dishes daily and the HACCP contribution to each was €0.01. The additional cost was insignificant considering the advantages of the HACCP programme, such as the safety of food products, an increase in confidence and fewer customer complaints.

2.3.4 Case Study – Implementation of HACCP System in a Pasteurised Milk Plant

The study was conducted in a dairy plant in Brazil, which supplied pasteurised milk fortified with vitamins A and D, yogurt, cream cheese and butter to the retail trade. This case study relates to the manufacture of homogenised, pasteurised milk, supplemented with vitamins A and D (Roberto et al., 2006). The company produced 4,500 l of this product daily with seven employees dedicated to this process. All stages from milking in the farm to the despatch of the finished product were included in the process. Data was collected over a period of three months.

The development of the HACCP system included the following stages:

1. Evaluation of existing pre-requisites in the plant: Evaluation of the Good Manufacturing Practices (GMPs) was performed against the International Dairy Foods Association (IDFA) criteria. The findings indicated the need for structural changes in the processing plant.
2. Development of the HACCP plan: During this stage, the significance of PRPs was assessed by evaluation of two HACCP plans: (a) a plan for actual processing conditions in a plant without previous compliance to GMP/Sanitation Standard Operating Procedures (SSOPs) and (b) a plan that considered compliance to GMP/SSOPs. The plan without previous compliance to GMP/SSOP requirements identified a large number of CCPs. However, by considering some stages of the process as pre-requisites, the number of CCPs was reduced to two, which was manageable.
3. Evaluating the cost of investments of implementation and maintenance of the HACCP system: The cost estimates considered all items necessary to assure food safety as well as those required by the CCPs:

a. Cost of recruiting employees for monitoring and maintenance of CCP records.
b. Cost of initial and periodical staff training.
c. Investment in new equipment, cleaning supplies and laboratory analysis.
d. Consultancy services.
e. Cost of hiring and 5S (Sort, Straighten, Shine, Standardise and Sustain) training of an employee to perform tasks related to GMP/SSOP requirements.

Implementation of the HACCP plan that considered compliance to GMP/SSOP requirements involved a higher cost during the first four months of implementation because of the need to adjust the PRPs. From the fourth month onwards, a reduction of the cost was expected. For this plan, 70.6% of the total cost was associated with the introduction of GMP/SSOPs, while only 29.4% was related to the cost of implementation itself.

The study showed that the estimated costs for the implementation and maintenance of the HACCP plan with previous compliance to the prerequisites were less than those spent on the plants without compliance to GMP/SSOPs. It was also observed that for the plan with eight CCPs, the implementation cost for the first year was RS177,538 (1 US$=3RS). After introducing the GMP/SSOP PRPs, it was possible to reduce the cost by 24.2%.

2.4 Impact of Environmental Management Systems

Many studies have been conducted to evaluate the impact of an EMS on environmental performance and business performance in organisations. A plethora of evidence indicates that the adoption of an EMS does improve environmental performance. For example, the results of seven out of 11 studies indicate that, in general, EMSs do provide environmental improvements. However, the results of four studies were inconclusive regarding an EMS's ability to provide legislative compliance. In Northern Ireland, three out of four studies demonstrated that an EMS has both a positive impact on environmental improvements and environmental legislation (NIEA, 2009).

However, the studies that evaluated the association between the organisation's environmental strategies and business performance have shown varied results. While some studies have demonstrated an improved business performance, others have shown either insignificant improvements or mixed results. As such, the impact of environmental activities on business performance has been a debatable issue (Darnall et al., 2008).

Organisations are driven (a) by the need for internal efficiency, external legitimacy and competitiveness (institutional approach); and (b) by complementary resources and capabilities (resource-based approach). Alternatively, they have been driven by both approaches to adopt EMSs and develop proactive activities (Darnall et al., 2008).

A study carried out in Canada, France, Germany, Hungary, Japan and Norway, which utilised data from a survey developed by the Organisation for Economic Cooperation and Development (OECD), measured the comprehensiveness of EMSs on the basis of nine different environmental practices and business performance in terms of profitability and growth (Darnall et al., 2008). This study demonstrated (a) facilities that experience greater institutional pressure are more likely to adopt a more comprehensive EMS; (b) facilities that have greater resources and capabilities adopt more comprehensive EMSs; (c) facilities that adopt more comprehensive EMSs gain positive business performance; and (d) facilities where EMSs are driven by a resource-based approach rather than institutional approach are more likely to gain positive business performance.

Russo and Fouts (1997) analysed the environmental activities of 243 firms in the Franklin Research and Development Corporation (FRDC) database over a period of two years using an independently developed environmental rating. According to this study, environmental performance and economic performance were positively related and industry growth improved this relationship. The results are consistent with the resource-based view that organisations with complementary resources and capabilities are more likely to adopt EMSs and develop proactive environmental management activities.

There are several EMSs that organisations could use to develop their own one. To identify the effects of certification of EMSs on financial performance, Ferron et al. (2012) studied the financial performance of 357 Brazilian firms, 52 of which have gained Norma Brasileira Regulamentadora (NBR) ISO 14001 certification for their EMSs. After controlling for macroeconomic movements, the increase in net income brought about by NBR ISO 14001 was 11%, while the increase in Earnings Before Tax, Interest, Depreciation and Amortisation (EBTIDA) was 25%. The results indicate NBR ISO 14001 having a positive effect on a firm's profitability.

A three-year study, which focused on high environmental impact business sectors such as air transport, construction, chemicals and pharmaceuticals, mining and metals, etc., explored the correlation between the quality of EMSs and environmental performance (Maier and Vanstone, 2005). The study included 18 such organisations in the *Financial Times* and the London Stock Exchange (FTSE) All World Developed Index representing medium- and large-sized capital companies. About 48% of high impact companies demonstrated some improvement over the previous three-year period. Analysis of data from the United Kingdom showed that the adoption of an accredited EMS improved the overall operational performance as measured by management indicators, such as commitment to training, awareness and operational risk management. However, the organisations certified to the Eco-Management Audit Scheme (EMAS) demonstrated a greater beneficial impact than those certified to the ISO 14001 standard. The association between EMSs and improved process efficiency was not found to be strong. This study concluded that the adoption of EMSs reduced the overall environmental impact in companies where no EMS was in place. However, to obtain a wider picture, greater transparency and monitoring effectiveness of EMSs and performance data is required.

A further study to ascertain the impact of EMSs on financial performance was carried out by Watson et al. (2004). In this study, they compared the financial performance of firms that have adopted EMSs (EMS adopters) against those with no EMS in place (non-adopters) on the basis of the Environmental Cost of Quality (ECOQ) framework, which extended the scope of cost estimates. According to the Cost of Quality (COQ) framework, process-driven, proactive quality costs are appraisal costs and preventive costs, and outcome-driven reactive costs are internal and external failure costs. The ECOQ framework includes extra cost items as shown in Table 2.5. Financial performance indicators were the price-to-earning ratio (P/E), the market-to-book ratio (M/B), the Return on Investment Capital (ROIC), the Return on Investment (ROI), the profit margin, the operating margin and Beta.

Although the implementation of EMSs involves substantial costs and provides some benefits to implementing firms, the paired comparison indicates that there is no difference in financial performance as measured by the ECOQ framework and financial performance indicators between EMS adopters and non-adopters.

The perceived benefits of adopting EMSs are as follows (Maier and Vanstone, 2005; Corbett et al., 2003):

■ Promotes greater awareness of legal requirements, thereby developing plans for implementation and compliance.
■ Ability to identify the potential for cost savings through improvement of efficiency.

Table 2.5 Environmental Cost of Quality Framework (ECOQ)

Type of Cost	Extended Items in ECOQ Framework
Internal failure	Workers compensation, injury costs, environmental clean-up costs at the facility, waste disposal, excess packaging, occupational safety and hygiene administration penalties, opportunity costs of underutilisation of resources, waste and pollutants
External failure	Loss of market share, waste disposal, including clean-up outside the facility, medical and environmental costs due to pollution in the community and disposal of near expiry or outdated products
Appraisal	Monitoring environmental activities
Preventive	Product design for sustainability, recycling, reassembly, product design to reduce environmental impact on operations, staff training, research and development activities associated with EMS

- Provides better understanding and control of activities, thereby reducing emissions and the risk of pollution incidents.
- Enhances the company's public image, enabling more detailed reporting and creating transparency to customers, insurers and local residents.
- Improves environmental performance.
- Improves procedures.
- Enhances the relationship with authorities and communities.

2.4.1 Case Study – Implementation of EMS on Gastonia Water Treatment Division

Background

The Waste Water Treatment Division of the city of Gastonia (GWWTD) in North Carolina is responsible for treating industrial, commercial and domestic waste water in its two treatment plants. The waste water treatment process ensures that the waste water discharged to the surface meets federal requirements. Waste water is tested in its own laboratories and the GWWTD also manages biosolids and by-products from waste water treatment. Currently, the plants are subjected to the provisions of the National Pollutant Discharge Elimination System (NPDES), biosolids discharge and air quality. In February 1999, the organisation entered into a contract with the Department of Environment and Natural Resources (DENR) in North Carolina to develop and implement an EMS (Eckert, 2001, January).

2.4.1.1 Planning and Implementation

The scope of the EMS included waste water treatment plants, laboratories, a resources recovery farm and pre-treatment facilities. The first part of the planning stage was the development of an environmental policy, which was approved by the Gastonia City Council. With the assistance of the EMS team comprising employees from both treatment plants, the city focused on identifying aspects and impacts and determining the significance of identified aspects using a form and a procedure devised by the Division of Pollution Prevention and Environmental Assistance (DPPEA). The process was completed in three months. Some of the identified aspects were metals in the effluent, laboratory waste, faecal matter, chlorine, oil and grease. The GWWTD held a meeting with the representatives of area industry to determine the significance of the aspects.

The objectives and targets for some of the significant aspects were established in terms of the ISO 14001 standard by considering the:

■ Legal and other requirements.
■ Significance of aspects and impacts.
■ Preventive efforts of pollution.
■ Technological options.
■ Financial, operational and other business requirements.

The action plan included: (a) tasks to be completed; (b) persons responsible for achieving the objectives and targets; and (c) the time within which the activities were to be completed.

2.4.1.2 Continual Improvement Programme

The continual improvement programme was an essential component of the development of the EMS. All employees were made aware of the importance of the environment policy, its impact on the activities and the EMS itself. The roles and responsibilities associated with the EMS were clearly defined. The competencies of employees who were involved with the EMS programme were developed, and the annual review ensured the continual improvement of necessary skills. As required by the ISO 14001 standard, the GWWTD developed: (a) procedures for external and internal communication; (b) monitoring and measurement of activities; (c) emergency preparedness and response; (d) documents for operational controls; and (e) EMS documentation.

An internal audit programme was carried out by four employees representing operations, biosolids, pre-treatment and the laboratories. Regular audits ensured that the EMS was effective, and the objectives and targets were met. Ready access to the EMS was made available to all employees with IT support. The GWWTD used the EMS approach to analyse spills during high rain periods to perform a root cause analysis and examine bypass systems, manhole height and control flow at lift stations.

The EMS was implemented in January 2000, and in 2001, the GWWTD's EMS was certified to the ISO 14001 standard. Among the benefits achieved were (a) improved management of environmental issues related to the operations of the waste water treatment facilities; (b) enhanced cooperation among team members within and across divisions; (c) public awareness of GWWTD's commitment for environmental excellence; (d) improved communication within GWWTD and other divisions; and (e) an effective system for continual improvement and pollution prevention.

Costs	
Staff time	$2,896.66
Internal auditor training	$1,400.00

2.4.2 Case Study – Implementation of EMS in Novozymes North America Inc.

2.4.2.1 Background

Novozymes North America Inc. is a biotech company with a strong focus on enzyme production for use in detergents, baking, beverages, textiles, pulp and paper, leather, starch, sugar and alcohol. Its manufacturing plant is located in Franklinton, North Carolina, employing 350 full-time staff and 50 contract workers. Regulatory requirements include a synthetic minor air permit, the National Pollutant Discharge Elimination System (NPDES) for cooling water and storm water discharge, permits for spray irrigation of treated waste water and the land application of spent biosolids. The Franklinton facility is also classified as a small quantity generator, and it must adhere to the Clean Air Act Resource Management Plan for the storage and use of ammonia. Franklinton facility's QMS has already been certified to the ISO 9001 standard and it embarked on a plan to implement an EMS (Blackmer, 2001 January).

2.4.2.2 Planning and Implementation

The Franklinton facility's EMS, which was integrated with the QMS, was designated an Environmental Quality System (EQS). Planning and implementation were carried out by the environmental management representative and several cross-functional teams comprising an eight-employee steering committee and a 16-employee committee in the facility. Each department analysed its activities to identify the aspects and impacts of each activity. Novozymes aspects included (but were not limited to) laboratory waste, solid waste, water consumption, erosion, odour, and energy and noise pollution. Its impacts included hazardous waste, air quality, depletion of landfill space and resources, soil and water quality, excessive noise, energy consumption and other environmental impacts. Aspects and impacts were identified in 10 months. The impact of each aspect was rated on the basis of existing controls:

1. Needs attention or room for improvement.
2. Possible opportunity for improvement.
3. Existing controls are sufficient and no further action is necessary.

All aspects that received a rating of one were categorised, consolidated and ranked on a scale of zero to five (zero being low and five being high) to obtain the significance score for each aspect according to the following five categories (Table 2.6):

- Area of impact.
- Quantity of impact
- Probability of impact
- Potential regulatory or legal issues
- Health risk.

Each of the environmental aspects was assessed for business practicability using the following categories (Table 2.7) on a scale of zero to five:

- Controls in place.
- Difficulty in reducing the impact.

Table 2.6   Significance of Environmental Aspects

	Environmental Aspects						
	Laboratory Waste	Solid Waste	Water Consumption	Erosion	Odour	Energy Use	Pollution
Impact area							
Quantity of impact							
Impact probability							
Potential regulatory/ legal issues							
Health risk							
Total score							

Scale=0–5 (zero=low; 5=high).

Table 2.7   Business Practicability Score

	Environmental Aspects						
	Laboratory Waste	Solid Waste	Water Consumption	Erosion	Odour	Energy Use	Pollution
Controls in place							
Difficulty of reducing the impact							
Impact probability							
Cost of reducing the impact							
Public relations/ community concerns							
Cost recovery period							
Total score							

Score=0–5 (zero=low; 5=high).

- Cost of reducing the impact.
- Public relations/community concern.
- Cost of recovery period.

The final ranking was obtained by subtracting the total business practicability score from the significance of aspects score.

2.4.2.3 Continual Improvement

Through written job descriptions and annual performance reviews, all staff were made aware of their environmental responsibilities associated with the EQS. Environmental performance was monitored quarterly and reviewed by the corporate head office management executives. Facility compliance improved with the implementation of EQS and potential non-compliances were identified, and this allowed corrective and preventive actions to be taken in a timely manner. Objectives and targets were achieved, thereby reducing company emissions and wastes. Facility performance improved as shown by the reduction of operating costs associated with materials and energy and water consumption. The programme extended to bulk raw material suppliers who were expected to meet new requirements and also to the environmental aspects of transportation of raw materials, products and waste products. Each member of the cross-functional team devoted three hours per month for the development and implementation of the EQS.

Benefits were apparent with the implementation of the EQS: increase in staff awareness of their impact on the environment and improvements in communication, work practices, new product evaluation, training and emergency preparedness. In May 2005, the EQS was certified to the ISO 14001 standard.

Costs	
Staff time	$175,000
Materials	$4,000
Consultants' fees	$20,000
Compliance audit costs	$3,000
Auditor training	$8,000
Other training	$3,000
Registration audit	$12,000

References

Arvanitoyannis, I.S. and Varzakas, T.H. (2008). Application of ISO 22000 and Failure Mode and Effect Analysis (FMEA) for industrial processing of salmon: A case study. *Critical Reviews in Food Science and Nutrition*, 48, 411–429.

Bas, M., Yuksel, M. and Cavusoglu, T. (2007). Difficulties and barriers for the implementation of HACCP and food safety system in food businesses in Turkey. *Food Control*, 18, 124–130.

Bata, D., Drosinos, G.H., Athanasopoulos, P. and Spathis, P. (2006). Cost of GHP improvement and HACCP of an airline catering company, *Food Control*, 17 (5), 414–419.

Blackmer, J.W. (2001, January). *EMS Case Study: Novozymes North America Inc.* Raleigh: Division of Pollution Prevention and Environmental Assistance.

Buchweitz, M. and Salay, E. (2006). *Analysis of implementation and cost of HACCP in food service industries in the county of Campinas, Brazil*. Retrieved February 12, 2018 from http://www.umass.edu/ne165/haccp1998/buchweitz.html

Casadesus, M., Karapetrovic, S. and Heras, I. (2011). Synergies in standardized management systems: Some empirical evidence. *The TQM Journal*, 23 (1), 73–86.

Corbett, C., Luca, A.M. and Pan, J.N. (February, 2003). Global perspectives on global standards: 15-economy survey of ISO 9000 and ISO 14000. *ISO Management Systems*, 1, 31–40.

Cusato, S., Tavolaro, P. and de Oliveira, C.A.F. (2012). Implementation of hazard analysis and critical control points system in the food industry. In A. McElhatton and P.J.do A. Sobral (Eds.), *Novel Technologies in Food Science: Their Impact on Products, Consumer Trends and the Environment*, pp. 21–38. New York: Springer.

Darnall, N., Henriques, I. and Sadorsky, P. (2008). Do environmental management systems improve business performance in an international setting? *Journal of International Management*, 14, 364–376.

Dick, G.P.M. (2000). ISO 9000 certification: reality or myth? *The TQM Magazine*, 12 (6), 365–371.

Donovan, J.A., Caswell, J.A. and Salay, E. (2001). The effect of stricter foreign regulations on food safety levels in developing countries. *Review of Agricultural Economics*, 23, 163–175.

Dragolea, L. and Cotirlea, D. (2009). Benchmarking: A valid strategy for the long term? *Annales Universitatis Apulensis Series Oeconomica*, 11 (2), 813–826.

Eckert, B. (2001, January). *EMS Case Study: City of Gastonia Waste Water Treatment Division*. North Carolina: City of Gastonia Wastewater Treatment Division.

Ehiri, J.E., Morris, G.P. and McEwen, J. (1995). Implementation of HACCP in food businesses: The way ahead. *Food Control*, 6 (6), 341–345.

Ferron, R.T., Funchal, B., Nossa, V. and Teixeira, A.J.C. (2012). Is ISO 14001 certification effective? An experimental analysis of firm profitability. *Brazilian Administration Review*, 9 (Special Issue), Art. 5, 78–94.

Food Safety Programme. (1999). Strategies for implementing HACCP in small and/or less developed businesses, *WHO/SDE/PHE/FOS/99.7. Report of a WHO consultation*. Ministry of Health, Welfare and Sports, June 16–19, 1999. Hague.

Food Standards Agency. (2011). *Foodborne Disease Strategy 2010–2015: An FSA Programme for the Reduction of Disease in the UK*. London: Food Standards Agency.

Gordon, D.K. (2002). Standards outlook: Where does quality begin? *Quality Progress*, 35 (3), 103–104.

Henson, S., Holt, G. and Northen, J. (1999). Cost and benefits of implementing HACCP in the UK dairy processing sector. *Food Control*, 10, 99–106.

Heras, I., Marimon, F. and Casadesus, M. (2011). Impact of quality improvement tools on performance of firms using different quality management systems. *Revista Innovar*, 21 (42), 161–173.

Hitt, M.A., Black, J.S. and Porter, L.W. (2005). *Management*. India: Pearson Education

Khatri, Y. and Collins, R. (2007). Impact and status of HACCP in Australian meat industry. *British Food Journal*, 109 (5), 343–354.

Levine, D.I. and Toffel, M.W. (2010). Quality management and job quality: How ISO 9000 standard for quality affects employees and employers. *Management Science*, 56 (6), 978–996.

Maier, S. and Vanstone, K. (2005). *Do good EMSs lead to good environmental performance?* Research briefings, Ethical Investment Research Services (EIRIS). Retrieved February 20, 2018 from http://www.eiris.org/files/research%20publications/emsperformanceoct05.pdf

Maldonando, E.S., Henson, S.J., Caswell, J.A., Leos, L.A., Martinez, T.A., Aranda, G. and Cadena, J.A. (2005). Cost-benefit analysis of HACCP implementation in the Mexican meat industry. *Food Control*, 16, 375–381.

McAloon, T.R. (2005). HACCP implementation in the United States. In T. Mayes and S. Mortimore (Eds.), *Making the Most of HACCP: Learning from Others' Experience*, pp. 61–78. England: Woodhead.

Mutlu, S., Bal, T., Say, D. and Emeksiz, F. (2003). The adoption and implementation of food quality system (HACCP) in Mediterranean region of Turkey, Cahiers Options Méditerranéennes, Vol. 61. In A. Nokolaidis, G. Baourakis, E. Isikli and M. Yercan (Eds.), *The Market for Organic Products in the Mediterranean Region*, pp. 201–217. Chania: CHEAM-IAMC.

Northern Ireland Environmental Agency (NIEA). (2009). Measuring the effectiveness of environmental management systems. *Phase 1: Desk top report, June 2009*. Retrieved February 20, 2018, from http://docplayer.net/2056526-Measuring-the-effectiveness-of-environmental-management-systems-phase-1-desktop-report-june-2009.html

Priskar, F. (2007). The impact of the quality management system ISO 9000 on customer satisfaction of Slovenian companies. *Managing Global Transition*, 5 (1), 45–61.

Rabinovitz, R., Glushkovsky, E.A., Shatzkin, A. and Sipper, D. (1998). Does ISO 9000 improve product quality? *ISO News, 4/1998*, 15–19.

Roberto, C.D., Brandao, S.C.C. and da Silva, C.A.B. (2006). Costs and investments of implementing and maintaining HACCP in a pasteurised milk plant. *Food Control*, 17, 599–603.

Russo, M.V. and Fouts, P.A. (1997). A resource-based perspective on corporate environmental performance and profitability. *Academy of Management Journal*, 40 (3), 534–559.

Saizarbitoria, I.H., Landin, G.A. and Casadesus, M. (2006). The impact of quality management in European companies performance: The case of the Spanish companies. *European Business Review*, 18 (2), 114–131.

Samad, S. (2009). Assessing the differential effects of quality management system on product quality and business performance. *International Review of Business Research Papers*, 5 (2), 283–292.

Sampaio, P., Saraiva, P. and Rodrigues, A.G. (2011). The economic impact of quality management systems in Portuguese certified companies: Empirical evidence. *International Journal of Quality and Reliability Management*, 28 (9), 929–950.

Scallan, E., Hoekstra, R.M., Angulo, F.J., Tauxe, R.V., Widdowson, M.A., Roy, S.L., Jones, J.L. and Griffin, P.M. (2011). Foodborne illnesses acquired in the United States – major pathogens. *Emerging Infectious Diseases*, 17 (1), 7–15.

Scharff, R.L. (2012). Economic burden from health losses due to foodborne illnesses in the United States. *Journal of Food Protection*, 75 (1), 123–131.

Semos, A. and Kontogeorgos, A. (2007). HACCP implementation in northern Greece: Food companies' perception of costs and benefits. *British Food Journal*, 109 (1), 5–19.

Six Sigma and Lean Resources. (2013). *History of Six Sigma*. Retrieved January 5, 2018 from https://www.isixsigma.com/new-to-six-sigma/history/history-six-sigma/

Suwanrangsi, S. (2000). HACCP implementation in Thai fisheries industry. *Food Control*, 11, 377–382.

Unnevehr, L. and Roberts, T. (1997). Improving cost/benefit analysis for HACCP and microbial food safety: An economist's view. In J.A. Caswell and R.W. Cotterill (Eds.), *Strategy and Policy in the Food System: Emerging Issues*, pp. 225–229. Proceedings of NE-165 Conference, June 20–21, 1996. Washington, DC: University of Connecticut and University of Massachusetts.

Wallace, C. and Williams, T. (2001). Pre-requisites: A help or a hindrance to HACCP. *Food Control*, 12 (4), 235–240.

Wang, Z., Weng, Y., Yutaka, T., Fukuda, S. and Kai, S. (2007). Cost-benefit analysis of food firms adopting HACCP system in different scale. *Journal of the Faculty of Agriculture, Kyushu University*, 52 (2), 475–479.

Watson, K., Klingenberg, B., Polito, T. and Geurts, T.G. (2004). Impact of environmental management system implementation on financial performance: A comparison of two corporate strategies. *Management of Environmental Quality: An International Journal*, 15 (6), 622–628.

Chapter 3

Strategic Planning

3.1 Introduction

Business organisations provide products and services not only to the community in which they operate but also worldwide through internet technology. Government changes and global events trigger changes to the economic environment. Progressive companies are able to meet the challenges and survive in the changing economic competitive environment. Strategic planning is the gateway to the mission, vision, objectives and goals of the organisation. It is the process of (a) identifying the organisation's external and environment in which it operates; (b) formulating a mission and vision; (c) developing goals to be achieved; (d) creating and selecting strategies to be followed and (e) allocating resources to achieve the goals. Critical and unexpected events such as earthquakes or floods demand a different type of planning – contingency planning.

As the organisation grows and the business environment become more complex, there is a greater demand for strategic planning. All the employees in the organisation need to understand the direction and the corporate mission of the organisation. Organisations that are able to adopt a disciplined approach to strategic planning evolve successfully as the market changes.

3.2 Definition

Strategy is a broad programme for designing and achieving the objectives of the organisation and its response to its environment over time.

3.3 Aims of Strategic Planning

The following are the aims of strategic planning (Koteen, 1989):

1. Establish strategic direction: Strategic direction (a) defines the goals that the company wants to reach; (b) indicates where resources need to be allocated; and (c) focuses on strategic goals as a priority.
2. Prioritise resources allocation: Effective allocation of human, financial and material resources.

3. Establish standards of excellence: The organisation is able to establish shared values and standards of excellence.
4. Meet the challenges of changing external environment: The strategic plan is flexible enough to manage contingencies for uncertainty and change.
5. Establish a basis for control and evaluation: Strategic planning allows the organisation to monitor success and failures. Performance measurements or monitoring of strategic objectives and action plans act as control mechanisms.

3.4 Benefits of Strategic Planning

Successful strategic planning helps an organisation in two ways: (a) creates an awareness of the company's priorities in its employees and (b) improves teamwork, enabling employees to achieve their goals effectively (Allison & Kaye, 2015; Bryson, 2004).

3.4.1 Improvement of Focus

It creates an understanding of the company's mission, values and corporate strategy among internal and external stakeholders.

■ Develops an action plan based on current information.
■ Establishes milestones to monitor achievement and assess results.
■ Creates information to promote the products and services of the organisation.

3.4.2 Improvement of Teamwork to Achieve Goals

■ Creates a forum to understand the purpose of the organisation and its values that should influence decisions.
■ Improves communication between the board and the rest of the staff.
■ Establishes a framework to understand change by encouraging strategic thinking and focusing on significant areas that contribute to the long-term success of the organisation.
■ Focuses on opportunities that accomplish the company's mission.
■ Encourages the use of the strategic plan to adapt to changing circumstances.

3.5 Progressive Evolution of Strategic Planning

Gluck, Kaufman and Walleck (1980) have examined the development of planning systems over time in large companies where formal planning and decision-making are closely linked. They identified four phases of strategic planning evolution in these companies. Table 3.1 shows the progressive evolution in terms of these four phases.

3.6 Strategic Planning Process

Bryson (2004) outlines a 10-step strategic planning process that links planning and implementation, enabling the organisation to manage on a continual basis:

Table 3.1 Four Phases of Strategic Planning

Phase	Features	Limitations and Positives
One: Basic financial planning	Operational control Financial focus Annual budget	• No consideration given to knowledge of company's products and markets • Unaware of major competitors' activities • Impact of products and market changes on plants, distribution, and sales force is not considered
Two: Forecast-based planning	More effective planning for growth Environmental evaluation Long-term forecasts Static allocation of resources	• Inaccuracy of forecasts • Predictive models fail to predict environmental changes • Portfolio analysis is based on current capabilities • Reward system is focused on short-term or medium-term operating performance Positives: • Forces the management to focus on long-term implication of their decisions • Effective resource allocation
Three: Externally oriented planning	Improved response to markets and competitions Effective situation analysis and competitive assessment Generating effective strategic alternatives Flexible allocation of resources	• Heavy burden on top management because of the large number of issues raised, alternatives generated and opportunities identified • Decisions are made by planner without top-level participation • Inability to segment into discreet strategic business units (SBUs) Positives: • Dynamic and creative resource allocation • Consideration given to competitors' products and services • Grouping of related business units into SBUs
Four: Strategic management	Consolidation of all resources to create strategic advantage Strategically chosen planning framework Innovative, flexible planning process Creating a supportive value system and environment	Positives • Planning framework that encompasses all organisational boundaries • Planning processes generate entrepreneurial thinking • Management commitment through a corporate value system

1. Initiate and decide on a strategic planning process.
2. Identify organisational mandates.
3. Establish the organisation's mission and value.
4. Evaluate the external and internal environments.
5. Identify the strategic issues facing the organisation.

6. Devise strategies to manage the issues.
7. Review and adopt the strategies or strategic plan.
8. Create an effective organisational vision.
9. Develop an effective implementation plan.
10. Monitor the strategies and strategic planning process.

3.6.1 Initiate and Agree on a Strategic Planning Process

The purpose of this step is to conduct a preliminary stakeholder analysis and identify the parties involved in the effort and the decision-makers. The concept of strategic planning is introduced so that the group can comprehend the applications and implications of the process and encourage a commitment to it. In this initial step, roles and responsibilities, the preferred steps in the process, the timeframe, the resources needed and the limitations are defined.

3.6.2 Identify Organisational Mandates

During this step, relevant regulations, policies, ordinances, charters, articles and contracts that have an influence on the organisation are identified to determine their influence on the organisation and restrictions placed on it.

3.6.3 Clarify Organisation's Mission and Values

The mission statement defines the purpose of the organisation. A proper stakeholder analysis is conducted to generate answers to the following questions:

■ Who are our customers?
■ What are their needs?
■ How can the organisation enhance customer satisfaction?

The mission statement leads to a proper understanding of the organisation's values.

3.6.3.1 Create a Mission

The mission statement outlines the purpose or the reason for the existence of the organisation. Its creation involves the people in the organisation and different constituents that it hopes to affect. Above all, it must inspire commitment, innovation and courage. A mission statement must define the purpose, the business and the values of the organisation (Patterson & Radtke, 2009; Angelica, 2001).

The organisation's mission statement contains three fundamental statements:

1. The purpose statement, which focuses on the reason for the existence of the organisation and what it hopes to achieve in the future.
2. The business statement, which outlines the activities or programmes of the organisation to be implemented to achieve the purpose.
3. The value statement, which includes the beliefs that the staff share in common, and these guide them in performing their work for the organisation (De Silva, 2013).

The mission statements of most companies fall short of these conditions. The statement is either a description of their intentions, with no indication about how these could be achieved, or a description of their products and services. A sample mission statement that fulfils the three conditions is given below:

> *ABCCL has been producing and selling premium wines to the local and the export market for over 22 years. We are dedicated to producing premium wines to satisfy all market segments by working with our grape growers to improve the quality of our grapes, adopting modern wine technology, enhancing the image of our products, while focusing on the social values of the community and minimising our environmental impact.*

3.6.4 Assess External and Internal Environment

This step involves the assessment of the internal and external environment using SWOT (Strengths, Weaknesses, Opportunities, Threats) analysis. Strengths and weaknesses define the present capacity of the organisation, and opportunities and threats reflect the external environment and future potential (Hill & Jones, 2008).

3.6.4.1 External Analysis

The purpose of external analysis is to identify significant strategic opportunities and threats in the organisation's operational environment that can influence its drive towards the mission. External analysis involves the assessment of three inter-related environmental factors: (a) the industry environment in which the firm operates; (b) the country or national government; and (c) the wider socioeconomic or macro environment. Analysis of the industry environment involves both an evaluation of the competitive structure of the organisation's industry and the competitive position of the company. Because of the proliferation of global markets, the company must examine the global competitors so that strategic decisions can be taken either to shift the market to another country or expand the current global market. Macroeconomic analysis involves a close examination of macroeconomic, social, government, legal, international and technological factors that can influence the company and industry sector.

3.6.4.2 Internal Analysis

Internal analysis focuses on evaluating the internal operational structure of the organisation. Resource needs, competencies and capabilities are reviewed. The aim of internal analysis is to identify and address a company's weaknesses.

3.6.5 Identify the Strategic Issues

Strategic issues are critical challenges facing the organisation. According to Bryson (2004), strategic issues are "the fundamental policy questions or critical challenges facing the organisation's mandates, mission and values, product or service level mix, clients, users or payers, cost, financing, structure, processes and management". They include (a) development issues that affect the core business; (b) issues that require no current action but need careful monitoring; (c) issues that may require some action now but are likely to require action in the future; and (d) urgent issues that need immediate attention. There are seven approaches to identifying strategic issues (Bryson, 2004):

1. Direct approach: Planners go straight from a review of mandates, the mission and SWOT analysis to the identification of strategic issues.

2. Indirect approach: Commences with brainstorming about different kinds of options before the identification of issues.
3. Goals approach: Initiates a discussion of goals and identifies issues that must be addressed before they can be achieved.
4. Vision of success approach: Identifies the issues that must be addressed before the vision is realised.
5. Oval mapping approach: Involves the creation of word-and-arrow diagrams indicating the potential actions an organisation might take, how they are taken, the reasons for taking these actions and the inter-relationship among them.
6. Issues tension approach: It is based on the premise that any strategic issue has four fundamental tensions: human resources (HR), equity concerns, innovation and change versus maintenance of tradition and productivity improvement.
7. Systems analysis approach: This approach involves using the best way to frame issues when issue areas can be considered as a system. A strategic issue contains three elements: (a) the issue itself is described accurately in a short paragraph; (b) factors that make the issue significant; and (c) the consequences of failure to address the issue.

3.6.6 Formulate Strategies

Strategy formulation is concerned with crafting and designing strategies and selecting the best for implementation, so as to achieve the goals and objectives of the organisation. Major areas where a business needs help from the external environment are identified. In this phase, the present issues and problems of the organisation are resolved first (Figure 3.1).

3.6.6.1 Development of Strategies

Strategies can vary by level and by timeframe. Strategy formulation involves the creation of a set of strategies that will effectively link the organisation to its environment and create public value (Bryson, 2004). Two approaches for developing strategies are the five-part process and the mapping process.

a. Five-part process: Each strategic issue is subjected to five basic questions:
   – What are the practical alternatives, expectations and vision that the organisation wishes to pursue to address the issue and reach the desired outcome?
   – What are the barriers to the realisation of these alternatives, expectations and vision?
   – How does the organisation hope to overcome these barriers to reach its goals?
   – What are the major actions that the organisation will implement for these proposals in the next one or two years?
   – What specific steps need to be taken within the next two to three years to implement the major proposal, and what specific actions must be taken to implement the proposals within the next 6–12 months?

b. Mapping process: This approach is used when the planning team needs or desires to express the relationship among the various options in order to demonstrate how they fit together as a part of a pattern. The approach is to:
   – Generate multiple options for addressing each strategic issue, expressed in terms of an action.
   – Link the various options using arrows to indicate how they influence each other – each option may be a part of more than one chain.

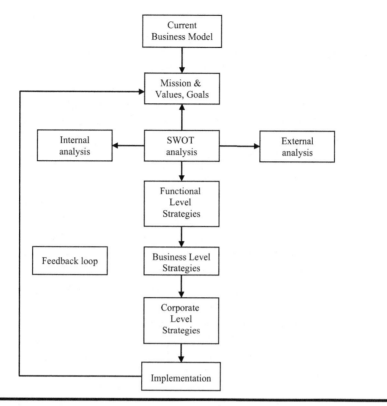

Figure 3.1 Strategy formulation.

- – The outcome is a map of cause and effect or means to an end relationship.
- – The options at the end of the chain of arrows are possible goals or even mission statements.

Effective strategies share the following features:

■ Technically and administratively feasible.
■ Acceptable to all stakeholders.
■ Results oriented.
■ Compatible with the philosophy and values of the organisation.
■ Ethical, moral and compliant with regulatory requirements.
■ Deal with strategic issues that the organisation intends to address.
■ Must create value and generate profit for the organisation.

3.6.6.2 Three Aspects of the Strategy

Three major aspects of the strategy are (a) corporate strategy; (b) business or competitive strategy; and (c) functional level strategy (Campbell et al., 2002).

a. Corporate strategy: The corporate strategy affects the entire organisation. It defines the business that the enterprise is engaged in, shows ways to acquire or divest businesses, outlines the allocation of resources among the businesses and gives ways to expand the knowledge base and synergy in those businesses. Organisations consist of many business units linked together in varying degrees in terms of ownership, objectives, products and activities such as finance, marketing and management, etc. The synergy among the business units can vary among various businesses due to the type of knowledge and core competencies that can be shared. In organisations where businesses have little in common, strategic decision-making occurs at the level of business or strategic business unit (SBU). An SBU is a business unit or a subsidiary of a firm that offers a distinct product or service and often has its own mission or vision in line with the corporate mission and vision (Hellriegel et al., 2002).

There are five types of corporate growth strategies: (i) forward integration strategy; (ii) backward integration strategy; (iii) horizontal integration strategy; (iv) centric diversification strategy; and (v) conglomerate diversification strategy. (Strategic Management MGT603 (n.d.))

i. Forward integration strategy: The company enters a business that brings the organisation close to its customers. In 2003, the acquisition of Direct TV (a satellite TV company owned by News Corporation) enabled it to use Direct TV as a medium to distribute news, movies and TV shows by managing the process itself (Sandilands, 2016).

ii. Backward integration strategy: The parent company usually enters the business of its suppliers to control the supply parameters. In 2001, Apple Computer entered the retail industry when it established a chain of Apple stores to sell its computers and iPods, a strategy already implemented by Dell (Hill & Jones, 2008).

iii. Horizontal integration strategy: The parent company acquires one or more of its competitors to consolidate the market share. In 2008, Pfizer acquired Wyeth Pharmaceuticals to create a very large prescription drug company and offered $68 billion (Hill & Jones, 2008).

iv. Centric diversification strategy: Also known as related diversification strategy, a firm acquires a business related to the existing business in terms of technology, products and markets. There are usually some common elements between the two companies, e.g. the same customer base and markets, similar technology, distribution networks, managerial skills and products and services. AT&T's acquisition of cable TV for $120 million enabled it to wire the United States with a fast internet service using cable rather than telephone lines (Ingram, 2017).

v. Conglomerate diversification strategy: A firm adds another unrelated business or service to its line of business. More often, the parent company purchases established companies. General Electric, popularly known as GE, is a good example of conglomerate diversification. Thomas Edison started his company in 1890 as a lighting business and since then it has expanded through horizontal mergers and acquisitions into radios, refrigerators and wind turbines. World War I aircraft were built by GE and the company eventually became the largest manufacturer of jet engines in the United States (Hudson, 2016). The GE strategy (GE, 2016) is:

> We are repositioning GE to be the world's best infrastructure and technology company, with a smaller financial services division. Our focus is on driving infrastructure leadership, investing in innovation and achieving a culture of simplification to better serve our customers around the world.

b. Business strategy: Business strategy defines the way the organisation competes in each of its businesses. Most strategic decisions are taken at the level of business or its SBU. This will, however, depend on whether there is synergy, economies of scale and scope among the various businesses. Although certain core competencies in marketing, finance, sourcing and distribution can be shared across the various levels of the corporation, each business will also require specific competencies, depending on factors such as demography, competition and industrial conditions (Campbell et al., 2002). Apple employs a differentiation competitive strategy that emphasises innovative products with creative design.

c. Functional strategy: Functional strategy defines how the various value-adding functional units such as design, purchasing, production, marketing, etc., support each of the business strategies. Functional strategy is important for the successful implementation of the business strategy and helpful for making changes and tactical management (Campbell et al., 2002). Proctor and Gamble invests large amounts of money in advertising to create customer demand.

3.6.7 Review and Audit the Plan

When strategies have been formulated, the planning team needs approval to adopt them and proceed with the implementation plan. For smaller organisations, this step may be merged with Step 9. Other relevant policy-making bodies and other implementing groups and organisations may also have to approve at least a part of the plan so that implementation can proceed effectively. Throughout the process, the planning team must pay attention to the goals, interests and concerns of both internal and external stakeholders.

3.6.8 Establish a Vision

Vision is a description of what the organisation will look like when the goals are achieved. Strategic planning is an iterative process, and therefore, it is difficult to have a vision of success until the final plan is realised. The description may include such elements as the organisation's mission, its values and philosophy, basic strategies and performance criteria, etc.

Martin Luther King was one of the great visionaries in the world. His speech, popularly known as the "The Dream Speech" delivered in Washington in 1963, has been translated to over 40 languages around the globe. His vision of the world where all human beings live in harmony without any prejudices or bias is reflected in his oration (King, Jr., 1963):

> ...I have a dream that one day this nation will rise up, live out the true meaning of its creed, – We hold these truths to be self-evident, that all men are created equal –...

An organisation's vision forms the roof of the strategic planning process (Butuner, 2015). Essentially it:

■ Describes the future of the organisation which is different from today.
■ Gives hope to employees that the vision can be achieved.
■ Inspires and motivates employees to achieve their objectives.
■ Is properly crafted, short, consistent, flexible and focused.
■ Helps define goals that are refined and achievable.
■ Guides the generation of strategy.
■ Is communicated to all in the organisation.

A good vision statement must be cordially developed and understood, has a clear association with the business of the organisation, differentiates the business from others and attracts the attention of internal and external stakeholders.

3.6.8.1 Vision Statement

The vision statement answers two basic questions: (a) What are the anticipated changes in the physical, economic, social environment in the next three to five years because of the presence of the organisation? and (b) what role will the organisation play in making the difference? The vision statement is a vision of the future, and it must inspire and challenge the staff so they firmly believe that it can be accomplished. For instance, a vision statement might be:

> ABC Company Limited will be the largest exporter of premium quality wines while maintaining high ethical standards and providing employment to local staff. We will generate an environment where staff will always feel proud to be an integral part of ABC Company Limited. They will work in close partnership with the grape growers and the local community in maintaining the beauty and the vibrancy of the environment in which our organisation operates.

The company's vision should be articulated to all the staff, and they should be aware of how it affects the customers and how their work supports the vision. Although it gives direction to the organisation, it should not be considered as a static statement. External factors such as an economic downfall, government policy changes and job opportunities can affect the role of the organisation in the community. As circumstances change, top management should be prepared to review the vision because the company exists for the good of the wider community.

3.6.9 Develop an Implementation Plan

The creation of an action plan for implementation may involve such details as implementation responsibilities, anticipated results, schedules, a communication process, allocation of resources, and review and accountability procedures. Four basic questions associated with implementation are (Hinsky, 2015):

- Are our products optimally placed in the market in which we operate?
- What are the strategies to convert the plan into specific results for growth and productivity?
- Do we have the skilled people to implement the plan?
- How do we determine whether we have specific programmes to deliver the outcome?

The "Big 8 Components" of implementation are as follows:

1. Competencies: Identify and provide the competencies, capabilities and resources needed for successful strategy implementation.
2. Resources: Allocate sufficient resources for critical activities.
3. Policies: Establish policies that support the strategies.
4. Best practices: Introduce best practices and drive towards continual improvement.
5. Systems: Develop information and operational systems to enable strategy implementation by company staff.
6. Rewards: Offer rewards and incentives to those who achieve the company's strategy targets.
7. Environment: Create a work environment and culture that fit the strategy.
8. Leadership: Demonstrate the leadership needed to drive the project forward.

3.6.10 *Strategy-Focused Organisation: Balanced Score Card*

Kaplan and Norton introduced the balanced score card (BSC) as a measure of both the financial and non-financial performance of the organisation (Kaplan & Norton, 1992, 2001). All the objectives and measures on a BSC are derived from the organisation's vision and strategy. Companies such as Mobil Oil Corporation's North America Marketing and Refining Division, CIGNA Corporation's Property and Casualty Division, the Chemical Retail Bank, and Brown and Root Energy Services' Rockwater Division are some of those who have successfully adopted the principles of the BSC. Based on the BSC, these companies developed a new kind of management system consisting of three dimensions: Strategy, focus and organisation:

- Strategy: The BSC enabled the organisations to describe and communicate the strategy in a way that could be understood and implemented.
- Focus: The BSC aligned every resource and activity to the company strategy.
- Organisation: The BSC created linkages across business units, shared services and individual employees to mobilise employees in different ways.

The success of the BSC depends on the following five principles:

3.6.10.1 *Principle 1*

Translate the strategy into operational terms: BSC integrates tangible and intangible assets in value-creating activities using strategy maps of cause and effect linkages. The strategy maps and the BSC create value by recognising the importance of intangible assets and quantitatively using non-financial measures such as cycle time, market share, innovation, satisfaction and competencies.

3.6.10.2 *Principle 2*

Align the organisation to the strategy: Organisations are structured around various business units such as production, sales, marketing, finance, engineering, purchasing, HR, etc. Each function has its own body of knowledge, language and culture. The BSC breaks down the silos and creates linkages between business units and shared services and strategy, thereby focusing on strategic ideas right across the organisation.

3.6.10.3 *Principle 3*

Makes strategy everyone's everyday job: Top executives with the help of the BSC communicate the strategy to everyone in the organisation. A strategy-focused organisation requires all employees to understand the strategy and perform their roles in a way that contributes to its success.

3.6.10.4 *Principle 4*

Make strategy a continual process: Strategy-focused organisations consider strategy to be an essential management tool and integrate the management of tactics such as financial budgets and monthly meetings with the management of strategy. First, the budgeting process is linked to the strategy followed by conducting regular strategy review meetings and learning and adopting the strategy.

3.6.10.5 Principle 5

Demonstrate leadership to drive change: The strategy requires change from every part of the organisation, and teamwork is essential to coordinate these changes. The executive team must be actively involved, and strategy implementations require continual attention to monitor change initiatives and performance measurements against strategy targets.

According to Kaplan and Norton (2006), the BSC framework is the best way to align the strategy with the organisation's structure. The two essential tools of the BSC framework are the strategy map and the score card. The former facilitates the managers to define and communicate the cause and effect relationships that deliver the value proposition of the business, while the latter provides a tool for implementing the strategy. The BSC framework has four perspectives: financial perspective, customer perspective, process perspective and learning and growth perspective (Kaplan & Norton, 1996).

a. Financial perspective: The financial perspective deals with measures which indicate whether the company's strategy, implementation and execution are contributing to the financial growth of the organisation. Financial objectives typically relate to operating income, return on capital invested and economic value added. Other financial objectives are sales growth or the generation of cash flow. The financial perspective deals with the way the organisation appears to stakeholders in order to succeed financially.

b Customer perspective: The customer perspective involves the identification of the customer and market segments in which the business unit operates and measures the business unit's performance in the particular market segment. Outcome measures include customer satisfaction, customer retention, new customers gained, customer profitability, and market and account share in the market segment. The customer perspective describes the way the organisation appears to customers in order to achieve the organisation's vision. Therefore, critical factors such as value propositions that the company will deliver to customers in the targeted market segment (short lead times, on-time delivery and the ability to offer innovative products and services) are also considered in the customer perspective.

c Process perspective: The process perspective describes the processes that an organisation should excel at in order to satisfy the needs of customers and shareholders. These processes enable the organisation to offer the value proposition that will attract and retain customers in the targeted market segment and satisfy shareholders' financial expectations. Internal business processes focus on processes that are critical to achieving customer satisfaction and financial profitability. Traditional approaches aim at improving existing processes, whereas the BSC approach identifies entirely new processes that are required for realising customer and financial objectives. Incorporating innovative processing to internal business processes is also a significant aspect of customer perspective.

d. Learning and growth perspective: The learning and growth perspective describes how enterprise value can be created by investing in HR development activities such as recruiting, training, continual professional development and leadership development, and knowledge management for capturing, storing and communicating knowledge and best practices across the many business units. It relates to the ability to change and improve continually according to the organisation's vision.

These four perspectives are illustrated in Figure 3.2.

Figure 3.3 demonstrates the alignment of strategies with the BSC. In the example, the organisation describes its mission and vision briefly. The strategies for a wine-making venture, e.g., are:

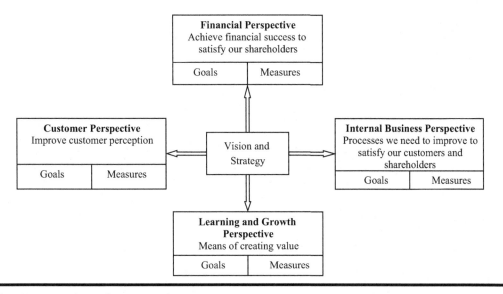

Figure 3.2 Balanced score card.

Mission: *We are dedicated to producing premium wines to satisfy all market segments by working with our grape growers to improve the quality of grapes, adopting modern wine technology, enhancing the image of our products while focusing on social values of the community and minimising environmental impact.*
Vision: *ABC Company limited will be the largest exporter of premium quality wines while maintaining high ethical standards and providing employment to the local staff.*

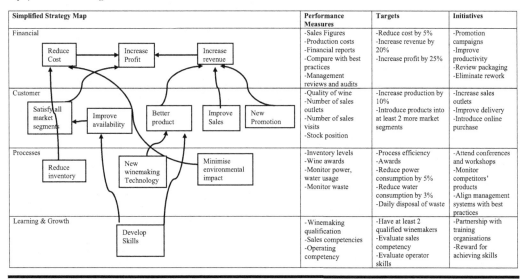

Figure 3.3 Strategy map; alignment of strategies with balanced score card.

- ■ Financial: Increase profit by reducing the costs and increasing the revenue.
- ■ Customer: Satisfying all market segments and improving the availability of its wine in the market to contribute towards the profit objective.
- ■ Processes: New wine brands are developed using new wine-making technology in order to introduce them to new market segments. Environmental factors are monitored to facilitate effective operational activities.

- Learning and growth: This involves improving wine-making skills and operating skills. Establishing partnerships with training organisations enables the organisation to adopt new operational as well as selling skills.

The metrics for monitoring, targets and the initiatives are described in Figure 3.3.

3.6.11 Final Assessment

This step is essential for the continuity of the strategic plan. When the strategies have been implemented for a reasonable length of time, the planning team should review each strategy, measure the results against the expectations (including establishing methodologies to measure them) and decide on a suitable plan of action in order to engage the team in a new cycle of strategic planning. The strategic plan should define the roles and responsibilities for the overall implementation of the plan and for achieving the goals and objectives (McNamara, 2007).

Key questions for evaluation are:

1. Are goals and objectives achieved within the timeframe? If goals and objectives have been achieved then acknowledge, reward and communicate the progress. If they are not achieved the following questions (2–6) should be posed.
2. Are deadlines not realistic? Should they be changed?
3. Has the organisation provided adequate resources?
4. Has the organisation correctly prioritised the tasks? Should the priorities be changed?
5. Should the goals be changed?
6. What are the learning experiences from monitoring activities?

3.6.11.1 Frequency of Monitoring and Evaluation

The frequency of monitoring depends on the type of organisation and the environment in which it operates. Organisations that experience rapid changes from the external and internal environment should monitor the progress monthly. The CEO should see the status of progress monthly and the board of directors quarterly.

3.6.11.2 Monitoring Reports

The report should include at least the answers to the above questions, trends relating to activities, recommendations on the status of implementation and any actions needed by the management.

3.6.11.3 Deviations from the Plan

Sometimes deviations from the plan are unavoidable because of external circumstances and/or customer needs. In such instances, goals may have to be modified and changes to the availability of resources should be considered. However, it is extremely important to determine the cause of deviations from the plan.

3.6.11.4 Changing the Plan

The organisation should establish a process for changing the plan. The change request should include what is causing changes to be made, why the changes should be made, and the necessary changes relating to goals, objectives, responsibilities and timeframes. For example, a new technology may be introduced to the market to manufacture a better product at a lower cost. Organisations embracing this technology need to change the strategic plan and resource allocation. Change is caused by new technology (what), and it is necessary to produce and market a better product (why).

3.7 Failure of Strategy Implementation

Although the difficulties of implementing a new strategy have been acknowledged, there is no consensus on the true rate of implementation failure (Candido & Santos, 2015). However, the focus has now shifted from cost reduction, downsizing, process re-engineering and increasing operating performance to build growth, expansion, strategy and its implementation (Corboy & Corrbui, 2007). The following are the seven pitfalls that organisations should avoid:

1. The strategy is not worth implementing: If the strategy has to gain the support of the management and staff, it has to be innovative, realistic, specific and should give the organisation and staff something to look forward to.

2. Lack of clarity of implementation: Implementation planning is often ignored by organisations, and there is an urgency to get started. But a number of issues have to be addressed prior to implementation such as priorities, timeframes, lessons learnt from previous strategy implementation exercises, impact on the organisation and staff, active participation by the staff and risks involved.

3. The stakeholders do not understand the strategy: There is a tendency for the CEO to communicate the strategy on a "need to know" basis. One of the functions of top management is to sell and explain the strategy to all. The frontline supervisory staff must understand the strategy, its importance and how it affects their work. The implementation plan should include not only senior management but also middle managers, supervisors, customers, suppliers and other stakeholders.

4. The responsibilities have not been clarified: People should be given specific and clear responsibilities for strategy implementation. The task of implementation is easier if the net is cast wide so that it creates ownership, commitment and responsibility for it to happen. Giving responsibility without authority ends in total failure. The management must give clear instructions and monitor the progress of implementation.

5. The commitment of the CEO and senior managers diminishes when implementation commences: For the implementation to be successful, senior management must be seen to be committed throughout the implementation phase by explaining the vision and communicating the importance of the strategy to the future of the organisation.

6. The hurdles are not recognised: In the changing external environment, organisations encounter hurdles during the implementation phase. They should be acknowledged as real and quickly addressed. The staff should be encouraged to seek innovative solutions to clear the hurdles.

7. Strategy implementation is focused on senior management. Organisations believe that strategy development and implementation are the concern of senior management. While the strategy is being implemented, the organisation has to run the business and meet targets to satisfy customer needs. Shareholders expect the strategy to be implemented without allowing profitability to drop and customer service to decline. Therefore, the implementation plan should be integrated with the daily activities of the organisation.

The company's strategy has a strong impact on its competitive advantage. Although it is an exhaustive and time-consuming process, it creates new energy, new ideas and teamwork. Strategic planning gives direction, vision and accountability to the organisation, while providing the organisation, its employees and stakeholders with a sense of direction to achieve the shared vision and goals that they themselves have defined.

References

Allison, M. and Kaye, J. (2015). *Strategic Planning for Non-profit Organisations: A Practical Guide for Dynamic Times* (3rd ed.). Hoboken: John Wiley & Sons.

Angelica, E. (2001). *The Fieldstone Alliance Non-profit Guide to Crafting an Effective Mission and Vision Statement*. Minnesota: Fieldstone Alliance.

Bryson, J.M. (2004). *Strategic Planning for Public and Non-profit Organisations: A Guide to Strengthening and Sustaining Organisational Achievement* (3rd ed.). California: Jossey-Bass.

Butuner, H. (2015). *Systematic Strategic Planning: A Comprehensive Framework for Implementation, Control and Evaluation*. Florida: CRC Press.

Campbell, D., Stonehouse, G. and Houston, B. (2002). *Business Strategy* (2nd ed.). England: Butterworth Heinemann.

Candido, C.J.F. and Santos, S.P. (2015). Strategy implementation: What is the failure rate? *Journal of Management and Organisation*, 21 (2), 237–262.

Corboy, M. and Corrbui, D. (2007). The seven deadly sins of strategy implementation. Retrieved January 8, 2019 from https://www.scribd.com/document/208301770/The-Seven-Deadly-Sins-of-Strategy-Implementation.

De Silva, T. (2013). *Essential Management Skills for Pharmacy and Business Managers*. Florida: CRC Press.

GE. (2016). Our strategy. *General Electric*. Retrieved March 12, 2018 from https://www.ge.com/sites/default/files/Strategy_Page_121714.pdf.

Gluck, F.W., Kaufman, S.P. and Walleck, A.S. (1980). Strategic management for competitive advantage. *Harvard Business Review*, 58 (4), 154–161.

Hellriegel, D., Kackson, S.E. and Slocum, J.W. (2002). *Management: A Competency Based Approach* (9th ed.). Ohio: South-Western.

Hill, C.W.L. and Jones, G.R. (2008). *Strategic Management: An Integrated Approach* (8th ed.). Massachusetts: Houghton Mifflin Company.

Hinsky, M. (2015). *Strategic implementation: The poor cousin*. Retrieved March 12, 2018 from http://doc-slide.us/documents/strategic-implementation-the-poor-cousin-strategic-implementation-importance-of-implementation-vs-strategy-development-issues.html.

Hudson, S. (2016). An example of a company conglomerate. *Demand Media*. Retrieved March 12, 2018 from http://smallbusiness.chron.com/example-company-conglomerate-14699.html.

Ingram, M. (2017). AT & T does the break-up dance. *The Globe and Mail*. Retrieved March 12, 2018 from http://www.theglobeandmail.com/report-on-business/att-does-the-breakup-dance/article20935814/.

Kaplan, R.S. and Norton, D.P. (1992). Balanced scorecard: Measures that drive performance. *Harvard Business Review*, 70 (1), 71–79.

Kaplan, R.S. and Norton, D.P. (1996). *Translating Strategy into the Balanced Scorecard*. Massachusetts: Harvard Business School Press.

Kaplan, R.S. and Norton, D.P. (2001). *Strategy Focused Organisation*. Massachusetts: Harvard Business School Press.

Kaplan, R.S. and Norton, D.P. (2006). How to implement a new strategy without disrupting your organisation. *Harvard Business Review*, 84 (3), 100–109.

King, Jr., M.L. (1963). The dream speech. *March on Washington*. Retrieved March 12, 2018 from http://archives.gov/press/exhibits/dream-speech.pdf.

Koteen, J. (1989). *Strategic Management in Public and Non-profit Organisations*. New York: Praeger Publications.

McNamara, C. (2007). *Field Guide to Strategic Planning and Facilitation* (3rd ed.). Minnesota: Authenticity Consulting LLC.

Patterson, S.J. and Radtke, J.M. (2009). *Communications for Non-profit Organisations* (2nd ed.). New Jersey: John Wiley & Sons.

Sandilands, T. (2016). Example of a company's forward integration. *Demand Media*. Retrieved June 21, 2016 from http://smallbusiness.chron.com/example-companys-forward-integration-37601.html.

Strategic Management MGT603. (n.d.). *Types of strategies*. Retrieved March 12, 2018 from http://www.zeepedia.com/read.php?types_of_strategies_diversification_strategies_conglomerate_diversification_strategic_management&b=58&c=21.

Chapter 4

Risk Management

4.1 Introduction

Inhabitants of our planet at various times have been exposed to natural disasters such as floods, earthquakes, volcanic eruptions, famine, drought, etc. It is widely believed that the extinction of the dinosaurs was due to the massive impact of an asteroid on earth. In more recent times, the south-east Asian tsunami affected 13 countries and killed nearly 250,000 people (BBC, 2014). The 2010 volcanic eruption in Iceland disrupted millions of air travellers and affected time-sensitive air shipments (Chopra & Sodhi, 2014). Although modern technology enables the prediction of some of these events, their potential impact cannot be estimated accurately. Businesses are also not immune to such natural disasters. Besides natural disasters, organisations have to guard against events that may have a negative impact on the whole organisation. The possibility of exposure to financial and technical risks, legal liability and human asset risks such as disability cannot be underestimated (Young & Tippins, 2000). Factors such as a change of government, the passage of laws and political uprisings have a significant impact on the global market (Bremmer, 2011). Fraud and corruption by top executives in leading organisations have led to the collapse of once reputed companies. The collapse of Enron in 2001 and Tyco in 2002 in the United States are classic examples of corporate fraud that put these organisations at great risk (Ritholtz, 2013).

Organisations worldwide have become aware of environmental pollution and now environmental risk management is a critical component of corporate strategy. Terrorist activities, sabotage, failure to design and implement safety procedures, and a lack of concern for regulations and the environment are all possible ways for an organisation to cause pollution. The Union Carbide tragedy in 1984 in Bhopal, India, caused the death of 3,800 people and left 11,000 with disabilities. According to the Union Carbide report, it was a result of sabotage (Browning, 1993). In 2010, 1,700 gallons of oil spilled into the Gulf of Mexico as a result of British Petroleum's Deepwater Horizon oil rig explosion. In the six months following the spill, more than 8,000 birds, sea turtles and marine mammals were found dead or injured (National Wildlife Federation, 2015).

Apart from business risks and natural disasters, consumers and food-producing companies face food safety risks. Throughout the value chain, the farmers, suppliers, distributors, manufacturers, retailers and consumers have responsibility for food safety. Risks to consumers can arise from equipment or process failures or from criminal intent. The incidence of foodborne illnesses is increasing globally as a result of failure to manage risks associated with food production, delivery, storage and consumption. In the United States, 76 million people suffer from foodborne illnesses annually (Scott, 2003).

Governments all over the world have introduced legislation to protect the consumer, other stakeholders and businesses from risks. A proactive approach has been adopted by regularly monitoring the relevant agencies in order to ensure that all types of risks are effectively managed. In April 2003, the National Nuclear Safety Administration (NNSA) in the United States identified 412 safety failures in a recent audit in the nuclear research facility, the Los Alamos National Laboratory (LANL) (Gunther, 2015). The US Department of Labour's Occupational Safety and Health Administration in their latest inspection of DuPont's chemical manufacturing plant in La Porte, Texas, found three "wilful", one "repeat" and four "serious" violations of workplace safety (Trager, 2015). In order to minimise and hopefully prevent a negative impact on the business and consumers, a well-managed risk management system should place a strong emphasis on targeting the risks that could arise and implement systems of metrics. This chapter describes the principles of risk management and measures to minimise or prevent the negative impacts of risks.

4.2 The Evolution of Risk Management

Risk management has been known to humans since the dawn of time. Early civilisations battled with harsh environmental conditions such as floods, famine, drought, invasions, etc., and they took steps to protect themselves from such disasters. During the mid-20th century, organisations realised the need to manage risks in a much narrower context than it is understood today. Organisations focused on establishing insurance policies to protect against adverse events. However, during the 1970s companies adopted a broader view of managing risk and sought alternatives to insurance policies, but the negative effects of risks were not addressed (Young & Tippins, 2000),

Following World War II, there was a great interest in studies such as strategic management, operations management, logistics and materials management, and operations theory. Publications in academic journals reflected this interest. Although these studies were not directly applicable to risk management, the interest in management science filtered into many business education areas. Of particular interest was the study of insurance, risk and uncertainty. Practitioners were then able to adopt a broader approach to managing insurable risk as well as insurance coverage, which led to a change in the role of the insurance buyer.

Due to changes in the internal and external market environment, insurance buyers had to exert some influence on the risks that were insured. The expanded role of the insurance buyer led to the emergence of policies and procedures for managing health, safety and engineering risks. It was only in recent years that the concept of risk management was applied to negative threats and positive opportunities. Organisations needed to adopt a proactive approach to understand the size of threats and opportunities to make appropriate decisions.

The first edition of the guide, *Management of Risk: Guidance for Practitioners*, was published in the United Kingdom in 2002 (Office of Government Commerce), and it suggested that company directors to implement a generic framework for risk management across all divisions of the organisation and to establish the necessary controls. Since then both the private and the public sector have embraced risk management to take their organisations forward. In many parts of the world, legislation has been introduced for corporate governance and internal controls, which requires organisations to focus on formal risk management techniques, and that now extends to enterprise risk management (ERM) (Office of Government Commerce, 2010; Young & Tippins, 2000).

4.3 Terminology

Risk: An unexpected event or a set of events, should it occur, that will have an effect on achieving the objectives of the company. It is measured by a combination of the probability of occurrence of the event(s) and the magnitude of the impact.

Risk management: A disciplined approach to the systematic application of principles, identifying and assessing the risks, and planning and implementing risk responses.

Risk measurement: The process of quantifying and communicating risk.

ERM: The process of planning, organising, leading and controlling the activities of an organisation in order to minimise the impact of risks on its capital and investments.

Hazard: A biological, chemical or physical hazard or any other property in a food product that can harm the consumer or cause illness.

Hazard analysis: The identification of biological, chemical or physical hazard or any other hazard associated with ingredients, production processes, storage, distribution, retail and use.

4.4 Benefits of Risk Management

Risk management offers numerous benefits to the organisation. They can be classified as (a) mandatory; (b) assurance; (c) decision-making; and (d) effective and efficient core processes. Mandatory benefits result from risk management activities that are designed to ensure that the organisation complies with legal and regulatory requirements and customer requirements. Identification of risks and the implementation of effective controls ensure that risk management activities are effectively managed. Risk management activities that provide additional structured information enable top management to make the correct business decisions. Risk management also enhances the efficiency and effectiveness of operations within the organisation. It provides inputs to strategic decision-making, which deliver exactly what is required by the organisation (Hopkin, 2014).

Both the public and private sectors benefit from risk management. The private sector is concerned with shareholders' value and returns, whereas the public sector focuses on delivering services cost-effectively in accordance with regulatory requirements. Both sectors improve performance against objectives through risk management activities by better service delivery, better management of contingent and maintenance activities. This enhances efficiency and reduces waste through the efficient use of resources, fewer surprises, better management of fraudulent activities, and reducing the cost of capital (Office of Government Commerce, 2010).

The greatest asset of any organisation is its reputation. Although it is intangible, it has an impact on every aspect of the business: perceptions internally and externally by customers and other stakeholders, credibility as an organisation and its performance, and values, culture, beliefs and social interaction. A good risk management programme promotes credibility and reputation by being friendly to the environment, providing safe and quality products and services to consumers at a fair price, and being transparent in fiscal activities (Revuid, 2009).

According to a survey by Zurich among 1,419 business executives, ERM has achieved better operational performance by improving communication and strategic decision-making (39%), improving governance (34%) and enhancing management accountability (31%) (Harvard Business Review Analytic Services, 2011).

4.5 Nature of Risk

The risks of fire and floods have been known to humans since time immemorial. Such risks were accepted as more or less natural, and our ancestors handled such events in the most basic ways, sometimes unsuccessfully. With technological progress, another set of risks evolved. This time the risks were associated with failures of systems or equipment. Accidents occurred at work during major construction works when travelling on land or at sea and during wars. The first-ever motor vehicle accident happened in Ireland on August 31, 1869, when a woman, May Ward, fell under the wheels of an experimental steam car built by her cousins (Hollnagel, 2008).

A significant change took place in the 19th century when accidents became associated with technological systems that people designed, built and used as a part of work. With progress and civilisation accidents increased, not only because people did something wrong or because of an act of nature but also because of man-made system failure. These events were no longer simple, but complex, and challenged the understanding of people at work. People knew how to perform their work, but they had a limited understanding of the nature of technology. Many of the responses to risks such as fire and road accidents were automatic. They always have negative outcomes and are referred to as hazard risks (Hopkin, 2014).

Compliant risks are sometimes viewed as hazard risks because of the negative outcome of failure to comply. However, achieving compliance bring benefits to the organisation and its people. As individuals, some situations require mandatory responses. Buying insurance for a vehicle is usually a legal requirement. Vehicles that are regularly serviced and maintained also occasionally break down. These types of risks, which have a great degree of uncertainty associated with them, are called controlled risks. Individuals who invest money expecting a good return and those participating in sports activities for pride and self-esteem take opportunity risks (Hopkin, 2014).

Recent events such as terrorism, the Ebola epidemic, extreme weather patterns and the global financial crisis brought risks to higher profile because of the borderless nature of such risks. The risks cited above have no boundaries, and they share the following features (Smith & Fischbacher, 2009): (a) they are unpredictable; (b) the impact is large in terms of the damage that they can cause and they can trigger further events down the timeline; and (c) their origin, evolution and final scale and form are frequently unknown.

The transboundary nature of risks causes complex situations, which makes risk management difficult. The global financial crisis is a perfect example of a risk that sent shock waves around the world. The failure of the financial institution was both swift and for many organisations catastrophic. Other institutions around the world that felt the ripple effect had to be rescued by their respective national governments.

The Ebola epidemic was another example of a risk that crossed international boundaries. The interconnected nature of societies enables the transmission of certain diseases faster than in previous generations. However, western nations enjoy greater prosperity and health and are safer as a society than at any time in our history.

Terrorist attacks are becoming more and more sophisticated. Despite enormous precautions taken by governments, vulnerabilities still exist within modern societies (and port cities in particular) because of the risks associated with international terrorism. The evolving nature of terrorist attacks, the sophistication with which they are carried out, and their unpredictable nature expose the vulnerabilities that will exist within organisations and government agencies for some time to come (Smith & Fischbacher, 2009).

4.5.1 Business Risks

Business organisations face a variety of risks and challenges that must be dealt with every day. Some of the risks and challenges are obvious and include the need to maintain demand for products and services, manage resources, and make strategic decisions such as changing or expanding the operation. Some other risks are less obvious but are critical for business success. The risks faced by organisations depend on the type of business. Financial institutions are exposed to risks that production facilities rarely encounter (Price Warehouse Coopers, 2008). A summary of business risks is presented in Table 4.1.

Table 4.1   Types of Business Risks

	Risk	*Description*	*Assessed by*
1	Strategic	Relates to the organisation's mission and objectives	Senior Management Teams
2	Operational	Loss due to poor financial performance and failure resulting from internal processes, people, systems and external events	Regulators and Management Team
3	Compliance	Failure to comply with regulations, processes, business conduct standards and strategic voluntary standards	Compliance Officers
4	Internal audit	Relates to value drivers covering strategic, financial, operational and compliance objectives	Internal Auditors
5	Financial	Relates to misinterpretation of financial statements	Financial Controller
6	Fraud	Associated with instances of fraud that could impact on the organisation's ethics and compliance standards, business practice requirements and financial reporting integrity	Compliance Officers
7	Market	Market movements that could affect the organisation's performance and risk exposure	Market Risk Specialists
8	Credit	Failure of a borrower or counterpart to meet its obligations	Credit Risk Specialist
9	Customer	Customer's risk profile and behaviour: customer intent, credit worthiness, affiliations and other relevant factors	Account Managers

(Continued)

Table 4.1 (*Continued*) Types of Business Risks

	Risk	Description	Assessed by
10	Supply chain	Associated with inputs and logistics necessary to support the company's production and services	Logistics Manager
11	Production	Failure to meet production and service delivery targets	Product Management Team
12	Security	Associated with potential breaches in the organisation's physical assets, information protection and security	Information Security Officer
13	Information Technology	Failure or breakdown of technology impacting on business activities	Information Technology Specialist
14	Project	Failure to meet the delivery of implementing a project	Project Management Team

4.5.2 Environmental Risks

Environmental risks are defined as actual or potential threats that have a harmful effect on living organisms and the environment by effluents, emissions, wastes, resource depletion, etc., arising out of an organisation's activities. Environment pollution can also be caused by natural disasters such as floods, earthquakes, volcanic eruptions, etc. They are transmitted through air, water, soil or the biological food chain eventually to humans (Whyte & Burton, 1980).

The causes and characteristics of such events are diverse. Some of the environmental disasters are created by humans through the use of new technology, products or chemicals, while others are natural disasters due to natural processes that impact on human activities and communities. Yet others produce unknown effects at the time a new technology or activity was developed, as shown by the harmful effects on the earth's ozone layer by fluorocarbon sprays or nitrogen fertilisers. While modern technology enables some of these events to be predicted with reasonable accuracy, the extent of damage cannot be easily determined as shown by the earthquake and tsunami that destroyed the entire Sukuiso area in Japan in 2011. These adverse events inflict harm on people who have to suffer the consequences but not by choice. Events such as resource depletion also affect the future generations of this planet.

Environmental risks in developed countries have received much attention because of the magnitude of their impact on the economy, and these risks have been associated with urbanisation and industrialisation. Other risks due to malnutrition, poor housing and sanitation are more prevalent in developing countries. Common categories of pollutants are emissions to air, water and soil, energy use, waste, noise vibration and odour, biodiversity and social issues (resource depletion). Munn (1973), on behalf of the Scientific Committee on Problems of the Environment (SCOPE) in his report on the Global Environmental Monitoring System (GEMS), lists 22 priority pollutants. They include emissions to air, water and soil such as sulphur dioxide, sulphates, carbon dioxide, carbon monoxide, hydrocarbons, toxic chemicals, asbestos, noise, waste, etc. Environmental issues created by companies have both positive and negative impacts on society (Table 4.2). Environmentally conscious companies develop policies, strategies and actions to address environmental and social issues in the workplace and among their stakeholders (World Bank Institute, n.d.).

Table 4.2   Environmental Impact and Social Responsibilities of a Business

Originator	Environmental	Social Responsibility
Producer	Pollution, effluent, use, misuse or excess use of water, consumption of energy resources, misuse or overuse of land, depletion of natural resources	Provision of health services, equal opportunity, occupational health and safety standards, promoting diversity
Consumer of raw materials	Contamination of drinking water, desertification and degradation of land	Raising awareness, educational campaigns, promoting community projects, resolving land disputes, effective use of natural resources
Operation	Odour, human, animal and plant effects from toxins and hazardous waste, indoor air quality, smog, noise	Contribution to economic development, raising the standard of living.
Role model	Waste management, efficient use of resources, use of alternative energy	Good practice of human rights, promoting cultural diversity

4.5.3 Food Safety Risks

The approach to food safety has evolved from a hazard-based approach to a risk-based approach. According to the hazard-based approach, the mere presence of a hazard is sufficient to declare the food as unsafe. But the risk-based approach is a more rational approach which considers whether the exposure to a hazard has a significant impact on public health. There are three types of food safety hazards: biological, chemical and physical (De Silva, 2007). The features of these hazards are shown in Table 4.3.

4.6 Principles of Risk Management

Designing a dynamic risk management system is an art as well as a science. There are 10 principles that govern the art of risk management (Plaschke et al., 2013):

1. Risk management starts at the top management. The CEO and the senior management must demonstrate a commitment to the risk management programme and lead it. The companies that focus on risk management usually have a Chief Risk Officer (CRO) who leads the risk function and is responsible for coordinating the line organisation and business units. Their role includes identifying and managing specific risks, enforcing risk policies and reporting to the board of directors.
2. Risk management has to be integrated with business activities including planning, capital allocation, controlling and reporting. The organisation should encourage participation at all levels so that they are involved in the decision-making process. The most effective approach is to integrate the central risk unit, which provides guidance with business unit risk experts who report to business unit managers and the CRO.

Table 4.3 Features of Food Safety Hazards

Type	Description	Contamination
Biological	Microbiological organisms: bacteria, viruses, fungi, parasites Bacteria: pathogenic bacteria in food cause foodborne illnesses Viruses: survive on living cells and are foodborne, waterborne or transmitted by human, animal or other contact and occur in uncooked meat products or contaminated ready-to-eat food Fungi: mould and yeast and produce mycotoxins	Survival and growth are due to (a) inadequate heat treatment; (b) slow acid production during fermentation; (c) unsatisfactory storage conditions; (d) high water activity; and (e) low levels of food preservation
Chemical	Pesticides application, food additives in formulations and during processing, heavy metals, colourings, solvents, cleaning agents	The types and concentrations of chemicals are important. May originate from contaminated soil or water or ineffective cleaning procedures
Physical	Foreign matter such as metal fragments, insects, machine parts, glass pieces, plastic objects, sand, stones, cigarette butts, plastic dressing strips	May be dissolved or dispersed in food. Physical form can vary from powder to particulate matter
Sources	Primacy source: raw materials Uncontrolled processing steps Unclean, unhygienic equipment, faulty setup, machinery not properly maintained Food handling during storage, transport and customer use Environmental conditions: pollution of water and soil, industrial waste Pests such as rodents	

3. Avoid relying on complex metrics and models for all situations. Complex mathematical models available as software complicate the risk management process, disguise the transparency and make it a black box. But complex businesses do require sophisticated models for risk analysis. Banks, e.g., rely on a vast amount of data for complex statistical analysis. They have long-term experience of interpreting complex metrics and such institutions have a legal obligation to use complex models for risk analysis. Therefore, the complexity of the business determines the appropriate level of risk management.

4. Align risk management with the company's strategy. The overall objective of both should be the creation of shareholder value. Organisations generally tend to focus on risks that can be easily quantified, but not all risks can be. Regulatory changes and serious product failure are risks that cannot be quantified yet are significant. Therefore, companies should focus on all relevant risks.

5. Risk management is a culture. Top managers of the company should create a risk-aware culture to create new sources of competitive advantage and realise new business opportunities. According to a *Harvard Business Review* survey (2011), 34% of the respondents reported that a risk-aware culture is the most important factor for the success of the risk management

programme. However, only 11% of them thought that their organisation was doing a good job of it.

6. Communication of risk information is an essential part of a risk-aware culture. An effective risk management programme requires the free flow of information throughout all levels of the organisation. Relevant information kept in one business unit is of no use to anyone. Employees need unrestricted access to risk-related information so that they can escalate problems quickly to top management. One-to-one meetings with business unit managers, web-based intranet systems and risk management software management systems are some of the tools that can be used to share relevant risk information.

7. Focus on creating an understanding of potential risks rather than on complex metrics. Employees should be made aware of the probabilities and potential impact of risks that impact on business activities and train them to take appropriate corrective and preventive actions. The organisations should establish processes to conduct open discussions and assessments of all types of risks.

8. Focus on the goal and continuous improvement. The assumptions, probabilities and impacts of the risk management programme should be regularly reviewed. Successful organisations refine their assumptions about its future and their impact on the business with the changing business environment. An incremental approach that is designed to meet the risks of day-to-day business and is tailored to business requirements is much better than creating a comprehensive plan at the start.

9. Companies can prepare for unknown risks. "Black Swan" events are environmental disasters that rarely occur but have disastrous consequences. The Japanese tsunami that affected the viability of their nuclear industry was a Black Swan event. Highly adaptive companies prepare for such contingencies by developing crisis management and business continuity plans.

10. Use negatives to focus on positives. It is easy for companies to focus on the negative consequences of risks, but the survival of a business depends on creating new opportunities. Successful companies take advantage of negatives to strengthen their competitive position and gain an advantage. By employing scientific planning in order to define both best-case and worst-case scenarios, and using latest market developments and trends, it is possible to quantify the metrics for future planning. Companies such as General Motors, IBM, DuPont, General Electric, and Proctor and Gamble that were prepared to take risks exploiting the disruption and turmoil during the Great Depression in the United States survived the crisis and its aftermath.

4.7 Categories of Risk

The first step in designing a risk management programme is to distinguish among the categories of risk that organisations face. Any type of risk challenges the strategy and the survival of a business. Kaplan and Mikes (2012) classify risks into three categories: preventable, strategy and external risks.

4.7.1 Preventable Risks

Preventable risks are controllable risks that arise from within the organisation and should be eliminated or avoided. They are associated with the day-to-day activities of the organisation such as employees' or managers' unauthorised, illegal, unethical, incorrect or inappropriate actions and risks due to the breakdown of routine operational activities. Complete elimination of errors or defects can be too costly, and therefore, the company should establish a zone of tolerance for these that would not have serious consequences. Generally, firms should attempt to eliminate them because preventable risks do not offer a strategic advantage. They are best managed by monitoring the operational processes and activities of employees.

4.7.2 Strategy Risks

In order to gain competitive advantage and generate good returns, businesses take calculated risks. Banks take credit risks when they lend money to customers. Research and development activities are associated with risks of failure or success. Strategy risks are not undesirable and, in fact, they are essential for a company's growth. Rule-based controlled models are not applicable to strategy risks. Instead, a risk management system that reduces the probability of occurrence of strategy risks enables the organisation to improve its ability to manage or contain such risk events should they occur. Such a programme would not prevent the organisation from taking risks, but permit it to take higher risks to gain a competitive advantage over companies that do not have plans to manage strategy risks.

4.7.3 External Risks

External risks are outside events that are outside the control of the organisation. Examples of external risks are natural disasters such as floods, tsunamis and earthquakes, political events, regulatory changes and economic shifts. An entirely different approach is required to manage such risks because companies cannot prevent the occurrence of external events. The management must focus on identifying such risks and minimising the impact on the organisation.

The three types of risks described above require different management approaches. A compliance-based approach is suitable for managing preventable risks but is inadequate for strategy risks or external risks. These risks require open discussion and the involvement of all the business units.

4.7.4 Pure versus Speculative Risk Exposures

Generally, risk is defined in terms of an expected deviation of an occurrence from what is anticipated. The insurance industry and education and training material use the term "exposure" to describe the property, enterprise, person or activity facing a potential loss. Risk professionals often categorise exposure in terms of pure risk exposure and speculative risk exposure. Exposure to pure risk causes a loss or no gain (e.g. fire, flood and earthquake), whereas exposure to speculative risk results in either a gain or loss. Examples of speculative risk include investment risk, reputation risk and strategy risk (Baranoff et al., 2009). Table 4.4 shows examples of pure versus speculative risk exposures.

4.8 Components of Enterprise Risk Management

ERM has three components (Mikes & Kaplan, 2014):

1. Strategic activity: Identifying the potential events that prevent the organisation from achieving its strategic objective.

Table 4.4   Examples of Pure versus Speculative Risk Exposures

Pure (potential loss or no gain)	Speculative (potential loss or gain)
1. Natural disasters (floods, fire, earthquakes)	1. Market risks (investment, interest, foreign exchange, stock market)
2. Products, premises, employee practice liability risk	2. Reputational risk
3. New product or technology failure or obsolescence risk	3. Brand failure risk
4. Mortality and morbidity risk of individuals	4. Product success risk
5. Intellectual property violation risk	5. Public image risk
6. Environmental risks due to pollution, depletion of natural resources, irreversible destruction of the food chain	6. Demographic changes
7. Risks due to man-made disasters (nuclear, political risks, unemployment, wars) 8. Societal risks (pandemics, healthcare risks)	7. Market position 8. Company survival risk 9. Regulatory changes 10. Political events and labour disputes 11. Investment risk 12. New product development risks 13. Accounting risk 14. Genetic engineering risk 15. Longevity risk

  2. Governance activity: Participating at all levels of management.
  3. Monitoring activity: Measurement, feedback and corrective actions to limit or prevent exposure.

The emphasis on the three components of ERM varies across companies. Some firms may focus on financial, insurable and measurable events that threaten the financial performance of the organisation. Others may focus on non-financial, qualitative issues. Employee and managerial participation in firms may also vary. Those who desire quantitative measures concentrate on numbers, while others emphasise learning from numbers. The emphasis on risk management may also depend on whether the risks are tangible and quantifiable.

4.9 Planning for Risk Management

An integrated risk management plan (RMP) has several components and the basis of such a plan is strong corporate leadership. The components of an integrated RMP are a process for understanding the risks and their significance, a plan for implementation and the implementation process. In order to design an integrated RMP, the organisation has to use appropriate metrics and tools, develop rules for governance, and create a company-wide risk mindset and a risk-aware culture (Pidun et al., 2017). Risk management process has three basic steps: (a) understanding; (b) planning; and (c) acting.

Understand: Identify the risks, classify the risks and create a risk map.

Plan: Integrate risk management processes into the company's business processes.

Act: Implement the plan to mitigate the impact or take advantage of risks should they occur. This can be achieved through specific strategic operational activities or broader crisis management activities. To be successful, the entire organisation should be encouraged to regularly consider issues of risks and their probability.

Figure 4.1 shows the components of a risk management process.

4.10 Risk Management Plan

The RMP provides the project team with direction and basis for planning. It is a consistent and comprehensive approach that ensures all aspects of the programme are examined for risk. Since it is a roadmap, it is specific in areas such as assigning roles and responsibilities and definitions, and general in other areas, thus allowing the user to select the most efficient way to proceed (Department of Defence, 2006; Molenaar et al., 2010).

Risk planning involves the development, implementation and monitoring of appropriate risk response strategies, including the prerequisite activities needed for a successful RMP. The sources of information necessary for developing the RMP are (a) a documented, comprehensive and intensive risk management strategy; (b) methods to be used to implement the strategy; and (c) the plan for the acquisition of resources. Risk planning is an iterative process, which includes describing and scheduling the activities and processes to assess, mitigate, monitor and document the risks associated with business activities. A risk register may suffice for minor or moderately complex projects, but for major projects or moderately complex projects with a greater degree of uncertainty, a formal RMP is warranted.

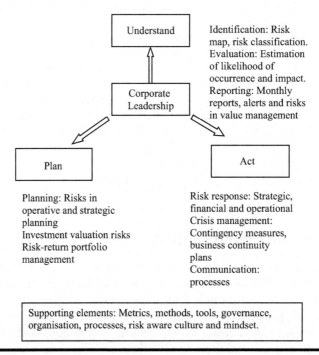

Figure 4.1 Overview of the risk management process.

The first step in the planning process is the development and documentation of a risk management strategy. During the early stages, the following activities take place:

- Establish the purpose and objective.
- Assign roles and responsibilities for specific areas.
- Identify the technical resources needed.
- Define the assessment process and areas to focus on.
- Outline considerations for mitigation planning.
- Select a risk rating scheme.
- Identify reporting and documentation needs.
- Establish reporting requirements.

The RMP should contain all or some of the following items:

- Introduction.
- Programme summary.
- Organisation and definitions.
- Risk management strategy and process.
- Risk management procedures.
- Risk planning.
- Risk allocation.
- Risk register and risk tracking.
- Risk management information system, documentation and reports.

The level of detail in the plan varies with the unique attributes of each project. Red flag items, lists, risk registers and formal RMPs allow flexibility in risk management documentation.

4.11 Identifying Risks

The first step in identifying risks is to assess the business. Focus on critical activities including key services, resources and staff and potential threats that could influence the operation. At the next stage, review the business plan and evaluate the threats that could prevent the achievement of company objectives (Queensland Government, 2014). The following questions are useful in identifying the risks:

- When, where, how and why are risks likely to happen?
- Are the threats internal or external?
- Should it occur who might be involved or affected by it?

Consider the consequences if essential services such as power and internet are disrupted, key documents and files are destroyed, infrastructure is damaged, the supplier goes bankrupt and/or key staff members quit (Queensland Government, 2014a).

4.11.1 Techniques for Identifying Risks

a. Brainstorming: Invite business unit managers, financial advisors, risk officers, suppliers and other stakeholders.

    b. Analyse other events: Consider previous threats that affected the business, the likelihood of a recurrence and the measures in place to deal with such events.

    c. Consider the activities: Review checklists, flowcharts and processes, and assess the associated risks that could prevent their performance, and the effect of these risks on other processes.

    d. Consider the worst-case scenario: Identify the worst things that could happen to the business. A single event may cause several other things to happen. A labour union strike by baggage handlers in the airport can trigger other events. Flights have to be cancelled or re-scheduled. Airlines may have to provide accommodation for transit passengers. Passengers whose holiday plans have been disrupted may claim compensation. Incoming flights have to be diverted to other airports (Queensland Government, 2014a)

4.12 Assessment of Risk

4.12.1 Risk Tolerance

The first step in the assessment of risk is to define the risk tolerance for each risk type. Risk tolerance is the acceptable level of risk that the organisation is willing to tolerate to achieve the organisation's objectives, e.g. a production facility may allow 15 minutes downtime for each operational shift. Reducing the downtime to an industry average of 10 minutes per shift may not offer any advantages so the company may specify 15 minutes per shift as tolerance. A downtime more than the specified tolerance will have a negative impact on performance (Price Waterhouse Coopers, 2008).

4.12.2 Assessment of Likelihood and Impact

Events identified that have the potential to inhibit the achievement of company objectives are assessed on the basis of the probability of occurrence and their impact on performance. This assessment should be conducted without considering the current responses and control activities (Queensland Government, 2014a). Various forms of risk matrices have been used in the assessment of risks for effective decision-making. Risk matrices involve the categorisation of probability of occurrence of risks and their impact based on a rating scale. They vary from 2×2 to 6×6 matrices. Generally, risk descriptors are sector-specific. For example, the health sector categorises the consequences of risk on the basis of fatalities, injuries, days off work, etc., whereas the financial sector's rating is based on investment failure, profit loss, fraud, etc. Cox (2008) presents the disadvantages of using risk matrices. Risk ratings do not necessarily support good resource allocation decisions because of the inherent subjective categorisation of uncertain events. Furthermore, he argues that quantitative and semi-quantitative matrices using numbers instead of categories cannot correctly reproduce risk ratings, especially if frequency and severity are negatively correlated. In adopting risk matrices, Cox (2008) recommends the following features (Olson & Wu 2010): (a) under weak consistency conditions no red cell should be placed next to a green cell; (b) no red cell should be placed on the left-most column or bottom row; (c) the matrix must have at least three colours; and (d) too many colours give a false resolution.

4.12.3 Risk Descriptors

Risk impact descriptors and risk likelihood descriptors are presented in Table 4.5

    The tsunami in 2011 that devastated a complete city in Japan created an entirely new perception of risk assessment. As the disaster began to unfold, governments and corporations realised

Table 4.5 Risk Impact and Likelihood Descriptors

Risk Category	Description	Impact
Catastrophic	Major disaster – Tsunami Earthquake Major flood	Huge fire Nuclear accident Explosion causing building collapse
High	Major financial loss Fatalities or permanent illnesses Major business interruptions Significant risk to the ecosystem	Major reputational damage High impact on the business strategy Significant harm to human health Major spillage
Medium	Moderate financial loss Single death or multiple injuries Critical systems unavailable for less than one day Leaking of contaminants from a site Pollution of non-sensitive waters	Moderate reputational damage Moderate impact on the business strategy Contamination exceeds generic or site-specific criteria Significant change in the ecosystem Significant damage to buildings making it unsafe to occupy
Low	Minimum financial loss Minor or no personal injury Critical systems unavailable for less than one hour Loss of plants in a land site	Insignificant reputational damage Issues resolved in day-to-day work Temporary adverse health effects Easily repairable damage to buildings

Likelihood

Estimation	Description	Indicators
High (Probable)	Likely to occur each year or more than 25% chance of occurrence within the next four months	Potential to occur several times within a four-year period Has occurred recently
Medium (Possible)	Likely to occur within a four-year time period or less than 25% chance of occurrence within the next 12 months	Could occur more than once within a four-year period Previous history of occurrence
Low (Remote)	Not likely to occur within a four-year time period or less than 2% chance of occurrence	Has not occurred Not likely to occur

that risks previously thought to be insignificant could not be ignored. Black Swan events have a very low probability of occurrence but they cause an enormous amount of damage to property, businesses and people when they occur (Taleb, 2007). Generally, Black Swan events trigger further events leaving no room for rescuing the situation.

Table 4.6 shows a generic matrix that satisfies the conditions described in Section 4.12.2 (Sadgrove, 2015). This can be easily adopted to suit the requirements of the organisation. In the matrix, some examples of risks are plotted and the assessment takes into account Black Swan events.

Table 4.6   Risk Matrix

IMPACT			
Catastrophic	Tsunami risk		
High	Mitigate or Transfer		Power failure risk
Medium		Information Technology risk	
Low		Minor product failure	
PROBABILITY ->	Low	Medium	High

Business continuity plan	
Eliminate	
Mitigate or Transfer	
Tolerate, monitor, manage	
No action	

Likelihood		
Estimation	*Description*	*Indicators*
High (Probable)	Likely to occur each year or more than 25% chance of occurrence within the next four months	Potential to occur several times within a four-year period Has occurred recently
Medium (Possible)	Likely to occur within a four-year time period or less than 25% chance of occurrence within the next 12 months	Could occur more than once within a four-year period Previous history of occurrence
Low (Remote)	Not likely to occur within a four-year time period or less than 2% chance of occurrence	Has not occurred Not likely to occur

4.13 Control and Treatment of Risks

The next phase of the RMP is to develop ways of responding to identified threats by controlling or treating the risks. The difference between control and treatment is subtle: Controls are *measures* that modify risks, whereas treatment refers to the *process* of modifying them (Department of Education, Training and Development, 2017; Praxiom, 2017; ISO, 2018). Both control and treatment share the following features:

- They modify the risk by reducing the likelihood of the occurrence of negative events and/or reduce the consequences of negative events should they occur, while at the same time they increase the likelihood and consequences of positive events.
- They address the root cause of the risk.
- They may not always be effective in modifying the risk.

The difference between them depends on whether they are established at the time of risk assessment. Controls are existing strategies and practices in place such as policies, systems and standard business procedures. A risk may have one control and a control may address more than one risk. On the other hand, treatments are the additional strategies and activities necessary to address unacceptable risks should they occur and if controls are not effective. Treatments are specific to a risk and become a control when it has been fully implemented and found to be effective. The treatment plan for ineffective controls includes strengthening controls and developing new controls.

4.13.1 Evaluation of Controls

Controls have to be carefully evaluated to ensure that they are effective, reliable and capable of being applied. Too many controls or too stringent controls can make them ineffective and waste valuable resources of the organisation. The following factors should be considered in evaluating controls: (a) fitness for purpose; (b) operational effectiveness; (c) relevancy; and (d) whether it is documented, used and up to date.

4.13.2 Evaluation of Treatments

Treatment options are evaluated on the basis of:

- Effectiveness of the modification.
- Cost–benefit analysis.
- Compatibility with company objectives.
- Compliance with legislation.
- Capability to introduce new or secondary threats.

Organisations should develop a treatment plan for complex events. Such a plan includes the target risk level, proposed action, resource requirements, responsibilities of personnel, timing, performance metrics, reporting and monitoring requirements. Organisations have little control or no control over some events such as earthquakes, floods, terrorist attacks, international financial markets and pandemics. The only action is recovery option after the event by proper business continuity planning.

4.13.3 Risk Treatment Options

An RMP should include the various options for treating the risks (Queensland Government, 2014b). The following are the options:

1. Eliminate the risk: High risks must be reduced to at least medium risk (reduce or transfer) before the work commences. Interim control measures should not be applied. Risk control measures should not be overly dependent on personal protective equipment (PPE) or appliances. Attempts should be made to eliminate the risk before commencing work. Management attention is needed.

2. Reduce the risk: The risk may be able to be mitigated through quality control procedures, performing audits, compliance with regulatory requirements, staff training, and maintenance or modifying the processes. A careful evaluation of the risk should be carried out to ensure that the level of risk is reduced to as low as reasonably practicable (ALARP) within a specified time period. Interim measures such as administrative control or PPE may be applied while longer-term measures are implemented. Management attention is required.

3. Transfer the risk: A risk may be transferred to another party through insurance coverage, outsourcing, joint ventures or partnerships. Cross-training of staff, identifying alternative suppliers and using manual methods are some other means of transferring the risk.

4. Accept the risk: The company may decide to accept the risk if it cannot be avoided, reduced or transferred. Generally, such risks have low probability of occurrence with a low impact on the organisation's activities. However, frequent review and monitoring of risks are required to ensure that the risk level assigned is accurate and does not increase over time.

4.14 Planning for Business Continuity

A business continuity plan is a collection of procedures and information designed and maintained for continuing the business operations in case of a disaster or an emergency. It has three essential elements (Doughty, 2001; Department of Education and Training, 2015): (a) preventing a disaster from occurring (prevention plans); (b) responding to a disaster during and after the event (emergency response plans); and (c) resumption of time-sensitive operations quickly after the event (resumption plans).

Prevention plans include risk management, facility plans and security plans. During the event an appropriate response to the risk, the protection of human lives and assets, and an assessment of damage are important. After the event crisis management plans, business unit plans and information system plans have to be put into operation.

The final phase of the business continuity plan is the resumption of operations and it includes a crisis management plan, business unit plans and information technology (IT) plans. A crisis management plan defines the methodology to respond to and manage a crisis situation. The objective of the crisis management plan is to gain control of the situation and minimise the negative impacts. Business resumption plans deal with the ways and means of resuming business operations after the event with support from the crisis management team and senior executives. The crisis management team also render support to the IT team to resume the operations.

A crisis is an abnormal situation that threatens the normal operations, staff, customers or reputation of the organisation. Some of the incidents that can escalate to a crisis include a product safety issue, damage to the reputation, a sudden market shift, a financial problem or trade union action. Volkswagen experienced a crisis situation when the US Environmental Protection Agency discovered that Volkswagen vehicles were fitted with a "defeat device" that detected the emission test, making the vehicle more environmentally friendly than it actually is (Geler, 2015). Eleven million vehicles were affected.

A disaster is a physical event that disrupts business operations sufficiently to threaten the viability of the organisation. Following a major earthquake, a 15 m tsunami disrupted the power supply and cooling systems of three Fukushima Daiichi nuclear reactors in Japan on March 11, 2011, causing a nuclear disaster. All three cores largely melted during the first three days (World Nuclear Association, 2017).

There is an essential difference between business resumption plans and crisis management plans. The former deal with events that cause damage to physical assets, whereas the latter manage the incidents that do not cause physical damage. Business resumption plans are non-specific and build on the basis of a worst-case scenario. On the other hand, crisis management plans have to be specific.

The planning process (SANS, 2002; Department of Education & Training, 2015) for developing a business continuity plan is shown in Figure 4.2. Six important steps are:

Step 1: Initiate the project
- Define objectives and scope.
- Appoint business continuity plan working group.
- Establish policies.

Step 2: Identify critical business activities
- Conduct risk analysis and business impact analysis.
- Establish a minimum acceptable outage (MAO) for each critical business activity.
- Consider alternative strategies for business continuity.
- Perform a cost–benefit analysis and select the most appropriate option to continue the business within the required MAO.

Step 3: Design the business continuity plan
- Establish a business recovery team and assign responsibilities.
- Design a plan structure and its components.
- Develop scenarios and execute the plan.
- Define escalation, notification and plan activation criteria.
- Develop general plan administration policy guidelines.

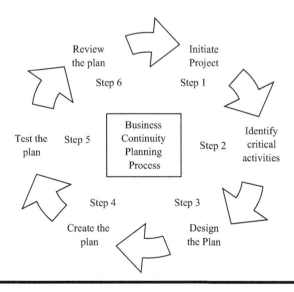

Figure 4.2 Business continuity planning process.

Step 4: Create the plan
- Develop an emergency response procedure.
- Prepare a command centre activation procedure.
- Prepare a detailed recovery procedure.
- Prepare the vendors' contracts and purchase recovery resources necessary to operate critical business activities.
- Prepare a list of contact details of all stakeholders.

Step 5: Test the plan
- Check the procedures to ensure that they are fit for purpose and can be activated easily and quickly.
- Ensure that the response and recovery results are within acceptable MAOs.
- Check that the staff are trained in the use of the plan and aware of their roles.

Step 6: Review the plan
- Review the plan periodically.
- Update and make the necessary changes.
- Distribute the plan among the recovery team members.

4.15 Measure, Monitor and Control

Measuring, monitoring and controlling the RMP are essential for continuous improvement of the programme. Monitoring and control during planning, programming and design phases provide a framework for managing risks through a planned process. Inputs during these phases are an RMP and a risk register. The output is a strategy, which (a) provides a consistent and comprehensive reporting procedure; (b) describes key milestones for resolving risks; (c) monitors changes to risk probabilities or impacts; (d) supports active contingency resolution procedures; and (e) provides feedbacks of analysis and mitigation for future risk assessment and allocation.

The objectives of monitoring and control are to (a) systematically track identified risks; (b) identify new risks that impact on business activities; (c) effectively manage contingency reserve, and (d) gain lessons learned for future risk assessment and allocation efforts. Monitoring and updating the risk management programme should occur during all its phases. Risks are dynamic in nature and risk strategies are bound to change as the project progresses, new risks develop and expected risks become obsolete. During any project review, phase risk identification, assessment, analysis, mitigation, planning and allocation are repeated. Risk monitoring and measuring also extend to the evaluation of the culture, performance and preparedness of the organisation, assessment of risk improvement recommendations, evaluation of the success of integrating risk management activities in the organisation and routine monitoring of risk performance indicators.

An essential task of monitoring and measurement is the evaluation of the effectiveness of the organisation to cope with major disruptions. This activity involves the testing of business continuity plans and disaster recovery plans. Existing controls should also be monitored in order to make recommendations for risk improvement. The results of measuring, monitoring and controlling should be recorded in the risk register (Molenaar et al., 2010; Institute of Risk Management, 2010).

4.16 Learning and Reporting Risk

Learning from experience and reporting complete the feedback loop on the risk management process. The results of risk performance and the measure of the effectiveness of ERM towards the success of the organisation are essential to gain learning experience. Learning from experience also requires the consideration of opinions of stakeholders, both internal and external. Internal audit results can provide useful feedback.

Risk reporting involves recording, maintaining and recording the assessment of the adequacy of existing plans and has several benefits:

- Provides a basis for programme assessments and updates.
- Ensures more comprehensive risk assessments.
- Provides a basis for monitoring mitigation and allocation actions and verifying the results.
- Can be used as a training tool and provides background material for new staff.
- It is a management tool for execution.
- Provides a basis for decision-making.
- Provides information on historical losses and trends.

In addition to internal communication, the organisation has to comply with the mandatory reporting requirements of regulatory bodies. External reporting provides useful information to stakeholders on the status of the risk management programme and the steps taken for continuous improvement (Molenaar et al., 2010; Institute of Risk Management, 2010).

4.17 Implementation of Risk Management Plan

A successful implementation of an enterprise RMP involves 10 steps under the following categories: (a) planning and designing; (b) implementing and benchmarking; (c) measuring and monitoring; and (d) learning and reporting.

The implementation of the plan is an ongoing process, and these 10 steps have to be reviewed regularly as a part of continuous improvement (Institute of Risk Management, 2010). The 10 steps are described in Table 4.7.

4.18 Creating a Risk-Aware Culture

An essential prerequisite for a successful risk management programme is the creation of a risk-aware culture, which is seen as a normal way of doing business. Management of risk has to be embraced by the management's philosophy. The first step in developing a risk-aware culture is to create among employees an understanding of company objectives, their risks and how they are managed. Useful practices are as follows (Graham, n.d.):

- Establish a risk management business unit and communicate risk management procedures and practices across the organisation.
- Risk management business unit should be prepared to offer support to employees for understanding risk issues.

Table 4.7 Implementation of the Risk Management Plan

	Activity		*Steps*
1	Planning and designing	1	Develop a risk management policy Provide the opportunity to focus on benefits, identify risk priorities and consider emerging risks Seek board approval
		2	Define the scope of the initiative, which depends on expected benefits
		3	Develop a risk management strategy and framework and define responsibilities
2	Implementing and benchmarking	4	Establish the risk assessment procedure and integrate with business activities
		5	Determine the significance of impacts, establish benchmarks and conduct risk assessment
		6	Establish the risk appetite and tolerances
3	Measuring and monitoring	7	Evaluate existing controls and their cost effectiveness and introduce improvements
		8	Demonstrate leadership and create a risk aware culture
4	Learning and reporting	9	Monitor risk performance indicators and evaluate the contribution of the risk management performance to the success of the organisation
		10	Report to regulatory bodies and other stakeholders and make improvements

- Involve the staff in all stages of the risk management programme.
- Recruit employees from a variety of units to serve in the risk management business unit.
- Encourage employees to see risks as something to manage and not something to avoid.
- Establish recognition and reward programmes to encourage employees to manage risks and take advantage of opportunities.
- Encourage team sessions and learn from experiences through story-telling.
- Discourage reckless risk-taking and design remuneration packages accordingly.
- Monitor employees' performance in managing risks.
- Establish risk management understanding and practices as essential for all management positions.
- Develop a code of ethics and communicate to all employees through training sessions, workshops or meetings.

4.19 Problems of Managing Risk Plans

The world has become a complex place because of the progress in communication, technology and globalisation. National and international relationships and interdependencies are more complex than ever before. Recent events such as the economic crisis clearly indicate the limited use of risk-predicting models. Low-probability/high-impact events, the so-called Black Swan events, are almost impossible to predict. Therefore, a clear understanding of the barriers to implementing an RMP is essential in reducing the vulnerability to major risks (Taleb et al., 2009).

The *Harvard Business Review* (2011) Analytic Services report involving interviews with executives at 13 companies worldwide identified 11 barriers to embedding ERM across organisations. Barriers range from the failure to adopt or effectively implement ERM software to an excessive focus on compliance with insufficient fundamental processes (Table 4.8).

Taleb, Goldstein and Spitznagel (2009) have identified six mistakes that executives make in risk management:

1. Too much focus on predicting extreme events: When organisations pay more attention to a few extreme events, they ignore other possibilities, thus leaving the organisation more vulnerable. Organisations are more concerned with issues such as global warming and its influence on new regulations about regulatory permits, energy consumption and fuel prices. However, companies ignore other unanticipated events which may have a greater impact on the business. A more effective approach is to focus on consequences to evaluate the impact of events and prepare for eventualities.

2. Dependence on past events to manage risks: History has shown that past events are not a good predictor of future events. The 9/11 attack on the World Trade Centre in the United States was unprecedented. Yet, financial risk experts depend on past events to predict future risks. They fail to take into account the randomness inherent in many economic variables.

Table 4.8   Barriers to Embedding Enterprise Risk Management (ERM)

	Barrier	*Overall Response %*	*CRO's Response %*
1	Excessive focus on compliance and insufficient fundamental processes	40	42
2	Lack of top management support	29	41
3	Reluctance to de-silo risk related information	31	35
4	Failure to integrate ERM to core business processes	24	35
5	Failure to set well-defined ERM goals and objectives	28	31
6	Failure to gain new skills and accept new roles	28	30
7	Lack of a practical decision-making process and structure	21	30
8	Failure to manage risk assessment and measurement	24	23
9	Lack of communication of goals, objectives and performance	28	20
10	Lack of suitable metrics for measuring the success of the ERM effort	20	19
11	Failure to adopt or implement the ERM software	11	18

Italian scientists failed to predict the seriousness of the earthquake that occurred in the mountain city of L'Aquila in 2009 based on past experience. It was a major catastrophe which killed more than 300 people. Scientists believed that the tremors which occurred weeks before the major event were not serious enough to warn the public and their decision was based on previous tremors in the area (Squires, 2014). Organisations cannot depend on "typical" failure or success because of the socioeconomic randomness.

3. Failure to listen to advice about what should not be done: The banks in the United States failed to take advice not to accumulate large exposure to low-probability/high-impact events, which resulted in the collapse of the banking sector. Managers generally focus on increasing profits rather than minimising losses. However, firms can be successful by preventing losses while their competitors fail and then take the market share from them. Companies should integrate risk management activities into profit centres and consider them as profit-generating activities so that companies can act on advice that may avoid a profit-destruction event.

4. Dependence on standard deviation (SD) for measuring the risk: SD is used extensively in finance as a measure of investment risk. SD is defined as the square root of average squared deviations and not average variations. The use of squares and square roots makes the measure complicated. Black Swan events do not necessarily follow the predictability of the bell-shaped SD curve. Therefore, SD models such as regression models, R-squares and betas are of little use in predicting risk.

5. Failure of properly communicating risk: People's understanding of risk is influenced by the way risk is presented. An investor who is told that all the money will be lost only every 30 years will not hesitate to invest. On the other hand, if they are told that there is a 3.3% chance of losing a certain amount each year, the investor will be reluctant to part with their money. People will be more likely to accept a risk if it is presented with a positive outcome (best-case scenario).

6. Assuming that efficiency and maximising shareholder value do not tolerate redundancy: Business managers equate redundancy to inefficiency – unused resources and money. Highly leveraged companies are more vulnerable to the external environment. In the risk management world, having an alternative plan, conducting frequent governance audits and establishing back-up emergency plans are essential to coping with extreme events.

4.20 Guidelines for Successful Risk Management

The events of the past three years from financial crisis to natural disasters have challenged the risk management practices in companies and now better best practices are beginning to emerge. *Harvard Business Review* Analytic Services and follow-up interviews have identified five distinct lessons that pave the way for better risk management (Harvard Business Review, 2011).

1. Risk management must have a clear owner: For the risk management programme to be effective, the company has to appoint a single individual, preferably a CRO who is responsible for risk management activities. The CRO should define standardised procedures for risk identification and management. They should work closely with the CEO and the line managers to create a risk-aware culture so that ERM is relevant to their business activities.

2. Risk management goals must be integrated with corporate goals: Organisations need to integrate risk-aware culture at all levels and link risk information to strategic planning and decision-making. This can only be achieved through the support and involvement of all the staff.

3. Companies must be proactive in managing risks: Often firms identify risks after the event when profits start to erode. Two changes are necessary to adopt a proactive approach: (a) establish active collaboration between the CRO and business units so that they can employ the CRO to assess potential risks before new projects are initiated; and (b) utilise better risk metrics that enable them to measure the potential impact of risk continuously. However, companies should avoid using complex procedures that hinder collaboration.

4. Determine the most serious risks in the long run: Recent events that had a major impact tend to mask reality, but there is only a very low probability of recurrence in the long run. Companies focus on major natural disasters ignoring many operational risks such as skill acquisition and retention, corporate or brand reputation and legal risks. It is important to manage these sequential risks because they can trigger further risks.

5. Discard the narrow view and overcome managerial problems: When the management focuses too much on compliance and not enough on fundamental processes, or the management is not sufficiently involved in ERM, organisations fail to realise potentially serious risks. An effective approach is for the CRO to facilitate communication between business units and management so that new potential risks are identified and acted upon quickly. ERM then becomes a company-wide collaborative approach consisting of three lines of defence: line management, risk management including legal and compliance, and audits.

The success of a business depends upon managing risks that impact on business activities. A commitment of effort and resources to integrate the risk management process with company-wide business units creates a successful risk-managing business environment leading to financial gains.

References

Baranoff, E., Brockett, P.L. and Kahane, Y. (2009). *Risk Management for Enterprises and Individuals. V. 1.0.* Washington, DC: Flat World Knowledge.

BBC (2014). *Case study: Tsunami.* Retrieved January 09, 2019 from https://www.bbc.com/bitesize/guides/zw7s4j6/revision/8.

Bremmer, I. (2011). *Thriving in Emerging Markets.* Brighton: Harvard Business Review Press.

Browning, J.B. (1993). *Union Carbide disaster at Bhopal.* Retrieved 20 September, 2015 from http://storage.dow.com.edgesuite.net/dow.com/Bhopal/browning.pdf.

Chopra, S. and Sodhi, M. (2014). Reducing the risk of supply chain disruptions. *MIT Sloan Management Review,* 55 (3), 78–80.

Cox, L.A. (2008). What's wrong with risk matrices? *Risk Analysis,* 28 (2), 497–512.

Department of Defence. (2006). *Risk Management Guide for DOD Acquisition* (6th ed.). Virginia: Defence Systems Management College Press.

Department of Education and Training. (2015). *Business Continuity Management (V. 3.2).* Australia: Queensland Government.

Department of Education, Training and Development. (2017). *Enterprise risk management.* Version 7. Queensland Government, Australia. Retrieved January 9, 2019 from http://ppr.det.qld.gov.au/corp/governance/Procedure%20Attachments/Risk%20Management/enterprise-risk-mgmt-procedure.pdf.

Department of Education and Training. (2018). *Business continuity management (ver 4.0).* Australia: Queensland Government, Retrieved January 09, 2019 from http://ppr.det.qld.gov.au/corp/governance/Pages/Business-Continuity-Management-(BCM).aspx.

De Silva, T. (2007). Hazard analysis and critical control point (HACCP). In M. Shafiur Rahman (Ed.), *Handbook of Food Preservation* (2nd ed.), pp. 969–1010. Florida: Taylor & Francis.

Doughty, K. (2001). *Business Continuity Planning.* Florida: CRC Press.

Geler, B. (2015). Everything to know about Volkswagen emissions crisis. *Fortune*, September 22, 2015. Retrieved January 10, 2019 from http://fortune.com/2015/09/22/volkswagen-vw-emissions-golf/.

Graham, A. (n.d.). *Integrated risk management implementation guide*. Retrieved January 09, 2019 from http://www.andrewbgraham.ca/integrated-risk-management-implementation-an-e-book.html.

Gunther, M. (2015). Safety lapses at US nuclear lab. *Chemistry World*, 32 (9), 10.

Harvard Business Review Analytic Services. (2011). *Risk management in a time of global uncertainty*. Harvard Business Review Survey. Retrieved January 09, 2019 from https://www.zurich.de/_/media/dbe/corporate/docs/general/risk-management-in-a-time-of-global-uncertainty.pdf?la=en.

Hollnagel, E. (2008). The changing nature of risk. *Ergonomic Australia Journal*, 22 (1–2), 33–46.

Hopkin, P. (2014). *Fundamentals of Risk Management: Understanding, Re-evaluating and Implementing Effective Risk Management*. UK: Kogan Press.

Institute of Risk Management. (2010). *A structured approach to enterprise risk management (ERM) and the requirements of ISO 31000*. Retrieved October 13, 2017 from https://www.theirm.org/media/886062/ISO3100_doc.pdf.

ISO (2018). *ISO 31000: Risk management guidelines* (2nd ed.). Switzerland: ISO copyright office.

Kaplan, R.S. and Mikes, A. (2012). Managing risks: A new framework. *Harvard Business Review*, 90 (6), 48–60.

Mikes, A. and Kaplan, R.S. (2014). *Towards a Contingency Theory of Enterprise Risk Management*. Massachusetts: Harvard Business School.

Molenaar, K., Anderson, S. and Schexnayder, C. (2010). *Guidebook on Risk Analysis Tools and Management Practices to Control Transportation Project Costs* (Vol. 658). Transportation Research Board. Washington: National Cooperative Highway Research Programme.

Munn, R.C. (1973). *GEMS. scope report No. 3*. Retrieved January 09, 2019 from http://dge.stanford.edu/SCOPE/SCOPE_3/SCOPE_3.html.

National Wild Life Federation. (2015). *How does the BP oil spill impact wildlife and habitat?* Retrieved January 09, 2019 from http://www.energybc.ca/cache/oilspill/www.nwf.org/Oil-Spill/Effects-on-Wildlife.html.

Office of Government of Commerce. (2002). *Management of Risk: Guidance for Practitioners*. UK: The Stationery Office.

Office of Government of Commerce. (2010). *Management of Risk: Guidance for Practitioners*. UK: The Stationery Office.

Olson, D.L. and Wu, D. (2010). *Enterprise Risk Management Models*. Germany: Springer-Verlag.

Pidun, U., Rodt, M., Ross, A., Stange, S. and Tucker, J. (2017). *The Art of Risk Management: CFO Excellence Series*. Massachusetts: Boston Consulting Group.

Plaschke, F., Rodt, M., Pidun, U. and Gunther, F. (2013). *The Art of Risk Management*. Massachusetts: Boston Consulting Group.

Praxiom. (2017). *Plain English ISO 31000-2009: Risk management dictionary*. Retrieved June 23, 2018 from http://www.praxiom.com/iso-31000-terms.htm#2.26_Control_.

Price Waterhouse Coopers. (2008). *A practical guide to risk assessment*. Retrieved Janary 8, 2019 from https://www.scribd.com/document/210408865/Practical-Guide-to-Risk-Assessment-PwC-2008.

Queensland Government. (2014a). *Identify risks to your business*. Retrieved January 9, 2019 from https://www.business.qld.gov.au/running-business/protecting-business/risk-management/preparing-plan/identify.

Queensland Government. (2014b). *Threat risks to your business*. Retrieved October 3, 2017 from https://www.business.qld.gov.au/running-business/protecting-business/risk-management/preparing-plan/treat.

Revuid, J. (2009). *Managing Business Risk: A Practical Guide to Protecting Your Business* (6th ed.). UK: Kogan Press.

Ritholtz, B. (2013). *10 Worst corporate accounting scandals*. Retrieved January 9, 2019 from http://www.ritholtz.com/blog/2013/03/worst-corp-scandals/.

Sadgrove, K. (2015). *The Complete Guide to Business Risk Management*. UK: Gower Publishing.

Scott, E. (2003). Food safety and food borne illnesses in the 21st century homes. *Canadian Journal of Infectious Diseases*, 14 (5), 277–280.

Smith, D. and Fischbacher, M. (2009). The changing nature of risk. *Risk Management*, 11, 1–12.

Squires, N. (2014, November 3). Italian scientists cleared of failing to predict L'Aquila earthquake. *The Telegraph*. Retrieved January 9, 2019 from http://www.telegraph.co.uk/news/worldnews/europe/italy/11221825/Italian-scientists-cleared-of-failing-to-predict-LAquila-earthquake.html.

Taleb, N.N. (2007). *The Black Swan: The Impact of the Highly Improbable*. New York: Random House.

Taleb, N.N., Goldstein, D.G. and Spitznagel, M.W. (2009). The six mistakes executives make in risk management. *Harvard Business Review*, 87 (10), 78–81.

Trager, R. (2015). US regulator slams DuPont's safety. *Chemistry World*, 32 (9), 19.

Whyte, A.V. and Burton, I. (1980). *SCOPE 15: Environmental Risk Assessment*. UK: John Wiley & Sons.

World Bank Institute. (n.d.). *Managing environmental and social impacts of local companies: A resource guide and tool kit*. Retrieved January 9, 2019 from http://siteresources.worldbank.org/CGCSRLP/Resources/EnvironmentalandSocialManual.pdf.

World Nuclear Association. (2017). *Fukushima accident*. Retrieved January 8, 2019 from http://www.world-nuclear.org/info/Safety-and-Security/Safety-of-Plants/Fukushima-Accident/.

Young, P.C. and Tippins, S.C. (2000). *Managing Business Risk: An Organisation-Wide Approach to Risk Management*. New York: Amacom.

Chapter 5

Good Manufacturing Practice

5.1 Introduction

Good Manufacturing Practices (GMPs), also known as current Good Manufacturing Practices (cGMPs), are a series of manufacturing and administrative procedures aimed at ensuring that products are consistently made to meet specifications and customer expectations. The regulations governing GMPs cover a variety of consumer goods such as manufacture, packaging or holding human food (21 CFR 110.3-110.110); manufacture, packaging or holding operations for dietary supplements (21 CFR 111.1-111.610); manufacture, packaging or holding of drugs (21 CFR 210.1-210.3); finished pharmaceuticals (21 CFR 211.1-211.208); cosmetic labelling (21 CFR 701.1-701.30) and medical devices labelling (21 CFR 801.1-801.437) (Government Publishing Office, 2018a). In relation to food, the implementation of GMPs results in safe and quality food. The revised Food and Drug Administration (FDA) Medical Devices GMP (FDA, 1996) places considerable emphasis on Quality Management Systems (QMSs). Quality policy, quality objectives and management commitment are all essential features of this programme (Carter, 1998).

In the United States, the FDA has issued these regulations about the minimum requirements for manufacture. Most countries have their own GMP regulations for pharmaceuticals and the first formal set of GMPs was published by the US FDA in 1963 as Part 133 (Karmacharya, 2012).

5.2 GMP Activities

Figure 5.1 shows the various activities of GMPs (Mendis & Rajapakse, 2009). It supports and brings together many programmes, systems and philosophies that lead to an effective food business providing safe and quality products. The three main elements of GMP are food safety, good practice and quality. Their relationship to each other is shown in Figure 5.2.

Food safety and QMSs and the standards provide a firm foundation for the survival of the business by adding the attributes of quality, safety and value to the product. This will enable the food business to gain competitive advantage. Companies who have implemented a successful GMP programme find that the journey to ISO 22000 is easy.

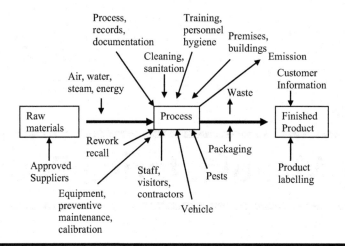

Figure 5.1 GMP activities.

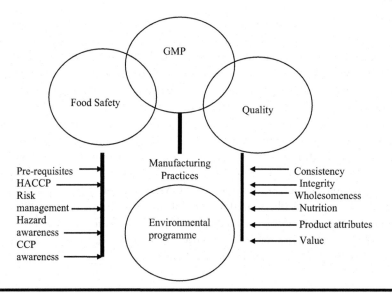

Figure 5.2 Core food business.

5.3 GMP Philosophy

The philosophy behind GMP can be summarised (Mead, 2012) as:

i. GMP is closely aligned with disciplines such as quality, management, food safety and food quality.
ii. GMP is designed by food manufacturers for food manufacturers.
iii. GMP involves the entire food business operation from establishment of policy to its implementation.
iv. GMP is a proactive and hands-on document.

v. GMP has provision to exceed customers' expectations and provides confidence in the product and consistency in the process.

vi. Every activity within the food business impacts on the finished product.

vii. Through GMP, value is built into the product and loyalty to the brand.

5.4 Foundation of GMP

GMP is based on two complementary and interacting components: effective manufacturing operations and effective food control operations. Complementary to these two components are the management functions of these two components (Manning, 2013).

5.4.1 Effective Manufacturing Operations

GMP requires that every aspect of the food manufacturing process is clearly defined and effective in achieving the desired result and that all necessary facilities are provided including (Manning, 2013):

i. Adequate premises and space.

ii. Correct and properly maintained equipment.

iii. Appropriately trained personnel.

iv. Correct ingredients and packaging material.

v. Suitable storage and transport.

vi. Documented procedures for all operations including cleaning.

vii. Appropriate management and supervision.

viii. Adequate administrative, technical and maintenance support.

Record-keeping is an integral part of the manufacturing operation, and records provide evidence of completed activities in the plant. Procedures are necessary for all processes, including training, written in a manner easily understood by the operators.

5.4.2 Effective Food Control

Effective food control can be achieved through having an efficient food control management plan by (a) management commitment and participation in the development and validation of process controls and specifications; (b) providing adequate facilities for inspection, sampling and testing; (c) monitoring process conditions and the production environment and (d) providing prompt feedback to manufacturing personnel to enable them to make adjustments, when necessary.

Control mechanisms are established for all tasks from receiving raw materials to the delivery of finished goods or the disposal of non-conforming goods.

5.4.3 Management Controls

The achievement of GMP objectives requires management controls that influence GMP compliance, but are not specifically required by GMP regulations. Issues such as the establishment of policies that communicate management's intentions or the establishment of a periodic review of quality data trends are specially designed to address GMP issues. Other management controls such as organisational structure, provision of resources, prioritising and performance management and incentive schemes are not specifically required by GMP regulations. Senior management must establish a clear vision to signify the importance of quality and compliance. Other management controls are:

i. Reporting structure of the organisation.
ii. Risk assessment and review of data.
iii. Prioritisation of the workload.
iv. Clear definition of roles and responsibilities.
v. Performance management.
vi. Resourcing.
vii. Method of escalating quality decisions.
viii. Internal audits.

Wise use of management controls will (a) ensure compliance; (b) protect the company and its executives from regulatory liability and (c) achieve business objectives (Chesney, 2004). The result of this attempt is the ISO 9000 series of standards.

5.5 The Preliminary Process

A manufacturing organisation adopting the GMP principles is able to (a) consistently meet its own and customers' requirements; (b) meet industry standards and codes of practice; and (c) comply with regulatory requirements. In order to achieve this, the organisation has to plan its activities. The preliminary process for GMP is shown in Figure 5.3. The scope of GMP is not only the production of a perfect end product but also the demonstration of activities that accomplish the end product.

5.6 GMP Requirements

GMP is intended to build quality into the product at all stages of the operation. The activities associated with GMP are given in Title 21, Part 117 of Code of Federal Regulations (CFR) – Current Good Manufacturing Practice, Hazard Analysis and Risk-Based Preventive Controls for Human Food. The main requirements are included in Subpart B and Subpart C of the regulations. Subpart B includes the following nine requirements for GMP (Government Publishing Office, 2018b,c):

1. Personnel.
2. Plant and facilities.
3. Sanitary operations.
4. Sanitary facilities and controls.
5. Equipment and utensils.
6. Processing operations.
7. Warehousing and distribution.
8. Storage and distribution.
9. Defect action levels.

Subpart C includes 15 specific requirements for assuring food safety:

1. Food safety plan.
2. Hazard analysis.

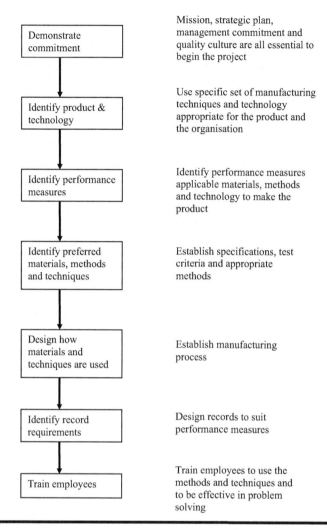

Figure 5.3   Preliminary process for GMP.

3. Preventive controls.
4. Circumstances which do not require preventive controls.
5. Provision of assurance required under section 117.136 (a) (2), (3) and (4)..
6. Recall plan.
7. Preventive control management.
8. Monitoring.
9. Corrective actions.
10. Verification.
11. Validation.
12. Implementation of verification and effectiveness.
13. Review.
14. Requirements for qualified personnel.
15. Record-keeping.

5.6.1 *Organisation and Personnel*

To implement the GMP programme effectively, it is necessary for the organisation to establish a structure appropriate for the business. It must have an adequate number of personnel who have the relevant qualifications and training to perform the required tasks. Their duties should be clearly explained before the commencement of the tasks. The training programme should cover the principles of GMP, specific tasks and personnel hygiene.

The three key personnel in a manufacturing organisation are the Quality Control/Quality Assurance (QC/QA) Manager, the Production/Plant Manager and the Purchasing Manager.

The QC/QA Manager has the authority to (a) approve materials and finished goods; (b) reject, hold or quarantine non-conforming products; and (c) recommend suppliers.

The Production/Plant Manager is responsible for production, personnel, equipment, operations and the management of records. It is the responsibility of the Production/Plant Manager to ensure that products are manufactured to the relevant specifications within the budgeted cost. In consultation with the QC/QA Manager, the Production/Plant Manager (a) generates specifications for materials and products; (b) trains manufacturing staff; and (c) controls manufacturing environment and hygiene.

The Purchasing Manager has the authority to order raw materials that comply with established specifications and initiate action with the suppliers when the purchased product does not meet product specifications.

The management must demonstrate support and commitment to the principles of GMP and create an environment where the employees take ownership. Leadership and motivation are key features of an effective business organisation. The managers must adopt a proactive approach and promote a quality culture within the organisation so that the employees take pride in their workmanship.

5.6.2 *Training and Personnel Hygiene*

The organisation has to ensure that the employees have appropriate facilities and are trained to promote personnel hygiene and safe food handling. The training programme has to reflect the type of operation and the level of education of its employees (Manning, 2013).

5.6.2.1 *Recruitment and Induction*

The basis of recruitment and selection process is the ability to do the task at the time, unless the organisation has a programme to train the new recruit. The organisation has to ensure that the person has the capability to perform the job either after training or with previous experience. The recruitment process and subsequent training is thus critical for food safety. Job descriptions have to be established for all positions. The relevant competence and/or training requirements are specified for each job.

The aim of the induction process is to prepare the new employee to the company culture and the process itself should commence with the introduction of the person to the business, its quality system, the organisation's expectations and the tasks. The person's responsibilities, reporting structure and the disciplinary process have to be clearly defined.

5.6.2.2 *Competence and Training*

Competence is the demonstrated ability to apply knowledge and skills to a task correctly and completely first time without assistance. The organisation should ensure that minimum levels of competence are maintained and that the employees perform the tasks without supervision.

The training programme should include the principles of GMP and the demonstration of competence in the company's hygiene practices, its QMS and the operating principles of the activity. It is essential that the trainer emphasises the reason for maintaining food hygiene and compliance with legal requirements. At regular intervals, it is the manager's responsibility to review the training requirements and address the deficiencies.

5.6.2.3 Food Hygiene Requirements

Training in food hygiene is an essential part of the training programme (Manning, 2013). The food hygiene requirements (Karmacharya, 2012) include:

  i. Clean protective clothing.
  ii. Hair and beard covers where necessary.
  iii. Washing hands before commencing work.
  iv. Keeping body, hands and clothing clean.
  v. Prohibition of smoking within the premises.
  vi. Exclusion of personnel suffering from infectious disease.
  vii. Covering wounds with water-proof plaster.
  viii. First aid material.
  ix. Prohibition of wearing jewellery or loose items.

5.6.3 Building and Facilities

Buildings should be located, designed and constructed to suit the type of operation that permits the separation of individual processing, manufacturing, packing, testing and storage operations to avoid mix-ups, cross-contamination and deterioration. At all times the premises should be maintained in a clean and tidy condition. The processing areas should have:

  i. Ceiling made out of materials that prevent mould growth or build-up of dust.
  ii. Floors made of impervious material free from cracks or open joints.
  iii. Walls of smooth impervious material to facilitate easy cleaning.
  iv. Environmental controls such as adequate lighting, ventilation, heating, cooling, proper washing and sanitary facilities.
  v. Entry points sealed off to prevent pest access and inhibit waste odours.
  vi. Drains that allow maximum flow of waste and have trapped gullies and proper ventilation.
  vii. Changing rooms segregated from processing areas.
  viii. Provision to contain waste in covered containers regularly disposed.
  ix. Protection for receiving and dispatch of materials and products in storage from weather.
  x. Written procedures for cleaning all processing areas.
  xi. Pest control devices placed at appropriate locations away from open product (Karmacharya, 2012; Food Supplements Europe, 2014).

5.6.4 Cleaning and Sanitation

Cleaning is the complete removal of food soil using appropriate chemicals as recommended. Sanitation is the process of reduction of microorganisms to a safe level (Karmacharya, 2012; Government Publishing Office, 2018b).

Cleaning and sanitation are the most important aspects of the hygiene programme. Detailed procedures have to be established for all surfaces, which come into contact with food products as well as for others such as overhead structures, walls, ceilings, etc. The objective of any cleaning and sanitisation programme is to remove food soil on which microorganisms can grow and kill those present. The cleaning programme has to be evaluated for its effectiveness by carrying out appropriate tests. The procedures should specify the cleaning and type of chemical for each production line.

Cleaning and sanitation consist of several steps (Cramer, 2007; Queensland Health, 2015):

1. Pre-clean – physically remove food particles and foreign matter by sweeping, wiping or scraping. Rinse any equipment containing high-protein substances with warm potable water.
2. Wash with hot water (60°C) and detergent. Soak if necessary.
3. Rinse with clean potable water to remove any loose dirt or detergent foam.
4. Sanitise to kill any remaining bacteria.
5. Final rinse – wash off sanitiser (if necessary, read manufacturer's instructions).
6. Dry – allow to drip dry or dry using a disposable towel.

5.6.4.1 Method of Sanitising

Most pathogenic bacteria are killed if they are exposed to chemical sanitisers or high heat or a combination of both:

a. Soak items in water at 77°C for 30 seconds, or
b. Soak items in water that contains bleach.

Water temperature will vary with the concentration of chlorine or use food grade sanitiser and follow the manufacturer's instructions.

5.6.4.2 Cleaning Methods

a. Mechanical cleaning, also referred to as cleaning-in-place (CIP), employs automated programmes and it does not require disassembly or partial assembly. The temperature and contact times are automatically controlled.
b. Cleaning-out-of place (COP) allows partial disassembly and involves cleaning in specialised pressurised tanks.
c. Manual cleaning requires total disassembly for cleaning and inspection.

5.6.4.3 Sanitisation Methods

Effective sanitisation of food product contact surfaces achieves a reduction of contamination level by 99.999% (five logs) in 30 seconds (Anderson, 2015). Non-product contact surfaces require a contamination reduction of 99.9% (three logs) using the test organisms, *Staphylococcus aureus* and *Escherichia coli*. There are two types of sanitisation methods:

a. Thermal sanitisation, which involves the use of hot water or steam at a specific temperature for a specific contact period.
b. Chemical sanitisation, which involves the use of an approved chemical sanitiser at a specified concentration and contact time.

5.6.5 Equipment

Equipment, utensils and containers for holding food must be cleaned and maintained in sanitary conditions. All equipment used in the manufacturing area should be suitable for its intended use and properly maintained and cleaned (Karmacharya, 2012). It is a good practice to use protective covers on equipment where there is a threat of contamination from external sources. All precautions must be taken to prevent contamination from hands and equipment during maintenance when processing takes place.

All surfaces which come into contact with food should be (a) inert to the food and should not contaminate it; (b) microbiologically cleanable, smooth and non-porous; (c) visible for inspection and cleaning; and (d) located to enable self-emptying or self-draining.

The equipment should be arranged to protect the contents from external contamination from leaking joints, lubricants and broken metal parts. A programme of preventive maintenance should be scheduled for all equipment, and during this, it is essential that the engineer reports missing parts such as nuts, bolts, springs, etc., so that appropriate action can be taken. Before and after every use, it is a good practice to clean all equipment. Documented cleaning procedures should be available at all work stations.

Power-driven equipment can sometimes generate fumes and appropriate precautions should be taken to prevent the food from contamination.

5.6.6 Production and Process Control

A fundamental requirement of any manufacturing organisation is that the processes are capable of consistently producing finished goods, which conforms to established specifications, and for food products, they are free from contaminants. The effectiveness of the process has to be determined prior to production by means of controlled trials. Similar evaluations are done whenever there is a change in the raw materials, methods of manufacture or equipment.

All manufacturing operations, processes, packing and holding food for consumption, including receiving, inspecting, transportation and segregation, must be conducted in sanitary conditions. Effective quality control procedures have to be employed to ensure that the food is safe for consumption. At all costs, allergen cross-contamination and contamination from chemical, microbiological and extraneous material should be avoided. Operations have to be performed under the supervision of competent staff (Iowa State University of Science and Technology, 2016).

a. Raw materials: Precautions must be taken to ensure that all raw materials and ingredients are inspected, handled and stored in a manner that protects them from allergen cross-contact and other contaminants. Raw materials must be inspected for microbiological contamination before being used. All ingredients and raw materials must comply with FDA regulations for poisonous substances or defect action levels. They are stored in appropriate temperatures and in bulk, or containers designed to prevent contamination. Water activity and pH should be controlled as necessary to prevent microbial contamination from reaching unsafe levels. Ice that comes into contact with food must be made from potable water (Iowa State University of Science and Technology, 2016).

b. Processing: Operations such as sterilising, irradiation, pasteurisation and cooking employed to prevent the growth of microorganisms must be validated. During processing, adequate precautions must be taken to prevent the introduction of extraneous matter such as glass fragments or metal pieces. Steps such as peeling, trimming, filling, assembling, packaging and other activities must be performed so as to prevent allergen cross-contact and contamination and the growth of microbes. Temperature and time of cooking are important considerations to destroy the microorganisms (Iowa State University of Science and Technology, 2016).

Before commencing production, checks should be carried out to ensure that (a) the processing area is free from potential contaminants; (b) correct materials and methods are used; (c) correct set-up procedures are used; and (d) all equipment is clean and ready for use.

Work instructions are kept at all work stations and are written in a clear and simple style for easy comprehension by the operators.

1. Controls during production: Accurate records have to be maintained of all production data including the operating conditions and quality parameters. Statistical control charts are used to identify deviations from normal. Problems that cause stoppages, breakdowns and emergencies are identified, recorded and promptly addressed.

    Process controls specify the type of tests to be conducted, the frequency of checks and the operating limits. Suitable methods should be used to identify the batches of production, delivery vehicles, container numbers, etc., to enable effective traceability. The controls ensure that the product is not contaminated and is capable of preventing the growth of microorganisms. This is achieved by careful monitoring of physical factors such as time, temperature, humidity, A_w, pH, pressure, flow rate and others as appropriate. Suitable conditions are maintained throughout the process to prevent the decomposition of the product and/or the growth of microorganisms (Iowa State University of Science and Technology, 2016).

    Ensure the processing areas used for food production are not used for the manufacture of non-human food.
2. Control of finished product: Finished products are not released until they are tested and approved by the authorised person. Non-conforming products are segregated and quarantined. Appropriate storage conditions are adhered to before and during the delivery of the finished goods.

5.6.7 Warehousing and Distribution

At all times keep food products in well-ventilated spaces protected from dust, condensation, fumes and pests. Ensure that transport vehicles are regularly cleaned and maintained in a manner compatible with the product and its specifications. Vehicles employed to transport food must not be used to carry items such as pesticides and fertilisers. Employ the stock rotation policy of first in and first out. Ensure that all warehouse operations are supervised by a competent person (Iowa State University of Science and Technology, 2016).

5.6.8 Storage and Distribution

Storage and distribution are significant elements in the food supply chain. The primary purpose of storage and distribution of food products, ingredients and packaging is to protect them against physical, chemical and microbial contamination, as well as against deterioration of the food and the container. The principles of good hygiene practice apply not only to food and ingredients but also to packaging components that come into direct contact with food. The buildings, grounds and equipment of food storage warehouses have to be designed, constructed and maintained in a manner that does not compromise food safety standards (Shapton & Shapton, 1998).

5.6.8.1 Storage

Storage, transport and distribution are important links between the producer and the consumers. Even if sufficient care has been taken to ensure the quality and the safety of food, uncontrolled storage and transport conditions can severely affect the food products. The storage conditions have to be appropriate for the type of food production facility, and the controlled conditions include:

   i. Regular inspection of material for signs of deterioration.
   ii. Maintaining correct storage conditions for the type of product.
   iii. Regular cleaning to maintain storage areas in hygienic conditions.
   iv. Pest control programme.
   v. Maintaining stock rotation.
   vi. Maintaining the integrity of the stock during internal and external transport.
   vii. Segregation of products which have not been released for distribution.

5.6.8.2 Distribution

It is essential that transport and distribution are carried out by approved suppliers. The organisation should ensure that vehicles used for transporting food products are not used for carrying animals, harmful articles, chemicals or biological products. It is a good practice to ensure that the transporting facility has a good cleaning programme, and it is the responsibility of the organisation to inspect the vehicle for general cleanliness, accumulation of water, presence of foreign material or damage that could cause contamination of the food product. The inspection checklist may include (a) openings that permit the entry of pests, rodents, birds and/or insects; (b) foreign odours; and (c) the presence of nails splinters, oil, grease, dirt and/or bird droppings. Security precautions deter any tampering with products during transport. Distributing the load in a uniform manner can avoid damage to the products and people or the vehicle during transport. All instruments necessary to maintain the environmental conditions inside the vehicle should be regularly inspected and maintained.

5.6.9 Defect Action Levels

Food products may contain natural or unavoidable levels that present no health hazard. The FDA has established maximum levels for these defects so that action can be taken to address the issues. However, the food processor must use effective quality control procedures to reduce natural or unavoidable levels to the lowest level possible. Mixing of food containing defects that render the food unsafe should be avoided (Iowa State University of Science and Technology, 2016).

5.7 Food Safety Requirements

Specific food safety requirements are discussed in other chapters in this book.

5.8 ISO 22000 Standard, ISO 9001 Standard, GMP and HACCP System

The ISO 22000 standard is a management system for controlling and improving the food safety practices of the organisation. On the other hand, GMP is a code of practice that controls all aspects of manufacture. The ISO 9000 standard provides a management structure for the effective implementation of the GMP programme.

The Hazard Analysis and Critical Control Point (HACCP) system is a food safety programme that gives an effective structure to GMP by providing a system that identifies, evaluates and controls hazards that are significant to the production of safe food. Prior to the development of HACCP plans, it is necessary to review the existing programmes and verify that all GMPs are in place and effective. The GMP programme ensures that HACCP plans focus specifically on Critical Control Points (CCPs) for product safety. If the GMP programme is not adequately implemented, the HACCP plan will be less effective in ensuring product safety.

The ISO 9000 standard, ISO 22000 standard, GMP and HACCP systems are thus complementary to each other, and together they contribute to the production of safe food while making a profit for the organisation by minimising waste and having effective systems.

5.9 Benefits of GMP

GMP is a dynamic programme that enables the organisation to make and maintain quality improvements (Gould, 1994). An effective GMP programme can offer several benefits to the organisation and some of these are summarised in Table 5.1.

Table 5.1 Benefits of GMP

	Benefit
1	Creates awareness of food quality and safety among staff
2	Increases confidence in product safety
3	Better products to meet competitors' demands
4	A more efficient food plant operation
5	Improves employee productivity
6	Provides a starting point for the HACCP programme
7	International recognition
8	Prevents regulatory non-compliances by meeting regulatory requirements
9	Prevents expensive failures
10	Reduces customer complaints and recalls
11	Fewer food plant incidents
12	Improves profits

References

Anderson, R. (2015). Sanitisers and disinfectants: Why the understanding is important. Retrieved April 24, 2019 from http://velocitychemicals.com/sanitizers-and-disinfectants-why-understanding-the-difference-is-important/.

Carter, J.E. (1998). Quality policies – key to GMP compliance. *Pharmaceutical Technology*, 22, 102–106.

Chesney, D.L. (2004). Management controls for GMP compliance. *Pharmaceutical Technology*, 29, 64–72.

Cramer, M. (2007). *Sanitation Best Practices. Food Plant Sanitation: Design, Maintenance and Good Manufacturing Practices*. Boca Raton: CRC Press.

FDA. (1996). 21 CFR Parts 808, 812 and 820, Medical devices: Current good manufacturing practices (cGMP); Final Rule, October 7, 1996. *Federal Register*, 61 (195): 52602–52662.

Food Supplements Europe. (2014). *Good Manufacturing Guide for Manufacturers of Food Supplements*. Brussels: Food Supplements Europe.

Gould, W.A. (1994). *Current Good Manufacturing Practices: Food Plant Sanitation*. Maryland: CTI Publications.

Government of Western Australia. (n.d.). *Cleaning and sanitising food premises and food equipment*. Retrieved March 20, 2018 from http://ww2.health.wa.gov.au/Articles/A_E/Cleaning-and-sanitising-food-premises-and-food-equipment.

Government Publishing Office. (2018a). *Electronic code of federal regulations*. Retrieved December 20, 2017 from https://www.ecfr.gov/cgi-bin/text-idx?SID=19a1cfc12f96b391bf4979c75e8a1b6d&mc=true&tpl=/ecfrbrowse/Title21/21chapterI.tpl.

Government Publishing Office. (2018b). *Electronic code of federal regulations*. Retrieved December 20, 2017 from https://www.ecfr.gov/cgi-bin/text-idx?SID=de87fc27ad65ed5bafddbf5ef7dc0614&mc=true&node=pt21.2.117&rgn=div5.

Government Publishing Office. (2018c). *Electronic code of federal regulations*. Retrieved December 20, 2017 from https://www.ecfr.gov/cgi-bin/text-idx?SID=e9cfc1921e0957cf6914c3b9ef59808f&mc=true&node=pt21.2.110&rgn=div5#se21.2.110_110.

Iowa State University of Science and Technology. (2016). FoodSafetyChecklist_2_16_16 GMP human food. Retrieved December 27, 2017 from http://www.fshn.hs.iastate.edu/wp-content/uploads/2016/05/FoodSafetyChecklist_5_3_16-GMP-Human-Food.pdf.

ISO. (2015). ISO 14001:2015 *Environmental Management Systems: Requirements with guidance for use*. Retrieved December 27, 2017 from https://www.iso.org/standard/60857.html.

Karmacharya, J.B. (2012). Good manufacturing practices (GMP) for medicinal products, promising pharmaceuticals. In P. Basnet (Ed.), *Promising-Pharmaceuticals/Good-Manufacturing-Practices-GMP-Formedicinal-Products*, pp. 1–148. Croatia: InTech.

Manning, L. (2013). *Food and Drink Good Manufacturing Practice* (6th ed.). Institute of Food Science and Technology. UK: John Wiley & Sons.

Mead, W.J. (2012). *Dietary Supplements Good Manufacturing Practices: Preparing for Compliance*. London: Informa Healthcare.

Mendis, E. and Rajapakse, N. (2009). *GMP and HACCP: A Handbook for Small and Medium Scale Food Processing Enterprises*. Sri Lanka: The Ceylon Chamber of Commerce.

Queensland Health. (2015). *Cleaning and sanitising: Food Act 2006*. Retrieved 26 March, from https://www.health.qld.gov.au/__data/assets/word_doc/0027/440919/cleaning-and-sanitising.doc.

Shapton, D.A. and Shapton, N.F. (1998). *Principles and Practices for Safe Processing of Foods*. UK: Woodhead Publishing.

CORE PROCESSES

Chapter 6

Purchasing

6.1 Historical Aspects

The purchasing function is vital to the success of an organisation. It has evolved from being a part of manufacturing or management to an extended financial contributor. The history and supply chain management provides a window to the growth, development and stature of the profession. Each historical period has made a unique contribution to the developments of purchasing that have shaped the modern purchasing and supply chain management system. The developments can be considered in terms of seven periods (Handfield et al., 2009; Pooler & Pooler, 1997; Lu Harding & Lu Harding, 2001), which are shown in Table 6.1.

Table 6.1 Evolution of the Purchasing

Period	Description	Developments
1	Early years 1830–1900	• Charles Babbage published his book on the economy of machinery and manufacturers in 1832 • "Materials Man" was responsible for several functions • Central officer operating the mines purchased materials and delivered the organisation's needs • Selling agent in the textile industry was responsible for purchasing, output, quality and style of cloth • In 1866 Pennsylvania Railroad created a supply department. Purchasing agent reported to the President • Comptroller of the Chicago and North-Western Railroads in 1887 published the book, *The Handling of Railroad Supplies – Their Purchasing and Disposition* • Late 1800s, purchasing was recognised as a separate corporate function

(Continued)

Table 6.1 (*Continued*) Evolution of the Purchasing

Period	Description	Developments
2	Development of purchasing fundamentals 1900–1939	• Journals and magazines other than Railroad Journals published articles on industrial purchasing • Engineering Managers emphasised the need for qualified personnel and development of material specifications • In 1905, *The Book on Buying* was published • During World War I purchasing function focused on buying raw material requirements for the war needs • From World War I to 1945, the development was gradual and uneven
3	War years 1940–1946	• Renewed interest in purchasing function • Colleges offering courses on purchasing • The National Association of Purchasing Agents was established • Purchase orders did not specify specifications or brands
4	Quiet years 1947 to mid-1960	• Ford Motor Company established a commodity research department to provide information on commodities • In 1947, General Electric developed the value analysis technique • Marketing and finance functions were seen as important
5	Materials management evolution Mid-1960 to late 1970	• Materials Man was responsible for purchasing and materials planning, inventory control and inward goods quality control and resolving material problems • Supplier was not considered as a value added partner • Purchasing Manager sourced materials from multiple sources • Role of purchasing was low in the management hierarchy
6	Entry of global market Late 1970–1999	• Severe competition, development of technology, purchasing through electronic media • Purchasing function extended to supply chain management
7	Integrated supply chain management Beyond 2000	• Growing emphasis on purchasing • Development of the supplier and long-term partnership • Involvement of the supplier in design • Service supplier selection • Strategic cost management • Enterprise resource planning

6.2 Definitions

Procurement: The act of obtaining goods and services in exchange for money or its equivalent. It includes sourcing, purchasing and all tasks from identifying potential suppliers through to delivery from suppliers to the user or beneficiary.

Purchasing: Specific role of actual buying of goods and services from the supplier.

Purchasing management: The management of the purchasing process and related management activities.

Purchasing agent: The person responsible for the selection and purchasing of goods and services using information on products, prices and suppliers.

Sourcing: Identifying suppliers for approval and working with them.

Vendor: A person who sells a product(s).

Buyer: The person or department that acquires or agrees to obtain ownership of goods or benefits or usage of services for money or other considerations under the terms of sale.

Supply chain: Parties directly or indirectly associated with fulfilling a customer's needs and includes manufacturers, suppliers, transporters, warehouses, retailers and end users.

Supply chain management: The management of materials and information in the supply chain to provide customer satisfaction at the lowest possible price.

Materials management (material planning): The planning and control of the functions involved with the complete flow of materials and associated flow of information.

6.3 Objectives of Purchasing

Traditionally, the main objective of procurement is stated as "to obtain the right quality of product at the right time, in the right quantity, from the right source at the right price". This simple objective provides a starting point for the development of appropriate objectives. Procurement in any organisation constitutes a major outflow of cash. Therefore, the CEO's goal is to balance the objectives for a reasonable return on investment. The Purchasing Manager must be cognisant of CEO's objectives when designing purchasing objectives. Purchasing decisions have a major impact on other functional activities of the organisation (Baily et al., 2015; Pooler & Pooler, 1997). A good approach is to define objectives in terms of (a) product, (b) cost, (c) supplier and (d) others.

6.3.1 Product

- Supply materials for the organisation to meet the needs of customers.
- Maintain continuity of supply: Purchasing function supports the organisation by purchasing raw materials, components, sub-assemblies, repair and maintenance items and services. An uninterrupted flow of high-quality goods is maintained by buying (a) the right quantity of goods that meet user needs at the right price from the right source and (b) by delivering to the right internal customer at the right time.
- Locate new and better materials and products.
- Ensure economic supply by procurement of goods, supplies and services for a diverse and globally competitive market.
- Identify critical materials and services essential to support company strategy in key performance areas.
- Maintain a low inventory without compromising the organisation's needs.

6.3.2 Cost

- Buying effectively and efficiently by ethical means to provide the best value for money.
- Maintain a healthy quality/value base by obtaining suitable quality at minimum cost.
- Negotiate and keep prices as low as possible in keeping with company commitments and optimal performance.

- Keep abreast of supply market to select new suppliers that are competitive.
- Carry out programmes to continually reduce purchasing costs.

6.3.3 Supplier

- Select best suppliers in the market that have the potential for excellent performance and for developing closer partnerships with them.
- Ensure optimal supplier performance through closer relationships and partnership.
- Facilitate the improvement of existing suppliers and help develop new suppliers that are not competitive.
- Negotiate effectively and develop partnership with suppliers to seek mutual benefit through excellent performance.

6.3.4 Others

- Develop staff, policies, and procedures to ensure the achievement of purchasing goals and company goals.
- Develop purchasing goals compatible with those of stakeholders and the organisation.
- Develop an integrated purchasing strategy that supports the organisation's strategy by involvement during the development of the company strategy.
- Provide information to functional departments on products and materials.

6.4 Features of Purchasing and Supply Organisations

Manufacturing and process industries are often considered as main organisations that purchase goods and services. However, purchasing activity is a function of several types of organisations and it will be greatly influenced by the type of organisation and its culture. Characteristics of purchasing and supply in different types of organisations are as follows (Baily et al., 2010):

6.4.1 Small Organisation Producing a Single Product, e.g. Fruit Picking and Packing

Small organisations employ few people with low status and receive poor pay. The purchasing activity does not usually influence company strategy. The Purchasing Manager is usually the head of the organisation and purchasing decisions are flexible. Purchasing and supply activities in these organisations do not require specialisation.

6.4.2 Assembly Industry, e.g. Motor Car Industry

Purchasing is a significant function in assembly industry and a director who has input into corporate strategy assumes the purchasing role. Purchasing activity is highly specialised involving functions such as inventory control, material control, maintaining delivery targets, etc. Functions within the purchasing activity are also specialised with a separate buyer for different types of goods such as electronic goods, chemicals, packaging, etc. Higher salaries and status are usually attached to the purchasing role. The process itself is technologically advanced.

6.4.3 Manufacturing Industry, e.g. Plastic Bottle Industry

The manufacturing industry consumes a wide variety of materials and constitutes a major proportion of production costs. A continuity of supply is required to maintain production. In dealing with internal and external issues, a strong professional approach is needed. Purchasing is an important function in the manufacturing industry and the head of the purchasing department reports to the board.

6.4.4 Processing Industry, e.g. Wine Industry

The processing industry consumes a large amount of raw materials and is a major component in production costs. Similar to the manufacturing industry, the processing industry also requires a continuity of supply. Purchasing is open to global bids. Purchasing Managers are specialists in processing categories.

6.4.5 Mining Industry, e.g. Gold, Coal, Oil Industries

The mining industry requires a high investment in capital equipment such as diggers, tractors, etc. Usually, the mining industry does not involve raw materials, but spares and maintenance costs are significant. These industries are located in remote locations. The emphasis of the mining industry is on plant, machinery and operations. The head of the purchasing function has a responsibility to keep the costs down and maintain the inventory.

6.4.6 Wholesalers and Retailers, e.g. Pharmaceutical Wholesalers, Supermarkets

Goods are sold as bought from primary producers, and there is no value-adding process. The entire operation is customer oriented with an emphasis on trends and fashion. Customers are attracted through advertising and promotions. About 80% of the total expenditure is for buying. The choice of goods and control of stock are important functions of wholesalers and retailers. Although there is a high turnover of goods, the profit margin is low, at around 5%. Buying is a specialist function and is represented at the highest level in the organisation. Due to the nature of the operation, the marketing and sales functions are closely linked.

6.4.7 Service Industry, e.g. Medical Service

An important component of the service industry is people who provide the know-how, technique, etc. Materials are not a large part of the service industry, which needs specialists to carry out the activities. Capital expenditure in some industries is high, e.g. in airlines. Where the cost of materials and equipment is high, purchasing is done by the functional department. For example, separate departments are responsible for the purchase of equipment such as computers and monitoring equipment.

6.4.8 Public Sector, e.g. Departments, Health Authorities, Municipal Authorities

The public sector comprises utility industries, local authorities, government departments, health authorities, the armed forces, etc. Apart from the utility industry, other public sector organisations have no sales role and therefore receive no income. Funds are provided by the government for the delivery of services. Purchasing accounts for a major portion of expenditure and therefore the role has a high status in the organisation. Often purchasing policies are influenced by politics.

6.4.9 Multifunctional Organisations, e.g. Ford Motor Company, Sony

These are worldwide organisations and a large proportion of expenditure is for the procurement of materials and supplies. The purchasing and supply functions are well developed.

6.5 Types of Purchases

All organisations require various types of goods and services for their operations. Companies do not produce all the necessary items themselves but depend on external sources of supply to purchase them as and when required. The selection of the sources of supply depends on the type of purchase (Monczka et al., 2009).

6.5.1 Raw Materials

The raw material category includes items such as fuel, metals, spare parts and packaging, etc. The food processing industry requires agricultural goods for the manufacture of food. Radioactive materials are necessary for the nuclear industry and the medical sector. Raw materials differ in their quality. For example, metals extracted from different locations may contain different impurities. Fruits grown in different regions have different taste profiles. Therefore, organisations have to decide on the quality before an item is purchased.

6.5.2 Semi-Finished Items and Components

Semi-finished items and components include component parts for machinery and equipment, sub-assemblies, assemblies and systems, etc. Automobile manufacturers need components such as tyres, seats, mirrors, electronics and many other items for assembling a motor vehicle. The quality of semi-finished products and components is very critical for the performance of the finished product. Space flight disasters due to faulty components have been well documented. Often motor car manufacturers recall motor vehicles to replace faulty components such as seatbelts and airbags free of charge. Both the Purchasing Manager and the supplier have a responsibility to ensure the correct quality is specified and supplied.

6.5.3 Finished Products

Organisations purchase finished goods either for internal use or for resale to the end user. Computers and stationery are bought as finished products for the operations of the organisation. Finished goods intended for resale do not require processing. An organisation may decide to purchase a finished item for resale for several reasons: (a) The buyer does not have the technical expertise or the capacity to produce the items; (b) lower cost due to bulk buying by the supplier; and (c) it can offer a wide range of products. However, the responsibility for the safe operation and quality of the finished product rests with the seller.

6.5.4 Items for Maintenance and Repair

Items used for the maintenance and repair of equipment and machinery do not end up in finished products. They are essential for effective operations in the organisation. Such items are very diverse and keeping an inventory is a difficult task.

6.5.5 Production Support Items

These are support items required for finished products such as tapes, pallets, bags, packaging material, etc. Production support items directly support the production operations of an organisation.

6.5.6 Services

Organisations utilise external sources for certain types of services they find necessary. Security operations are handled by security firms. Professional cleaning companies offer cleaning services. The maintenance and repair of equipment that cannot be performed by the organisation is done by external sources.

6.5.7 Capital Equipment

Capital expenditure is used to purchase assets for the operation of the organisation. Organisations allocate an annual budget for capital expenditure. Standard general equipment does not require special design features. Material handling equipment, computer systems and furniture are examples of standard general equipment, although computer systems may be customised for the organisation's requirements. Specialised production machinery such as bottle fillers, special machine tools and power-generating equipment are specialised capital equipment that requires technical know-how. Capital expenditure items are not purchased regularly, rather as and when required. These items have a long "operational life", and some may last up to 10 years. The purchase of capital expenditure involves high costs and therefore executive approval is necessary, and it is usually purchased from suppliers who have a long relationship with the purchaser.

6.5.8 Transportation

Purchasing transportation service is a specialised function and the evaluation of logistics service providers is similar to the evaluation of suppliers for production. Organisations are selecting logistics service suppliers who can provide a coordinated service including warehousing, packaging and even assembly.

6.5.9 Outsourcing

Outsourcing purchasing is the process of selecting an expert third party for the purchasing function. The driving force to outsource purchasing is the need to reduce costs. Outsourcing provides better value for money. However, it can be expensive if it is done without proper planning.

Effective communications have to be established between the outsourcing unit and the organisation to ensure that the product meets its needs.

6.6 Centralised Versus Decentralised Purchasing

The decision to centralise or decentralise the purchasing function depends on several factors: (a) the distance between the central location and other business units; (b) the nature of the material (bulky, heavy or fragile); (c) transport issues; and (d) company policies. The purchasing function of large organisations is generally performed by a central authority, which coordinates the procurement requirements of individual divisions or units. But with smaller organisations, the purchasing function is decentralised to individual plants or divisions (Lamming, 2002; Benton, 2014; GopalaKrishnan, 1990). Tables 6.2 and 6.3 show the advantages and disadvantages of centralised and decentralised purchasing.

6.7 Purchasing Strategy

The traditional view of purchasing did not consider it as a value-added activity. It was considered as a support to the value chain comprising inbound logistics, operations, outbound logistics,

Table 6.2   Advantages and Disadvantages of Centralised Purchasing

	Advantages		*Disadvantages*
1	Total requirements for the entire organisation can be consolidated and procured for a specific period – economies of scale	1	High initial investment in purchasing
2	Ability to standardise leading to reduction of operating costs and lower prices	2	Delay in distribution from central purchasing unit (it is possible to arrange delivery direct to individual business units)
3	Purchasing policies are deployed throughout the various business units	3	Geographical locations of individual units can be a barrier for centralised purchasing
4	Can exercise better financial control over purchases	4	In case of emergency, materials cannot be purchased from local suppliers
5	Auditing purchasing activities in one central unit is easier	5	Replacement of defective materials is difficult
6	Monitoring is easier		
7	Common IT systems		
8	Staff in the central unit develop skills and expertise, and exchange of staff does not cause problems		

Table 6.3 Advantages and Disadvantages of Decentralised Purchasing

	Advantages		*Disadvantages*
1	Autonomy enables divisional units to exploit the diversity and variety of local supplies	1	Coordination is difficult with different sites of the organisation
2	Information on good suppliers and materials can be shared through cross-communication	2	Decreased leverage that exists with consolidated procurement and the cost of purchasing is usually high
3	Individual units in better contact with suppliers	3	Focus on local rather than corporate goals
4	Awareness of local conditions and the ability to adjust purchasing conditions accordingly	4	Reporting structure is lower in the management hierarchy
5	Buyers are often located together, and the company has the ability to integrate with other functions	5	Expertise is limited to local requirements and fewer opportunities for cross-functional collaboration
6	The local purchasing reduces the time of communication with suppliers	6	Lack of standardisation of procurement procedures
7	Response time is rapid		
8	Possibility of lower transportation costs		

marketing and sales and service. The purchasing strategy was designed within the framework of corporate strategy, but it is now considered to be an essential contributor to the corporate strategy (Harland, 2002). A purchasing strategy should consider the following factors:

1. Decisions about sourcing:
   - Make, buy or lease.
   - Single or multiple sources of suppliers.
   - Varieties: reduction, management and standardisation.
   - Responsibility, storage and ownership of incoming material.
   - Timing of procurement.
   - Using distributors or manufacturers from local, domestic or global market.
   - Relationship with suppliers.
   - Responding to market trends.

2. Budgetary provisions: A budget provision is the amount of finance designated to each expenditure line and it defines the maximum amount of funding available for a given item or project, which should not be exceeded by employees, authorised to spend.

   The budget is usually divided into several cost centres for easier identification of the resources available for a specific programme. Each cost centre can be made up of several budget allocations. For example, the quality assurance (QA) budget may be included in the production cost centre. Sometimes, the allocations may have to be changed because of the failure to predict the expected expenditure or if a downturn occurs after the budget is adopted.

3. Extent, type and level of supply intervention required: The organisation has to intervene if the market is dominated by a single supplier. The extent of intervention affects the purchasing strategy and the choices are do nothing, respond to cope, counteract by locating alternative suppliers, being proactive and dominating.

The types of interventions are operational (basic transaction of buying and acquiring), managerial (planning and controlling for a specific period), strategic (taking strategic decisions) and policy (considering the impact on the environment or the community).

The level of intervention refers to the system level at which it takes place. It may be individuals or teams within the organisation, individual organisations, supply networks, regional supply units, government supply or divisional, national or global.

6.8 Purchasing Process

All organisations have to depend on suppliers for the raw materials, products, services and equipment needed for day-to-day operations. The purchasing function has an impact on many areas in the organisation such as product design, processes, supplier processes, supplier evaluation and selection. Therefore, suppliers have to be carefully selected on the basis of their ability to meet the requirements of the organisation. A failure to select the correct supplier will have an impact on production and the final product. An effective purchasing procedure (Monczka et al., 2009; Baily et al., 2015) includes the following activities:

■ Developing specifications for raw materials, products and services which may be generated in-house or may refer to national or international standards (sometimes it may be necessary to establish specifications or standards in consultation with the supplier).
■ Selection of suppliers on the basis of criteria established by the organisation.
■ Offer of contract.
■ Placing the order for materials or services
■ Receipt of supplies or services and delivery of materials.
■ Agreed method of verifying the purchased product which includes specifications, QA, test methods to be used, and resolving conflicts.
■ Management of non-conforming product.
■ Risk assessment.

Traditionally, organisations focus on quality parameters in the purchasing process. With an emphasis on environmental impact, organisations have realised the significance of environmental management performance in their purchasing decisions (Akili, 2008). A study of large and medium-sized organisations in China by Zhu and Geng (2001) found centralised purchasing was beneficial in overcoming the failure of senior managers to integrate environmental performance in the purchasing process.

6.9 Approval of Suppliers

Supplier selection and approval is a process of evaluating and selecting suppliers on the basis of a set of pre-established criteria. It is a useful and objective way of identifying the most appropriate supplier(s) to deal with in the supply chain. An organisation may use standard selection criteria or criteria developed to satisfy the process requirements of the organisation. Standard selection criteria generally include factors such as quality, capability, financial status of the supplier, delivery, responsiveness and business ethics. Since the 1990s, organisations have incorporated "green supplier selection criteria" into their selection processes in response to environmental issues related to business management processes. Purchasing Managers are key personnel who are best placed and best qualified to adopt a more environmental-friendly purchasing practice (Akili, 2008).

Environmental purchasing has been defined by Carter et al. (1998) as purchasing behaviour that includes the reduction, reuse and recycling of material. Life-cycle issues relating to the final disposal of material also have to be considered as an integral part of the purchasing procedure. The concept of Total Quality Environmental Management (TQEM) includes continuous environmental management through TQM activities. The improvements include the reduction of waste water, air emissions, solid waste and energy consumption (Lee, 2008).

6.9.1 The Process

The process of supplier selection (Mendoza, 2007) is shown in Figure 6.1.

Step 1: Recognise the need: The supplier selection process commences with the identification of a need for a specific product or a service. Activities such as new product development, searching for an alternative supplier or a supplier with a higher capability and renewal of a contract may trigger the search for new suppliers.

Step 2: Identify main sourcing requirements and establish criteria for election: The decision process generally involves multiple criteria which may conflict with each other. Traditionally, organisations focused on quality criteria until the 1990s. Since then environmental criteria have

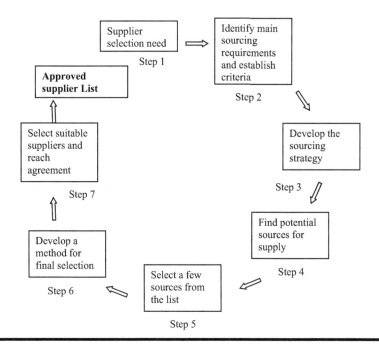

Figure 6.1 Evaluation and selection of suppliers.

been integrated into the selection process. Food processing organisations incorporate food safety criteria into the evaluation process.

Selection criteria

Suppliers are evaluated on the basis of following criteria (Egerod & Nordling, 2010):

1. General considerations.
2. Production.
3. Logistics.
4. Product development.
5. Purchasing.
6. Environmental impact.
7. Food safety.

Step 3: Develop a sourcing strategy: A sourcing strategy is different from the procurement process. It deals with planning, developing and creating a reliable competitive supplier base, designing a strategy for purchasing and defining pricing policies and supply chain requirements. It involves aligning procurement objectives with those of stakeholders in operations, financing, marketing and distribution. A sourcing strategy also involves planning to procure raw materials, components and services from competitive sources.

Step 4: Find potential sources of supply: During this step sourcing strategies are defined. This may involve a decision between a single source and multiple sources. If a single supplier is selected for a specific product, a better deal can be negotiated. With single suppliers, the organisation is exposed to greater risk of supply interruption due to unforeseen circumstances. Multiple suppliers offer the advantages of being competitive and ensuring continuity of supply. Other factors to consider are geographical location, national or international suppliers and duration of the contract (short or long term).

The location of potential suppliers that satisfies the organisation's requirements is a major responsibility of the Purchasing Manager. It is often believed that there are many suppliers at the "door step" of the buyer who are willing to meet the needs of the organisation. In actual fact, to find suitable suppliers is a major challenge. Difficulties of locating potential suppliers are summarised as follows (Baily et al., 2010):

1. Technological advances: Buyer needs are becoming more complex and difficult due to advances in technology and only a few suppliers are available to meet such demands.
2. Fewer suppliers actively seek business: Mergers and acquisitions have created a situation where the few large suppliers do not actively pursue business which will eventually come their way.
3. Increased specialisation: Manufacturing organisations are becoming more specialised and tend to buy rather than make. Therefore, a greater proportion of their needs are acquired from external sources that are not aware of the developing needs. Buyers have to actively seek such suppliers.

Buyers have to consider the following factors (ASQ, n.d.) when sourcing potential suppliers:

■ Find out the reputation of the supplier.
■ Conduct a detailed investigation of potential suppliers.
■ Evaluate the past performance from buyers who have been served by the supplier.

- Study approved supplier lists (ASLs).
- Consult catalogues, price lists and other literature.
- Refer to trade directories and industry sources.
- Communicate with sales personnel.
- Visit trade exhibitions.
- Talk to colleagues, other buyers and agents of suppliers.
- Contact trade consulates.

Step 5: Select a few suppliers from the identified sources.

Step 6: Supplier evaluation methods.

Two widely accepted methods of supplier evaluation are the categorical plan and the weighted point plan (Chary, 2007):

6.9.1.1 Categorical Plan

The categorical plan depends on a list of factors identified for each supplier by the organisation's departments such as production, quality, engineering, warehousing, purchasing, etc., based on the importance from the point of view of use. At the meeting of managers, each supplier is evaluated against these factors and given the subjective overall group evaluation in terms of categories: good (+1), unsatisfactory (−1) or neutral (0). Although the categorical plan has some disadvantages, it is very easy to administer.

Worked example is shown in Table 6.4

6.9.1.2 Weighted Point Plan

The weighted point plan involves (a) identifying factors important for the evaluation of suppliers; (b) assigning weightages for each factor (all of which should add up to 100); and (c) establishing a procedure for evaluating the performance of the vendor. The supplier's performance is quantified in terms of an index (from 0 to 5), which is then multiplied by the weightage for that factor. The individual results are added to arrive at an overall score.

A working example is shown in Table 6.5.

Step 7: Analyse the data and select suitable suppliers.

Step 8: Add the new supplier to the ASL.

6.10 Contract

The contracts offered by supply managers may differ in their specific words and details. But the structure of contracts employed in purchasing products and services are fairly standard and have

Table 6.4 Categorical Method of Rating Suppliers

Attribute	Supplier A	Supplier B	Supplier C
Cost	Good (+1)	Neutral (0)	Neutral (0)
Quality	Unsatisfactory (−1)	Good (+1)	Unsatisfactory (−1)
Speed	Neutral (0)	Good (+1)	Neutral (0)
Total	0	++	−

Table 6.5　Weighted Point Method of Rating Suppliers

Attribute	Weight[a]	Performance	Supplier A Performance	Supplier A Score	Supplier B Performance	Supplier B Score
Quality	40	1–5 worst–best	2	(2/5)×40=16	4	(4/5)×40=32
Delivery	30	1–5 worst–best	3	(3/5)×30=18	3	(3/5)×30=18
Cost	20	1–5 worst–best	3	(3/5)×20=12	4	(4/5)×20=16
Service	10	Good – 100% Fair – 70% Poor – 40%	70%	(70/100)×10=7	10%	(10/100)×10=1
Total	100			53		67

[a] Change as necessary.

several common features. These features are generally developed by the legal department of the organisation and then modified to suit different types of suppliers. Contracts create legal rights between the buyer and the supplier (Handfield, 2009). The essential features of a contract are:

a. An offer: Clearly defined offer to supply products and/or service of specified quality.
b. Acceptance: The offer is accepted unchanged without conditions. New terms offered are considered as counter offers which can be accepted or rejected.
c. Parties enter into a legal binding contract.
d. Consideration: Buyer gives the supplier an agreed price on delivery.

6.11 Green or Sustainable Procurement

Green procurement or sustainable procurement is the selection of the organisation's requirements of products and services that minimise environmental impact. Purchasing environmentally friendly products and services promotes the productive use of resources. This is achieved by integrating environmental considerations into all stages of the procurement processes. Green procurement avoids unnecessary purchases and identifies greener products according to the specifications used for contractors and whole-life costing (Environmental Protection Department, Hong Kong, 2018).

6.11.1 Green Products

"Green" products use fewer natural resources, contain fewer hazardous or toxic materials, have longer lifespans, consume less energy and water during production or use and can be reused or recycled on disposal.

6.11.2 Checklist for Procurement

Table 6.6 shows a checklist that can be adopted for green procurement (UNIDO, 2019).

Table 6.6 Checklist for Green Procurement

Get an overview of the raw and process materials used in the company Examine the raw and process materials listed in the worksheets and determine their environmental relevance and possible substitution	☐
Ask the supplier for product information (e.g. safety data sheets)	☐
Collect information on environmental or sector-specific labels for materials used in the company and ask the suppliers for site certifications	☐
Use the criteria and guidelines of environmental labels to define guidelines for the company's tenders	☐
Ask the supplier to offer environmentally friendly alternatives	☐
If the company has a quality management system, examine the purchasing procedure	☐

(Continued)

Table 6.6 (*Continued*) Checklist for Green Procurement

Does the company's environmental policy mention green procurement?	☐
Do employees know who exactly is responsible for which type of procurement in the company?	☐
Are the Environmental Manager and the Safety Manager integrated in the procurement activities?	☐
Is there a central purchasing unit in the company?	☐
Are products examined by a central unit before they are used in the company for the first time?	☐
If cleaning is carried out by an external cleaning team, does the company know which detergents are used?	☐
Are the procurement activities of the company documented?	☐
Does the company inform its employees in time if a new product will be used?	☐
Does the company train its employees in the handling of a new product?	☐
Are all environmentally friendly purchased products marked and are the underlying criteria applied?	☐
Does the company have a list of products for which no environmentally friendly alternative has been found to date?	☐
Does the company regularly check the product packaging in view of environmental friendliness (multi-way packaging system, recyclability)?	☐

Source: Reproduced with permission of UNIDO, 2019. Copyright at UNIDO.

6.12 Procurement of Products for Food Processing

Products needed for food processing require special consideration. In the food processing industry, raw materials constitute one of the most important aspects that must be carefully controlled. Food manufacturers have limited control over the quality of incoming raw materials. The supplier of these raw materials should establish adequate controls to prevent the entry of, or eliminate, harmful or potentially harmful organisms and contaminants. This topic will be discussed in detail in the chapter on Hazard Analysis and Critical Control Points (HACCP).

Some of the controls that can be established to ensure that incoming food ingredients and raw materials do not cause health hazards are shown in Table 6.7 (De Silva, 2007)

6.13 e-Procurement

e-Procurement is the combined use of electronic information and communication technology to conduct the transactional aspects of requisitioning, authorising, ordering, receipting and payment processes for the required goods and services. Since adopting e-procurement, many countries have realised enormous savings in transaction costs (Hunja, n.d.). In 2006, Korea realised savings of US$4.5 billion out of total transactions of US$44 billion. Between 2000 and 2006,

Table 6.7 Controls of Incoming Raw Materials to Ensure Food Safety

1. Be highly selective of sources/suppliers of materials and their ability to produce and deliver a safe product consistently by implementing an approved supplier policy
2. Establish specifications for raw materials taking into consideration those characteristics that are critical to quality and food safety
3. Avoid using the cheapest price as the sole criterion for purchase. Relate the price to risk assessment and quality
4. Review any new ingredients introduced into the system. Instruct the supplier to inform you of any change in the characteristics of the raw material, since even minor changes may affect the final quality of the end-product
5. Carry out periodic audits at the supplier's premises
6. Instruct the supplier to have a HACCP and a QA programme in place. Provide encouragement and support, if necessary. Developing a partnership can be mutually beneficial
7. Inform the supplier to label the raw materials accurately and provide assurance in the form of compliance certificates
8. Carry out periodic tests on raw materials on delivery
9. Monitor the storage conditions of raw materials, both at the supplier's end and at the producer's premises
10. Encourage the raw material supplier to develop safe packaging for ingredients
11. Encourage supplier to develop environmentally friendly products

Brazil made 51% in savings in transaction costs with 25.5% in price reductions. Transaction costs in India amounted to US$3.6 billion in 2005 with savings of US$238.2 million due to tender discounts. According to a study conducted by the Aberdeen Group (2007), enterprises realised a 35% improvement in spend under-management, with a 41% reduction in maverick spend, a reduction of requisition-to-order costs of approximately 100% and a reduction of transaction cycle time by more than half.

6.13.1 Objectives of e-Procurement

In order to realise the full potential of e-procurement, its options and opportunities must be realistic. They must focus on practicable and achievable options so that they add value in terms of improvement in effectiveness and efficiency, while minimising the risk to the organisation (Shakya, 2003). Some of the objectives of e-procurement are the following:

a. To make the best use of information and communication technology to reduce the cost of procurement process for the organisation and its suppliers and contractors.
b. To realise savings from all procurement processes.
c. To improve efficiency in online procurement, staff time and the speed of procurement process.

6.13.2 Seven Categories of e-Procurement

e-Procurement is conducted electronically, and it enables organisations to focus on their suppliers and maintain communication throughout the procurement process. Information is available in digital form, and it allows ready comparison of prices and reliability, eliminating paperwork and improving the relationship with suppliers. There are seven types of e-procurement (Baily et al., 2015):

1. Web-based ERP (Enterprise Resource Planning): Generating and authorising purchase requisitions, placing purchase orders (POs) and receiving materials.
2. eMRO (Maintenance, Repair, Overhaul): Creating and approving purchase requisitions, placing POs and receiving non-product-related MRO supplies.
3. eSourcing: Identifying new suppliers for a new category of purchasing needs.
4. eTendering: Requesting information and prices from suppliers and receiving quotes.
5. eReverse auctioning: Using internet technology to buy goods and services from a number of known or unknown suppliers.
6. eInforming: Collecting and sharing purchasing information between external and internal parties.
7. eMarket sites: Buying communities can access preferred suppliers' products and services, add to the shopping cart, generate requisition, seek approval, receipt POs, and process electronic invoices through the integration of suppliers' supply chains and buyers' financial systems. Each of these applications has a role to play in the e-procurement cycle (Inter Agency Procurement Working Group (IAPWG), 2006) (Figure 6.2).

6.13.3 Benefits of e-Procurement

Yearly reductions in purchase prices and savings from processing costs are undisputed benefits of e-procurement. However, key saving drivers of e-procurement include transactional payments, management information and price benefits. Benefits of e-procurements can be classified as hard benefits, soft benefits and intangible benefits (Eakin, 2003; Baily et al., 2015):

a. Hard benefits are directly measureable and deliver enhanced shareholder value. They include price savings, process cost reductions (head count), reductions in cycle times (days/weeks) and consequent reduction in inventory level (value/stock turnover ratio).
b. Soft benefits are indirectly measurable and include benefits such as staff time freed up due to more efficient processes. Therefore, they are able to spend more time on the value-added aspects of procurement such as supplier development and contract management. Soft benefits are also effective indicators of improvement and should not be ignored just because they are difficult to measure.
c. Intangible benefits are not directly measureable in financial terms and include the following:
   i. The ability to consolidate purchasing across multiple departments while maintaining individual control.
   ii. The enhanced possibility of buying goods that conform to specifications from approved suppliers.
   iii. The ability to identify the best price and quality from a wide range of suppliers.
   iv. Demonstration of disparity among price, quality and delivery of required goods.

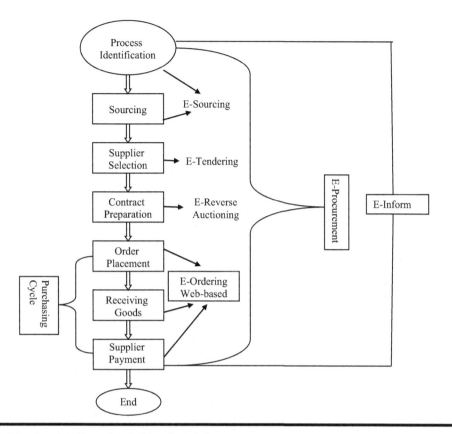

Figure 6.2   Application of web-based tools in e-procurement.

    v. Improved communication between the organisation and the supplier.
   vi. A common set of standards for procurement.

6.13.4   Challenges of e-Procurement

Although much progress has been made in improving e-procurement, there are significant challenges ahead (de Pablos et al., 2013):

1. Supplier enablement: During the early days of implementing e-procurement, the buyer, supplier and technology provider under-estimated the time, effort and resources to conduct transactions electronically. Best practice organisations employ a combination of supplier-enablement approaches. All involved parties – supplier, buyer and the technology provider – strive to improve e-procurement approaches.
2. User adoption: Individual users and business units have resisted change that altered their buying power and buying flexibility. However, the buyer's task has been made easier with the availability of more products and suppliers to choose from. Inadequate representation of spending categories within the system, inconsistent purchase requirements, not enough procedure and supply bases, and lack of executive commitment are some of the reason for not embracing supplier adoption.

3. Budget constraints and policy support: Lack of top management support and an inadequate level of investment needed to demonstrate the benefits of e-procurement are some of the reasons for the failure to adopt e-procurement in organisations.

4. Many factors shape the way that purchasing contributes to the performance of the organisation. Competent purchasing professionals with the necessary skills can play a vital role in enhancing the performance of the organisation and meet competitive challenges.

References

Aberdeen Group. (2007). *E-Procurement: Trials and triumphs*. Retrieved January 10, 2019 from http://www.enporion.com/media/whitepapers/eprocurement_trials_and_triumphs.pdf.

Akili, E.A. (2008). Green supplier selection criteria. *Supply Chain Systems*. Retrieved January 11, 2019 from http://www.uww.edu/supplychain/761Green/Select.pdf.

ASQ. (n.d.). *Supplier selections strategies and criteria*. Retrieved April 5, 2018 from http://asq.org/learn-about-quality/supplier-quality/overview/tutorial.html.

Baily, P., Farmer, D., Crocker, B., Jessop, D. and Jones, D. (2015). *Procurement Principles and Management* (11th ed.). Harlow: Pearson Education Limited.

Benton, W.C. (2014). *Purchasing and Supply Chain Management* (3rd ed.). New York: McGraw Hill Education.

Carter, C.R., Ellram, L.M. and Ready, K.J. (1998). Environmental purchasing: Benchmarking our German counterparts. *Journal of Supply Chain Management*, 34 (4), 28–38.

Chary, S.N. (2007). *Theory and Problems in Productions and Operations Management*. India: Tata McGraw-Hill.

de Pablos, P.O., Lovelle, J.M.C., Gayo, J.E.L. and Tennyson, R.D. (2013). *E-Procurement Management for Successful Electronic Government Systems*. Pennsylvania: Information Science Reference.

De Silva, T. (2007). Hazard analysis and critical control point (HACCP). In M.S. Rahman (Ed.), *Handbook of Food Preservation* (2nd ed.), pp. 969–1011. Florida: Taylor & Francis.

Eakin, D. (2003). Measuring e-procurement benefits. *Summit: Canada's Magazine on Public Sector Purchasing*, 16–19.

Egerod, J. and Nordling, M. (2010). *Strategic supplier evaluation: Considering environmental aspects*. (Masters Thesis). LIU-IEI-TEK-A-10/00974-SE. Department of Management and Engineering Logistics Management, Linkopins Universitet, Sweden.

Environmental Protection Department, Hong Kong. (2018) *Green procurement*. Retrieved January 12, 2019 from https://www.epd.gov.hk/epd/english/how_help/green_procure/green_procure.html.

GopalaKrishnan, P. (1990). *Purchasing and Materials Management*. India: Tata McGraw-Hill.

Handfield, R.B., Monczka, R.M., Giunipero, L.C. and Patterson, J.L. (2009). *Sourcing and Supply Chain Management* (4th ed.). Ohio: South-Western Cengage Learning.

Harland, C. (2002). Purchasing strategy process. In M. Day (Ed.), *Handbook of Purchasing Management* (3rd ed.), pp. 23–36. UK: Gower Publishing Limited.

Hunja, R. (n.d.). *E-Procurement: Opportunities and challenges*. Retrieved January 10, 2019 from http://www.europarl.europa.eu/document/activities/cont/201207/20120710ATT48625/20120710ATT48625EN.pdf.

IAPWG. (2006). *UN Procurement Practitioner's Handbook*. Austria: IAPWG.

Lamming, R. (2002). Purchasing and organisational design. In M. Day (Ed.), *Handbook of Purchasing Management* (3rd ed.), pp. 9–22. UK: Gower Publishing Limited.

Lee, C.W. (2008). Green suppliers with environmental performance in the supply chain perspective. *Asia Pacific Management Review*, 13 (4), 731–745.

Lu Harding, M. and Lu Harding, M. (2001). *Purchasing* (2nd ed.). New York: Barron's Education Series.

Mendoza, A. (2007). *Effective methodologies for supplier selection and order quantity allocation.* Doctor of Philosophy Thesis in Industrial Engineering and Operations Research, Pennsylvania State University, Pennsylvania.

Monczka, R.M., Handfield, R.B., Giunipero, C. and Patterson, J.L. (2009). *Purchasing and Supply Chain Management* (5th ed.). Ohio: Cengage Learning.

Pooler, V.H. and Pooler, D.J. (1997). *Purchasing and Supply chain management: Creating the vision.* New York: Chapman & Hall.

Shakya, R.K. (2003). *Theme Paper on e-Procurement.* Nepal: The Asia Foundation.

UNIDO. (2019). Volume 6: Green procurement and hazardous material. *CP Tool Kit English.* Retrieved January 12, 2019 from https://www.unido.org/resources/publications/safeguarding-environment/industrial-energy-efficiency/cp-toolkit-english.

Zhu, Q. and Geng, Y. (2001). Integrating environmental issues into supplier selection and management: A study of large and medium-sized enterprises in China. *Greener Management International,* 35, 27–40.

Chapter 7

Production and Provision of Services

7.1 Definitions

Good Manufacturing Practices (GMPs): This is a part of quality assurance which ensures that products are manufactured in a consistent manner and controlled to quality standards appropriate to their use.

Process: It is a set of interrelated operations that transform inputs to intended outputs adding value.

Quality assurance: It is the organisation of all activities necessary to ensure that products are of the quality required for their intended use.

Quality control: It is the performance of necessary and relevant tests to ensure that products are released for use only after ascertaining their quality.

Validation: "Act of confirming a product or service meets the requirements for which it was intended" (ASQ, n.d.).

Verification: "Act of determining whether products and services conform to specified requirements" (ASQ, n.d.).

7.2 Concept of Production

Production is the step-wise conversion of inputs in one form into outputs of another form through chemical, mechanical or other processes to create products in sufficient quantities to meet customers' requirements. Although the conversion process itself is simple, the demands by the customer for better quality, fast and rapid delivery and competitive prices make the process rather difficult. Customers also expect the supplier to make changes to order quantities, delivery dates and product specifications at short notice. While meeting these requirements, the Production Manager has to utilise the resources effectively to reduce the cost of production. Production is essentially a value addition process, and at each step of the process, value is added. Figure 7.1 shows a production model. Inputs such as materials, labour, information, capital and land are converted to outputs

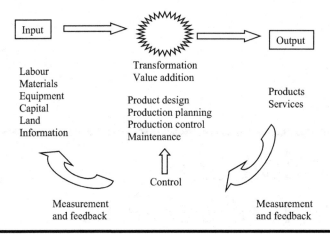

Figure 7.1 Production process.

(goods and services) using one or more transformation processes. At various stages of the process control measures are applied to ensure that established standards are met (control). Corrective actions are implemented to resolve any deviations (feedback).

7.3 Provision of Service

7.3.1 Differences between Production and Service Operations

Organisations exist to provide goods and services to customers. The features of production are quite different from those of service (Kumar & Suresh, 2008; Stevenson, 2012). Table 7.1 shows the distinguishing features of production and service.

1. Tangible nature of output: Production of goods results in tangible outputs such as furniture, machines, motor vehicles, etc., that we can see and touch. On the other hand, a service is an act. A medical practitioner's examination of a patient, advice on tax matters by a tax consultant and a lawn-mowing service are some examples of services offered to customers.
2. Contact: Generally production occurs in a facility away from the customer, and there is little or no contact with customers. Many services involve a high degree of interaction with customers. However, some services such as the provision of internet services or the delivery of mail do not involve the participation of the customer. Only when problems occur there is direct contact with the customer.
3. Labour content: Production requires more equipment and less labour. However, some production jobs such as the sorting of fruits involve more manual labour. Although services generally require more labour and less equipment, automated services such as telephone and rail road services are equipment-based and services such as hair styling and taxation services are people-based.
4. Variability of inputs: Inputs required for production operations can be carefully controlled by verification activities, whereas those for a service are more variable. For example, patients consulting a medical practitioner may have widely different illnesses and a TV repair person may have to deal with TVs having simple to major defects.

Table 7.1 Features of Production and Service

Feature	Production	Service
Tangible nature	Tangible	Intangible
Contact	Away from the customer	Direct contact
Labour content	Low	High
Inputs	Can be controlled	Less control and variable
Productivity	Easy	Difficult
Mistakes	Can be corrected	No opportunity for correction
Storage	Can be stored	Immediate consumption
Inventory level	High	Low
Wages	Uniform	Variable
Patenting ability	Can be patented	Cannot always be patented

5. Measurement of productivity: Uniformity of production activities permits the simple evaluation of productivity. Due to the large variation of inputs, measurement of service productivity can be difficult.
6. Correction of mistakes: Mistakes identified during production, which usually occur away from the customer, can be corrected before the goods reach them. But when consumption and delivery of service take place at the same time, there is no opportunity to identify and correct mistakes.
7. Storage: Goods produced can be stored for future use. Services cannot be stored and consumption and delivery take place at the same time.
8. Inventory: Many services require fewer inventories than production and therefore the cost of having inventory on hand is less than for production operations. Services have to be performed on demand and unlike manufactured goods services cannot be stored.
9. Wages: Production jobs are better paid, and there is less variation in the job market. The service sector workers vary from minimum wage workers to highly paid professional and technical staff.
10. Patenting ability: Production designs can be patented, making it difficult to copy. On the other hand, some services cannot be patented, making it easier to copy.

7.3.2 Similarities between Production and Service Operations

Production and service operations vary in terms of what has to be accomplished but are quite similar in terms of how it is performed. Some of the similarities between production and service operations are (Stevenson, 2012):

- Management of processes.
- Controlling variation.
- Monitoring and controlling the cost of operation.

- Supply chain management.
- Location planning, planning for production and/or service, scheduling the tasks.
- Managing inventory levels.

Production and service operations do not exist in isolation. Production operations involve some degree of service and some equipment is needed for the delivery of services (Stevenson, 2012). The continuum between production and service operations is shown in Figure 7.2.

The goods content of automobile manufacture and production of steel is very high and the service component is low. On the other end of the spectrum, teaching and lawn-mowing need less material and more labour. Having a meal in a restaurant and the repair of a computer involve almost equal elements of goods and services. Song writing and software development have more of the service component and automobile repair, fast food service, home redesigning and retail sales have more of the goods component (Stevenson, 2012). Table 7.2 shows two examples of transformation processes.

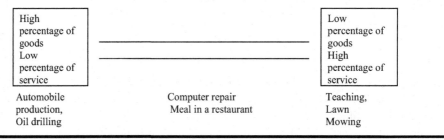

Figure 7.2   Production – Service interaction.

Table 7.2   Transformation Processes

Provider	Input	Transformation Processes	Output
Beverage production	Grapes Chemicals Filter aids Water Information Testing equipment Bottles Corks Capsules Labels Packaging Labour	Crushing Processing juice Fermentation Testing Filtering Centrifuging Filling Corking Capsuling Labelling Packing	Cases of wine bottles
School	Labour Equipment Information	Teaching Examining	Learnt student

7.4 Types of Production

Productions systems can be categorised as job shop, batch, flow line or mass and continuous production systems (Stevenson, 2012; Mapes, 1992).

7.4.1 Job Shop Production

A job shop facility is often a subcontractor producing a small number of items made to order according to a design specified by a customer. Repeat orders are few and far between, and the product mix is continuously changing, causing fluctuations in production. However, the customer still expects the rapid and reliable delivery of orders. Job shop operations need general-purpose machines and facilities, skilled labour, large inventory levels and detailed planning. Major limitations of job shop productions are higher costs due to frequent set-up changes, the need to hold higher inventory levels and large space requirements.

7.4.2 Batch Production

Batch production is used when an organisation has a range of standard products in quantities not large enough to adopt continuous production. Batches of various products are manufactured according to demand and held in stock for future use. In order to avoid "out of stock" situations, organisations using batch production have to depend on accurate forecasting and ensure effective utilisation of capacity and other resources. Batch production facilities incur lower costs of production and lower investments in plant and machinery. Resources are better utilised, and there is the flexibility to accommodate a number of products and services. Limitations of batch production are (a) complex material handling and production planning due to frequent changes in production and (b) higher set-up costs and higher levels of in-process stock.

7.4.3 Flow Line or Mass Production

Flow line or mass production is a cost-effective method of manufacturing high volumes of a limited range of products. Production operations consist of a number of simple operations setup in line. A beverage production consists of filling, capping labelling, packaging and palletising operations setup in a line. Each station of the process is dedicated to a single operation, and because of the repetitive and simple nature of the operation, unskilled labour can be often employed. The work is monotonous and it is important to motivate the workforce to maintain the output. Since the equipment is arranged in line, each machine depends on the previous operation. Therefore, continuity of material supply is essential to avoid any "bottlenecks". The speeds of operation of the machines have to be synchronised to maintain continuity of production. With flow line or mass production operations, higher production rates are possible with lower costs of production. All resources are effectively utilised, and the process inventory is low. The limitations of flow line or mass production operations are (a) a hold-up or a breakdown of one machine will stop the entire production operation, so some facilities employ extra space in the line to hold accumulated in-process stock to avoid stopping the line; (b) the line layout needs major changes; (c) often flow line or mass production operations use automated systems and therefore incur high investment costs; and (d) the slowest operation determines the cycle time.

7.4.4 Continuous Production

Continuous production is used when a single undifferentiated product is manufactured in high volumes. Sugar refining, steel production and flour production are examples of continuous production. The production facility is dedicated to the manufacture of a single product continuously and therefore tends to be economical. Continuous production has several unique features: Material handling is fully automated, the process involves a predetermined sequence of operations, and planning and scheduling are simple. Major limitations are inflexibility to accommodate changes which require additional resources, high investments for setting flow lines and limited product differentiation.

7.5 Effect of Processes on Production Management

The organisations which focus on quality, speedy and reliable delivery, design and quantity flexibility and lowering costs are more likely to gain orders. Besides these criteria, the nature and the variety of processes have a strong influence on production management. Figure 7.3 shows the relationship between process and product mix and the job types. The four types of production can be placed on a diagonal scale and production units placed on the same position on the scale meet similar challenges (Mapes, 1992).

7.6 Types of Service

7.6.1 Classification of Services

Services can be classified on the basis of labour content and capital investment. Table 7.3 shows the four types of services (Schmenner, 1986). The classification is based on the labour content

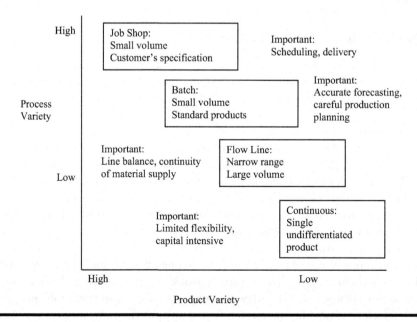

Figure 7.3   Effect of process variety and product mix on production management.

Table 7.3 Types of Services and Management Challenges

	Low Customisation	*High Customisation*	
Low labour intensity	• Airlines • Transport • Event management • Entertainment • Hotels	• Auto repair shops • Hospitals • Restaurants • Travel agencies	**Low labour intensity challenges:** • Capital expenditure • Technological developments • Managing demands to prevent peaks • Promote off peaks • Planning service delivery
High labour intensity	• Supermarkets • Rail services • Schools • Retail services in banks	• Medical professionals • Engineers • Lawyers • Accountants	**High labour intensity challenges:** • Recruitment • Training and development • Development of methods and monitoring • Staff welfare • Workforce planning • Managing distant operations • Establishment of new units • Managing growth
	Low customisation challenges	**High customisation challenges**	
	• Marketing • Improving service • Focus on physical environment • Managing rigid organisation hierarchy • Standard operating procedures	• Cost increases • Managing quality • Responding to customer needs • Staff development • Managing flat organisation hierarchy • Loose subordinate – supervisor relationship	

measured in terms of the ratio of labour costs/capital investments and the customer interaction and the degree of customisation, which is a marketing variable that determines the extent of customer interaction that affects the nature of service. When the service is standardised, such as in KFC restaurants where meals are prepared from assembled items, very little interaction with the customer is required.

Service factory: Examples of services with high capital investment and low labour content are airlines, trucking and rail services, and hotels and recreation facilities. They incur high capital investment in machinery and equipment, but the degree of labour intensity is low compared with capital expenditure. Customisation is also low and a standard service is delivered.

Service shop: These provide a higher degree of customisation for the consumer. They have a high degree of plant and equipment relative to the labour content and offer higher opportunities for interaction with consumers. The concept of a service shop is similar to a job shop in manufacturing where customisation is required. Garage workshops offer a range of services such as wheel balancing, tuning up, repairs, oil change, etc., which require a high degree of interaction with customers and special equipment. Other services in this category are hospitals and some restaurants.

Mass service: Schools and commercial aspects of businesses provide services high in labour content with minimum capital investment. They offer standard services with little or no customisation. Many of the traditional services and routine services such as cleaning, laundry service, computer software and data processing functions fall into this category.

Professional service: Lawyers, dentists, accountants provide customised solutions to client's problems. The client or the patients must actively participate to discuss various courses of action. The ratio of labour content to capital investment is high.

7.7 Challenges for Service Providers

The four types of services offer various challenges (Table 7.3) depending on the degree of labour intensity, interaction with customers and the extent of customisation (Schmenner, 1986). In low-intensive services, such as airlines and hospitals, investment in capital is important with emphasis on technological advances. Inflexibility of capacity of such services means that demands have to be managed to encourage off-peak service by effectively scheduling service delivery.

Managing and controlling the workforce is essential in services where the degree of labour intensity is high. Human resources (HR) aspects such as training, hiring, personal development and employee welfare are critical elements. Controlling the workforce and managing work in other geographical locations are further challenges. If new units have to be established, the start-up and growth of such units can be difficult.

Services with high and low levels of customer interaction present other challenges. Airlines and hospitals that offer services where customer interaction and customisation is low have to develop an effective marketing strategy to remain competitive. Services have to be offered in a warm and friendly manner in a pleasing physical environment. Standard operating procedures are easy to develop because the services are standardised. In this type of service, levels of managerial hierarchy are rigid.

A talented specialised workforce is essential to provide professional services where the levels of customer interaction and customisation are high. Managing the cost, quality and reacting rapidly to customers' requirements are challenges faced by service providers. Professional employees demand career advancement in the organisation. The managerial hierarchy is flat where the power distance is low.

7.8 Production Planning

The functions of an organisation involve effective planning, scheduling and coordinating production and service activities. During the planning stage, the level of demand is determined for each product or service, and the demand forecast is translated into a plan that optimises the organisation's objective of maximising profit while satisfying the needs of customers. However, these two objectives are not always compatible. The scheduling stage involves the translation of the production plan into a day-to-day work schedule of products to be made or services to be offered. The coordination stage is a feedback loop, which compares the actual output with the scheduled output to make necessary adjustments to the plan. The Production Planner has to assess the capacity of each work centre and produce a plan in which the load does not exceed the capacity. The capacity is the maximum rate at which a given output can be produced under standard operating conditions, while the load is the required output for a given period measured in the same units as capacity (Mapes, 1992).

7.8.1 Objectives of Production Planning (Dalal, 2011)

■ Cost considerations.
  – Achieve cost reduction and cost control.
  – Achieve goals at minimum cost.

■ Resource considerations.
  – Achieve maximum utilisation of resources.
  – Maintain optimum inventory levels.

■ Operational considerations.
  – Minimise production cycle time.
  – Maintain flexibility of operations.
  – Maintain quality.
  – Remove bottlenecks in operations.

■ Management considerations.
  – Achieve coordination among employees, machines and other supply departments.
  – Prepare and maintain production schedule.

A production plan establishes production rates, workforce levels and on-hand inventory levels for product families. Product families include products with similar demand requirements that share common processes, HR and materials. In a winery, a product family of coolers, ciders and sparkling wines has similar processing requirements. Similarly, a product family of different still wines needs similar resource requirements for bottling. A careful analysis of each product family is conducted considering the differences among product groupings including forecasts, resource usage and inventory investment policies and objectives (Duchessi & O'Keefe, 1990). The unit measurements are man-hours, machine-hours, facility-hours or another measure of output. Product families' requirements are combined to establish an estimate of the total resource requirements for one or two years. If the load exceeds the capacity, one or more product family plans are modified to strike a balance between load and capacity. This aggregated production plan forms the basis for creating a master schedule.

7.8.2 Limitations of Production Planning (Dalal, 2011)

■ Production planning is based on assumptions of demand forecast, availability of resources, technological progress, government policies, etc., and these assumptions can change making the original production plan ineffective.
■ It is costly and time-consuming.

- External environmental factors can also change, making the plan ineffective.
- Employees may resist any changes introduced as a result of implementing the plan.

7.9 Scheduling

Scheduling is defined as the time required to perform each operation and routing the entire series. It is a process for establishing targets for all production operations, including times for setting up machinery and other preparations required for completing a manufacturing order (Dalal, 2011).

The following are the objectives of scheduling:

- Perform the operations to meet the delivery dates.
- Make the maximum use of machinery and employees to minimise costs.
- Smooth out unbalanced allocation time (capacity/load combination) amongst various departments and work centres.
- Minimise storage costs and working capital investment in inventory.
- Prevent or minimise work-in-progress (WIP).

7.9.1 Types of Scheduling

Three types of scheduling are recognised in the manufacturing sector (Dalal, 2011):

Operation schedule: It determines the total time required to complete a piece of work using a specified process and machine(s).

Master schedule: It is a list specifying the quantity of each item to be produced in a specified period of time in the future.

Sequential schedule: It is a plan defining the sequence of operations for multiple products that go through several units or departments.

7.9.2 The Process of Scheduling

The process of scheduling commences with the creation of a master schedule using the data presented in the master production plan. It is a record of what the organisation expects to produce within a given period. The master schedule is prepared by breaking down the demands of each product family into specific end items and the quantities required each week. It is, therefore, a detailed manufacturing plan. It is used for material requirement planning for estimating the materials and components needed to produce items in the master schedule. Capacity plans are then developed for both the master schedule and material requirement plans considering the lead times and routings. They determine capacity needs for both machine centres and labour skills (Duchessi & O'Keefe, 1990).

7.9.3 Limitations of Scheduling

1. When the appropriate production rates, labour requirements and inventory levels required to meet the product family demands are determined, managers have to make trade-offs. Maintaining a stable labour force reduces the costs of recruitment and dismissal, but as demands decrease, inventory investment and under-time costs tend to increase.

2. The maximum output for a specific period is limited by capacity constraints.
3. Financial constraints may inhibit the acquisition of resources required to support a given level of production.
4. Policy constraints may limit the amount of overtime permitted and specify minimum inventory levels to maintain safe stock levels.

The strategies to combat the limitations include the reduction of production, workforce and inventory costs by (a) varying the labour costs by hiring and firing employees as demand fluctuates; (b) adjusting the production rates through overtime and under-time while maintaining a stable work force; and (c) varying the inventory levels to absorb fluctuations in demand. Typically, organisations employ a combination of these strategies (Duchessi & O'Keefe, 1990).

7.10 Management of Processes

All processes are managed through the application of quality assurance and quality control principles. They include the availability of specifications at the correct location, validation of the processes and verification of products while in process and prior to release, analysis of operations and maintenance, performance of risk assessment, investigations and corrective actions. Quality has to be built throughout the process. Inspection activity has some drawbacks: (a) It does not add value; (b) defects are observed only after the problem has occurred; (c) it is costly; and (d) it is subject to human error. However, quality assurance does not completely eliminate the need for inspection (quality control). A certain degree of inspection is involved in process management activities.

7.11 Maintenance Management

Equipment, machinery and facilities are essential to produce goods and deliver the services required by customers. Their idleness or failure is costly and therefore organisations have to ensure that they are properly maintained for effecting functioning. The main objectives of maintenance management are (Kumar & Suresh, 2008) to (a) minimise breakdowns and keep the equipment and machinery in good working condition to avoid unnecessary costs; (b) enable optimal capacity without interruptions; and (c) ensure the availability of facilities, machinery and equipment in good condition for other sections of the organisation.

7.11.1 Types of Maintenance

Organisations adopt different approaches to manage the maintenance programme of facilities, equipment and machinery to ensure they reach or exceed their design life. Three main maintenance programmes are (1) reactive or breakdown maintenance; (2) preventive maintenance; and (3) predictive maintenance (Kumar & Suresh, 2008).

1. **Reactive or breakdown maintenance**

    According to reactive or breakdown maintenance, no maintenance or repair is carried out until there is a breakdown or failure. Recent studies have shown that this is the predominant mode of maintenance.

2. **Preventive maintenance**

Equipment, facilities and machinery are maintained according to a time or machine-run-based schedule. The aim of preventive maintenance is to detect, prevent or reduce the degradation of components or systems to ensure the reliability and extension of the design life. Estimated savings of a preventive maintenance programme compared with a reactive maintenance programme are about 12–18%.

3. **Predictive maintenance**

Predictive maintenance aims to detect the onset of degradation mechanisms that cause the breakdown or failure of equipment, machinery or facilities. Elements that cause deterioration are detected before a failure occurs. Unlike preventive maintenance, predictive maintenance is need-based rather than time-based. Estimated savings are about 8–12% over a preventive maintenance programme and, depending on the facility, it can be as much as 30–40%.

The advantages and disadvantages of the three programmes are presented in Table 7.4.

Table 7.4 Advantages and Disadvantages of Maintenance Management Programmes

Programme	Advantages	Disadvantages
Reactive or Breakdown	• Low maintenance costs • Less staff for managing	• Unplanned downtime leading to higher costs • Increase in overtime • Higher costs for maintenance and repair • Inefficient utilisation of staff
Preventive	• Cost effective • Able to adjust the programme • Energy savings • Decrease incidence of equipment and machinery failure • Cost savings about 12%–18% over reactive maintenance programme	• Possibility of major failures or breakdowns • More staff needed • Includes unnecessary maintenance of some parts or machinery which can lead to incidental damage
Productive	• Increase in operational life/availability • Enables corrective action • Decrease in downtime, labour costs and costs of parts • Improved employee and environment safety • Energy savings • Cost savings about 12%–18% over preventive maintenance programme	• Requires expensive diagnostic equipment • Increase in the cost of staff training • Savings potential is not transparent to management

7.11.2 *Scientific Maintenance Management Programmes*

There are several scientific maintenance management programmes, and they are described briefly here (Kumar & Suresh, 2008):

Reliability-focused maintenance: It is based on the fact that equipment and operations and the degradation mechanisms of different equipment differ and financial resources have to be effectively managed. According to this programme inexpensive equipment and those that are unimportant to the facility are managed by a reactive maintenance approach.

Six Sigma maintenance: This programme focuses on reducing business process variation. The programme involves (a) defining benchmarks, availability and reliability; (b) failure of measurement techniques; (c) analysing and verifying data and drawing conclusions; (d) the creation of a model equipment and maintenance process, a total maintenance plan and schedule, and implementing the plan; and (e) monitoring the improvement programme.

Enterprise asset management: It is an information management system (IMS) that creates an integrated unit of all departments and disciplines. It monitors the utilisation of all physical assets (plant, equipment and facilities) that generate useful data at the point of performance for necessary action.

Lean maintenance: It focuses on the reliability of equipment and aims to reduce waste in maintenance such as over-production, waiting, transportation, process waste, inventory, waste motion and defects.

Computer-aided maintenance: It is a well-designed information system that captures a large volume of data about labour, finance and equipment. A properly designed computerised maintenance programme includes (a) development of a database; (b) analysis of previous records; (c) the creation of a maintenance schedule; (d) the availability of maintenance material; (e) a monitoring system; and (f) project management.

7.12 Management of Specifications

Specifications perform an essential function for producing goods and delivering services in a consistent manner in business organisations. It is defined (ISO, 1992) as "a collection of features and characteristics of a product or service that confer its ability to satisfy stated or implied needs". A specification for a food product includes two sensory elements: (a) objective sensory properties of a product (the collection of features) and (b) the subjective observation of the consumer (satisfaction of consumers' needs) (Carpenter et al., 2000). A specification for sensory attributes clearly identifies the essential sensory qualities of the product, which can be used as a basis for agreement between the supplier and the buyer. The quality attributes associated with sensory aspects are appearance (colour), organoleptic features, texture and size. A comprehensive specification includes many other attributes not related to sensory qualities.

There are several features of specifications (Swoffer, 2009):

■ A document that clearly specifies essential technical attributes or requirements for a product or process.
■ A contractual agreement between the supplier and the buyer that provides clarity and transparency to both parties.
■ A document that confirms understanding.
■ Provides protection and forms a part of the legal defence.

The design of specifications depends on the nature of the product and is stated in terms of buyers' and suppliers' requirements. Organisations develop specifications for raw materials, ingredients, chemicals, packaging, rework and finished products.

A specification should include but is not limited to (Swoffer, 2009):

■ Product details – name and size of the product.
■ Supplier information – name of location of the supplier and other contact information for the consumer.
■ Date of issue.
■ Food safety and legal requirements.
■ Labelling requirements.
■ Composition
■ Quality standards including packaging requirements.

7.12.1 Standards

1. Specifications may refer to external standards such as British Pharmacopoeia (BP), United States Pharmacopoeia (USP) and the Industry Codes of Practice, etc.
2. The supplier may create specifications for their own products such as glass bottles. Manufacturers of glass bottles maintain a comprehensive specification, including drawings and their performance, which can be used by the buyer.
3. An organisation may develop specifications for a product in consultation with the supplier. Cases for packaging are often custom-made to buyers' requirements using the expertise of the supplier about board type, dimensions and performance.
4. An organisation may develop specifications in-house, e.g. specifications for product labels are often custom-made.

7.12.2 Control of Specifications

■ Specifications must always be brief, but both accurate and explicit.
■ Organisations must ensure that the specifications used by the supplier are current and not obsolete.
■ The control of specifications generated according to customers' requirements should reflect the accuracy of information provided by the customer and ensure that quality can be achieved consistently.
■ The organisation should specify the review date and identities of signatories for preparing and checking the document on creation and review.

A sample specification for wine is shown in Form 7.1, and the packaging specification for wine is presented in Form 7.2.

Form 7.1 Packaging Specifications for Sparkling Wine

ABC COMPANY LIMITED

Specification no:...............	Date of Issue:
Product: Sparkling Wine	Pack size: 750 ml
Production volume: 9,000 Litres	Tank:

Wine release no:

Production location:..Work order No:

....

Product Code	Unit	Description	Inventory ID No:	Batch No.	Quantity issued	Quantity used	Cost
SW 001		Sparkling wine			9,000 Litres		
B 001	1	750 ml sparkling wine glass bottles			12,000		
C 001	1	Plastic corks			12,000		
M 001	1	2-post muselets			12,000		
S 001	1	Sparkling wine shrouds			12,000		
NL 001	1	Neck label			12,000		
BD 001	1	Body label			12,000		
BK 001	1	Back label			12,000		
SC 001	1/12	Sections			1,000		
CS 001	1/12	Cases			1,000		

Line Supervisor..........

Instructions:

1. Fill level.............
2. Carbonation:..............
3. Neck label position:.................
4. Body label position.......
5. Back label position................
6. See test methods for carbonation, cork depth, muselet application, shroud application and label application.
7. See palletising pattern for palletising.
8. Write the pallet number on a case at the bottom layer on all 4 sides.
9. Shrink wrap the pallet.
10. Write the pallet number on the warehouse docket.
11. Sampling: remove 2 samples from each line at start up and after every break.
12. See laboratory manual for finished goods inspection.

....

....

....

....

Prepared by   Checked by   Date

Form 7.2 Sample Specification Sheet for a Wine

Attribute	Description
Composition	Variety Region Vintage Available volume
Chemical analysis	pH Alcohol Reducing sugar Preservatives Total acidity
Certification	Export SWNZ
Physical properties	Cold stability Protein stability Racked Filtered Malolactic fermentation Oak

SWNZ: Sustainable Wine Growing New Zealand

7.13 Food Processing

In addition to maintaining quality during food processing operations, quality assurance and quality control activities should ensure food safety during processing. Food safety is assured through the implementation of Hazard Analysis and Critical Control Point (HACCP) principles (see Chapter 14). Organisations should also have operations for sanitation, pest control, waste management, maintaining the health and safety of workers, and a safe and hygienic work environment.

7.14 Environmental Concerns

Processing operations should also consider the impact that the operations have on the environment. Environmental monitoring describes the processes and activities that need to take place to monitor the impact of production activities on the environment. The factors to monitor include emissions during production and transportation, water and energy use, discharges, waste disposal, and noise and odour from the facility. A risk assessment should be carried out to determine the significance of the impact by evaluating the size of the impact and the likelihood of occurrence (Chapter Four).

7.15 Risk Assessment during Production

All manufacturing and service organisations have established and maintained procedures for managing risks. It involves the following activities:

- Assigning responsibility for managing risks.
- Defining risk criteria.
- Identification and communication of risks to stakeholders.
- Identification, implementation and management of actions to prevent or mitigate the identified risks.
- Acceptance of risks remaining after prevention and mitigation actions.
- Reviewing the risks.

An effective risk management programme (Brown, 2009):

- Adds value.
- Is an integral part of the organisation's procedures and decision-making process.
- Is a structured and systematic programme.
- Addresses uncertainty.
- Is tailored to meet the needs of the organisation and is based on available information.
- Considers human factors.
- Is responsive to change and capable of continual improvement.

Some of the risks to be considered in a production environment are as follows:

1. Spillages.
2. Inability of suppliers to produce and deliver supplies.
3. Floods, fire and earthquake.
4. Glass contamination in bottled products.
5. Microbial, physical and chemical contamination.
6. Equipment breakdown and lack of spare parts.
7. Failure of storage facility to maintain the storage temperature.
8. Cancellation of orders.
9. Sanitation failure and intrusion of pests.

7.16 Case Study: Bottling Operation of Sparkling Wine

West Winery Limited is a medium-sized winery producing about 2,500 cases of wine daily. Its peak bottling period is after June following the harvesting of grapes and wine-making. The winery cellar operations and other activities are included in a quality manual and its Quality Management System (QMS) and food safety programme have been certified to external standards. It has a stable, competent and skilled workforce. West Winery Limited has a major market share in sparkling and white wines. Recently, it has acquired a large order from Japan. Earlier in the year, it undertook a major overhaul of machinery and equipment, and the winery manager, Daniel Bonkovich, is confident that the winery can meet the increasing demand for sparkling and white wines.

Fully maintained cellar operations produce wine for bottling according to established specifications. Each year the management team evaluates and selects suppliers to be included in the approved suppliers list (ASL). Packaging, bottles, labels, corks and muselets are all purchased from approved suppliers. In-process controls are performed by the line staff under the supervision of a supervisor. Laboratory tests are conducted in the fully equipped laboratory. The sequence of operations is shown in Figure 7.4.

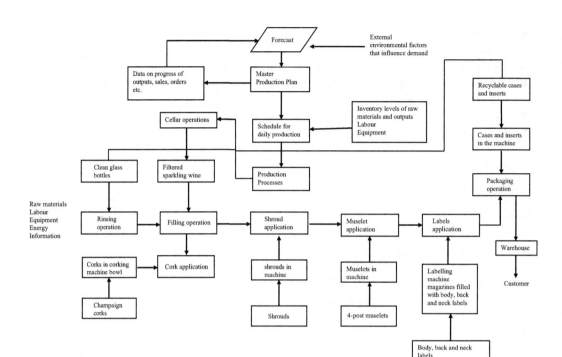

Figure 7.4   Sparkling wine production (packaging).

7.16.1 *Monitoring the Quality of Raw Materials*

Ingredients and packaging are visually examined, measured and tested or accepted on the basis of a Certificate of Quality (COQ) from the supplier. These requirements are specified in the test methods manual.

Bottles: Bottles arrive from the glass factory in pallet loads. On arrival, the inward goods person visually examines the stock for any breakages, torn plastic wrapping and dirty bottles. The pallet label is checked against the stock to confirm the identity and quantity. The reject sticker is applied to rejected stock to be returned to the supplier.

Corks, muselets and capsules: They are accepted on the basis of a COQ.

Labels: Random samples of body, back and neck labels are thoroughly examined for the accuracy and style of text and for their performance. They are measured to ensure that they meet the requirements in the specifications.

Cases: Random samples are measured and the consignment is accepted on the basis of measurements and the COQ.

Grapes: Representative samples are crushed and the juice is tested. Payment is based on the sugar content of the grapes.

7.16.2 *Monitoring the Food Safety Issues of Raw Materials*

Food safety issues relating to raw materials are physical, biological and chemical contamination according to the HACCP plan. The significance of these hazards in raw materials is discussed in Chapter 14.

7.16.3 Monitoring the Environmental Issues of Raw Materials

Materials received by the organisation for incoming inspection include some of the following documents (Culley, 1998), as applicable:.

- Results of Failure Mode and Effects Analysis (FMEA)
- Design of FMEA.
- Material Safety Data Sheets (MSDS).
- Packaging details.
- Labelling and product information.
- Use of ozone-depleting substances (ODSs)
- Physical and chemical characteristics.
- Other hazard warning requirements.
- Material testing and data reports.
- Recyclable nature of material.

7.16.4 The Process

The bottling process goes through the following steps:

1. The supervisor examines the inward goods received for production for accuracy against the specification sheet for production given by the Quality Control Officer.
2. The filler is sterilised and filtered wine that meets the specifications (chemical and organo-leptic tests) and is pumped to the filler (control 1).
3. Bottle rinsing (control 2).
4. Filling operation commences (control 3, 4, 5).
5. Corking operation (control 6).
6. Muselet application (control 7).
7. Capsule application (control 8).
8. Label application (control 9).
9. Packaging (control 10).
10. Finished goods on pallets destined to the warehouse (control 11).
11. Final release (control 12).

7.16.5 Control Operations

7.16.5.1 Control Operations for Quality

The control operations, tests and specifications for monitoring quality are presented in Table 7.5.

7.16.5.2 Control Operations for Food Safety

Control operations for monitoring food safety are based on control methods and the Critical Control Points (CCPs) specified in the HACCP plan.

7.16.5.3 Control Operations for Monitoring the Environmental Impact of Processing

The Environment Manager must monitor chemicals and materials waste, the waste water discharged, emissions to air, water and energy usage, and recyclable material used in processing.

Table 7.5   Example of In-process Controls for Sparkling Wine Production

Test Method No.	Operation	Test Method	Description	Samples	Limits	Frequency of Checks
1	Wine release for bottling	Organoleptic and chemical tests	Check wine from the filler before filling commences	Sample from the filler	Complies with specifications	Before commencing filling
2	Bottle rinsing	Temperature of bottle rinsing water	Measure the temperature with a calibrated gauge	From the rinser	Complies with specified temperature	At start up
3	Filling	Carbonation volume (use Zahm carbonation tester)	Measure the carbonation	2 from the filler	… – … gas volumes	Hourly
4	Filling	Fill volume	Measure the fill height using the gauge	5	750 – … mL	Two hourly
5	Corking	Cork depth	Measure the cork depth using the ruler	5	… – … mm from the top	Two hourly
6	Muselet application	Muselet application (visual)	Correct application	5	Tucked under all round	Hourly

(Continued)

Table 7.5 (*Continued*)   Example of In-process Controls for Sparkling Wine Production

Test Method No.	Operation	Test Method	Description	Samples	Limits	Frequency of Checks
7	Shroud application	Shroud application (visual)	Correct application	5	See reference sample	Two hourly
8	Labelling	Glue coverage (remove a label and look for glue coverage)	Measures glue coverage of labels	3	Complete coverage with no bubbles	Hourly
9	Labelling	Label height	Measure the label position and application (absence of wrinkles or bubbles)	3	See reference sample	Hourly
10	Insertion of section and packaging	Label damage (open two cases and examine all bottles in the case)	Evaluate label damage due to wrong insertion of the section	2	No label damage	Hourly
11	Finished products	Microbiological contamination	Microbiological test procedure	2	No growth	At start up and after every break

7.16.6 Assessment of Risk

See Section 7.15.

7.16.7 Records

1. Wine release for bottling.
2. Bottle rinsing.
3. Fill chart.
4. Bottle breakage chart.
5. Corking, muselet and capsule inspection chart.
6. Label application.
7. Packaging checks.
8. Final release record.
9. Machine stoppages.
10. Labour record.
11. Production figures.
12. Reject stock record.

References

ASQ. (n.d.). *Quality Glossary – V*. Retrieved May 17, 2018 from http://asq.org/glossary/v.html.

Brown, D.J. (2009). *ISO 13485 and risk analysis: Why does risk analysis matter?* Paper presented to ASQ Fox Valley Section 1208 on behalf of Eagle Registrations, Carol Stream, Illinois.

Carpenter, R.P., Lyon, D.H. and Hasdell, T.A. (2000). *Guidelines for Sensory Analysis in Food Product Development and Quality Control* (2nd ed.). Gaithersburg: Aspen Publishers.

Culley, W.C. (1998). *Environmental and Quality Systems Integration*. Florida: Lewis Publishers.

Dalal, J. (2011). Production management or production planning, controlling and scheduling. *Introduction to production planning*. Retrieved May 18, 2018 from http://www.slideshare.net/jasmindalal/introduction-to-production-planning-by-jasmin-dalal.

Duchessi, P. and O'Keefe, R. (1990). Knowledge-based approach to production planning. *Journal of the Operational Research Society*, 41 (5), 377–390.

International Organisation for Standards. (1992). *Sensory analysis vocabulary*. ISO 5492.

Kumar, A.J. and Suresh, N. (2008). *Production and Operations Management* (2nd ed.). India: New Age International Publishers.

Mapes, J. (1992). Managing a production department. In D.M. Stewart (Ed.), *Handbook of Management Skills* (2nd ed.), pp. 305–317. England: Gower Publishing.

Schmenner, R.W. (1986 Spring). How can service businesses survive and proper? *Sloan Management Review*, 27 (3), 21–32.

Stevenson, W.J. (2012). *Operations Management: Theory and Practice* (11th ed.). New York: McGraw-Hill.

Swoffer, K. (2009, December). *FSKN 7 – Specifications*. Paper presented at Coca Cola Conference, Shanghai, China.

Chapter 8

New Product Development

8.1 Introduction

With the globalisation of the world economy, companies are facing intense competition. Advances in technology enable consumers to obtain accurate information on products and services at the touch of a button. Therefore, consumers have become more knowledgeable, and consumer markets have become more difficult to satisfy and more susceptible to change. The key to staying in business in the 21st century in an ever-changing economic environment is to offer product quality, competitive cost, rapid delivery and flexibility. Although the innovative approach to the development of an enterprise can enhance flexibility and improve product quality, it can be time-consuming and uneconomical. Consumers demand new products that will meet their needs. Organisations looking for quick profits can implement a fast innovation approach, which can have undesirable impact on the innovation process. However, successful innovators focus on (Barclay et al., 2000):

- Developing a strategic plan with new product development (NPD) as a key element.
- Striving to reduce the time to market and improve a "right first time" approach.
- Creating high-quality team leaders and providing essential training.
- Preparing product development guides and procedures.
- Applying performance measures to product development activities.
- Integrating post-development reviews as a part of product development.
- Developing a thorough understanding of the NPD process.

8.2 Definitions

8.2.1 New Product Development

NPD is a process that is designed to develop, test and consider the viability of new or changed market offerings over time in order to ensure the growth and survival of the organisation. The activities include the generation of market opportunities, their selection and conversion into manufactured products and/or activities offered to customers, as well as providing improvements in NPD activities themselves (Loch & Kavadias, 2008).

8.2.2 Innovation

Innovation is the process of transforming an idea or invention into a product or service that adds value or for which the customer will pay. The idea must be capable of being produced at an economical cost and must satisfy the specific needs of customers. It involves the application of information, imagination and initiative in delivering a better product or a product with different values. Often in the business sector, innovation results when new ideas are applied to further satisfy the needs and expectations of customers. Innovation facilitates alliance creation, joint-venturing and the creation of buyers' purchasing power (Business Dictionary, n.d.). There are two broad categories of innovation:

■ Evolutionary innovation: Continuous or dynamic innovation made possible by several incremental advances in technology or processes.
■ Revolutionary innovation: Discontinuous innovation, which is often disruptive and new. For example, in the 2000s cathode ray tube (CRT) TVs were replaced with improved image quality LCD screens.

Organisations take greater risk when they innovate revolutionary products because they create new markets. However, organisations that copy and produce an imitation product take less risk. Such imitation products are freely available in the Asian market.

Two important elements in the innovation field are skills and decision-making in uncertain conditions. Skills help identify market opportunities, create environments for innovative solutions and organise innovation processes. The latter involves implementing actions of unique solutions that have not been tried before and this can bring surprising results (Chwastyk & Kolosowski, 2014).

8.2.3 Design

The design is the transformation of a concept or idea into a configuration, drawing, model, mould, pattern, plan or specification which helps achieve the product's design objective. It is a unique solution to a problem (Business Dictionary, n.d.).

8.3 Reasons and Uses of New Products

Creating new products is not a luxury. It is necessity arising out of the need to change to meet the challenges of the economic environment, competition, technological advances and increasing consumer demands. Therefore, new products are needed for (Fripp, n.d.; Jaideep, n.d.):

■ Growth and development.
■ Marketing environment changes.
■ Embracing new technology.
■ Maintaining or increasing the market share and maintaining competitive advantage.
■ Variety as consumer needs and wants change.
■ Replacing mature products.
■ Replacing end of life-cycle products.
■ Diversification of risk.

Organisations take advantage of new products for:

- Improving or defending the market share by offering greater choice or upgrading tired products.
- Appealing and diversifying into new market segments.
- Improving relationships with distributors.
- Maintaining the reputation of the organisation as a leading edge company.
- Maintaining uniformity in demand.
- Making better use of the organisation's resources.

8.4 Difference between Production and Product Development

Most managers who are production oriented in their role in product development struggle to complete projects on time and within budget. Allocated resources are often insufficient and they demand predictable schedules and deliveries from their development team. Teams are pushed to be frugal, to create detailed plans and to minimise schedule variations and waste. A new approach is required to manage product development (Thomke & Reinertsen, 2012).

In production, the activities are often repetitive, predictable and the created items can be in only one place at a time. In contrast, product development activities are unique and constantly change and the output can reside in more than one place.

8.5 New Product Categories

There have been several classifications of new products, but often the various categories are not clearly demarcated. These various categories are defined on the basis of the market the product is entering into, whether the product is new or existing, and the level of product innovation. Only 10% of all new products are truly innovative. Greater risk is involved in developing such products, and they are new both to the company and the market. In 70% of cases new products involve changes within the current product lines of a firm, and in 30% of the cases new products are new to the firm as well (Wang & Lee, 2011; Trott, 2010). Table 8.1 illustrates a profile of new products (Saxena, 2008).

Table 8.1   Profile of New Products

Type of New Product	% of Each Category	
Breakthrough	10	New to the organisation (30%)
New product lines	20	
Extensions to product lines	26	Changes to existing product lines (70%)
Product modification	26	
Repositioning	11	
Cost reduction	7	

1. New to the world products. These are innovative products, e.g. high definition TV, iPod, flat screen TV, etc. They are breakthrough products that represent a small proportion of new products and they are the first of their kind. Often, a new discovery or manipulation of existing technology in a different way leading to a new design involves breakthrough products.
2. New product lines (new to the firm): These products, which target an existing market, are new to the company. They enter an established market for the first time. For example, Sony-Erikson, Alcatel and Samsung have all entered the mobile phone market to compete with market leaders like Motorola.
3. Additions to existing product lines: The company already has a line of products in this market. In this category, the company introduces a new item that is sufficiently different from the present offering, but it is not truly a new item. For example, Hewlett Packard introduced the colour inkjet printer, which was an addition to their established line of black and white inkjet printers.
4. Improvements of revisions to existing products: Products in this category are replacements of existing products in a firm's product line. Laptops are being replaced with newer versions with extra features, and with each revision, performance and reliability have been improved. In the process of revision or modification, cost reductions are also possible, providing added value. A good proportion of new products fall into this category.
5. Cost reductions: From a marketing perspective, these are not new products. They do not offer anything new other than reduced cost, but from a manufacturing perspective, they are significant because they offer similar performance at a lower cost to the customer. Cost reductions are achieved through improved manufacturing processes, cheap labour, use of different and/or cost-effective materials, or reducing the number of moving parts. Products in this category bring greater financial returns. The distinction between the products in this category and improved or revised products is that cost reduction may not achieve product improvement. The Dell Computer Corporation used improved technology to lower manufacturing and administrative costs and offered computers at a lower price than those of its competitors. The banking sector has reduced the cost of serving customers by introducing automated teller machines (ATMs), toll-free call centres and the web.
6. Repositioning: Repositioned products are created from the discovery of applications for existing products. Consumer perception and branding are important elements in repositioned products. Napisan was originally introduced in 1980s as a sterilising agent for diapers. However, when disposable nappies were introduced into the market, the product was repositioned as a sanitising agent and a detergent. Similarly, Kellogg's cereal was repositioned as a snack bar.

8.6 Case Study

In the 1980s and the early 1990s, Montana Wines Limited in New Zealand was the largest winery with wineries in four other regions. Its success was due to their innovative approach in developing new products. They were leaders in premium wines, coolers and on-tap wines.

In order to revamp the whole range of premium wine lines, the CEO appointed a well-known label designer from Italy and he redesigned the entire range. In other areas too there were problems. Wine bags with taps were leaking, causing storage problems in warehouses. At the lower end of the market, there was nothing to compete with "coolers" – a mildly sparkling, low alcohol sweet wine which was very popular amongst the young generation.

Although the quality of the premium wines received accolades, the presentation was very disappointing. A fair proportion of the products displayed in shelves had labels that were torn, damaged or scuffed. At the monthly meeting, the marketing and the sales team expressed their dissatisfaction with the presentation and demanded a quick resolution. As Corporate Quality Assurance Manager, I was involved with a team of production specialists to lead the project.

a. **New product**

The problem of torn and damaged labels was a factor that was affecting the sales of premium wines. Label damage had occurred while inserting the labelled bottles between the sections in the box. Our team carried out a number of trials led by the box supplier, and our suggestion to make the dividers in the sections movable in the box was taken up by the supplier. Eventually they developed an improved version of sections, the dividers of which could move when the bottles were inserted into the box. On our part we developed a technique to properly insert the bottles.

The scuffing problem was yet to be solved. Our quality assurance (QA) team formed an alliance with the label printer and the Technical Manager of Panprint, the sole supplier of labels to Montana Wines Limited, led the project. Panprint examined the damaged and scuffed labels and it was soon realised that a protective coating was necessary. Our team carried out the trials on coated labels, which included rigorous transport trials. The supplier produced a new coating which resisted even the most rigorous transport conditions.

Following these changes, the problem of label damage completely disappeared.

b. **New product line**

In the 1980s, a cooler market was growing. Winemakers were given the responsibility to come up with a new cooler that could successfully compete with the existing product. In collaboration with the Food Research Institute in Auckland, a number of formulations were tested by an expert panel. The most successful product was labelled MIAMI. It was an instant hit and at the time MIAMI become the best cooler on the market.

c. **Product improvement**

Twenty litre wine bags with taps were very popular in the South Island in New Zealand. However, disaster struck when they were transported to Christchurch as bags started to leak causing enormous problems in the warehouse. The QA team was dispatched to Christchurch to study the problem. The team examined the bags and located the positions where leaking had occurred and a pattern started to emerge. The bags were taken to the production plant in Auckland where engineers thoroughly examined the damaged positions. The automatic filling machine was designed to fill 3 l and 4 l bags and not 20 l bags. The engineers were able to locate the places in the machine where the damage occurred. Modifications to the machine eliminated the problem altogether.

8.7 Innovations and Risk

New products on the level of innovations can be classified into three types (Wang & Lee, 2011):

1. Highly innovative products: These include new to the world products and new to the company product lines. Highly innovative products yield great rewards for companies and are evaluated on financial criteria such as sales volume, profit objective and sales objectives. They carry the greatest risk for the company.

2. Moderately innovative products: These consist of products new to the firm, but not to the world, and improvement items in existing product lines. These are assessed on sales objectives, profit objectives and internal rate of return. A moderate risk is involved with products in this category.
3. Low innovative products: These include all product modifications, repositioned products and cost reduction items. They are evaluated on sales volume, profit objectives and marginal rate. These products carry the lowest risk to the firm.

8.8 New Product Development Strategy

The NPD strategy provides a unifying direction and serves as a road map for product development activities. The strategy specifies the areas to be focused on and those that should be avoided. It also adds other areas appropriate and relevant to the firm to be explored (Crawford, 1972). A company product strategy serves as a guide for decisions and actions relating to NPD activities, such as the development of new products, entering into new markets, improving or deleting existing product lines, taking risks, etc. (Karol & Nelson, 2007).

To be successful, a product development strategy must be aligned with the business context. Different business contexts need different product development styles. A best match between the business context and the product development style allows opportunities to develop and thrive and mature opportunities to be managed to produce the best value for the company. On the other hand, a mismatch between the approaches and business context can generate threats for the very viability of the company (MacCormack, Crandall, Henderson & Toft, 2012).

Therefore, careful consideration must be given to the development of a strategy statement. A good product development strategy will help avoid (Queensland Government, 2014) overrating and misjudging the target market, launching a poorly designed product that does not meet customers' requirements, over-committing resources, subjecting the business to risks and threats from unexpected competition, and incorrectly pricing new products.

Companies have adopted different product development strategies, depending on the business context, and some of the approaches are presented in Table 8.2.

For over 160 years, Corning in the United States has been a leading innovator. Their inventions include a manufacturing process for the mass production of light bulbs, cellular ceramic substrates for catalytic converters, glass optical fibres for telecommunication applications and liquid crystal display glass for consumer electronic goods. Corning's growth was due to the optical fibre industry, and in 2001 after the global economic crisis, the demand for the product plummeted. Correspondingly, sales decreased by $1 billion in 2001 and $3 billion in 2002. The share process dropped from $130 to $1.20 per share. However, Corning survived and its success was due to a strategy focused on consolidating and strengthening R&D, assessing its core competencies, improving and expanding innovation processes, and developing an innovation plan to help identify new opportunities for growth (Miller, 2011). Drawing on Corning's experience, Cooper and Edgett (2010) presented a plan to develop an NPD strategy:

8.8.1 New Product Development Strategy Plan

8.8.1.1 Step 1 – Establish Goals and Objectives

The first step in developing an NPD strategy is to establish clear goals for the company's product innovation efforts, which must align with the broad business goals of the organisation. The most

Table 8.2   New Product Development Approaches

References	*Approach*
MacCormack et al. (2012)	Define the business context Select appropriate development style Define and implement the style Monitor and review
Wang and Lee (2011)	Highly innovative Moderately innovative Low innovative
Karol and Nelson (2007)	Assess the market Market direction Assess competition Compare the market with portfolios
Crawford (1972)	Technology Market mix Market width and competitive situation Degree of innovation and R&D commitment Price/quality ranges, pay back conditions and promotional requirements, minimum sales Internal and external facilitation Product, patent and speed requirements Product service mix Risk assessment
Queensland Government (2014)	Define the product Identify market requirements Establish the time frame Identify key issues and approaches
Cooper and Edgett (2010)	Establish business goals and objectives Define focus arenas and R&D effort Evaluate arenas Develop an entry strategy Define spending conditions Create the roadmap

commonly used objective is the contribution to the annual revenue from the sale of new products. Another metric sometimes used is sales revenue from products launched only in order to ignore the revenue from replacements and extensions. The team must be made aware of the role of new products in realising business goals.

8.8.1.2 Step 2 – Identify Arenas to Focus on and the R&D Effort

The product development strategy clearly specifies the markets the company intends to enter and those that are of no interest to it anymore. Strategic arenas include the markets, industry sectors, applications, product types and technologies on which the company intends to focus its NPD efforts. In-bound and out-bound limits are established through identifying and assessing innovation opportunities at the strategic level. In this way, possible arenas that offer opportunities are identified.

Companies use a product-market matrix to identify new opportunities for NPD (IES Development Institute, n.d.). Such a matrix is shown in Figure 8.1. Each cell is assessed on the basis of its potential value to the growth of company's business. For example:

- The company is the market leader in the homes sector in TVs and DVDs and in the universities sector in telephones.
- It is one of the leaders in supplying DVDs to offices and telephones to homes.
- The company follows the market leader in the offices sector in TVs, in the homes sector in microwaves and in the schools sector in supplying telephones.
- It plays a minor role in supplying DVDs to universities and telephones to offices.
- It has no presence in the microwave market in universities or offices, the DVD market in schools and the TV market in universities.

Therefore, to penetrate large markets possible growth areas are TVs and DVDs in offices and homes, telephones in offices and the microwave market in homes.

8.8.1.3 Step 3 – Evaluate the Arenas

Potential arenas are evaluated in two dimensions: (a) arena attractiveness and (b) business strategy strength.

a. Arena attractiveness: This is a measure based on the size and growth of the market, and technological advancements of the arena or the location of the arena in the technology S curve.
b. Business strength: This is measured in three dimensions: technological leverage, marketing leverage and competitive advantage.

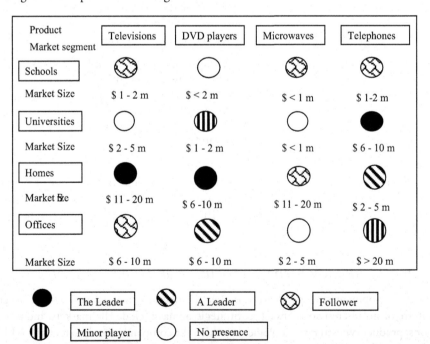

Figure 8.1   Product-Market matrix.

Table 8.3 Criteria for Evaluating Strategic Arenas

Arena Attractiveness		Business Strength		
Market	Technological Opportunities	Technology Utilisation	Marketing Utilisation	Competitive Advantage
Strength Growth rate Intensity and the strength of competition Margins of competitors	Technological advancement Location on the S curve	Ability to utilise development skills Production capability	Ability to utilise sales force and/or distribution channels Ability to utilise customer relationships Ability to utilise marketing skills	Uniqueness of new products Advantages over competitor's products

Table 8.3 presents the criteria for evaluating strategic arenas (Cooper, 2008). This is essentially a strategic map that facilitates idea generation, the funding of specific projects and a focus on R&D efforts.

8.8.1.4 Step 4 – Develop Competitive and Entry Strategies

Competitive and entry strategies may include (a) becoming the industry leader in innovation; (b) being the first in the market with new products; (c) following the competition with improved competitive products; (d) offering low cost products as a differentiator; and (e) taking advantage of strengths, core competencies and product attributes. Competitive strategies might also consider global markets. If the company intends to enter new arenas, strategies such as joint-venturing, partnering, seeking alliances or open innovation must be defined for more productive NPD. Key factors for selecting competitive strategies are the knowledge of the businesses' core competencies and drivers that are essential to succeed in industry.

8.8.1.5 Step 5 – Implement Decisions, Allocate Funds, Establish Priorities and Strategic Buckets

In order to align NPD strategy with the business strategy, funds are allocated to the right areas and the right strategic projects through portfolio management. As a result, there is a right balance between strong portfolios containing high-value projects with a few low-value projects. The strategic bucket method is used to help in resource allocation decisions. These decisions define how the funds are allocated based on project type, market geography and product area (Cooper & Edgett, 2010).

8.9 New Product Development Process

In 1999, Marc Benioff co-founded SalesForce.com, which started from an idea to become a billion-dollar company revolutionising the cloud computer industry. Since then SalesForce.com has been recognised as an industry leader in cloud computing. In 2008, it received the prestigious *Wall Street Journal* Technology Innovation award and was one of *Business Week*'s Top 100 Most

Innovative Companies (2006). It was also No. 7 on the *Wired 40* list (2007). The success was due to the courage to pursue innovations before it is obvious to the market, investing in the long term with a robust prototype, following market leaders who are close to customers and reusing technology in novel ways (Benioff & Adler, 2009).

NPD is an iterative process that begins with idea generation and ends with a new product available for purchase, and it differs from the further development of an existing product. Product development strategy and product complexity have a significant impact on the NPD process. Companies that have been successful in product development have transformed the development process from a process-based approach to an information-based one. In a process-based approach timelines and design review gates are important for decision-making, while the latter responds to information throughout the development stages (Jauregui-Becker & Wits, 2013). There are several models of NPD, and a summary of these models is presented in Table 8.4 (Trott, 2010). The linear NPD model and Stage-Gate model are described here.

8.9.1 Linear NPD Model

The NPD planning and systematic customer-driven product development process is crucial for NPD. In general, an NPD process has eight steps (Kotler & Armstrong. 2012) as illustrated in Figure 8.2.

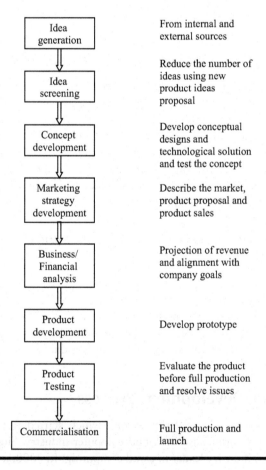

Figure 8.2 NPD process.

Table 8.4   Models of NPD

Model	Description	Comments
Departmental stage	Based on the linear model of innovation. Each department is responsible for specified tasks. Project is passed from department to department	Involves much reworking and consultation between functions. Marketing provides input continuously. Control of project changes according to the stage of the project
Activity stage	Activities take place concurrently using cross-functional approach. Focuses attention on the whole project. Need for management philosophy to change from a functional to a project orientation	High technology businesses with specialised knowledge are more difficult to manage. Requires project teams
Stage-Gate	Has several time-sequenced stages with decision gate at each stage. The framework includes work flow and decision flow paths. Also includes supporting systems and practices for smooth operation	The process is sequential and tends to be slow. Focus is on gates rather than on customer's needs. Product concept can be stopped prematurely. Not suitable for projects with high uncertainty. May lead to poor decisions at the gates due to insufficient knowledge
Cross functional	Has a dedicated project team from all functional departments. Emphasises project management and interdisciplinary approach	Improved communication amongst functional groups. Avoids passing of the project back and forth between various functions. Reduces changes to the project because of team approach
Decision stage	Progress of the project depends on a series of decisions	Facilitates iteration through feedback. Emphasises interaction among the functions.
Conversion process	Conversion of inputs into outputs. Inputs are technical requirements, customers' needs and feasibility of manufacturing. Output is the product	Lack of details at various stages is a limitation
Response	Uses behaviour approach to analyse change. Focuses on an individual's or organisation's response to a new product proposal	Reveals factors that influence the decision to accept or reject a proposal especially at the screening stage
Network	Most recent model. Acquires information from a variety of inputs to gather knowledge as the project passes from stage to stage	Emphasises external and internal activities that contribute towards successful NPD. External linkages provide additional knowledge to improve the NPD process

8.9.1.1 Step 1 – Idea Generation

Ideas for new products can originate from staff at many levels in the organisation. A company generates a large number of ideas to identify a good one. The sources include internal sources and external sources such as customers, competitors, distributors, suppliers and others.

8.9.1.1.1 Internal Sources

Major internal idea-generating sources originate from employees and customers. New ideas also originate through the R&D process. Successful companies encourage employees to come up with new ideas for which they get rewarded. Breakthrough products are the result of scientific research in the improvement of products and processes. Another internal idea source is top managers. However, they can be a valuable source or a disruptive influence. The usefulness of such ideas has a limitation if the supporting data, primary customer feedback, and due diligence are ignored and glossed over by top managers exercising executive privilege (Annacchino, 2003; Kotler & Armstrong. 2012; Pahwa, 2018).

8.9.1.1.2 External Sources

Direct customer surveys: These are valuable sources to engage customers, solicit feedback and obtain information in a systematic manner.

Forced group discussions: These are discussions for generating ideas involving several individuals.

Suggestions from customers: This method involves discussions with customers and users to obtain unsolicited ideas and suggestions.

Customer complaints: Often customer complaints are frowned upon as source of new ideas. But successful companies listen to customers and address the issues quickly through correction and product implementation.

Competitors: They provide useful information on market activities and how your products measure against the competition.

Company dealers and representatives: Although the sales representatives bring customer feedback ideas and ideas of their own for new products, they should be evaluated carefully. Sales staff are driven by sales orders and their suggestions can be biased towards their own advantage.

Miscellaneous sources: Inventions, patents, government licensing offices, individual consultations, marketing research companies and industry sector journals can also provide ideas for product development.

8.9.1.2 Step 2 – Idea Screening

The purpose of the idea screening stage is to reduce the number of ideas by promoting good ones and eliminating bad ones as soon as possible. The new product idea proposal describes the product or the service, the proposed customer value proposition, the target market, competition, market size, product price, development time, cost of development and production, and the rate of return. The proposal is evaluated by the NPD team.

Another approach used for screening is called R-W-W (real, win, worth doing). It is based on the assessment of the real need for the product, competitive advantage (win), the resources required, alignment with the company product strategy (worth doing) and potential profit (Kotler & Armstrong. 2012).

8.9.1.3 Step 3 – Concept Development and Testing

The product concept is the result of transforming the idea into a product that consumers can perceive. It is different from product idea and product image. The former is an idea for a potential product that the company can offer to consumers. Product image is the way a consumer perceives the product in the market.

During the concept development stage, customer needs and target specifications are converted into a set of conceptual designs and technological solutions that can be presented to consumers. They describe approximate form, working principles and product features. Often the designs are supplemented with industrial design models and experimental prototypes.

The purpose of concept testing is to determine whether the consumer needs or wants the product or service. It is presented to groups of consumers to evaluate their attitudes and buying intentions. The concept may be in the form of text or pictures. However, a physical presentation will enhance the reliability of the concept test. If a physical form has not been presented, consumers may not be able to understand the concept and express any opinion. The answers to the following questions will provide information on attributes and benefits that customers feel are important:

1. Would you buy the product?
2. Would you replace the current product with the new product?
3. Would this product meet your real needs?

8.9.1.4 Step 4 – Marketing Strategy Development

Marketing strategy development includes the development of a three-part strategy plan:

Part 1: Describes the market size, structure and behaviour, planned positioning, estimated sales, market share and profit goals for the next few years.
Part 2: Defines the planned product price, distribution strategy and the marketing budget for the first year.
Part 3: Describes the long-run sales and profit goals and marketing mix strategy.

8.9.1.5 Step 5 – Business and Financial Analysis

Business and financial analysis is a projection of revenue in terms of the sales and profits generated by the new product to determine whether they meet the company's financial objectives. The analysis includes the estimation of selling price based on competition and customer feedback, sales volume based upon the size of the market, and profitability and breakeven point.

8.9.1.6 Step 6 – Product Development

The product development phase is the most complex stage of the product development process. The object is to develop a product based on the specifications and development plans approved at the business and financial analysis stage. This stage calls for a major injection of capital to develop software, hardware, tooling, packaging and prototypes. Output during this stage includes:

- Complete design review and resolution of issues.
- Hardware and software development.

- Manufacturing processes and test methods.
- One or more prototypes to reduce technical and market risks.
- Technical documents.
- Packaging design.
- Business plan and marketing/product introduction plan.
- Final cost estimates.

Products undergo rigorous tests to ensure safety, reliability and effectiveness so that consumers find value in them.

8.9.1.7 Step 7 – Product Testing

This stage involves the introduction of the new product and its proposed marketing programme in a real marketing setting. The object is to evaluate the product before going to full production. It gives the opportunity to test the product itself and the entire marketing programme including targeting and positioning strategy, advertising, distribution, pricing, branding, packaging and brand levels. Outcomes at this stage are pilot manufacturing, validation of the manufacturing process, completion of tests, assessment of product against specifications and previously defined criteria, and updated marketing introduction launch plan. An alternative to extensive and costly test marketing is testing under controlled or simulated conditions. In controlled tests, the product is tested amongst a controlled group of customers or stores. In simulated test marketing, researchers measure responses to new products and marketing in a simulated marketing environment such as malls, supermarkets, etc.

8.9.1.8 Step 8 – Commercialisation

The final stage of the NPD process involves the full release of the product. It includes production, implementing marketing and launch plans, distribution and support. The company must decide when and where to launch and be aware that competitors may also be in a position to release their new products.

Part of the final stage is post-launch activities, which must take place three to six months following the initial release of the product. At the post-launch review, the NPD team evaluates the overall product performance, product-related issues, possible product enhancements, the NPD process, in general, and any recommendations for corrective action.

8.9.2 Stage-Gate Process

The Stage-Gate process is an operational plan to develop new products from the initial concept to production leading to post-launch activities. It is a management process to improve the efficiency and effectiveness of the NPD process. A series of stages and gates are the key elements of the Stage-Gate process. Various stages define the work to be undertaken, provide the necessary information, and analyse and integrate the data. At each gate Go/Kill decisions are made on the future of the project (Cooper, 2008). The Stage-Gate system is illustrated in Figure 8.3.

8.9.2.1 Stages

The Stage-Gate process has five stages: scoping, business case, development, testing and validation and product launch. The discovery stage precedes Stage 1 and the post-launch review follows Stage 5 (launch). The following are the features of the various stages:

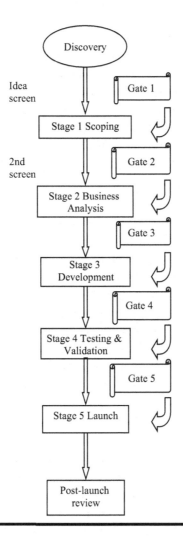

Figure 8.3   Stage-Gate process.

- At each stage, information is gathered to reduce uncertainties and risks and defines the purpose of each stage in the process.
- The cost increases in incremental stages and uncertainties are reduced to manage the risks involved.
- Activities are performed concurrently by functional department.
- The stages are cross-functional and at each stage, marketing, production, R&D and engineering provide a team effort.

8.9.2.2 The Gates

The gates are Go/Kill decision points. Each gate consists of (a) deliverables, which are the output of the previous gate defined by agreed output standards; (b) criteria against which the NPD product is assessed, including those that must be met and should be met; and (c) outputs, which define the Go/Kill/Hold/Recycle decision and an action plan for the next stage (timeline, resources and deliverables).

8.10 Product Service Model for NPD

Traditionally, product development centres on value creation through production, sales and delivery with limited technical support and short- or medium-term warranty. Competition is no longer restricted to product differentiation. There is a radical shift of competition to product-service differentiation. Customers demand the total package of product and service. A classic example is a wireless broadband service. Users select the service provider on the basis of product offerings, as well as on the ability to quickly resolve common issues with the service. Therefore, competitors who offer an integrated product-service package are at a distinct advantage (Marques et al., 2013).

In the product service model proposed by Marques et al. (2013), product development activities of idea generation, planning, concept development, prototype testing and implementation are integrated with service development activities of the identification of needs, feasibility analysis, concept development, modelling, realisation plan and testing. The proposed model includes four phases: organisational preparedness, planning, design and post-processing.

8.10.1 Organisational Preparedness

A set of prerequisites has to be established to provide solutions to customers which include the offer of service. In order to provide the necessary service, changes are necessary in planning, design and integrating the product-service process. The output of this phase is a review of current design processes, the implementation plan for design service, and organisational and modular processes.

8.10.2 Planning

The planning stage involves the identification of new customers' ideas and customer/market requirements. Ideas for the new product-service model are developed on the basis of external and internal inputs. Internal inputs originate from the company's strategy to validate the product position in the portfolio. External inputs result from customers' needs and expectations identified by analysing the external environment. It is important to develop and evaluate ideas against the expectations and goals of customers. Both product and service requirements have to be integrated in the development of the product-service mode.

8.10.3 Design

The design phase of the integrated product-service model refers to the integrated management of product and service elements. From a product perspective, the design phase involves concept development and the completion of preliminary and detailed design. A prototype is created based on detailed specifications of each component and the product itself, the raw materials to be used and the suppliers. The service aspect of the design phase includes both physical and non-physical properties of the service element. Physical properties are documents describing the designed service and guidelines and checklists for follow-up service. A non-physical property is the provision of training for staff to provide the service to customers. The prototype, which includes both product and service components, is tested with key customers to receive feedback for further enhancement or improvement of product and/or service.

8.10.4 Post-processing

The post-processing phase includes full production according to established specifications and design features, product commercialisation, validation and documentation. Product installation on the customer's site, providing documents relating to safe operation, and recording all activities are the service elements in the post-processing phase. Technological aspects of service are also considered in order to ensure the complete integration of service elements amongst the manufacturers, customers and service providers. If a third party is involved in the provision of service further education and training are necessary to deliver an efficient service. Changes may also be needed to configure and adapt to the environment where the service is provided.

8.11 Design Mix and Characteristics of Good Design

The three features of design mix are functional design, aesthetics and economy of manufacture (tutor2u, 2015):

1. Functional design is concerned with performance and reliability.
2. Aesthetics is concerned with the way appeals to the customer and their subjective judgement.
3. Economy of manufacture is concerned with production efficiency and cost-effectiveness.

The criteria of good design (Chary, 2007) are:

■ Functionality: how well a product functions.
■ Compliance: conformance to set specifications, standards or customer requirements.
■ Features: the number of secondary features in addition to basic functions.
■ Aesthetics: attractiveness.
■ Reliability: performance over a given period.
■ Durability: lifespan of the product.
■ Serviceability: ease of maintenance.
■ Safety: safety in use and during disposal.
■ User-friendly: ease of operation.
■ Customisability: ability to modify.
■ Environmentally friendly: impact on the environment.

8.12 Factors Influencing NPD

In NPD, organisations generally focus on the various stages of the NPD process. However, the preparation for NPD and follow-up after the introduction of the new product are also crucial for the success of the project. Three factors influence the speed and efficiency of the process: (a) organisation structure; (b) leadership; and (c) teamwork (Mayo, 2014).

8.12.1 Organisational Structure

The organisational structure affects the efficiency, autonomy and coordination of various functions in NPD. The structure must ensure direction and guidance, promote internal and external communication, decision-making at lower levels and material flow. It allows more time for planning, leading to competitive advantage and reduction of costs because of lower overheads and a work-in-progress (WIP) inventory. The structure should permit effective coordination amongst the engineering, product design, manufacturing and marketing functions.

8.12.2 Leadership

Leadership influences the NPD strategy, culture and organisations' ability to undertake the development of new products. Top management must demonstrate a commitment to the project by recognising individual skills, providing professional development and motivating the team. Clarity and vision are essential for creating a good strategy. Risk taking, trial and error, and flexibility must be encouraged to promote individual initiatives. The process of NPD has to be recognised as an iterative and dynamic process capable of adapting to change. Initiatives prompt creativity, and problem-solving skills are essential elements of NPD. Above all, the top management must coordinate and integrate the various functions of NPD so that the entire team functions as a coherent unit.

8.12.3 Teamwork

Successful teams reduce conflicts that may arise amongst the various functions. Top management must provide direction, promote shared understanding about the objectives and the purpose of the project, and communicate clearly the tasks to be accomplished. This social unity is created amongst the team members of the project.

8.13 Addressing Complexities in NPD Projects

A study involving interviews with 10 project managers dealing with different degrees of complexities in internal improvement and product development projects has shown that in product development projects, major sources of complexities include interdependency between tasks and the novelty of the project. The complexities are addressed through (a) reducing the number and interdependency between tasks; (b) a proper understanding of the project, its scope and objectives; (c) understanding the customer and their needs; (d) establishing good project management methods; (e) understanding the weaknesses and strengths of the project team and the correlation between technical and organisational aspects; (f) applying appropriate leadership styles; and (g) appointing skilled project managers (Hussein, Pigagaite & Silva, 2014).

8.14 Evaluation of NPD Projects

A survey of 87 successful NPD projects in Taiwan has shown that the projects are evaluated in five categories: market, financial, technical, time and opportunity (Wang & Lee, 2011).

Market category: customer acceptance and satisfaction, sales objectives, growth and volume, market share and potential.

Financial category: breakeven time, profit objectives, internal rate of return and margin rate.

Technical category: product quality, uniqueness and its performance and technical feasibility.

Time category: performance against the budget, launched on time and time to market.

Opportunity category: marketing opportunity and intuition.

8.15 Failure of NPD Projects

There are several reasons for the failure of new products. Kotler and Armstrong (2012) have summarised the causes of failure:

- Product may be good, but the company has overestimated the market size.
- Product is poorly designed and positioned incorrectly in the market.
- Product has been introduced at the wrong time.
- Price of the product is too high to attract customers.
- Promotion has been ineffective.
- Unhelpful management influence in the NPD process
- Cost of development is too high
- Ineffective competition strategy.

Other reasons for failure are:

- Poor distribution of the product.
- Product performance falls below expectations and is too complex.
- The market is not ready for the product.
- Inability to supply the demand of customers.
- Unforeseen reasons.

8.16 Success Factors for NPD

Cooper (2013) has formulated eight factors that drive successful NPD projects:

1. A unique superior product: A product that differentiates itself from competitors' products and offers unique benefits and features and a compelling value proposition to the consumer.
2. Alignment with the needs of customers: The product is market-driven and the process is customer-focused.
3. Completion of preparatory work: Homework, front-end loading and due diligence are essential preparatory tasks before the NPD project starts.
4. Clear product and project definitions: Clarification of both the product and project definitions during the early stages of NPD avoids scope creep and ensures reliable specifications.
5. Spiral development: Design, build, test, review and revision based on customers' feedback. Involving customers in the early stages is a key to success.
6. Target the global market: Targeting the international market is more profitable.
7. Good launch plan: A well-executed launch plan and a solid marketing plan are essential for the success of the NPD project.
8. Speed: The project is accelerated without compromising quality.

8.17 Addressing Environmental Issues in NPD

Global warming, pollution and environmental disasters in the world have created an awareness of environmental damage caused by products, their use and disposal, and the processes that develop them. Consumers too have become more environmentally conscious and demand environmentally friendly products. To meet these challenges, organisations have developed new products that minimise the harm to the environment. For example, the small "nano car" is more efficient in non-renewable fuel consumption. Similarly, the electric car runs on batteries without fuel consumption. Multifunction products such as computer printers with built-in facilities for printing, scanning and photocopying consume less raw materials and are easy to assemble and use. Packaging utilises recyclable materials and self-erecting boxes for packaging have no glue.

All stages of a product's life-cycle have different types of environmental impacts. Most of them occur during the early phases of designing a product. In fact, approximately 80% of the product's environmental profile is associated with the concept creating in product development (McAloone & Bey, 2009). Designers have a role to play in minimising the environmental impact by providing solutions to environmental issues without creating problems in other areas. Traditionally, designers have focused on functionality, appearance and financial considerations. Now it is necessary for them to take a more proactive holistic approach to design. In assessing the environmental impact, the entire life cycle of the product has to be considered, which includes all stages from extracting raw materials to final disposal of the product. Marketing too plays a crucial role in product development activities by encouraging changes in individual behaviour. Marketers realise that environmentally friendly products have a competitive advantage.

Some of the eco-design principles (Deniz, 2002) are as follows:

- Manufacturing
  (a) Use of clean technologies without producing hazardous materials; (b) use of non-hazardous recyclable material; (c) use of recyclable material and reusable components; (d) improving efficiency in the use of materials, energy and other resources; and (e) minimising the damage from the use of materials.
- Process
  Reduce chemical emissions and energy consumption.
  Minimise pollution due to small and noise.
- Use
  Minimise long-term harm to the environment caused by the product.
  Ensure that the life of the product is appropriate and fully functional during its lifespan.
  Ensure that the packaging instructions and overall appearance encourage efficient and environmentally friendly use.
  Analyse and eliminate or reduce potential safety hazards.
- Disassembly
  Consider the effects of the end disposal of the product.
  Design for easy disassembly.
  Consider product reuse and recycling at the end of its life.
  Facilitate longer life by minimising the need for repairs and upgrading.

These principles are considered in the design analysis stage, which includes three parameters for design: (a) process design; (b) material design; and (c) energy consumption design. Process design focuses on reducing the energy consumption during processing and minimising waste and pollution. Material design takes into consideration the selection and the use of raw materials to minimise hazardous waste, pollution and the amount of raw materials used. Energy consumption design is associated with the selection of materials and processes that minimise energy needs during manufacture and use (Deniz, 2002; Gungor & Gupta, 1999).

8.17.1 Seven-Step Approach for Environmental Improvement

The seven-step approach provides an overview of the environmental effects, details of the product's environmental impacts, its use and the end consumer, and creates solutions to minimise environmental harm and help build an environmental strategy. The first six steps identify the environmental effects, and the last step provides a framework for an action plan to integrate environmental improvements into the NPD process (McAloone & Bey, 2009).

Step 1 – Use context: Identification of environmental impacts associated with the product use, e.g. how is it used, by whom and for how long (life expectancy)?

Step 2 – Overview: Life-cycle information, e.g. how is it manufactured, distributed and disposed of?

Step 3 – Eco-profile: Identifies the origins of environmental impacts by materials, energy, chemicals and others.

Step 4 – Stakeholder network: Identifies all who have an influence on the product and their connections and the environmental impacts, e.g. consumers, distributors, internal and external influences.

Step 5 – Quantification: Determines the likelihood and effect of each environmental issue. Consider alternative processes, materials and life-cycles.

Step 6 – Conceptualisation: Provides solutions to reduce the environmental impacts on products or life-cycle changes. Use eco-design principles.

Step 7 – Eco-strategy: Create an action plan.

By adopting an innovative and creative approach to environmental improvements in product development, it is possible to integrate environmental concepts into the NDP process. By involving many functions and professions, there is a greater likelihood of success.

8.18 New Food Product Development

New food product development is a basic activity in the food sector. The product mix of a food company involves a vast range of products that are constantly evolving, and it includes unprofitable food products, those reaching their maturity, those that show growth and new products. To maintain the array of product mix, companies have developed product development programmes that include product improvements, line extensions, re-launches and product innovations.

The food product development process known as the Milestone process formulated by Arthur D. Little Inc. (Rudolph, 2000) is similar to the Stage-Gate process described earlier. It established clear, consistent milestones for the entire development process with well-defined outcomes at each milestone. Milestones permit review of the outcomes against the established goals and initiate changes, if necessary. The advantages of milestone-driven food product development process are that it is flexible and continuously evolving. It consists of three phases: (a) product definition; (b) product implementation; and (c) product introduction. The process is presented in Table 8.5.

8.18.1 Product Testing

Product testing is an integral part of the design and development process and the testing activities and techniques are presented in Table 8.6 (Earle & Earle, 2000).

Table 8.5 Milestone Process of New Food Product Development

Phase	Milestones	Activities
1 Product definition phase	Strategic plan	Creating a vision and direction, identification of markets served, market positioning, competition, regulatory issues, core competencies, profitability, etc.
	Market opportunity assessment	Consumer research, which identifies market opportunities
	Product business plan	Describes market opportunities and project requirements to achieve opportunities
	Product definition	Consumer perceptions, business objectives, product definition requirements and regulatory requirements are integrated
2 Product implementation phase	Prototype development	Development of a model, which aligns with business objectives and consumer needs
	Market strategy and testing	Long-term forecasts are made using market test analysis to predict trial and repeat purchasing pattern
	Scale-up trial production	Resolution of conflicts amongst consumer expectations, R&D functions and manufacturing, manufacture the new product and develop a total quality package. Hazards are identified with a Hazard Analysis and Critical Control Point (HACCP) programme and controls are established to eliminate or minimise risks
3 Product introduction phase	Product introduction	Led by sales and supported by marketing and distribution functions. Field trials have been completed. The product is designed to meet consumer's needs and has been packaged and priced appropriately to convey the message of quality and value to consumers. Transport trials have been conducted and the product is distributed to select outlets. The success or failure of the product depends on the initial consumer response
	Production support	Consumer feedback is used to build product support and repeat business. Feedback is communicated to other functions in the organisation for future application

Table 8.6   Product Testing

Stage	Input	Tests			Output
		Technical	Consumer	Cost	
Initial	Product design specification	Reliability Training	Ideal profile	Cost analysis	Product mock up
Screening	Product mock up	Sensory	Difference testing	Material cost comparison	Elementary product prototypes
Preliminary studies	Elementary product prototypes	Sensory Statistical testing	Acceptance Preference panel	Preliminary product costs	Acceptable product prototype
Optimisation	Acceptable product prototype	Control testing Shelf life testing	Competitive comparison Product improvement using test results	Cost comparison	Optimum product prototype
Scale up	Optimum product prototype	Raw material testing Product study Process study	Buying predictions Market survey Attitude panel Large consumer tests	Yields Materials Equipment comparison Total capital and operational costing	Final product prototype Product and process specifications Market strategy Financial analysis

8.18.2 Product Formulation

Many food products are made by combining raw materials in specific proportions according to a recipe. Food product developers conduct research on the effects of various formulations on product quality. The five steps in formulation are (a) establish product qualities; (b) establish data for the raw materials compositions, qualities and costs; (c) set limits for the raw materials and process variables; (d) employ quantitative techniques, linear programming, experimental designs and mixture designs; and (e) make changes to formulations using a product profile test and technical test results that relate to product quality.

Generally, raw materials are considered in two categories: basic raw materials and those that add aesthetic value to the product.

The goal of NPD is to increase profits while simultaneously maintaining an internal structure that promotes innovation and continuity. In the process, the NPD team meet numerous challenges, and to meet them successfully, the top management must communicate a shared vision to the middle and lower management and to the individual members of the project team.

References

Annacchino, M.A. (2003). *New Product Development: From Initial Idea to Product Management*. Boston: Elsevier.

Barclay, I., Dann, Z. and Holroyd, P. (2000). *Product Development*. UK: Butterworth-Heinemann.

Benioff, M. and Adler, C. (2009). *Behind the Cloud*. San Francisco: Jossey-Bass.

Business Dictionary. (n.d.). *Definitions*. Retrieved September 15, 2018 from http://www.businessdictionary.com/.

Chary, S.N. (2007). *Production and Operations Management* (3rd ed.). India: McGraw-Hill.

Chwastyk, P. and Kolosowski, M. (2014). Estimating the cost of the new product development process. *Procedia Engineering*, 69, 351–360.

Cooper, R.G. (2008). The Stage-Gate idea to launch process update: What is new and NextGen systems. *Journal of Product Innovation Management*, 25 (3), 213–232.

Cooper, R.G. (2013). New products – What separates winners from losers and what drives success. In K.B. Kahn (Ed.), *The PBMA Handbook of New Product Development*, pp. 3–34. New Jersey: John Wiley.

Cooper, R.G. and Edgett, S.J. (2010). Developing a product innovation and technology strategy for your business. *Research Technology Management*, 53 (3), 33–40.

Crawford, C.M. (1972). Strategies for new product development: A guideline for a critical company problem. *Business Horizons*, 15 (6), pp. 49–58.

Deniz, D. (2002). *Sustainability and environmental issues in industrial product design*. (Master of Industrial Design Thesis). Izmir Institute of Technology, Turkey.

Earle, M.D. and Earle, R.L. (2000). *Creating New Foods: The Product Developer's Guide*. UK: Chadwick House Group.

Fripp, G. (n.d.). Why do companies introduce new products? *The Marketing Study Guide*. Retrieved January 10, 2019 from https://www.marketingstudyguide.com/companies-introduce-new-products/.

Gungor, A. and Gupta, S.M. (1999). Issues in environmentally conscious manufacturing and product recovery: A survey. *Computers & Industrial Engineering*, 36, 811–853.

Hussein, B.A., Pigagaite, G. and Silva, P.P. (2014). Identifying and dealing with complexities in new product and process development projects. *Procedia – Social and Behavioral Sciences*, 119, 701–710.

IES Development Institute. (n.d.). *Product/market matrix*. Retrieved November 10, 2018 from http://strategictoolkits.com/strategic-concepts/productmarket-matrix//.

Jaideep. (n.d.). *Developing new products: Definitions, features, reasons and constraints*. Retrieved January 9, 2018 from http://www.yourarticlelibrary.com/products/developing-new-products-definitions-features-reasons-and-constraints/48617.

Jauregui-Becker, J.M. and Wits, W.W. (2013). An information model for product development: A case study at Philips shavers. *Procedia CIRP*, 9, 97–102.

Karol, R. and Nelson, B. (2007). *New Product Development for Dummies*. New Jersey: Wiley Publishing.

Kotler, P. and Armstrong, G. (2012). *Principles of Marketing* (14th ed.). New Jersey: Pearson Education.

Loch, C.H. and Kavadias, S. (2008). *Handbook of New Product Development Management*. UK: Butterworth-Heinemann.

MacCormack, A., Crandall, W., Henderson, P. and Toft, P. (2012). Do you need a new product development strategy? Aligning process with context. *Research-Technology Management*, 55 (1), 34–43.

Marques, P., Cunha, P.F., Valente, F. and Leitao, A. (2013). A methodology for product-service systems development. Forty-sixth CIRP Conference on Manufacturing Systems 2013. *Procedia CIRP*, 7, 371–376.

Mayo, C.M. (2014). New product development. *Encyclopedia of Business* (2nd ed.). Retrieved October 20, 2014 from http://www.referenceforbusiness.com/management/Mar-No/New-Product-Development.html.

McAloone, T. and Bey, N. (2009). *Environmental Improvement through Product Development – A Guide*. Denmark: Svendborg Tryk.

Miller Jr., J.A. (2011). Out of a near-death experience into a chaotic global economy: How Corning rediscovered its innovation roots. *Research Technology Management*, 54 (6), 26–31.

Pahwa, A. (2018). 8 Steps of new product development: Marketing before introduction. *Feedough*. Retrieved January 10, 2019 from https://www.feedough.com/new-product-development-npd/.

Queensland Government. (2014). New product development strategy. Business and industry Portal. Retrieved September 20, 2018 from http://www.business.qld.gov.au/business/business-improvement/new-product-development/new-product-development-strategy.

Rudolph, M.J. (2000). The food product development process. In A.L. Brody and J.B. Lord (Eds.), *Developing New Food Products for a Changing Market Place*, pp. 87–101. Florida: CRC Press.

Saxena, R. (2008). *Marketing Management*. India: Tata McGraw-Hill.

Thomke, S. and Reinertsen, D. (2012). Six myths of product development. *Harvard Business Review*, 90 (5), pp. 84–94.

Trott, P. (2010). *Innovation Management and New Product Development* (4th ed.). India: Dorling Kindersley.

tutor2u. (n.d.). *Product design*. Retrieved January 8, 2018 from https://www.tutor2u.net/business/reference/product-design

Wang, K.J. and Lee, Y.H. (2011). The impact of new product strategy on product performance and evaluation criteria. *British Journal of Arts and Social Sciences*, 1 (2), 106–117.

Chapter 9

Warehousing and Logistics

9.1 Evolution of Warehousing

The history of warehousing can be traced back to the early years of evolution of humans. In early writings, humans were described as having stored excess food and kept animals for future consumption. There have been three notable periods in our civilisation. The first period, the age of agriculture, lasted from the dawn of recorded history until two centuries ago. The second period was the industrial era which evolved during the Renaissance period (around 1,400–1,600). During the last three decades, the age of information has played a vital role in business transactions (Ackerman, 2000).

Genesis describes the role of granaries for storing food to prevent famine in Egypt, and the concept of warehousing has been thought of as originating during this period of agriculture. The use of transport has also been associated with the age of agriculture. Oriental spices were used to preserve meat and vegetables, and early explorers went to Asia to trade for spices. The early Chinese used some sort of "bank notes" in place of gold and silver for commercial transactions. A negotiated receipt called a "Lombard", named after the province of Lombardy, was used when goods were stored in warehouses.

Further developments in transport occurred during the industrial era. Local warehouses were built to store merchandise and manufacturing items. There was no inventory control and often appliance manufacturers stockpiled excess quantities of goods to enable them to respond to customers' demands quickly. During this period, transporting goods by ships was the norm and consolidation and distribution warehouses were constructed at piers to store goods arriving by ships. The first major commercial warehouse was built in Venice, a centre for major trade routes. Such warehouses were operated for profit by a brotherhood of merchants known as the guild. Commercial activities expanded beyond the Mediterranean and territorial warehouses proliferated at each port city. Warehouses at port cities reduced the waiting time for ships that unloaded the cargo (Tompkins, 1998).

In the United States, terminal warehouses were built at rail centres for merchandise, and these served as transit points for storage, awaiting movement to the final destination. Railroads held the monopoly for storing and transporting goods. In the 1880s, the Interstate Commerce Act was passed in the United States to prevent discriminatory pricing practices. As a result of lobbying by a small group of businessmen, further legislation was enacted to prevent railroads offering free warehouse services. Thus, one of the oldest trade unions, the American Warehouse Association was formed.

The industrial era also brought new modes of transport and competition, and so government intervention was no longer necessary. In the 1980s, all modes of freight transport were deregulated. With deregulation logistics, services offered warehousing as a part of the package. At the same time, warehouse designs began to change. The use of forklifts led to the conversion of multi-storey terminal warehouses to high-bay single-storey buildings. Forklifts had a huge impact on materials handling which had previously relied on manpower and some horse-drawn gantry arrangements. Forklifts enabled logistics units to increase the load from a maximum of ~20 kg which a man could lift to more than 1,000 kg per movement. This resulted in a steep change in efficiency and consequential labour and cost reduction. Fewer people were needed and this impacted the wider community as less labour was needed to be located near wharves, railway depots, etc.

Further developments in warehousing occurred during the age of information. Hand-held terminals introduced around the 1980s eliminated the need to read product codes manually and enabled the use of the barcodes as a distribution tool. Real-time communication between the warehouse driver and the warehouse system through radio frequency (RF) transmission allowed location and product verification, dramatically increasing the efficiency and accuracy of warehouse operations. Computer programmes today can handle a very large amount of warehouse information.

Goods held in quarantine are designated unavailable until quality checks are completed. Information systems also allow goods to be moved from the receiving area directly to another distribution centre, eliminating the need to move stock from the receiving area to the storage area (Ackerman, 2000; Tompkins, 1998).

In 1999, the United States spent $75 billion (0.8% of GDP) on warehousing for a total space of 6.1 billion ft², an increase of 700 million ft² within a span of nine years (an increase of 13%) (Coyle et al., 2003).

9.2 Definitions

9.2.1 Warehousing

Warehousing refers to the storage of all varieties of goods from iron ore in open mining fields to finished goods, raw materials, industrial goods, appliances, etc., in storehouses and locations suitable for the business.

9.2.2 Picking

Picking is the process of filling a customer's order from component items stored in the warehouse and accumulating them for shipment.

9.2.3 Kitting

Kitting is the process of assembling complete units from items stored in the warehouse. It allows related or co-dependent items to be picked in prescribed proportions before the time of shipping.

9.2.4 Cross-Docking

Cross-docking is the process of unloading materials from an incoming vehicle (trucks or rail wagons) and loading directly into outbound trucks or rail wagons without the need to store them in the warehouse. Inventory is generally recognised in the transit warehouse as inwards goods but then immediately picked and despatched on the pre-arranged distribution or sales order (Van den Berg, 2007).

9.2.5 Logistics

According to Rushton, Goucher and Baker (2010), logistics is "The efficient transfer of goods from the source of supply through the place of manufacture to the point of consumption in a cost-effective way whilst providing an acceptable service to the customer".

9.2.6 Supply Chain

The supply chain is the process of integrating, coordinating and controlling the movement of goods and materials from a supplier to a customer and then to the final consumer.

9.2.7 Supply Chain Management

"Supply chain management is the integration of these activities through improved supply chain relationships to achieve a sustainable competitive advantage" (Handfield & Nichols, 1999).

9.3 The Need for Warehousing and Holding Inventory

Warehousing is a core function that companies utilise to enhance their competitive advantage. It is an essential link in the supply chain and is undergoing enormous challenges to achieve excellence. Increasing consumer awareness of products and services and the demand for greater choice have resulted in a proliferation of product ranges and size, with the need to expand the storage capacity to hold higher inventory levels (Tompkins, 1998; Van den Berg, 2007; Richards, 2011). However, with the proliferation of internet trading, many small goods purchases now bypass the legacy procedure, which uses distribution warehouses and takes advantage of improved courier services to supply goods from a manufacturer direct. This provides reduced costs for the consumer because of the lower inventory in the supply chain and more variety.

9.3.1 Reasons for Warehousing

Warehousing is a planned process to bridge over time and status. Some important reasons to implement warehouse and distribution systems to cater to the supply chain include (Hompel & Schmidt, 2007):

1. Optimising logistic performance: In order to fulfil customer requirements, sufficient quantities of items must be available. Since ordered quantities cannot be forecast accurately, organisations must keep a forecast quantity of goods ready for delivery. When the distance between the customer and the organisation is large, warehousing becomes a reasonable solution. However, there is a trend towards more frequent orders of small quantities, and therefore, good logistic decisions should be considered in selecting suppliers.
2. Supporting productivity: Organisations that design processes for just-in-time (JIT) delivery along the supply chain deal with minimised stocks. In such instances, inventory control is

subject to many interruptions in the environment. Efficient stock-keeping ensures the maintenance of productivity levels.

3. Providing additional services: An organisation's marketing channel demands a wide variety of items and assembly services in warehouses, and such services are offered in goods distribution centres.

4. Minimising transport costs: Transport costs are significant in warehouse operations; and therefore, in order to keep the costs down, warehouses optimise the loading capacity. Consolidated lots are more efficient to handle than a large number of small lots. Since the retail trade cannot handle frequent deliveries because of staffing and the availability of gates, warehouses must be prepared to customise delivery quantities to suit their customers.

5. Balancing ordered and delivered quantities: The market has changed in logistics methods from a push environment to a pull (customer responsive) environment. The production environment often encounters irregularities in the requirements which cannot be influenced; and therefore, it does not correspond to a continuous or sporadic demand. Warehouse management systems (WMSs) must be designed to meet these challenges.

6. Using the market position: Warehouses experience demands due to quantity discounts at retailers, and this adds to administrative costs such as the execution of orders, price negotiations, etc.

7. Warehousing as a processing step: For some products or processes, warehousing is a value-adding process by assembling and customising products moving through a distribution facility, thus improving product flow. This reduces and eliminates storage while enabling customisation to suit the needs of customers.

8. Availability of reliable, responsive and efficient third-party warehouses.

9. Technological advances enabling fast response times through integrated up-line and down-line communications, electronic data interchange (EDI), automatic identifications and compatible information systems.

10. Importance of global marketplace for business and the challenges that result from the multiplicity of shipping requirements.

9.3.2 Reasons for Better Inventory Management

Consumers have a greater choice of products leading to a demand for a wider variety. In order to meet such demands, warehouse needs huge storage capacities. The reasons for holding stock are (Richards, 2011):

1. Unpredictable and erratic demand patterns, depending on the changeability of the external environment and the launch of new products.

2. Buying in larger quantities reduces the unit rate. However, the decision to purchase larger quantities depends on storage and handling costs, working capital interest, and possible discounted sales and disposal costs.

3. Trade-off between transport costs and shipping costs: The trade-off is between the cost of storing large quantities against the cost of transport of smaller quantities and more frequent deliveries. If the transport cost is favourable, additional storage space is required.

4. The distance between manufacturers and consumers requires a greater amount of safety stock to be held in the warehouse: A greater distance between the warehouse and the customer requires the warehouse to hold large stocks. The trade-off is between more expensive local suppliers and producers against the increased costs of transport and inventory holding costs.

5. Production shut down for maintenance, breakdowns, stock counts and staff shortages requires additional stock to be held in the warehouse.
6. The need to adjust production and storage during changes in models, colour, design features, etc. Longer production runs reduce the production costs and the trade-off is between the lower cost per unit versus the cost of holding additional stock.
7. The need to respond to customer demands due to seasonality such as summer, winter, Easter, Christmas, Valentine's Day, etc.
8. Spare parts storage: To maintain uninterrupted production, manufacturers need to store a stock of spare parts, just in case an item becomes defective. Although it can be expensive, the trade-off is between the cost of the part and its holding cost versus the potential breakdown in production and the consequences that follow.
9. Work-in-progress (WIP) storage: Parts of an item are held in storage for future assembly until required.
10. Holding stock for investment: Goods such as wines and spirits, cigars, precious metals and fine arts increase in value with time.
11. Document storage: A wide variety of documents are stored for future retrieval and some of these are stored as required by regulations.

9.4 Types of Warehouses

9.4.1 Based on Ownership

The three types of warehouses – public, private and contract – differ in ownership and the extent of user control (Bowersox et al., 2012).

9.4.1.1 Public Warehouses

These are storage facilities which anyone can use for storing goods. They offer inventory management, physical inventory counts and shipping facilities. The owner of the warehouse charges the client for the storage space and the services used. They operate as independent businesses offering a range of standardised services. Public warehouses have been classified on the basis of operational specialisation such as (a) general merchandise such as paper, food and small appliances; (b) refrigerated foods, medical, photographic items and chemicals requiring temperature control; (c) special commodities such as bulk material and clothing; (d) bonded goods; and (e) household goods and furniture. The users of public warehouses do not have to employ staff, own inventory software or warehouse equipment. Although public warehousing is a short-term solution, clients often use them for long-term storage because of convenience. Public warehouses invest significantly in modern facilities to maintain a competitive edge, as well as offer flexibility and a range of labour solutions.

9.4.1.2 Private Warehouses

Private warehouses are owned and operated by the user for their own distribution activity, and they offer total control to the user. A major retail chain may own several regional warehouses supplying their stores. Similarly, a wholesaler may operate a warehouse to receive and distribute its products. The Warehouse Manager is responsible for the storage of goods. Private warehouses are the most economical means of handling large and constant volumes of goods. They are not operated for profit and hence both fixed and variable costs are lower than for-hire facilities. The main advantage is total control of operational activities including leasing out unused space. In addition, they offer more flexibility since operating policies, hours of operation and procedures can be adjusted to meet the requirements of the user. The intangible benefit of enhancing customer perception of responsiveness and stability is achieved by having its name on the sign. The capital needed to acquire space and cash flow is a major disadvantage. The perceived cost-benefit is offset by the public warehouse's ability to achieve operational economies of scale and scope because of the broader client base.

9.4.1.3 Contract Warehouses

Contract warehouses are owned by a third party and combine the features of public and private warehouses. Unlike public warehouses, which offer month-to-month contracts, they offer long-term contracts. They allow the client to store goods and provide facilities like cross-docking, packaging, inventory control, JIT management, local transportation and quality control (QC). Additional activities handled by contract warehousing are receiving incoming goods and import and export. These warehouses are centrally located for maximum transport efficiency. Multiple clients of contract warehouses enable better use of the assets lowering overhead costs. This provides the benefits of expertise, flexibility, scalability and economies of scale by sharing management, labour, equipment and information resources across a wide spectrum of clients. Contract warehouses are typically designed for a particular type of storage, which naturally restricts the goods they will accommodate, e.g. chilled or frozen, food or non-food products, pharmaceuticals, etc.

9.4.2 Classification Based on Roles

Warehouses can be classified on the basis of the roles they play in the supply chain (Frazelle, 2008).

9.4.2.1 Raw Material and Component Warehouses

These warehouses hold raw materials and components in locations close to manufacturing facilities.

9.4.2.2 WIP Warehouses

Partially completed assemblies and products are stored in WIP warehouses at various points in the assembly or production line.

9.4.2.3 Finished Goods Warehouses

Completed products awaiting distribution are held in finished goods warehouses and they balance the variation between production schedule and demand forecast. They are generally located near the point of manufacture and enable receiving and despatching, even for small pallet loads of goods. The inventory is replenished monthly or quarterly depending on the demand.

9.4.2.4 Distribution Warehouses

Distribution warehouses accumulate and consolidate stock from various points of manufacture within a single company or several companies with a similar customer base for consolidated shipment. They are located near manufacturing facilities or customer bases. These warehouses cater to weekly or monthly orders of full or less than full case quantities.

9.4.2.5 Fulfilment Warehouses

Fulfilment warehouses receive, pick and ship small orders to individual customers (e.g. Amazon.com).

9.4.2.6 Local Warehouses

These centres respond to rapid demands of customers and are conveniently located in order to reduce transportation costs. Generally, orders are fulfilled daily.

9.4.2.7 Value-Added Service Warehouses

These are centres where customisation of packaging, labelling, marking, pricing and return goods handling takes place.

9.5 Warehouse Operations

A warehouse performs a number of operations from receiving goods to safe, secure storage, product monitoring, order picking, marshalling and despatch to wholesalers, retailers or customers (Coyle et al., 2003; Frazelle, 2008; Cullinane & Tompkins, 1998; Rushton et al., 2010). Basic warehouse operations are shown in Table 9.1 and Figure 9.1.

9.5.1 Receiving

Receiving goods is the basis for all subsequent activities in the warehouse, and it is the interface between manufacturing control and warehouse control. At the receiving point, the control of goods is given to the warehouse. However, when WIP or finished goods are received the transfer of control is not clearly defined. Clearly defined operating procedures that specify at which point WIP goods belong to a WIP warehouse, and finished goods belong to a finished goods warehouse enable effective inventory control. Procedures for receiving WIP and finished goods should not be different from those for receiving raw materials. For efficient manufacturing operations, the receiving point and storage of raw materials should be located as close as possible to manufacturing operations. If materials are received JIT for assembly, inventory levels can be reduced. On receipt of the goods, the assigned person in the warehouse should unload, inspect for damage and compare with the packing slip. Any discrepancies should be recorded and notified to the supplier immediately. Receiving perishable items (called perishables) is a special process. All documents relating to temperature control of the carrier and cleaning prior to loading should be examined by the assigned person.

9.5.2 Storing

Basic operations on storage are (a) identification of the product and storage location; (b) moving the product to the location; and (c) updating the records. Materials are stored as they arrive as raw materials, WIP goods and finished goods. Storage locations also have to be allocated to hold goods

Table 9.1   Basic Warehouse Operations

	Warehouse	Operations
1	Raw material	Receiving
		Storing (includes stock control, rearrange for space and task optimisation)
		Kitting
		Releasing
2	Work-in-process	Receiving
		Storing (includes stock control, rearrange for space and task optimisation)
		Kitting
		Releasing
3	Finished goods	Receiving
		Storing (includes stock control, rearrange for space and task optimisation)
		Picking
		Despatch

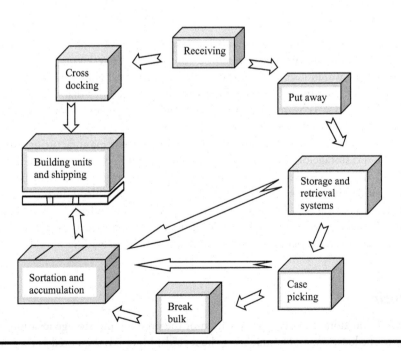

Figure 9.1   Common warehouse functions.

on hold, goods awaiting QC inspection (quarantine area) and for returned goods. Materials are usually taken to the reserve or bulk storage area awaiting the movement to the final location in the warehouse or bulk (full pallet) picking. When required, goods are taken from the reserve storage area to replenish picking stock. Goods awaiting QC inspection are clearly identified as quarantine stock with appropriate stickers or container labels flagged in the WMS. The warehouse computer system prevents picking any goods from these locations. Some packages may require additional work such as barcoding, palletising, repalletising or placing in tote bins. When goods are ready to be moved into the final location (put away), the computer system identifies and recommends the most appropriate location.

9.5.2.1 Storage Policies

Storage policies determine the allocation of locations to put away received goods (Lee, n.d.; Cullinane & Tompkins, 1998). There are different types of storage:

a. Randomised storage: Goods are stored in the closest possible location and retrieved on the basis of first-in first-out. This method maximises space utilisation but it involves longer travel times between order picking locations. Therefore, it suits a warehouse where inwards and outwards goods are in close proximity to a low number of fast-moving stock-keeping units (SKUs). It is ideal for the generic storage requirements for most products.

b. Dedicated storage: Items are stored in permanent dedicated locations in the warehouse. Popularity, unit size, cube, compatibility and complementarity are examples of the criteria used to allocate fixed locations. Items stored according to popularity are located in the vicinity of shipping area which minimises the travel distance for order picking. According to the unit size criterion, smaller items are stored near the shipping area and larger items away from it. Therefore, more items can be stored near the shipping area. A cube is an extension of the unit size criterion. Items with smaller cubic volume are located close to the shipping area. Compatibility storage refers to the method of storing complementary items close to each other. Pharmaceuticals cannot be stored together with agricultural chemicals. Hence, such storage also requires specialised features for hazard management, dangerous goods, etc. Warehouses store items that are ordered together (e.g. disk drives and CD/DVD discs, a variety of stationery items and different cleaning products) are stored in close locations.

9.5.3 Order Picking

Picking is the process of extracting from the inventory the products required by customers and accumulating them to form a single shipment. In manufacturing, the term "kitting" is used to describe the picking of items to form a handling unit of items to be assembled. For example, disposable coffee cups are picked with a corresponding number of lids to fit. Sequential kitting in raw material or WIP warehouses requires the picker to select units and pick them to form a kit. Batch kitting permits the selection of items and sorting them for a specific manufacturing kit. The zone picker requires the picker to pick units from assigned zones and kits are only completed when all the zones have kitted the customer order. Order picking is the most labour-intensive activity in warehousing and accounts for 50% of labour costs in warehouse operations. Picking also involves break-bulk operations when pallet quantities are received from suppliers and ordered by customers in less than pallet quantities. As a consequence, there is a great deal of technology available to enhance the efficiency, accuracy and quality of picking.

9.5.4 Sortation

When small quantities are ordered, it is convenient to batch a number of orders together and treat them as a single order for picking purposes. Picked batches then have to be sorted down to individual orders before despatch. This is called "wave picking", which is a two-stage process (pick then pack) that offers efficiency in some circumstances. It also has the advantage that, as a two-stage process, pick accuracy can be verified by the packers.

9.5.5 Consolidation

When a customer orders a large product range from a single source, items are consolidated and delivered to the customer as a single delivery. Consolidation improves the efficiency of outbound transportation. Palletised product may also require stretch and shrink wrapping for extra protection and stability of the load.

Consolidation centres receive goods from different sources and hold them for on-delivery to a customer or a production line. Retail warehouses stock a wide range of items from different suppliers so that customers can pick their selection as a single order.

Cross-docking involves the movement of items directly from the receiving bay to shipping boxes. In cross-docking, items remain in the warehouse for a very short period. The process requires the items to be labelled by the supplier to allow particular groups of goods to be identified and consolidated with other deliveries ready for despatch in the transit warehouse.

9.5.6 Marshalling and Despatch

Pre-shipping operations involve staging, packaging and labelling. Picks are dropped off at the pre-assigned staging area. In the despatch area, goods are marshalled together to form vehicle loads. Prior to despatch the following tasks have to be completed:

- The order is checked for completeness.
- Ensure that goods are consolidated and packed in appropriate containers.
- The load is weighed – freight is usually based on pallet quantities and airfreight on weight.
- If applicable, shipping charges are established.
- Orders are accumulated in lanes according to the destination or outbound carrier.
- Trucks are loaded onto outbound vehicles for transportation to a port or airport for the next transport leg or directly to the final customer or destination
- Shipping documents, packing lists, address labels and bills of lading are prepared.

9.6 Logistics

The Chartered Institute of Logistics and Transport (2014) defines logistics as: "Getting the right product to the right place in the right quantity at the right time, in the best condition and at an acceptable cost is the challenge of logistics". The importance of logistics and supply chain in business has led to the adoption of a scientific approach towards the subject, which has addressed the need for and means of planning logistics and supply chain and some operational issues (Rushton et al., 2010; Prince, 1998).

Logistics and supply chain are concerned with the integration of order processing, inventory transportation and the combination of warehousing, material handling and packaging

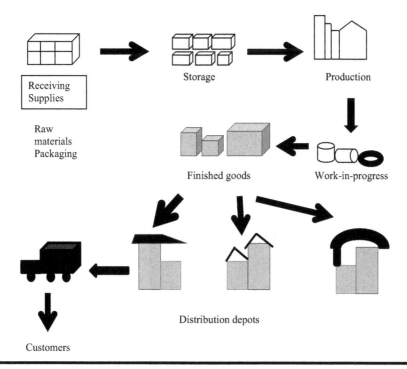

Figure 9.2   Physical flow of materials in a supply chain.

throughout a network facility. The goals of logistics are (a) support procurement; (b) manufacturing; and (c) customer service requirements. Logistics performance is measured by the optimum delivery service, which can only be achieved when material flow and information flow are well coordinated and information flow precedes material flow. To achieve the lowest cost, financial and human costs allocated to logistics must be held to an absolute minimum. (Bowersox et al., 2012). Service reliability, availability of inventory to consistently meet customer needs, cost efficiency and enhanced operational performance are benefits of lean logistics. Key components of logistics and distribution are (a) physical flow of information; (b) order processing; (c) inventory; (d) transportation; (e) warehousing, material handling and packaging; and (f) facility network. To provide service at competitive rates, cost management at each step is also critical to effective supply chain management. Figure 9.2 shows the physical flow of materials in a supply chain linking all the activities between suppliers and customers to the consumer in a timely manner. The supply chain comes into force following initial customer/consumer demands. Companies may have more than one supply chain depending on the number of suppliers and customers.

9.7 Distribution

During the post-war period, a number of trends emerged which saw the need for an increased focus on the distribution of goods (McKnight, 1998). They included:

■ Increased focus on the customer: Customisation of products and adoption of value-added activities with no extra cost to the customer satisfying the demands of customers.

- Control changes in inventory management: Control procedures were introduced which placed the burden of finished product inventories on the distributor, with retailers playing a minor role.
- Network planning: An effective network system not only optimises customer service and achieves maximum profitability but also designs the system to adapt to changing requirements of customers.
- Changes in transportation systems: The fuel crisis in the 1970s and the deregulation led the companies to examine the costs of transporting goods closely.
- Introduction of new technologies and innovations: Planning and tracking tools such as Manufacturing Resource Planning II (MRPII), Distribution Resource Planning and WMSs provided accurate information on physical distribution data on a real-time basis.
- Outsourcing: Third-party logistics enabled the restructuring of the physical design of a warehouse to enhance and focus on key competencies.
- Global environment: In order to remain competitive, borders of trade have to be extended beyond one's own territory.

Distribution is the activity of moving a product physically from one location to another as part of the process of selling it to a customer in the supply chain (Newton, 1992). An assessment of distribution as a key activity depends on the following factors:

1. Cost of distribution: Generally, if the cost of distribution is approximately 10% of the turnover, distribution is considered a key operation.
2. Competitive edge: Companies that use distribution as a marketing edge offer reliability, faster availability, a fresher or a wide range of products and can adapt to customers' demands.
3. Type of product: Organisations recognise the risk associated with handling hazardous or perishable products through distribution and take steps to minimise risk or the failure of the product.

9.7.1 Complexity of Organising the Distribution Department

The distribution function cannot be considered in isolation. Functions such as storage, order processing, order picking and transport are closely integrated with distribution. Therefore, operation planning involves the provision of facilities to meet the requirements of the sales plan and the allocation of budget for internal and external distribution services.

The functions of a distribution department depend on the complexity of the operation (Newton, 1992). The following are the functions of the distribution department, although they may not be under the direct control of the Distribution Manager:

- Inventory holding.
- Picking and packing.
- Depot and transport operations.
- Order processing.
- Customs and exercise.

Support functions include (a) packaging design; (b) material handling; (c) information technology (IT) programmes; (d) compliance with safety and regulatory requirements; and (e) customer service.

9.7.2 Training the Distribution Team

The warehouse employs various categories of employees: warehouse staff, machine operators, administrative staff, computer operators, vehicle drivers, freight buyers, sales liaison staff, customer service staff, and specialists in customs and regulatory affairs.

Training should include, but is not limited to, (Newton, 1992) the following:

- Product knowledge, awareness of intended markets and special characteristics of products and markets. Includes idiosyncrasies of products types and handling requirements.
- Safety training: Lifting and handling, operating power-handling equipment such as forklifts.
- Customer service: Staff should create an image of caring and efficiency and should be able to respond to complaints about stock availability, delivery delays or supply failure.

9.7.3 Golden Rules

1. Handle complaints by trainer personnel and discuss them with staff who are responsible for resolving issues.
2. Never ignore complaints, however, trivial they may look. Satisfactory resolution leads to more efficient operations.
3. When problems occur promptly inform the sales staff or the customer. Prompt notice provides the greatest opportunity to resolve the issue satisfactorily.
4. Communicate with sales staff regularly and make them aware of positive developments as well as potential problems and possible solutions.
5. Encourage teamwork.
6. Never make promises you cannot keep. For example, in adverse weather conditions such as storms and snow the delay of delivery is inevitable so explain the delay in advance.
7. Offer tangible rewards for exceptional performance.
8. Acknowledge tasks well accomplished, however, small they may seem.

9.8 Transportation

The business environment is changing rapidly in response to emerging technologies, global trading patterns and deregulation nationally and worldwide. Warehousing and distribution play a key role in the systems approach to business. Transportation involves a single mode or multiple modes such as air, road, rail, etc. Intermodal transfer is the movement of goods between two modes. There are several issues that apply to all modes (Muller, 1998) including:

1. Type of cargo: General cargo consists of goods such as machinery, packaged goods, vehicles and equipment. Coal, petroleum, gases and flour fall into the category of bulk cargo. A third category is neo-bulk which includes bulk and other homogeneous types of cargo in one shipment. Parcel tankers are used to transport different grades of petroleum.
2. Interchange points: Airports, harbours, railroad stations are interchange points. There is intense competition between airports/ports and inland terminals.
3. Government regulations: Deregulation of transport in the United States, the European Common Market (now EU) and other economic block countries led to competition in world markets (Tompkins, 1998).

4. Economic impact: Deregulation removed restrictive trade barriers and allowed supply and demand in the transport sector, including warehousing, to adjust the rates. The shippers had the option of selecting and using modal and intermodal carriers based on rates and service.
5. Communication advancement: Deregulation of the communication industry and advances in communication technology such as EDI enabled paperless warehouse activities and tracking shipments through the supply chain.
6. Need for warehouse and logistics facilitators: Niche markets that have opened as a result of globalisation of world markets require specialists in customer service, JIT, and manufacturing and customer delivery concepts.
7. Relationship with distribution management: The evolving nature of warehousing and distribution roles, and their relationship with distribution management, increased the need for the complete management of all these activities.

9.8.1 Modes of Transportation

Three possible modes of transport are (a) land; (b) water; and (c) air. On land, trucks, rail and tractors carry goods. Trains, buses and cars carry passengers and also goods. On water, ships and steamers carry passengers as well as goods. In the air, helicopters and planes carry passengers and goods. The advantages and limitations of various modes of transport are shown in Table 9.2 (National Institute of Open Schooling, n.d.).

9.9 Food Safety: Refrigerated Storage

Many products such as fish, meat, dairy products and some pharmaceutical products require temperature-controlled storage and distribution to allow them to be considered as part of the mainstream food supply chain. With the proliferation of retail outlets, more and more food products are manufactured and distributed in temperature-controlled vehicles or containers to ensure they arrive in peak condition. At present, storage at a constant temperature applies to frozen products such as fish, ice cream and meat, as well as to many vegetables, fruits and prepared meals that can be defrosted and cooked.

Retail outlets may have cold storage and distribution centres which include frozen, chilled and ambient facilities as in-house operations. However, third-party contractors are playing a significant role in specialised storage and distribution for chilled and frozen food (Young, 1997). Temperature-controlled warehousing generally includes the following services:

- Appropriate stock rotation.
- Warehousing of whole packages through pick 'n pack operations and pre-packaging.
- Maintenance of a range of internal temperatures recommended for various food products.
- Continuous monitoring of temperature using microprocessor digital temperature control.
- Forced air cooling for temperature stability and recovery.
- Audio and/or video signals to warn temperature deviation.
- Chlorofluorocarbon (CFC)-free refrigeration system and insulation.

The British Retail Consortium (BRC) Global Standards for Storage and Distribution (BRC, 2010) specify the following requirements during the storage of food products:

1. Monitor as specified by product specifications and procedures.
2. Install automatic or manual temperature/time recording equipment linked to an automatic alarm system where temperature control is necessary.

	Land				Water	Air
	Road	Rail	Pipeline	Ropeway		
Comment	Connect one place to another	Transport of people and goods by train	Transport of liquids, gases in large quantities	Connects two places on hills or across a valley	Movement of goods and passengers on waterways	Carry goods and passengers on airways
Examples	Cars, cycles, trucks, buses	Local trains, metro rails, goods trains	Petroleum, natural gases, water	Trolley moving on wheels connected to a rope, bucket conveyor	Boats, steamers, ships	Aircrafts, helicopters
Advantages	Perishable goods can be transported faster Flexible mode for loading and unloading They can deliver goods to areas not served by other modes Relatively cheap	Low cost and convenient for long distances Relatively faster Suitable for heavy goods in large quantities over long distances Less affected by adverse weather	Low operating costs Low product losses	Can operate in deep and long valleys Suitable for ropeway buckets Low operating costs Low product losses	Most economical form of transport Suitable for bulky and heavy goods Safe mode of transport Low maintenance costs Promote international trade	Fastest mode of transport Can reach inaccessible areas using helicopters Convenient modes of transport in disasters Provide support for national defence
Limitations	Limited capacity Not suitable for long distances Transporting heavy goods and bulk is costly Affected by weather conditions	Relatively expensive for short distances Does not serve remote areas Loading and unloading have to be planned according to the schedule High risk of damage due to multiple transfers	Suitable for liquids and gases High capital investment Suitable for single product movement only	Suitable for solids High capital investment Suitable for single product movement only	Limited to ports and harbours Slow moving Not suitable for perishable goods unless refrigerated Adversely affected by weather Large capital investment	More expensive Not suitable for heavy and bulky goods Affected by adverse weather Not suitable for short distances Heavy losses of life and property in case of accidents

3. Provide facilities to maintain the temperature control necessary for the product.
4. Install the equipment necessary to maintain temperature control, where necessary, during handling and transfer operations. Specify the maximum period of time that a particular type of food may remain outside the temperature control environment.
5. In the case of equipment failure, specify the safety and quality status before releasing the product.
6. Specify the level of uniformity of condition under control (temperature and/or humidity).
7. Determine the performance capability when changes to equipment are made.

9.10 Environmental Impact

A warehouse is amongst the largest consumers of energy in the logistics sector and organisations, in general, are concerned with the environmental impact of warehouse activities. Companies are now moving towards a reduction of carbon emissions. It is possible to minimise carbon emissions and reduce environmental pollution by adopting green warehouse practices.

Environmental issues associated with warehousing are (a) hazards due to stored materials such as toxic chemicals, corrosive substances and flammable substances; (b) in case of a fire, the emission of toxic fumes released into the atmosphere by stored materials such as household cleaning products, home improvement products, cosmetics and personal hygiene products; (c) noise and/or exhaust fumes from lifting equipment and vehicles; (d) energy consumption; and (e) packaging material (Mapfre, n.d.).

Organisations can implement measures to reduce the environmental impact by:

a. Classifying stored goods and labelling them adequately to identify hazardous material.
b. Providing safety data sheets (SDSs) in easily accessible locations.
c. Providing information and training for workers handling these products.
d. Installing safety guards or rails on shelving or racking to prevent them from being knocked or struck by forklifts.
e. Ideally locating these warehouses away from other warehouse facilities.
f. Installing systems to limit the damage caused by toxic spillages.
g. Constructing battery charging areas with acid-resistant floors with a slope which allows easy removal and cleaning.
h. Using electric forklift trucks.
i. Reducing energy consumption, e.g. lighting.
j. Utilising biodegradable or recyclable packaging material.

9.11 Health and Safety Issues

Health and safety issues in warehousing involve pedestrian movement, movement of forklift trucks, falling objects and a cold working environment. The effects of cold temperature and cold environment on people depend on the type and size of the facility, the operations being undertaken, the quality of protective gear provided and the time spent in a demanding environment (Richards, 2011). Some of the issues are as follows:

■ Accidental lock-in in cold stores requiring alarms and quick response equipment.
■ Accidental release of refrigerant, particularly ammonia.

- Material-handling equipment on slippery floors where ice build-up occurs causing machinery skids, personnel slips, trips and falls.
- Ice build-up on panels may lead to ice falling and roof panels to collapse, causing injury to warehouse operators.
- Product falls from pallet racks due to misplaced stock.
- Risk of falls while working at heights.

The Health and Safety Authority (HSE) in the United Kingdom has identified the top five safety issues to be addressed in the warehouse environment (n.d.): (a) accidents due to vehicle movement in the warehouse; (b) poor management of the pedestrian–vehicle interface; (c) accidents while loading and unloading goods; (d) falls from equipment and vehicles; and (e) slips, trips and falls due to slippery floors. An action plan to prevent health and safety issues involves:

- Conducting a risk assessment of warehousing operations.
- Carrying out inspections of the warehouse, particularly warehouse transport arrangements.
- Regular maintenance and inspection of forklift trucks and delivery vehicles.
- Racking inspections.
- Preventive maintenance of forklift trucks and vehicles and compliance to regulatory requirements.

9.12 Impact of Information Technology

Advances in IT in the 1990s had a significant impact on all business operations. Organisations embraced IT to improve their operations (Tompkins & Smith, 1998).

9.12.1 Applications of IT

1. Distribution Requirements Planning (DRP): DRP is a global planning concept to manage and integrate closely with the total logistic network. It can be used for planning transportation costs, warehousing requirements and inventory management. An effective DRP programme enables increased inventory turnover, rapid response to market changes, assists the JIT programme, and reduces obsolescence and the prediction and minimisation of future inventory issues.
2. EDI: EDI is the electronic transfer of information from one computer system to another. There is no human intervention; and therefore, EDI provides the accurate transfer and receipt of information. Organisations that embrace EDI can integrate closely with trading partners. A further advantage of EDI is that it reduces information lead times and therefore allows a rapid response to customer requirements.
3. Applications in the WMS: The WMS is used to maximise space, equipment and labour utilisation by directing labour and providing inventory and location information. The advantages of the WMS are (a) reduction of operating costs; (b) improvement in productivity; (c) elimination of non-value-added steps; (d) reduction in lead times; and (e) improvement in the accuracy of inventory management, picking and data management.
4. Application in transport management system (TMS): A TMS performs many administrative tasks through automation which include (a) planning loads and routes; (b) transport performance; (c) trailer loading; and (d) freight management.

5. Order processing: The nature of a pull system and improvement of the logistics network allows the organisation to remain competitive by processing orders more quickly. IT is being applied to speed up the real-time order processing system.

6. Electronic purchasing: A reduction in inventory and improving the time associated with purchasing can be achieved through a rapid information exchange between trading partners.

7. Application in automatic identification technologies (Auto ID): The technology in auto ID can be applied to print and read barcodes and RF identification with great accuracy. Barcoding technology allows information to be processed quickly and accurately between trading partners, reducing the non-value-added steps associated with inaccurate information.

9.13 Performance Assessment

Assessing the effectiveness and efficiency of warehouse operations is a major challenge for warehouse managers. The assessment tool is based on a factor-rating method consisting of 11 areas (De Koster, 2008). This tool is briefly described here. Following are the 11 categories:

1. Customer satisfaction.
2. Cleanliness, environment, ergonomics, safety and hygiene.
3. Utilisation of space, building condition and technical installation.
4. Condition and maintenance of material handling equipment.
5. Team work, management and motivation of staff.
6. Storage systems and strategies including inventory management.
7. Order picking methods and strategies.
8. Supply chain coordination.
9. Use of technology.
10. Commitment to quality.
11. Managing efficiency and flexibility.

A warehouse performs a very important function of creating a time utility for raw materials, industrial goods and finished products. The management and improvement of warehouse operations needs a professional approach.

References

Ackerman, K.B. (2000). *Practical Handbook of Warehousing* (4th ed.). Norwell: Kluwer Academic Publishers.

Bowersox, D.J., Closs, D.J. and Cooper, M.B. (2012). *Supply Chain Logistics Management* (4th ed.). New York: McGraw-Hill.

BRC. (2010). *Global Standard for Storage and Distribution*. UK: TSO (The Stationery Office).

Chartered Institute of Logistics and Transport. (2014). *What is logistics?* Retrieved January 10, 2018 from https://ciltuk.org.uk/Careers/Online-Careers-Service/Career-Pathways/Logistics-Management.

Coyle, J.J., Bardi, E.J. and Langley, C.J. (2003). *Management of Business Logistics* (7th ed.). Ohio: South Western Learning/Thomson.

Cullinane, T. and Tompkins, J.A. (1998). Warehousing and manufacture. In J.A. Tompkins and J.A. Smith (Eds.), *The Warehouse Management Handbook* (2nd ed.), pp. 43–50. North Carolina: Tompkins Press.

De Koster, M.B.M. (2008). Warehouse assessment in a single tour. In M. Lahmar (Ed.), *Faculty Logistics: Approaches and Solutions to Next Generation*, pp. 39–60. New York: Taylor & Francis.

Frazelle, E.H. (2008). *World-Class Warehousing and Material Handling*. UK: McGraw-Hill.

Handfield, R.B.A. and Nichols, E.L.A. (1999). *Introduction to Supply Chain Management*. New Jersey: Prentice Hall.

HSE (n.d.). *Warehousing and storage*. Retrieved February 20, 2018 from http://www.hse.gov.uk/pubns/indg412.pdf.

Hompel, M.T. and Schmidt, T. (2007). *Warehouse Management: Automation and organisation of warehouse and order picking systems*. Germany: Springer.

Lee, S.H. (n.d.). *Chapter 4 Warehousing*. Retrieved February 10, 2018 from http://www.iems.co.kr/CPL/lecture/part4/4.%20Warehousing.pdf.

Mapfre (n.d.). *Warehouse safety guide*. Retrieved February 20, 2018 from http://www.mapfre.com/ccm/content/documentos/mapfrere/fichero/en/safety-guide-warehouses.pdf.

McKnight, D. (1998) Warehousing and distribution. In J.A. Tompkins and J.A. Smith (Eds.), *The Warehouse Management Handbook* (2nd ed.), pp. 19–42. North Carolina: Tompkins Press.

Muller, G. (1998). Transportation modes. In J.A. Tompkins and J.A. Smith (Eds.), *The Warehouse Management Handbook* (2nd ed.), pp. 89–138. North Carolina: Tompkins Press.

National Institute of Open Schooling (NIOS) (n.d.). *Lesson 10 Transport*. Retrieved February 29, 2018 from http://old.nios.ac.in/Secbuscour/cc10.pdf.

Newton, K. (1992). Managing distribution. In D.M. Stewart (Ed.), *Handbook of Management Skills* (2nd ed.), pp. 377–388. UK: Gower.

Prince, M. (1998). Logistics excellence. In J.A. Tompkins and J.A. Smith (Eds.), *The Warehouse Management Handbook* (2nd ed.), pp. 51–62. North Carolina: Tompkins Press.

Richards, G. (2011). *Warehouse Management*. India: Kogan Press.

Rushton, A., Groucher, P. and Baker, P. (2010). *Handbook of Logistics and Distribution Management* (4th ed.). UK: Kogan Press.

Tompkins, J.A. (1998). The challenge of warehousing. In J.A. Tompkins and J.A. Smith (Eds.), *The Warehouse Management Handbook* (2nd ed.), pp. 1–18. North Carolina: Tompkins Press.

Tompkins, J.A. and Smith, J.A. (1998). *Warehouse Management Handbook* (2nd ed.). North Carolina: Tompkins Press.

Van den Berg, J.P. (2007). *Integral Warehouse Management: The Next Generation in Transparency, Collaboration and Warehouse Management*. Netherlands: Management Outlook Publications.

Young, M. (1997). The cold storage chain. In C. Dellino (Ed.), *Cold and Chilled Technology* (2nd ed.), pp. 1–52. UK: Blackie Academic and Professional.

Chapter 10

Sales Management

10.1 Introduction

Marketing and sales are complementary business functions. The strategy of marketing is to utilise the resources of the company so that the needs and requirements of customers can be satisfied by offering an appropriate product and/or service. The sales function, on the other hand, makes customers understand the benefits of the offer and encourages them to purchase it while making a profit for the organisation. Several tactical tools are used to implement the marketing strategy. The needs are identified through market research. Product development and testing activities ensure that the product or service is right. Tools are also used in presenting the offer to customers. The sales function is a major tactic in presenting the offer while having a role to play in the first two.

In companies that offer industrial, speciality and consumer goods, most of the presentation effort is carried out by the sales force. In fact, in the office equipment and life insurance markets, the quality of the sales force is a major factor in purchasing decisions. The sales process involves interpersonal interactions such as one-to-one meetings, cold calls and networking. New prospects or potential customers are driven to sales through marketing efforts. Therefore, selling is the ultimate result of marketing (Wilson, 1992).

10.2 Definitions

Personal selling is the personal interaction with one or more buyers for the purpose of completing a sales transaction.

"**Sales management** is the process of planning, organising, directing, staffing, training, motivating and controlling the sales operations to achieve the company objectives through the sales team" (Donaldson, 2007).

"**Salesmanship** is a seller initiated effort that provides prospective buyers with information and motivates them to make favourable decisions concerning the seller's products or services" (Still et al., 1988).

Sales funnel is a metaphor used in the sales process. At the top of the funnel are unqualified prospects. These are customers to whom the company product or service is applicable and with whom the company has not made an initial contact. At the bottom of the funnel are customers who have ordered, paid for and received the company's products and services. Along the sales process not all potential customers will make it to the bottom and some will fall out (Mind Tools, 2014).

10.3 Sales Management

Sales management comprises five key elements: planning, organising, staffing, directing and controlling performance (Donaldson, 2007; Jobber & Lancaster, 2012). It also includes:

- Defining the roles and tasks of the sales force in relation to overall corporate and marketing objectives.
- Selecting, training, motivating and delegating subordinates.
- Time management.
- Allocating time to reflect and plan.
- Demonstrating leadership.
- Maintaining control.

The planning process is a repetitive and basic management activity in any organisation and is necessary for its growth. It involves setting corporate objectives, corporate plans and policies and corporate control mechanisms. The organising function essentially drives the business through tracking, planning activities, reviewing, reinforcing expectations, forecasting, managing the sales funnel and budgeting.

Staffing activities include identifying and sourcing talent, selecting sales staff, identifying training needs and leading discussions. The sales team expects the management to create an environment that provides fair and consistent management, offers sufficient support through leadership and direction, and enables them to realise their personal goals and be accountable. Performance reviews evaluate the performance of the sales team against established standards, recognise talent and offer counselling when necessary. The core of sales management is a winning environment comprised of the four proactive disciplines (hiring, training, driving business and evaluating) that create motivation and encouragement amongst the staff (White, 2004).

10.3.1 Sales Management Process

Calvin (2007) has incorporated the key elements of sales management in the sales management process/model. The key pieces of this process/model are presented in Table 10.1.

10.3.2 Management Activities

Management activities involved in the sales management process/model fall into three conceptual decision levels: (a) strategic level; (b) tactical level; and (c) operational level (Donaldson, 2007).

10.3.2.1 Strategic Level

Strategic-level decisions are concerned with the identification of existing and future business through defining the current and future markets to be served, the products and services needed to satisfy the requirements of the customers in those markets and the areas of business that the

Table 10.1   Sales Management Process Model

	Description	*Associated Items*
1	Set strategy and objectives	Using data such as sales and profit margins, description of available product range with additions and deletions, price structure, promotional support, tactics, etc.
2	Recruiting	Preparation of job descriptions, creating a candidate profile, sourcing talent, interviewing, reference checking and final selection
3	Training	Knowledge of product range, competitors and customers, selling skills, field coaching, sales meetings
4	Compensation	Fixed or performance pay, total dollar level
5	Organisation	Channel choice – direct or indirect, geographic, product or functional architecture, deployment and sizing of territory boundaries, managing time within the territory
6	Forecasts	Method: bottom-up or top-down forecasts, format, preparation of sales plan and actions that drive forecast numbers
7	Non-monetary motivating factors	Consider the usefulness, challenge, achievement, belonging, personal growth, leadership
8	Sales force automation	System applications, e-commerce, internet, implementation of automation
9	Performance review	Consider results, activities, skills, knowledge, personal characteristics, self-evaluation, review interval setting and achieving goals, productivity measurements

company does not want. The sales function has an input into this process and the outcome is to define the role of this function in the marketing mix.

10.3.2.2 Tactical Level

Tactical-level decisions are concerned with what to do, who will do it and how to do it within the defined timeframe. The role of the sales team is determined and goals have been established. The management tasks include structuring the sales force in terms of size and organisational design, developing the sales force in terms of recruitment, selection and training programmes and policies, and motivating the team by supervising, demonstrating leadership and offering remuneration, and by evaluation and control.

10.3.2.3 Operational Level

Management decisions at the operational level are concerned with assessing the performance of the sales force and encouraging the sales people to manage themselves and their territories as far as possible. The type of person in terms of personality, knowledge, skill and motivation are important factors in decision-making at the operational level. The management must be able to evaluate and respond to competitors' sales strategies and environmental factors, understand the customers they serve, and be aware of the procedures and policies that apply to the sales organisation.

10.3.3 Factors that Influence the Sales Management Process

A number of major environmental (behavioural, technological and management) forces impact the sales management process (Jobber & Lancaster, 2012; Calvin, 2007).

10.3.3.1 Behavioural Forces

a. Customers' behaviour changes with the environment and therefore, the sales management function needs to adapt to several key influences:
1. Consumers' awareness of products and services raises their expectations. With easy access to information on products and services, customers are becoming more knowledgeable and can make informed decisions.
2. Customer avoidance of buyer–seller negotiations. Owing to intense competition, sales people are trained in the art of negotiation and high-pressure sales tactics. Purchasing a motor vehicle is a classic example of this approach. Customers, therefore, perceive purchasing as an ordeal to be tolerated.
3. Exercising the power of major buyers in many sectors enables them to demand and get special customer status and other facilities. Successful sales people respond to the increasing demands of customers and coordinate the efforts of selling and technical teams in the organisation to meet their needs.
4. Globalisation and fragmentation of markets. As domestic markets saturate, companies are moving abroad to reduce costs and achieve sales and gain profit. Such companies face numerous challenges such as cultural differences, lifestyles, languages, competing against established brands and building global relationships across many countries.
5. Shorter product/service life-cycles make them more difficult to differentiate. Because of the shorter life-cycle, products such as medical devices, telephone services, computers or bakery products will be quickly imitated and improved on. Therefore, the sales force needs improved product knowledge and skills.
6. Larger, more complex, life-cycles expand the steps from customer search to purchasing. Often this involves developing a prototype and demonstrating the product before the customer decides to buy.
7. Buying from overseas markets. In order to gain a competitive advantage, the training programme should emphasise product knowledge and knowledge of the competition and customers.
8. Group decisions. In some organisations, major purchasing decisions are made by groups to minimise the risk. Sales people should be able to understand the needs of the groups, benefits from the purchase and who the decision-makers are. In such situations, forecasting and planning will be difficult.
9. Intense competition. In the global marketing environment, competition is intense due to new marketing channels such as the internet, eBay, etc. New technology allows smaller companies to compete with larger companies, and therefore, the sales force should understand the competitors' issues and how customers choose between vendors.

10. Less customer loyalty. Buyers are becoming less loyal to a particular vendor because the internet can provide competitive products and price information. Sales people should be able to demonstrate, quantify and prove customer benefits, allowing the customer to rationalise their choice of vendors.

10.3.3.2 Technological Forces

The three major technological forces are sales force automation, virtual sales offices and electronic sales channels. Electronic equipment such as laptops, mobile phones, email and advanced sales software are essential tools for sales activities. Purchase orders, invoices, quotes, delivery dates, various reports and promotional material can now be transmitted to retailers, wholesalers and distributors through electronic data exchange devices. Technological advances have made video-conferencing possible for conducting sales meetings, training sessions and communicating with customers.

Virtual offices in homes or cars allow sales people to communicate with their head office, customers and co-workers. Sales staff can, therefore, manage their time more efficiently, thus looking after the needs of customers.

The internet has become the fastest-growing electronic sales channel. By encouraging customers to use the internet for their shopping, the sales force size can be reduced and they can spend more time closing major orders. Television home shopping has now become popular, and customers can order their requirements as and when needed in the comfort of their home.

10.3.3.3 Managerial Forces

Sales managers have to respond to changes in the commercial environment by developing strategies to promote their sales through direct marketing tactics, improving cooperation between marketing and sales, and encouraging the sales force to attend training programmes to improve their skills and acquire professional qualifications.

Direct marketing tactics include direct mail and telemarketing. Some organisations have installed computer stations in their outlets where customers can obtain product and price information, compare features of competitive models, calculate running costs and place orders.

Poor communication is often the cause of a lack of cooperation between the sales and marketing functions. Setting up an intranet can not only improve communication and information between the two functions but also enhance the effectiveness of the sales force.

Sales people have to keep up with the developments in the market and gain skills to convince customers about the benefits of their products and services to their customers. Training programmes can be designed to improve their knowledge and obtain professional qualifications.

10.3.4 Problems Related to the Study of Sales Management

The study of sales management presents several issues (Donaldson, 2007):

1. Implementation issues

Traditionally, the sales management process focused on implementation and tactical operations rather than on strategic planning and policy, which are the essentials of marketing. Many factors other than selling effort influence the sales response, and therefore, it is difficult to separate sales function and its causes. The environmental factors such as territories, personnel and customers in which sales operations take place are continually changing.

2. Assessment issues

There is a narrow perception that behavioural relationships and interactions in selling are not open to classification and the variables are impossible to measure. The data on principles of sales organisation, deployment and motivation are highly specific and anecdotal, and some of these are difficult to assess.

3. Issues relating to research

Much of the input on sales management issues originate from dissimilar areas of research, behavioural sciences, operational research and economics. Evidence from many studies is based on research conducted in the United States, and the findings cannot be extrapolated to other countries.

10.3.4.1 Addressing the Problems

1. Consider the position and the roles of selling as a part of the promotional mix. All the elements in the marketing mix have to be managed successfully better than competitors to satisfy customer demands. When all the elements are integrated and coordinated, the synergistic effort is greater than maximising individual elements in isolation.
2. Understand the individual sales person's motives and actions that affect their performance. By establishing a successful style for a sales person, many of the sales management problems can be easily eliminated.
3. Adopt and interactive approach. A sales transaction takes place between two personalities, the buyer and the seller. The greater the similarity of characteristics between the buyer and the seller, the greater is the chance of a successful transaction.
4. Focus on the economics of selling by considering measurements such as sales force size, the profit and sales from sales effort, return on investment and the value of the sales force. For example, new or modified organisational systems such as customer relationship management (CRM) can be implemented using the lifetime value of the customers.
5. Study the decisions the sales managers are expected to make and assist them in decision-making using sound judgement and realistic data. These decisions may not be applicable in all situations, but better planning of territories, establishing sales targets and selecting, and training and motivating sales people will result in enhancing real productivity gains.

10.4 Sales Strategy

The sales strategy is an operational plan that defines the customer segments that a company targets, its value proposition for each segment, its sales force structure and its selling processes. Basically, sales strategies include measures to gain customer orders. This provides a basis from which a sales plan can be created and the sales plan includes the short-term tactical plan for attracting customers and making the sales process far more efficient. Both are influenced by the company's corporate strategy and market analysis (Sales Benchmark Index, 2014; VP of Strategy, n.d.).

Typical issues that a sales strategy can resolve are:

■ Merger of sales forces after acquisition or merger.
■ Declining sales revenue and market share.

- Increasing the cost of sales.
- Changing the market-product mix.
- New product that did not meet sales expectations.
- New entries to the market that pose a threat to the company.

10.4.1 Sales Strategy Development

Effective marketing is essential to the success of any business. In order to increase revenue and maximise profits, both marketing strategies and sales strategies have to be implemented correctly. Sales people contribute to strategy-making in five ways: (a) involvement is strategy formulation; (b) intelligence gathering; (c) working across functions; (d) relationship development; and (e) internal marketing of customers to colleagues (Rogers, 2007). While marketing strategies are utilised to inform the customers of your business and offerings and clarify the benefits of patronising your company instead of another, sales strategies help identify and take advantage of the best opportunities (BHP Information Solutions, 2010). Five key steps are involved in sales strategy development: (a) setting objectives; (b) decide how to reach target customers; (c) plan and support the sales staff; (d) prepare the sales plan; and (e) measure performance.

10.4.1.1 Objectives

Clarify and establish sales objectives. They must be **S**pecific, **M**easureable, **A**chievable, **R**ealistic and **T**ime-bound (SMART). An example of a sales objective might be "To increase the sales revenue from computer sales by 10% at the end of the second quarter within the education sector". This statement incorporates all the elements of a SMART objective.

10.4.1.2 Key Elements of a Sales Strategy

The key elements of a sales strategy are (a) target market; (b) prospect segmentation; (c) sales distribution model; (d) sales process; (e) sales funnel calculation; (f) pricing strategy; and (g) upsell strategy (VP of Strategy, n.d.; BHP Information Solutions, 2010).

10.4.1.2.1 Target Market

This step involves developing a clear understanding of the customers by identifying their needs, products and the expected level of service, and communicating this to the entire sales team. With this knowledge, a target customer profile can be generated which identifies the typical customer(s) in the core market(s) that the product or service is being sold in.

10.4.1.2.2 Prospect Segmentation

Top prospects in a given market are identified through market research in various industry sectors. In this step, the prospects are segmented on the basis of region and quality so that the sales team can approach them efficiently. Regional territory is then assigned to a specific sales person who may or may not be located in that region. The ideal customer profile is generated and ranked according to the size of the company or profitability.

10.4.1.2.3 Sales/Distribution Model

An effective distribution model enables the sales team to develop and maintain a close relationship with the target customer. The choice of a distribution model depends on solution complexity and marketing complexity. The former denotes the ease of installation, deployment and use while the latter refers to the problems of sourcing, purchasing and after-sales service. The use of an intermediary to sell the product may also be considered by the company.

10.4.1.2.4 Sales Channels

This step involves the selection of sales channels to reach your target customers. Use a direct face-to-face method to sell high-value products. This method is the most expensive sales method, and the sales people need to have sufficient experience to explain and demonstrate the product. For lower value products, direct mail and telesales methods can be employed. The cheapest method of selling is through the company's web page. The design and layout of the web page have a strong impact on the sales. Individual customers can also be reached through retailers. For the global market, an experienced agent can be employed. Another method to boost the sales effort is to join with non-competing companies, which requires customers' permission to share information.

10.4.1.2.5 Sales Funnel Calculation

The sales funnel calculation is a model for estimating the number of "unqualified leads" required to be included in the sales cycle and converting this into sales to reach sales targets. This is also useful for sales managers in evaluating the performance of the sales force. An "unqualified lead" (also known as a cold lead) is a potential customer who would be interested in the offers but has not yet been contacted by the sales team. When the cold leads pass through each stage of the sales cycle and turn into closed sales, they become "qualified". However, some potential customers will fall through, and therefore, estimates have to be adjusted as more data on conversion rates become available.

10.4.1.2.6 Pricing Strategy

Pricing is a major element in the marketing mix. The product or service has to be positioned effectively to gain customers and challenge the competitors. Several factors affect the pricing strategy:

- Positioning: The choice is between pricing the product and/or service higher if the products or services have sufficient product differentiation/competitive advantage, or lowering the prices compared to competition expecting to build a market.
- Demand/price sensitivity: The issue here is whether the customers are price conscious so that their selection is based solely on price, or whether they are willing to pay a higher price for the product of their choice.
- Cost: In order to gain a profit, the price should be higher than the cost per customer, which is calculated using all fixed and variable costs.
- Competitive/environmental factors: These are factors that influence market perception of pricing a product or service higher or lower than the competition.
- Maximisation of revenue and profits: In order to achieve maximum revenue and profits, revenue and expense projections have to be considered.

10.4.1.2.7 Upsell Strategy

An upselling strategy is a systematic plan for increasing the average sales revenue per customer by using a variety of sales techniques to encourage customers to buy more than what they intended to buy. Although upselling is the easiest method to increase the sales revenue, a proper plan should be designed to maximise sales opportunities. The techniques will be different for every industry and every kind of product or service. Some of the techniques are offering complementary products, additional service at a discount, bundled packages, upgrades at a discount, 24-hour service, a product free of charge when the same product is purchased (buy-one-get-one-free) and online support.

10.4.1.3 Resources

Sales tools including access to databases and equipment such as mobile phones, laptop computers and transport facilities are provided to sales staff to facilitate their activities. Standard documents such as call sheets, standard contracts and promotional material enable sales people to record the results of their sales activities. It is essential that the management support the sales force by explaining the benefits and value of the company's products over competitors' products and communicate key sales information to them.

10.4.1.4 Training of Sales Force and Customer Support

Training of sales people and customer support are important elements of the sales strategy. An effective training programme makes the customers happy, differentiates them from the competition and generates new business. It will reduce the internal workload and eliminate redundancies. Common elements of an effective training and support programme include product/customer knowledge, 24-hour service and quick response to problems, online knowledge base/company website, frequently asked questions (FAQs) and best practice information, and a customer forum.

10.4.1.5 Performance Measurement

Measure the performance of the sales team at regular intervals using profitability analysis and conversion rates. Identify problems such as a reduction in sales to key customers and dead accounts. Determine the cause and be prepared to address the issues.

10.5 Common Mistakes Made by Sales Managers

In most organisations, sales managers are the essential link between the company's sales goals and the realisation of these goals. The sales objectives are met by chance rather than by proper planning, and the sales people are not developed to their full potential (Miller, 2007; Kahle, n.d.). The mistakes made by sales managers are:

1. Lack of a focused sales structure. The structure of the sales force consists of rules, policies and procedures that influence the behaviour of sales people. An improperly designed sales structure fails to support essential sale activities.
2. Sales managers often avoid coaching and managing the sales force and remain in the selling mode. This is particularly true of those who have been trained by a great sales person.

3. They focus on bottom performers and ignore middle and top performers. As a result, those who are actually producing results are alienated.
4. They fail to understand what motivates individual sales people.
5. Sometimes the right person is not recruited or the recruitment policies are not robust enough to attract top sales people.
6. The sales managers fail to demonstrate leadership qualities to earn the confidence of the sales force. They fail to evaluate the environment properly, make changes without addressing the real issues, and create a plan that brings poor results.

10.6 Sales Planning

The JWPM consulting firm (n.d.) based in Australia with expertise in business-to-business marketing defines a sales plan as: "An operational plan that identifies how the annual sales revenue budget will be achieved by aggregating sales budgets by customer, territory, and sales representative and listing the week-to-week activity required to achieve the sales budget". A sales plan allocates resources for achieving the sales budget and specifies the tactics, tools and training. It is a management tool used to resolve several basic sales management problems:

1. Forecasting annual sales revenue: A sales revenue budget includes an annual sales revenue forecast based on customers, territory, product and sales representatives.
2. Achieving face-to-face visits: The sales plan is used as a tool to provide direction to the sales staff to focus on profitable customers.
3. Sales force numbers: The sales plan identifies the number of sales people required to achieve the target sales revenue.
4. Purpose of the sales visits: Sales calls are expensive, and therefore, each call must have a purpose. Generally, calls are made to sign up a new customer, maintain relationships with existing customers for support or for identifying new opportunities, or to close a sale, resolve a problem, deliver product(s) and collect the payment. Sales modelling, which varies from industry-to-industry, defines the processes required to close a sale.

10.6.1 Sales Plan Elements

There are five key elements of a sales plan (Hudson & Smith, n.d.): (a) sales goals, targets, challenges and investments; (b) revenue model; (c) fill the funnel; (d) selling culture; and (e) execute and measure.

10.6.1.1 Sales Goals, Targets, Challenges and Investments

Sales goals and targets: The first step of the plan is to establish the goals and targets. These two terms are often used synonymously. Goals define a sense of direction, i.e. where the company wants to be while the targets are specific results the company wants to achieve. Toyota's company goal was to offer hybrid alternatives for every model that was sold in the market. Its target was to sell one million hybrid vehicles within a year, and this was achieved in 2012 (Barcelona, 2014).

Challenges: These are issues that prevented the company from achieving the sales targets during the previous year. Consider their impact and priority and specify the approaches to overcome the barriers.

Investments: Some changes are necessary to achieve sales success. Long-term systemic improvements are necessary for the sales team to perform at their full potential and for hiring best-in-class sales personnel. Investments in the sales process area include establishing a formalised sales process and targeted account planning, training programmes to improve sales manager effectiveness and industry-specific knowledge for the sales team, creating a lead management process and market automation system, and providing sales knowledge management, sales intelligence, prospect profiling and industry monitoring.

10.6.1.2 Revenue Model

This step involves establishing a total qualified value of the company's sales pipeline and generating a revenue projection from that data. The following data should be considered when forecasting the revenue potential of the company's sales pipeline:

- Current sales pipeline to calculate the total value of qualified customers.
- Annual revenue target for the coming year.
- Targeted winning percentage of new customers.
- Revenue conversion factor that defines the rate of conversion of prospects to qualified customers.

This model forecasts the revenue the company expects to close by each quarter based on its current pipeline. It is now possible to determine how much more pipeline is needed and by when to meet the specified targets.

10.6.1.3 Fill the Funnel

In order to win customers, the company has to define the perfect prospect. This may have been generated during the strategy creation stage. A survey of 473 companies having a formal prospect definition, compared with 216 companies with no prospect definition, found that a company with a formal prospect definition generated 9% more leads from marketing than others (CSO Insights, 2011). The five dimensions of prospect profiling are:

1. Target industries that the company understands.
2. Target company sizes that can be most successful.
3. Identify companies that can generate the company's goal for average deal values.
4. Identify prospects that are looking for a solution that the company can solve.
5. Identify the titles and roles of decision-makers.

The lead funnel concept identifies the customers who fit the definition of an ideal prospect, and for the sales plan to succeed, there must be sufficient qualified leads above the sales funnel.

10.6.1.4 Selling Culture

In organisations with strong selling cultures every employee "sells". All employees recognise that they have a vested interest in selling their organisation's products and services. They are proud of their company's achievements and become champions, both inside and outside the organisation. Therefore, they help the company's sales efforts and build a strong selling culture. It refers to the environment, belief system and framework in which sales people operate. The elements of a strong selling culture (Rabbage, 2011) are:

■ Top commitment from senior management to achieve sales excellence.
■ Creating a sales-related mission statement which is ambitious, motivational, powerful and reinforces sales excellence.
■ Does not tolerate consistent failure.
■ Offers incentives to the sales force to facilitate sales excellence.
■ Implements sales practices which introduce accountability, encourage creativity and motivate the sales force.
■ Effectively manages poor performers.
■ Encourages growth so that the sales force can operate at their full potential.

10.6.1.5 Execute and Measure

The process of execution translates a sales plan to effective sales. It holds sales people accountable, communicating actions and results across the business, and is a key to increasing sales and improving productivity. Measures of sales performance should provide a vision into the future performance of the business. It should be unique to the business and business practices and should enable the organisation to align with future goals.

The Vantage Point Performance and Sales Education Foundation (Jordan, 2004) has conducted a study on the measurement and management of sales forces using thousands of data points from sales leaders in various industries. The survey identified the sales metrics they monitor in their dashboards from top-line revenue growth down to the number of monthly sales calls made by the sales force. Three hundred and six metrics were found to be the most effective in sales management, which were classified into three different levels of metrics, each with its own management value and purpose.

At the highest level are business results such as revenue growth, number of units sold, percentage of market share, gross profit and customer satisfaction ratings. These metrics are influenced by factors such as manufacturing, finance, marketing and the external commercial environment. While the outcome of these factors can be influenced, they cannot be directly controlled by the organisation. Business results are uncontrollable and what cannot be controlled cannot be managed.

Sales objectives such as the number of new customers, percentage of customer retention and percentage of target customers contacted are goal posts of sales activities that show where the company is heading. These metrics fall into the second level, and while not directly manageable could be easily influenced. For example, to acquire new customers or sell certain types of products requires consent from buyers and the sales force has no direct control over the process, although it can be influenced.

The third level of metrics is sales activities which can be controlled. Sales activities such as the number of calls made per representative, percentage of sales people using CRM programmes, number of accounts assigned per representative, etc., are used to track the progress of these activities.

These three levels of metrics are interrelated. More sales calls (a sales activity) will probably generate new customers (a sales objective). This, in turn, leads to more sales (a business result). If the sales force has better account management (a sales activity), there will be a greater chance of retaining and growing the company's customers (a sales objective), which, in turn, will expand the customer base (a business result).

10.7 Sales Process

The sales process is a set of distinct stages that follow interactions with prospects from their first point of contact with the business through to a closure and delivery (Pipeliner, 2013). The stages are represented in Figure 10.1.

The sales person needs to have a thorough knowledge about the product, its operation, features and particularly the benefits. Armed with this knowledge, various tools are used to identify prospects and decision-makers in the organisation. After initial contact has been made, the sales person presents themself to assess whether the prospect has financial resources to invest, sufficient time to discuss the proposal, and whether they have the commitment for a trial or a demonstration. At this stage the prospect's needs or problems can be identified. When the sales person can confirm that the prospect is a qualified lead the next step is to demonstrate in detail the proposed solution and possible benefits to the prospect. A sale can only be successful if the sales person can anticipate and handle the prospect's objections satisfactorily, and the end result is a closed sale or a rejection. The sales process does not end after closure. At the final stage, the product has to be delivered as promised, which lays the foundation for a close relationship and repeat buying.

Figure 10.1   Selling process.

Apart from selling, the sales person supports the customer in many ways (Donaldson, 2007). For example:

■ Solving customers' problems.
■ Retaining and improving current business.
■ Providing quotations, advice and resolving complaints.
■ Representing the company.
■ Taking orders.
■ Displaying and demonstrating products.
■ Advising distributors and users.
■ After-sales service.
■ Collecting payment.
■ Checking stocks and removing outdated items from the shelves.
■ Undergoing training.

10.8 Sales Forecasting

A sales forecast is an essential tool for managing a business. The primary goal of sales forecasting is to identify the full range of possibilities facing the organisation, society or the world at large. Traditionally, a sales forecast is defined as a prediction of the level of sales that the company expects to achieve. However, the well-known futurist Paul Saffo (2007) dispels this myth. According to him "The goal of forecasting is not to predict the future but to tell you what you need to know to take meaningful action in the present". A prediction is different from a forecast. The former is concerned with certainty, whereas the latter identifies how current uncertainties affect possible changes in direction. A forecaster, therefore, maps uncertainty. The user of the forecast must understand the forecasting process and logic to assess its quality and manage the opportunities and risks it presents. Saffo presents the following six rules for effective forecasting:

Rule 1: Define a cone of uncertainty: The breadth of the cone, which is a measure of the overall uncertainty, is a critical factor in defining the cone of uncertainty. In sales forecasting, external factors to be considered are consumer attitudes toward the environment, price trends, environmental impact and economic trends. Inside the cone are uncertainties such as competing technologies, consumer preferences, production issues, shortage of raw materials and labour disputes, etc. The edges of the cone are defined by extreme events such as terrorist attacks or wars and surprises. Factors to be considered in defining the cone are (a) it should be wide enough to capture many uncertainties; (b) a narrow cone leads to many surprises; and (c) a hollow cone will result in being surprised by a neglected or entirely overlooked certainty.

Rule 2: Look for the S curve: Important changes never occur suddenly. They follow an S curve by starting slowing in increments, then accelerating and finally tapering off. Often the initial flat line of the S curve is mistaken for a trend. Hence, a good forecaster will identify the inflection point of the S curve before it emerges. The production of TV sets in the United States illustrates the application of S curve as a tool in forecasting (Radio Electronics Manufacturers' Association (RETMA), n.d.). There was a slow growth in TV set production from 178,571 in 1947 to 975,000 black and white sets in 1948. This period was followed by an upsurge in production from 3.0 million sets in 1949 to 7.4 million in 1950 (Figure 10.2). The forecasters who identified the inflection point in 1948 were able to capitalise on the rapid growth. There was a decline in growth in 1950 and 1951 because there were no advancements in black and white TV technology.

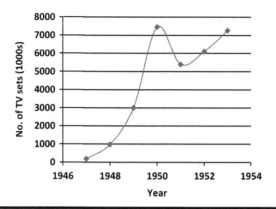

Figure 10.2   Total TV sets production in the United States.

The year 1951 marks another inflection point where there was a steady growth from that year with the evolution of colour TV transmission in 1954 in the United States (Santos, 2013).

Rule 3: Embrace the things that do not fit: Odd events are important signals for forecasters who should become accustomed to abnormal things, those that could not be classified or even rejected. They are early signals that the S curve will soon reach the inflection point.

Rule 4: Hold strong opinions weakly: Generally strong opinions reinforce one's own judgement. We tend to ignore contradictory evidence that does not agree with our views. In forecasting, lots of interlocking weak information is more important than one or two strong opinions. Strong opinions tend to be used for reaching quick conclusions, but holding weak opinions allows one to reject them when contradictory evidence appears. Therefore, good forecasting is built on a process of strong opinions that are held weakly.

Rule 5: Look back twice as far back as you look forward: Past events, if one looks back far enough, signal the present and can be reliably used to forecast the future. The recent past is never a reliable indicator of the future. By looking back at least twice as long as one is looking forward, a good forecaster can find patterns or rhythms that shape the future.

Rule 6: Know when not to make a forecast: There are times when forecasting is difficult or even impossible. The cone of uncertainty is an ever-changing entity, expanding and contracting as the past moves into the future. Certain possibilities are realised while others are closed out of reach. Under certain circumstances, the cone of uncertainty is so broad and the edges are blurred to such an extent that a good forecaster will refrain from making a forecast.

10.8.1 Forecasting Process

Forecasting accuracy decreases as the time horizon for the forecast period increases. A good forecast should be timely, reliable, accurate, meaningful, simple to use and cost-effective (Stevenson, 2012). The following steps are involved in the process:

Step 1: Determine the purpose of the forecast, level of detail and units of analysis.

This step establishes the resources required that can be justified and the level of accuracy required.

Step 2: Estimate the time horizon.

Note that the accuracy decreases as the time horizon increases.

Step 3: Choose a forecasting technique.

    Review the data to remove outliers obviously incorrect data before analysis.

Step 4: Collect and analyse the data, then identify the needed data and find out whether it is available.

Step 5: Prepare the forecast.

Step 6: Monitor the forecast.

    Monitor to determine whether it is performing as intended. If it is not, review the method, assumptions, validity of data, etc., modify as needed and prepare a revised forecast.

10.8.2 Forecasting Techniques

There are two approaches for forecasting: qualitative and quantitative (Stevenson, 2012). Qualitative approaches are judgemental methods and forecasts are generated subjectively without numerical data. On the other hand, quantitative methods include hard data and are based on mathematical models. The techniques used for forecasting can be classified as (a) judgemental; (b) time series; or (c) associative models.

Judgemental forecasts: Depend on analysis of subjective input from sources such as customer surveys, sales staff, executives and panels of experts.

Time series forecasts: These forecasts are projections of past experience into the future. The forecasters smooth out random variations or look for patterns.

Associative models: Associative models use mathematical models that include one or more explanatory variables such as price, advertising costs, or specific characteristics of the product to predict the demand.

10.8.3 Forecasting Sources

Four major components are used in formulating effective sales forecasts (Gilmore, 2006): (a) sales pipeline (high probability opportunities); (b) historic run rate; (c) field forecasts; and (d) sales management discretion.

Sales pipeline denotes the opportunities that pass on the way to becoming a sale. It can be segmented, depending on the company's life-cycle. When opportunities pass from stage-to-stage, the opportunities that are likely to become a sale can be identified. Some opportunities will not be able to go through all the stages and they can be eliminated. A probability metric includes those with approximately 80% or greater chance of success.

Historic run rate refers to sales data from past sales performances. The past review period may be a few months or a year, depending on the business cycle of the company. Several factors have to be considered when selecting historic data. Typically, a longer period is more useful to identify random variations and month-to-month patterns.

Field forecasts originate from the sales people in the field and are reviewed by the sales management team. The field-level staff have a greater visibility in their sales performance and are often aware of deals that may not have been included in the pipeline. This represents a bottom-up approach.

Sales manager's discretion provides a review of forecast data from the other three sources. The review can identify situations where the historic data includes a set of transactions that are unlikely to occur, a product line that has been discontinued, a major client is no longer prepared to buy, or data from sales people may have been duplicated. Management discretion can be applied to make the necessary adjustments.

10.8.4 Developing the Forecast

Developing a sales forecast as accurately as possible helps the company avoid unforeseen cash flow problems and manage the company's production, staff and financial needs more efficiently. It involves the accumulation of critical data, analysing them and compiling future projections (Smarta Enterprises, 2013). The elements that go into a sales forecast are shown in Figure 10.3.

Essentials: These are data from the business and include the prices of everything that is offered, the units (number of units sold multiplied by the price of each unit) and the cost of sales (cost per unit multiplied by the total unit sales). A good forecast also considers three scenarios: best, middle and worst cases. The timespan may extend from one year to two to five years. Monthly figures are shown for the first year.

Assumptions: In making the forecast, a number of assumptions have to be made. The environmental factors include threats from competitors, market changes, seasonal changes, consumer preferences and demographics, etc. These assumptions have to be justified and considered together with the data from market research.

Formulation: The data collected needs to be formulated into a forecast. It may be necessary to break the data into smaller units such as the number of calls made per day, the number of customers coming into the shop at a given time of the day, and how many of these customers make purchases, etc. Use historical data to help project future sales. Although a very accurate forecast is impossible, a good forecast includes realistic figures.

10.8.5 Measuring Success

Several elements of the forecast can be measured to evaluate the level of success (Gilmore, 2006): (a) forecast accuracy; (b) meeting a deadline; (c) participation rate; and (d) value of the forecast. The accuracy of the forecast can be measured by comparing the actual results with previous time

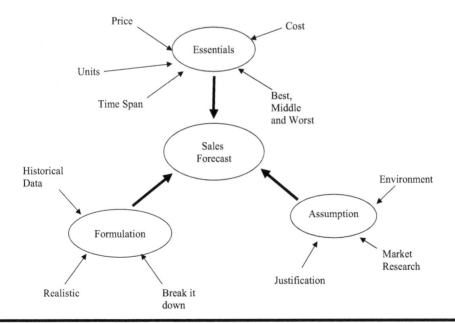

Figure 10.3   Developing a sales forecast.

period forecasts. Not only will it demonstrate visibility, but it also shows individual contributions. Such feedback encourages contributors to improve the accuracy of their forecasts and makes them aware that the management is monitoring their performance.

Deadlines for various stages of the forecast process ensure that the participants have adequate opportunities to develop, review and submit their forecast reports.

The participant rate is a measure of the amount of forecasts submitted by the sales staff. By using forecasting responsibility as sales compensation, the sales staff will be encouraged to participate and meet forecasting deadlines.

Forecasting data should contain actionable and useful information for the company and has to be evaluated by the sales management. The assessment ensures that the forecasting tool is current, compatible with the needs of the company, and capable of adapting to changes in the sales mode.

10.9 Sales Management Skills

In order to perform management activities at the strategic level, tactical level and operational level, different types of skills are required (Donaldson, 2007).

First-line managers require strong personal management, communication and team-building skills to lead the sales force into the future. They require a sound understanding of the business dynamics and competitive forces that influence the sales strategy. The emphasis is on production, company and customer knowledge, and the ability to demonstrate selling skills and train the sales force.

Essential skills for tactical decision-making are organisation capability, ability to create job specifications and job descriptions, arranging payments for training, and developing incentive packages and control systems.

Strategic decision-making requires a much higher degree of conceptual thought, excellent organisational abilities and a corporate perspective. Sales managers should be competent at all three levels and they should provide technical, human and conceptual skills to the sales force so that the sales staff can progress to sales management positions.

10.10 Impact of Sales Activities on the Environment

Among the tasks carried out by the sales force, the following activities have an impact on the environment. Table 10.2 lists these activities and the possible means of minimising the impact.

10.11 Food Safety Issues

Sales people are the buffer between the company and the customer. They are the last line of defence to protect the consumer from unhygienic food products. Therefore, they have a responsibility to ensure that food hygiene practices are maintained throughout the selling process.

Stock control: Ensure that products are stored on the basis of first-in first-out. Remove outdated and damaged products.

Storage: Products are stored at correct temperatures. Check the temperature control log book.

Complaints: Address any complaints from customers. Check the complaints log book.

Table 10.2   Environmental Impact of Sales Activities

Activity	Impact	How to Minimise
Promotional activities (printing material)	Paper use	Use recyclable paper Select alternative methods of promotion
Delivering goods	Vehicle use	Use fuel economy vehicles Clean driving training
Working in the office	Lighting Air conditioning	Use low-energy bulbs Switch off when not necessary
Advising customers	Waste accumulation	Advise on waste disposal
Communication with customers	Knowledge of environmental friendly products	Promote clean green image of environmentally friendly products and recyclable packaging

Promotion: If there is a promotion of a new product and samples are issued to customers for tasting, ensure that all utensils containing the food item are clean and kept covered to prevent the entry of insects.

Handling food items: Ensure that products such as meat or bakery items are not handled with bare hands.

References

Barcelona, J.D. (2014). *Marketing plan for Toyota motor company*. Retrieved May 14, 2018 from http://www.academia.edu/4784977/Running_Head_MARKETING_PLAN_FOR_TOYOTA_MOTOR_COMPANY.

BHP Information Solutions. (2010). *Directors' Briefing: Your Sales Strategy*. London: BHP information solutions.

Calvin, R.J. (2007). *Sales Management Demystified*. New York: McGraw-Hill.

CSO Insights. (2011). *Sales performance optimisation report*. Retrieved May 14, 2018 from http://www.nomorecoldcalling.com/wordpress/wp-content/uploads/2011/03/BarryTrailer_ROI_on_Prospect_Definitions.pdf.

Donaldson, B. (2007). *Sales Management*. UK: McMillan Publishers.

Gilmore, L. (2006). *How to develop an effective sales forecast*. Retrieved May 20, 2014 from http://www.gilmorelewis.com/storage/salesforecast.pdf.

Hudson, D. and Smith, M. (n.d.). *The B2B sales planning handbook*. Retrieved May 14, 2014 from http://www.usdatavault.com/library/sales_planning_handbook_3forward_ch%201-3.pdf.

Jobber, D. and Lancaster, G. (2012). *Selling and Sales Management* (9th ed.). UK: Pearson Publishing.

Jordan, J. (2004). *In sales, can you manage what you're measuring*. Retrieved March 20, 2018 from https://hbr.org/2014/01/in-sales-can-you-manage-what-youre-measuring.

Jordan, J. and Vazzana, M. (2012). *Cracking the Sales Management Code: The Secrets to Measuring and Managing Sales Performance*. New York: McGraw-Hill.

JWPM. (n.d.). *Getting gritty with sales plans*. Retrieved May 14, 2018 from http://media.wix.com/ugd/a3c9af_a7139d3c121cffd67d24afcc184c9141.pdf.

Kahle, D. (n.d.). *Three most common mistakes Most sales managers make*. Retrieved January 15, 2019 from https://www.davekahle.com/article/managermistakes.html.

Miller, H. (2007). *Best practice in sales management: A resource guide for sales managers*. Retrieved January 10, 2018 from http://www.academia.edu/5290636/Best_Practices_In_A_Resource_Guide_for_Sales_Managers.

Mind Tools. (2014). *The sales funnel: Keeping control of your sales pipeline.* Retrieved May 20, 2018 from http://www.mindtools.com/pages/article/newLDR_94.htm.

Pipeliner. (2013). *5 crucial sales process steps explained.* Retrieved May 30, 2018 from http://www.pipeliner-sales.com/sales-process-steps/.

Rabbage, P. (2011). *What are the elements of a winning sales culture?* Retrieved May 14, 2018 from http://moresalesneast.wordpress.com/2011/05/16/what-are-the-elements-of-a-winning-sales-culture/.

RETMA. (n.d.). Television receiving set production 1947–1953. *TV Fact Book No.18.* Retrieved May 28, 2018 from http://www.tvhistory.tv/1947-53-USA-TV-MonthlyProduction.JPG.

Rogers, B. (2007). *Rethinking Sales Management.* UK: John Wiley & Sons.

Saffo, P. (2007). Six rules for effective forecasting. *Harvard Business Review*, 85, 122–131.

Sales Benchmark Index. (2014). *How to set up 2013 for sales success.* Retrieved May 10, 2018 from http://www.slideshare.net/salesbenchmarkindex/sales-strategy-2013-success.

Santos, T. (2013). *The evolution of TV.* Retrieved May 28, 2014 from http://www.techgeeze.com/2013/06/evolution-of-live-tv.html.

Smarta Enterprises. (2013). *Mind map: How to make a sales forecast.* Retrieved, May 20, 2018 from http://www.smarta.com/advice/business-planning/business-plans/mindmap-how-to-make-a-sales-forecast/.

Stevenson, W.J. (2012). *Operations Management* (11th ed.). UK: McGraw-Hill.

Still, R.R., Cundiff, E.W. and Govoni, N.A.P. (1988). *Sales Management: Decisions, Strategies and Cases.* India: Prentice-Hall International.

VP of Strategy. (n.d.). *Sales strategy.* Retrieved May 11, 2014 from http://vpofstrategy.files.wordpress.com/2012/02/vpos_salesstrategy_feb_2012.pdf.

White, M. (2004). *Welcome to Sales Management: The First 90 Days and Beyond.* Indiana: AuthorHouse.

Wilson, M.T. (1992). Managing a sales force. In D.M. Stewart (Ed.), *Handbook of Management Skills* (2nd ed.)., pp. 362–377). UK: Gower Publishing.

Chapter 11

Initial Environmental Review

11.1 Introduction

The conservation movement and the need for sustainable growth have received the attention of business organisations so that they are beginning to consider environmental management as a key issue in business development. Companies are increasingly interested in understanding the impact of the environmental issues associated with their sites and activities on competitiveness and business strategies. An initial environmental review (IER) provides a solid foundation for the environmental management system (EMS) of the business. This is an opportunity for businesses to consider all the interactions between the manufacturing system and the external environment. It highlights a company's environmental aspects, applicable legislation, environmental management practices in place already and lessons learnt from previous incidents. Therefore, an IER plays a crucial role in building the foundation for policy, programmes and target development.

11.2 The Purpose

An IER is a comprehensive analysis of the problems, impact and environmental performances associated with a company's activities. It is an assessment of company's commitment towards environmental issues (Waste and Resource Action Programme (WRAP), 2013). An IER is designed to (a) identify activities that have an impact on the environment; (b) evaluate the significance of these impacts and identify those that need improvement; (c) identify violations or potential violations of legislature; (d) identify applicable documentation for the EMS; (e) quantify discharges, emissions and utility/material use; and (f) identify opportunities for improvement of environmental performance to reduce waste.

11.3 Outcome of an IER

The outcome of an IER is a document describing the key issues, opportunities in terms of standards and benefits that could be achieved, requirements to ensure legal compliance plus and IER "determination" (Stoughton & Fisher, 2003). An IER determination can be:

- A positive determination where the activity is likely to have significant environmental impacts which require a full environmental assessment or project redesign, or
- A negative determination where the activity presents no significant impact, or
- A negative determination with the activity having adequate mitigation and monitoring and causing no adverse environmental impact, or
- A deferral determination applicable to activities with inadequate information to evaluate the impact (in this case, the project must be defined and an IER finalised before resources are committed).

The terms "negative" and "positive" are similar to the negative and positive tests applied to medical tests. A negative determination is the best outcome, and a positive determination is an unsatisfactory outcome. An initial IER will identify good environmental practices and those that need improvement. If there are management practices that help a business to run smoothly, it will probably help the EMS as well. The review will reveal the following (Price, 2014): (a) performance of the organisation and the EMS; (b) goals to achieve; (c) gaps between existing practices and EMS requirements; and (d) existing programmes that can serve as a basis for improvement.

11.4 Main Features of an IER

The method used to carry out an IER dictates the coherence of the chosen process and the reliability of the results. Several factors have to be considered in the development and implementation of the method (Cagno et al., 1999):

1. Exhaustive: A wide initial scope of potential environmental aspects requires an exhaustive IER, which provides a broad knowledge base for later simplification.
2. Complete: The study should cover different operational conditions such as normal, accidental and emergency situations.
3. Selective: The methodology adopted must be capable of identifying as quickly as possible the significant environmental aspects associated with the study. The selectivity influences the time required to complete the analysis and the overall cost, which can be managed by the correct restricting of the process.
4. Process modelling-based: An IER requires the modelling and description of the processes at the site. The level of detail must recognise factors such as the size of the site, the complexity of the processes, the level of environmental impact of the technologies used, the expected results, and the stage of development of the EMS, etc. An effective model should link site activities to environmental impacts and appropriate corrective measures to be taken, and it enables modification to be made when circumstances change.
5. Transparent: The transparency of the study refers to the documentation and justification of intermediate phases of the study in order to facilitate and communicate between all

stakeholders. Therefore, the essential factors are correct documentation, consistency in the methods adopted, and management involvement in the final phase to evaluate the data.

6. Integrity: During the data collection phase of the study, the information already available in the organisation should be explored. The quality system often provides information on process efficiency, material waste, etc. Materials and substances safety data sheets (SDSs) can be found in the safety management system. Production management and management control systems can also yield useful information.

11.5 Preparation

Before an IER is undertaken, it is necessary to obtain management commitment. Top management should be aware of the benefits of implementing an EMS so that the necessary resources can be committed to the project. These resources include (RRC International, n.d.) the commitment of staff time to develop and maintain the system, training for those leading the project, auditors and other staff, external resources such as environmental consultants and reference material, and financial resources to implement the programme.

11.6 The Process

Several approaches have been employed to conduct IERs. One possible approach includes the following steps (RRC International, n.d.): (a) Select a review team; (b) preparation; (c) conduct a site review; and (d) prepare a report.

11.6.1 Selection of the Team

The team can be drawn from inside and outside the organisation, but they should possess the necessary skills, knowledge and experience to undertake an IER. However, there are some essential conditions (Sheldon & Yoxon, 2008):

a. Ensure top management is involved and committed at all stages in the review process.
b. The team should have access to specialist skills that may be required. Specialists or technical staff within the organisation, or environmental professionals outside the organisation who have established close relations with it, may possess the necessary skills. Regulatory authorities may also be contracted.
c. Create an awareness of environmental requirements among the staff. The success of the project depends on the commitment of the staff.
d. The roles and responsibilities of those involved in the project must be clearly defined so that they are aware of what is expected of them.

11.6.2 Preparation

This step involves several activities such as establishing the project outline, defining the roles and responsibilities of the team, collecting background information and methods of communicating, and developing a plan (RRC International, n.d.). The IER methodology includes methods for collecting data through interviews, observations and documentation reviews, methods for identifying aspects and impacts, evaluating their significance, and methods of communicating the results in the report.

The collection of background information depends on the processes within the scope of an IER and associated risks. Background data may include site permits and monitoring data related to waste, energy utilisation, water use, emissions to air, etc., financial reports relating to energy and water use and waste disposal, existing relevant procedures, and communications with regulatory agencies and interested parties relating to compliance and concerns.

11.6.3 Identification of Processes

Analysis by processes enhances the quality of an IER. This involves the identification of relationships between specific impact categories and the existence of activities and processes causing the impacts. An effective environmental evaluation of impacts takes into consideration major upstream (e.g. raw material purchases) and downstream processes (e.g. use and disposal of materials) following a life-cycle management approach (Cagno et al., 1999).

11.6.4 Site Review

A major portion of the review is site review, and it includes the following (Zackrisson et al., 2004; Sheldon & Yoxon, 2008):

1. Site history.
2. Company description.
3. Organisation's operations and activities.
4. Legal and other requirements.
5. History of accidents.
6. Raw material and component usage.
7. Chemical and chemical products usage.
8. Energy consumption.
9. Waste and recycling.
10. Indoor and outdoor emissions.
11. Impact on surrounding area.
12. Transportation.
13. Company products.
14. Summary of emissions and consumption of resources.

1. Site history
 - Date of acquisition.
 - Expansions since acquisition.
 - Known contaminants.
 - Details of any contaminated site survey.
 - Details of warnings and regulatory non-compliances.
 - Complaints from the community.

2. Company description
 - Company's products, services and volumes.
 - Company location: proximity to buildings, natural areas of beauty, water courses, etc.
 - Size and design of the premises.

- Purpose for which the premises were used prior to current occupation.
- Any extensions to premises.
- Type of facilities.
- Type of plants and machinery.
- Type of goods supplied by major suppliers.
- Activities planned for the future.
- Number of employees.
- Turnover.
- Limitations of the review: Specify the limitations if the scope of the review does not include the whole company as described here.

3. Organisation's operations and activities

The organisation's operations and activities refer to the processes required to offer products and services to customers, as well as those needed to maintain the business. Although an activity is independent, it may be linked to other supporting activities. The accomplishment of an activity requires planning, design and implementation such as the selection of suppliers, choice of materials and equipment, staff training, etc. Most activities also require maintenance. Information about the activities, including background and their major components, will be useful in the evaluation phase of an IER. Physical details and quantitative data will strengthen the quality of the report. The activity description of an IER should also include all the components and phases of the life-cycle of the product (Stoughton & Fisher, 2003).

4. Legal and other requirements

This section includes environmental laws, statutes, regulations, general provisions, customer demands and other demands that influence the business. An overview may be obtained from industry sector organisations. Other avenues of information are suppliers, auditors, authorities, specialists, municipal authorities and health and environmental officers. Then build the repository of laws and other requirements based on this overview. The following steps may be helpful:

- Review the descriptions and gather only those requirements applicable to the organisation.
- Identify people who are knowledgeable about the statues and other requirements.
- Obtain documents relevant to the organisation's activities.
- Determine for each statute how compliance could be achieved and assign responsibilities.
- Summarise the findings (Table 11.1).

Table 11.1   Legal and Other Requirements

	Requirements and Responsibility	*Description*	*Current Status*
1	Authorisations	Municipal authorities Health regulators Environmental officers Certifying bodies	
2	Legal and other requirements applicable to the product/service	State all regulations and requirements applicable to the product/service	

(Continued)

Table 11.1 (*Continued*) Legal and Other Requirements

	Requirements and Responsibility	*Description*	*Current Status*
3	Customers' demands and their preferences	Review complaints from customers on quality, food safety and environmental issues and identify their demands	
4	Suppliers' demands and preferences	Determine how suppliers can help in supporting the company's environmental demands	
5	Community demands and preferences	Determine whether the community is affected by noise, pollutants, waste, etc.	
6	Employees' demands and preferences	Obtain employees' feedback on health, safety and environmental issues	

Table 11.2 History of Accidents

Date of Occurrence	*Location*	*Cause of the Accident*	*Environmental Damage and the Extent (Include Penalties, If Any)*	*Corrective Actions*

5. History of accidents

This section deals with accidents that have occurred during the last five years (Table 11.2).

6. Raw material and component usage

This is an inventory of raw materials and components used in the company's products and services. The inventory could be easily compiled using each process as the basis. A detailed description is not necessary, and it is the order of the size of the impact that is important (Table 11.3).

7. Chemical and chemical products usage

Most industries use various types of chemicals in their processing environment. Legislation often requires companies to use environmentally friendly products. The users are expected to have sufficient knowledge about the products so that harmful effects can be prevented during their use (Table 11.4). General requirements include the use of chemicals that comply with quality requirements, as well as products that are environmentally friendly,

Table 11.3 Raw Materials and Components

Process	Raw Material Component	Amount	Use	Environmental Impact

Table 11.4 Chemicals and Their Usage

Type (According to the Classification)	Amount (Annual Quantity)	Use (Location of Use)	Destination (During Use and after Use)	Environmental Impact

Table 11.5 Energy Use

Type of Energy	Usage (MWh)	Cost	Use	Fuel Conservation Measures

maintaining an inventory of chemical used for procurement, maintaining health and safety information applicable to each chemical, and making this accessible to those who use them, and strictly following appropriate storage and handling requirements.

8. Energy consumption

Power bills produce the usage of energy, which includes electricity and fuel-fired boilers. Table 11.5 shows a template for recording energy use.

Table 11.6   Waste and Recycling

Type (Waste Water, Chemicals, Solids)[a]	Sources	Characteristics Quantity[b]	Treatment (Waste Water) Handling (Chemicals) Disposal (Solids)	Recycling (Waste Water, Chemicals) Disposal (Solids)	Discharge (Waste Water) Disposal (Chemicals, Solids)	Permits Approvals Licenses	Records of Discharges (Waste Water) Disposal (Chemicals, Solids)

[a] For solids, specify the type, e.g. wood, metal, paper, etc.
[b] For waste water, use waste water analysis reports; for chemicals, specify the type of chemicals; and for solids, specify the quantity.

9. Waste and recycling

Waste materials include water waste, chemical waste and solid water. In this category, recycling and/or disposal methods are important. Permits may be required to dispose of some waste material. The required information may be captured using the template shown in Table 11.6.

10. Indoor and outdoor emissions

Emissions to air can originate from a wide variety of industrial activities and can come from a single source (e.g. boiler or furnace) or from multiple sources (e.g. application of solvents in a production line). Organisations should avoid, minimise and control the adverse effects of emissions to air on health, safety and the environment. Therefore, air emissions should be carefully monitored according to standard methods.

Noise levels should not exceed the applicable noise level guidelines. Methods of preventing and controlling noise levels depend upon the source and proximity of recipients. The best method for controlling noise from a single source is to implement suitable measures at the source. Table 11.7 template can be used to review emissions to air and noise levels.

11. Impact on surrounding area

This section describes the activities and their impact that adversely alters the physical environment. Adverse effects include soil erosion, land pollution, ground water contamination, and effects on plants and animals (Table 11.8).

Table 11.7 Emissions to Air and Noise Levels

Type of Emission (Gas or Noise)	Origin	Mass (tonnes/year)[a]	Reduction Method	Emissions Monitored? (Yes/No)	Annual Cost of Reduction Methods	Proposed Reduction Methods

[a] For gaseous emissions.

Table 11.8 Impact on Surroundings

Impact on (Land, Water, Plants, Animals, etc.)	Source	Effect of the Impact	Remedial Measures	Penalties, If Any

12. Transportation

Transport effects include emissions of gases such as carbon dioxide (CO_2), carbon monoxide (CO), oxides of nitrogen and sulphur (NO_x, SO_x), particles, and other gases such as benzene and butadiene. Traffic also causes other effects such as noise, traffic congestion resulting in air pollution and nuisance, possible changes to the landscape, land acquisition for parking, and spillages of fuel polluting the soil and ground water (Table 11.9).

13. Company's products

Packaging constitutes a major component of products, and through proper design, it is possible to reduce the environmental impact from the start of a product's life to its final disposal or reuse (Table 11.10).

14. Summary of consumptions and emission

This section presents a summary of overall findings (Table 11.11).

11.7 Communication

A short briefing paper should be presented to management, which covers the purpose of an IER, a summary of findings and the benefits of the report.

An IER is a critical step in the environmental management programme, and the information will provide a basis for measuring its future progress. Therefore, top management must ensure that an IER is conducted efficiently and effectively so that accurate information is available for decision-making.

Table 11.9 Transportation

Number of Vehicles	Monthly Mileage	Fuel Usage	Emissions	Other Effects	Mitigating Efforts

Table 11.10 Company's Products

Product	Annual Usage	Weight Per Product	Packaging (Type and Weight)	Recycling or Efforts to Reduce

Table 11.11 Summary of Consumption and Emissions

Input	Type and Amount
Raw materials including packaging	
Energy consumption	
Water usage	
Transportation Total mileage Total fuel consumption	
Output and Source	*Type and Amount*
Emissions to air	
Waste water discharge	
Solid waste discharge	
Soil pollution	

References

Cagno, E., Di Giulio, A. and Trucco, P. (1999). A methodological framework for the initial environmental review (IER) in EMS implementation. *Journal of Environmental Assessment Policy and Management*, 1 (4), 505–532.

Price, T. (2014). *Environmental Management Systems: How to Boost Your Organisation's Environmental Performance*. Washington: Amazon Publishing.

RRC International. (n.d.). *Tools for assessment and interpretation of environmental performance*. Retrieved May 27, 2017 from http://www.rrc.co.uk/media/623035/iema_fc.pdf.

Sheldon, C. and Yoxon, M. (2008). *Environmental Management Systems*. UK: Earthscan.

Stoughton, M. and Fisher, W. (2003). *USAID environmental procedures manual for USAID environmental officers and USAID mission partners*. Retrieved May 26, 2017 from http://pdf.usaid.gov/pdf_docs/Pnacy577.pdf.

WRAP. (2013). *Your guide to an environmental management system: Business resource efficiency guide*. Retrieved May 26, 2017 from http://www.wrap.org.uk/sites/files/wrap/WRAP%20EMS%20guide%20June%202013.pdf.

Zackrisson, M., Bengtsson, G. and Norberg, C. (2004). *Measuring Your Company's Environmental Impact: Templates and Tools for a Complete ISO 14001 Initial Review*. UK: Earthscan.

Chapter 12

Impact of Business and Industry on the Environment

12.1 Introduction

During the years following World War II, the world has witnessed several major environmental disasters. Although the casualties due to disasters have been disputed, the impact on the environment cannot be ignored (Table 12.1) (Open University, 2016).

Table 12.1 Major Environmental Disasters after World War II

Location	Date	Business	Cause	Impact
Seveso, Italy	July 10, 1976	Pesticide and herbicide plant	Dense vapour cloud containing tetrachlorodiben-zoparadioxin (TCDD)	3,000 animals died and 450 people experienced skin lesions
Three Mile Island, Pennsylvania	March 28, 1979	Nuclear Plant	Partial meltdown releasing radioactive gases and iodine	No health effects reported
Bhopal, India	December 2–3, 1984	Union Carbide Pesticide Plant	Released 30 tons of toxic gas methyl isocyanate	Over 500,000 people were exposed and there were 3,787 deaths due to exposure (disputed)
Chernobyl, Ukraine	April 26, 1986	Nuclear Plant	Radioactive fallout across Western Europe	3964 deaths directly attributed to radiation

(Continued)

Table 12.1 (*Continued*) Major Environmental Disasters after World War II

Location	Date	Business	Cause	Impact
Exxon Valdez, Alaska	March 24, 1989	Crude oil	Grounding of the tanker Exxon Valdez off Prince William Sound, Alaska	Spillage of 260,000 to 750,000 barrels of crude oil. Marine and wild lives were the hardest hit
Deepwater Horizon, Gulf of Mexico	April 20, 2010	Oil	Explosion of the platform	Killed 11 workers and 5 million barrels of crude oil were released into the gulf. Marine and wild lives were the biggest casualties
Fukushima, Japan	March 11, 2011	Nuclear Plant Fukushima Daiichi	Earthquake and tsunami caused reactor meltdown releasing radioactive gases	No confirmed casualties due to radiation. Mortality due to "evacuation stress" from the area around Fukushima had reached more than 1,600. This includes deaths from suicide and lack of access to critical health care, but not from radiation such as increased cancer or any other direct result of the nuclear accident

More recently, in 2008, a fatal explosion in the CropScience pesticide plant in Institute, West Virginia killed two people and injured eight others (Davis, 2016). A chemical spill of 4-methylcyclohexyl methanol from a storage tank in the Freedom Industries chemical plant in Charleston, West Virginia, leaked into the Elk River contaminating the tap water for 300,000 inhabitants. In 2015, across China, five separate chemical explosions caused the deaths of many people. Enormous amounts of toxic waste were released into the River Doce in Southeast Brazil in November 2015 as a result of the collapse of two mining dams (Mussarani, 2016), killing 18 people and destroying villages, vegetation and wildlife. Therefore, the year 2015 will be remembered as a bleak one that reminded the chemical industry about its social and ethical obligations to protect the environment, the people and conserve its resources.

12.2 Environmental Movement

The environmental movement refers to any social or political movement aimed at the conservation, restoration or enhancement of the natural environment. It is difficult to establish where the environmental movement began. In the United States until the late 1800s, any available resources were utilised by industries for profit. However, during the late 1800s, Americans began to focus their attention on depleting natural resources giving rise to the conservation movement, which aimed at the protection of public land. The environmental movement aimed at protecting both resources and species. Both movements were concerned with natural resources. The conservation movement directed their attention to efficient human use of resources, whereas the environmental movement was more concerned with the depletion of any resource or species (Stanko, 2011; Encyclopedia.com, 2003; Vault, 2019).

The modern environmental movement had its roots in the 1960s, the period of social change in the United States. An increase in public awareness about environmental issues triggered by events such as the four-day smog that killed 80 people in New York, the publication of the book *Silent Spring* by Rachel Carson emphasising the harmful effects of pesticides such as DDT on human health, and the Santa Barbara oil spill that dumped 200,000 tons of crude oil along the California coastline can be considered to be milestones in the modern environmental movement. Other countries around the globe experienced similar events. In the first wave of the environmental movement, countries such as England, Germany and Japan became aware of the depletion of natural resources and introduced measures to manage them. In the second wave, organisations around the world joined hands with experts to create an awareness of environmental issues leading to the modern environmental movement (Stanko, 2011; Encyclopedia.com, 2003; Vault, 2019).

12.2.1 Developments in the United States

In the United States, the 1960s was a period of growth for the environmental movement. Conservation societies gathered pace and there was a rapid increase in their membership. President Lyndon Johnson took a keen interest in preservationist issues and introduced almost 300 beautification and conservation measures with $12 billion in authorised funds (Encyclopedia.com, 2003). The most significant during President Johnson's term was the Wilderness Act of 1964. The Federal Government also took a new interest in controlling pollution and Congress passed laws such as the Clean Air Acts of 1963 and 1967, and the Clean Water Act of 1960. During the terms of subsequent presidents, the environmental movement has had its ups and downs.

12.2.2 Global Concerns

From the first Greenpeace protest involving six people and a boat, the environmental movement made considerable progress drawing the attention of world leaders to the issues and commanding action. Universal concerns about the environment and natural resources prompted the United Nations to convene several summits (United Nations, 2018; European Commission, 2016):

1. UN Conference on Human Environment 1972.
2. World Commission on Environment and Development 1987.
3. UN Conference on Environment and Development 1992 (also called the Earth Summit or Rio Conference).
4. General Assembly Special Session on the Environment 1997.
5. World Summit on Sustainable Development 2002.
6. UN Conference on Sustainable Development 2012.
7. UN Conference on Climate Change 2015.

Table 12.2 World Summits on Environmental Issues

Conference	Outcome
UN Conference on Human Environment (1972)	Establishment of the United Nations Environment Programme (UNEP)
World Commission on Environment and Development (1987)	Developed the theme of sustainable development
UN Conference on Environment and Development (1992)	Rio declaration on environment and development, a series of principles defining the rights and responsibilities of states Global plan of action to promote sustainable development (Agenda 21) Statement of forest principles, a set of principles to underpin sustainable management of forests worldwide
General Assembly Special Session on the Environment (1997)	Programme for the further implementation of Agenda 21
World Summit on Sustainable Development (2002)	Reviewed the progress on the implementation of Agenda 21 Johannesburg declaration of sustainable development Plan of implementation
UN Conference on Sustainable Development (2012)	The future we want
UN Conference on Climate Change (2015)	Global action plan to limit global warming to well below 2°C

Table 12.2 shows the outcome of these summits.

12.2.3 *Kyoto Protocol*

The Kyoto Protocol is an agreement negotiated by many countries in December 1997, which sets out mandatory targets for reducing greenhouse gas (GHG) emissions. It was implemented following Russia's ratification in 2005. The protocol was developed by the United Nations Framework Convention on Climate Change (UNFCCC). The signatories to the Kyoto Protocol have committed to cut emissions of not only carbon dioxide (CO_2) but also other GHGs: methane, nitrous oxide, hydrofluorocarbons, perfluorocarbons and sulphur hexafluoride. The goal of the Kyoto Protocol was to collectively reduce GHG emissions by 5.2% below the emission levels of 1990 by 2012. Although the target of 5.2% is a collective one, individual countries were assigned higher or lower targets. For example, the United States was expected to reduce GHG emissions by 7%. The protocol also allows emissions trading, i.e. buying "credits" from other participants who are able to exceed their reduction targets in order to offset. Currently, there are 192 parties (191 states and one regional economic integration organisation) to the Kyoto Protocol (United Nations, 2019; Johnston, n.d).

12.2.4 *Montreal Protocol*

The ozone layer on the planet has existed throughout the history of mankind, and it had been taken for granted. However, in 1970, scientists suggested that this vital protection from the sun's radiation by the ozone layer could be adversely affected by man-made actions. Soon afterwards, scientists discovered that the use of man-made chemicals known as ODS (ozone-depleting substances) has been damaging the ozone layer. Professor Paul Crutzen who shared the Noble Prize in Chemistry with Professor Mario Molina and Professor F. Sherwood Rowland in 1995 for their work in atmospheric chemistry, particularly concerning the formation and decomposition of ozone (Royal Swedish Academy of Science, 1995), described it as the worst disaster to hit the global environment (European Commission, 2007). Against this backdrop, the Montreal Protocol on substances that deplete the ozone layer was agreed on September 16, 1987, and it entered into force January 1, 1989.

The Montreal Protocol has been amended a number of times, and the focus was to reduce and phase out several ODS such as chlorofluorocarbons (CFCs) found in spray cans, methyl bromide used as a pesticide and halon used in fire-fighting applications. The Montreal Protocol targets 96 chemicals in thousands of applications across more than 240 industrial sectors. Both developed and developing nations are obliged to progressively phase out the entire major ODS. It was the first international environmental treaty to achieve complete ratification (Ozone Secretarial, 2018).

12.3 Environmental Issues

Activities of a business include material purchasing, design and development, production, logistics, sales, consumption and recycling and waste disposal. All these activities have an impact on the environment. The impact of business activities on the environment falls into three major categories:

1. Resources: Timber, oil, metals, water and other resources are used in the manufacture of goods.
2. Pollution and noise: These are the spill-over effects of manufacturing activities.
3. Land use: Manufacturing facilities, houses, roads and landfills destroy the ecology and available land.

Specific technologies used in these activities have a significant impact on the amount and types of materials that go through the production cycle of extraction, manufacture, use and waste. The Citizen Group, a global leader in miniaturising and precision technology in Japan, has monitored the environmental impact of its activities in Japan and overseas. Input and output data for 2015 is presented in Table 12.3 (Citizen Group, 2016).

12.4 Resources

The increased use of resources in industrial countries coupled with population growth has put enormous pressure on worldwide natural resources including air and water, arable land and raw materials. Over the 20th century, there has been increased activity in the global industrial sector. Global production has increased by a factor of 40, energy use by 16 and ocean fishing by 35.

Table 12.3 Environmental Impact of Business Activities of Citizen Group, Japan

	Input			Output	
Environmental Factor	*Japan*	*Overseas Companies*	*Environmental Factor*	*Japan*	*Overseas Companies*
Total energy (GJ)	2,136,797	1,148,626	CO_2 emissions (tons CO_2)	83,875	42,953
Water resource (km³)	1,757	995	NO_X emissions (tons)	4	0
Repeated use of water within the organisation (km³)	55	85	SO_X emissions (tons)	2	0
Chemical substances handled (tons)	141	2,239	Water drainage (km³)	1,177	574
Containers and packaging used (tons)	77	1,631	BOD emissions (tons)	15	7
			COD emissions (tons)	8	17
			Waste generated (tons)	6,662	7,864

CO_2: carbon-di-oxide
NO: nitrous oxide.
SO: sulphur oxide.
BOD: biochemical oxygen demand.
COD: chemical oxygen demand.

The global population has increased from 1.5 to 6 billion people. Material flows in industrial nations too have increased, and today, it amounts to 60 tonnes of material per capita per year. This is far above the production area available on the planet. Renewal resources can be replenished, while non-renewal resources are only present on finite quantities and cannot be replenished once removed from the geosphere. Renewal resources cannot be extracted from the earth at a rate faster than the renewal process. Therefore, the message is clear: The use of resources should be reduced (Nilsson et al., 2007).

12.4.1 Water Consumption

Humans, plants and animals require water for their very existence, but it is not an unlimited resource. Only 2.5% of total world water is fresh water. Out of this, 70% is ice and snow in mountainous regions, and about 30% present is ground water and only 0.3% is fresh water in lakes and rivers (Open University, 2016). Industries depend on water for their activities. It can be used as a raw material, solvent for dissolving chemicals, a coolant, transport agent and as an energy source. Water is used for three main purposes: agriculture, industry and domestic. According to the UN World Water Association Programme (2017), the consumption and waste water generation by major water use sectors in 2010 were as follows:

- Agriculture consumption 38%
- Industry consumption 32%
- Municipal consumption 3%
- Municipal waste water 8%
- Industry waste water 16%
- Agriculture drainage 32%

The trends in developed and developing countries show that the global water withdrawal will increase from 3,800 km³ to 4,300–5,000 km³ by 2025. In some developed countries, 70% of industrial wastes are dumped into untreated water where they pollute the drinking water. Each year, industrial waste accounts for million tons of heavy metals, solvents, toxic sludge and other wastes which find their way into the fresh water supply (Cosgrove, 2001).

12.4.2 *Energy Use and Consumption*

An adequate energy supply is necessary not only for industrial activities but also to meet consumer demands. Energy resources include oil, electricity, coal, hydroelectric, solar and nuclear. Oil and coal are non-renewable energy resources. While solar energy is inexhaustible, it is currently expensive. Lignite, black coal and gas are fossil energy resources, which were formed hundreds of millions of years ago, are non-renewable. However, their use is millions of times higher than their renewal. Although many countries have high levels of energy production, world demand for energy continues to spiral upwards. The global consumption of energy by industry, transportation and households amounts to 12 billion toe (tonne of oil equivalent) per annum and is expected to rise to 15 billion toe per annum by 2020 with an annual growth rate of 2%. This increase is mainly due to population growth and the advanced industrialisation of emerging economies. Fossil fuel extraction and use is considered to be the second largest resource flow in the planet. It is estimated that oil will be depleted by the year 2040 (Chen, 2011). Peak oil is designated as the year when half the existing oil reserve has been used up and is estimated to have occurred in 2008–2010. Fossil oil combustion pollutes the atmosphere. The process releases large quantities of CO_2, oxides of sulphur and nitrogen. CO_2 release contributes to global warming. Other energy resources include the following resources:

1. Flowing energy resources – solar heat, solar electricity and photosynthesis.
2. Streaming energy resources – waves, wind and flowing water: They are used in wave energy, wind energy and hydro power. These resources also have environmental problems. Hydro power requires large water reservoirs and flowing natural water streams. Wind power utilises large land spaces (Nilsson et al., 2007; McKinsey Germany, 2009). World supply and consumption of energy balance is shown in Table 12.4 (International Energy Agency (IAE), 2017). Total primary energy supply (TPES) includes imports, exports and stock changes. Generally, from 1973 to 2014, energy supply and consumption have almost doubled and oil products and natural gas are major consumption items.

The industrial sector is a major energy user and all industrial processes require energy to convert raw material into the desired products. The main consumers of energy in the industrial sector are (Cong et al., 2012) chemicals and petroleum (29%), iron and steel (20%), non-metallic minerals (10%), paper, pulp and printing (6%) and food and tobacco (5%). Other industries consume the balance.

Table 12.4 World Supply and Consumption of Energy Balance

Energy Source	1973 (Mtoe)		2015 (Mtoe)	
	TPES	Consumption	TPES	Consumption
Coal	1,496.19	631.43	3,836.09	1,044.09
Crude oil	2,867.64	22.14	4,442.11	19.10
Oil products	−49.73	2,230.28	−107.83	3,820.49
Natural gas	976.73	651.57	2,943.72	1,401.13
Nuclear	53.05		670.73	
Hydro	110.31		334.40	
Biofuels and waste	640.84	609.10	1,323.47	1,052.21
Others	5.96	516.76	204.68	2,046.58
Total	6,100.99	4,661.28	1,3626.37	9,383.60

Mtoe: million tons of oil equivalent.
TPES: total primary energy supply.

12.4.3 *Mineral Use and Depletion*

With the rapid growth of the human population and expansion of the world economy, humans extract and harvest increasing amounts of natural resources from the ecosystem and mines in order to meet the increasing demands of consumers. According to the estimates about 60 billion tonnes of material are extracted annually (Nilsson et al., 2007).

Natural resources fall into two categories: renewable and non-renewable. Renewable resources, e.g., are agricultural products, fish for food and timber used in furniture and paper manufacture. Fossil fuels, metal ores used for manufacturing cars and computers, and minerals for building houses and constructing roads are non-renewable resources. Although not used in production processes additional materials are extracted or removed from the soil surface in order to gain access to valuable resources. They constitute about 40 billion tonnes annually. Therefore, the total drainage of resources amounts to 100 billion tonnes per year. There has been a steady increase in the rate of extraction from 40 billion tonnes in 1980 to 58 billion tonnes in 2005 (Friends of the Earth Europe (FoEE), 2009).

Different types of resources have specific characteristics that impact on the environment. Four main types of resources are (1) bulk materials; (2) macronutrients; (3) mineral compounds; and (4) biotic resources (Nilsson et al., 2007).

1. Bulk materials: These are extracted from the uppermost layer of the ground and constitute the largest material flow. They are used in the building industry.
2. Macronutrients: Nitrogen, phosphorus and calcium are macronutrients used in agriculture and chemical compounds, e.g. phosphorous compounds in detergents and nitrogen compounds in the plastic industry.
3. Mineral compounds: They are minerals extracted from bedrock and they are employed to produce metals such as iron, the most heavily used metal. They are also used to make alloys

with iron called ferro-alloy metals contain, in addition chromium, nickel, titanium, vanadium and magnesium. Non-ferrous metals extracted are aluminium, copper, lead, zinc, tin and mercury. Metals are non-renewable resources, but iron and aluminium (which are abundant) will not be depleted at the current rate of use. Others are being used at a rate much faster than the natural weathering process. Some rare earth metals are almost depleted.

4. Biotic resources: These are obtained from the biosphere (living and organic material) and used as food for consumption. They are also used in the production of pharmaceutical substances and in landscapes. Although these resources are renewable, they have a limited carrying capacity, which is the rate of production of biotic resources that depends on the area considered. Biotic resources are used in several industrial sectors, e.g. food processing industry, timber in the building industry, wood in paper and pulp production, etc.

12.4.3.1 Environmental Damage

Mining operations cause immense environmental damage worldwide. Water, air, soil, wildlife and social values are all affected by different stages of mining operation. A mining project involves the following phases (Environmental Law Alliance Worldwide (ELAW), 2010):

1. Exploration: During this phase, information about the location and value of mineral ore deposits is gathered using surveys, field studies, drilling test boreholes and other exploratory studies. This phase requires the clearing of wide areas of vegetation for heavy equipment access.
2. Development: Access roads are constructed, and the site is prepared and cleared.
3. Active mining: The active mining phase involves open-pit mining, placer mining, underground mining and/or reworking inactive or abundant mines and tailings.
4. Disposal of waste rock.
5. Ore extraction.
6. Beneficiation: separation of metal from non-metal material.
7. Disposal of tailing.
8. Site reclamation and closure.

12.4.3.2 Impact

Some of the major effects of mining operations are (1) water consumption; (2) soil erosion; (3) mine dewatering; (4) air quality; (5) release of mercury; (6) release of cyanide; (7) noise and vibration; (8) degradation of wildlife and habitat; (9) energy use; and (10) social effects (Environmental Law Alliance Worldwide (ELAW), 2010).

1. Water use: Mining operations affect both the quality of water and its availability in the area of operation. Ground water supply will be contaminated and may not be fit for human consumption. Surface water may not be adequate to sustain the ecosystem. Rainwater seeping through metal heaps will form an acidic solution called acid drainage containing high levels of sulphate and metals. Leaching of toxic substances such as arsenic, selenium and metals can occur even in the absence of acid conditions. Water near mine sites will contain high levels of cyanide and nitrogen compounds from heap leaching and blasting.
2. Erosion of soils and mine washes into surface water: Where mining areas are large and when large quantities of materials are exposed, soil erosion can be a major problem. Erosion may cause sediment to deposit in nearby water sites, especially during stormy periods.

3. Impact of mine dewatering: Pumping and discharging mine water causes several environmental issues: (a) reduction or elimination of surface water; (b) degradation of surface water quality; (c) degradation of habitat; (d) reduction or elimination of producing domestic supply wells; and (e) water quality problems associated with discharge of pumped mine water back to the surface water.

4. Impact of air quality: Mining operations produce a large amount of waste piles containing small particles that are easily carried by the wind. Particulate matter is produced as a result of excavation, blasting, transportation of material, wind erosion, fugitive dust from tailings, stockpiles, waste dumps and haul roads. Gas emissions from vehicles, both stationary and mobile, explosions and mine processes also pollute the atmosphere.

5. Release of mercury: During the roasting or autoclaving process of ore to recover the gold, mercury is vaporised and enters the atmosphere. This is particularly evident in small-scale mining operations. It is estimated that 10–15 million small-scale gold miners operate in 70 different countries. Mercury pollution is not a localised issue as it is transported around the globe by winds and major ocean currents. Mercury that enters the water or soil is converted into methylmercury by anaerobic bacterial action. This is absorbed by phytoplanktons, which gets ingested by zooplankton and fish, thereby contaminating the food chain (Norman, 2016).

6. Release of cyanide: Some gold mining operations use cyanide to recover gold from ore. During the leaching process nearby soil and water can get contaminated with cyanide.

7. Noise and vibration: Noise pollution originates from vehicle engines, the loading and unloading of rock into steel pumpers, chutes, power generation and other sources. Cumulative noise from shovelling, ripping, drilling, blasting, transport, crushing, grinding and stockpiling can adversely affect wildlife and the nearby community. Many types of mining operations cause significant vibration and the worst is blasting. Vibrations affect the stability of the infrastructure, building and homes of people living near mining operations.

8. Impact on wildlife and habitat: Mining operations have a major impact on flora and fauna through the removal of vegetation and topsoil, the displacement of fauna, the distribution of pollutants and the generation of noise. Disturbing, removing and redistributing the land threaten the survival of wild species. While some of the effects are short-lived, others may cause long-term effects. During the excavation and piling of mine waste, mobile species leave their territories and sedentary animals suffer the consequences. In streams, lakes, ponds or marshes which are filled or drained aquatic animals disappear. The reduction of land space creates a food shortage. When land is fragmented into smaller and smaller portions, migration becomes difficult and as a result species which require large areas simply disappear.

9. Energy use: Mining operations consume a large amount of electricity. Smaller operations are more energy efficient than large-scale mining operations as they are less mechanised and rely on manual labour. But small operations use older and less energy efficient equipment. Energy consumption differs between open-pit and underground mining operations. Ventilation, cooling and lifting ore from underground mines requires much electricity. Open-pit mines use a considerable amount of diesel for transporting ore in large trucks.

10. Social effects: The resettlement and redistribution of land during mining operations creates tension among the community, and community harmony is often disturbed. Communities have to adjust to changes in water quality and availability, public health facilities and other amenities. Sacred sites and sites of historical interest may simply disappear from the planet.

12.5 Pollution

Pollution is the process of introducing a substance (gas, liquid or solid) or energy (heat, noise, radiation) that directly or indirectly harm or has the potential to cause harm to the environment, causing hazards to human or animal health, harm to the ecosystem, damage to the infrastructure, including building and amenities, and interference with light levels. According to Belcham (2015), pollution can be represented by a model known as the source–pathway–receptor model. The source defines the origin of the pollutant, the pathway represents the mode of transmission and finally, the receptor signifies the recipient (Table 12.5). Traditionally, organisations have focused on pathways to control the impact on the environment. More recently, attention has been focused on the source of pollution. The impact on the environment can be described as acute or chronic. The features of acute and chronic pollution are presented in Table 12.6.

Some Asian countries completely ignore the serious consequences of water pollution. Beaches are littered with plastic bottles, plastic bags, household waste and animal waste. According to an environmental project carried out by the University of Moratuwa in Sri Lanka, deterioration of ground water quality was observed in the Dehiwala-Mt.Lavinia suburb with high faecal coliform levels due to the discharge of pollutants from unsewerage houses, businesses or industries to local canals and rivers. In addition low dissolved oxygen levels were also observed (Uni-Consultancy Services, 2019).

Pollution has been classified in many ways. A common approach is to classify them on the basis of origin: point and non-point source pollution. Point source pollution occurs when pollutants originate from a single source and is pollution that can contaminate air, water and soil. Toxic chemicals released into the air and/or water as a result of industrial activity and waste oil from a garage are examples of point source pollution. Non-point source pollution occurs when contaminants are introduced into the environment over a wide spread-out area (Mirsal, 2008).

Table 12.5   Source–Pathway–Receptor Model of Pollution

Source (Examples)	Pathway	Receptor (Examples)
Emissions	Typically through air, land, water or biological systems transferring through the food chain	Humans
Liquid waste		Flora and fauna
Solid waste		Land
Chemicals		Soil
Radiation		Water
		Climate

Table 12.6   Acute and Chronic Pollution Impacts

Acute	Chronic
Impact felt immediately after the incident	Develops sometimes after the incident
Generally straightforward	Often long-term
Sometimes fatal	Less clear-cut
Generally non-reversible	May lead to death ultimately
E.g. Exposure to nuclear radiation	Affects growth or behaviour functions
	May be reversible
	E.g. Particulate matter

12.6 Types of Pollution

Pollution can be classified according to the environment in which it occurs (e.g. air, water and soil) or according to the type of pollutant (e.g. lead, mercury, sulphur dioxide, solid waste, heat etc.) responsible for the pollution. It is also classified as natural pollution caused by natural processes and artificial pollution caused by humans. Pollution caused by humans (Khopkar, 2004) include air, water, soil, solid waste, noise, thermal, light and radiation.

12.6.1 Air Pollution

Air pollution is not new to the planet. Humans have experienced smoke from burning coal, intense fog, and sulphur dioxide in the air since early times. Technological advancements have enabled the extent and location of air pollutants to be determined accurately. Two main types of air pollutants are (Nibusinessinfor.co.uk, n.d.) fumes, which include vapour, gases, smoke and odours, and dust as dry particles. These are produced mainly by chemical manufacturing processes and equipment and less by cleaning and packaging processes. Air pollution affects the environment in several ways: GHG emissions contribute towards climate change and ODS damage the ozone layer. This type of pollutions causes acid rain, which causes damage to buildings, land, fresh water, sea water, wildlife and plants. Respiratory problems can develop in people exposed to polluted air. Toxic pollutants in the air can cause wild species to migrate to new locations and change their habitat. They affect the health of aquatic animals when deposited over the surface of water. In areas where air is polluted, smog is a common occurrence in the mornings (Nilsson et al., 2007).

Oxides of nitrogen originate from power stations and vehicle emissions. They contribute less to acid rain. Three oxides of nitrogen are primary pollutants: nitrous oxide, nitric oxide and nitrogen dioxide. Nitrous oxide is a GHG found in small quantities and it contributes to global warming. The other two are highly reactive gases with short residence time. They are secondary pollutants and their action is due to the oxidation products.

The main sources of air pollution are (nibusinessinfo.co.uk, n.d.):

■ Emissions from burning fuels in furnaces and boilers.
■ Open air burning.
■ Dust and fumes from poor waste storage and ventilation systems.
■ Ozone from office equipment such as copiers and laser printers.
■ Exhaust fumes from equipment and vehicles.
■ Sulphur oxides and nitrogen oxides from mining operations.
■ Radioactive elements from nuclear plant incidents.

Those who are exposed to air pollutants can face harmful health effects such as skin conditions, breathing difficulties and lung conditions, allergic reactions and cancer.

12.6.1.1 Particulate Matter

Particulate matter (Nilsson et al., 2007) is a solid or liquid matter dispersed in the atmosphere, and it ranges in diameter from 0.005 to 100 μm.

Aerosols: Tiny liquid or solid particles dispersed in the atmosphere.

Dust: Solid particles that range in size from 1.0 to 1,000 μm caused by grinding or construction operations.

Fumes: Fumes are formed when vapour condenses and range in size from 0.03 to 0.3 μm.

Mists: Mists are liquid particles of the size 0.07 to 10 μm. Fogs are concentrated mists.

Sprays: Sprays are formed by atomisation of liquids and range in size from 10 to 1,000 μm.

Smoke and soot: Smoke (0.5 to 1.0 μm) and soot are formed from carbon as a result of the incomplete combustion of gases in burning coal.

Fly ash: Non-combustible particles (1.0 to 1,000 μm) connected with combustible gases in coal burning.

Particulate matter directly enters the air by sources such as combustion processes, wind-blown dust formed in the atmosphere and by the transformation of emitted gases such as sulphur dioxide.

12.6.1.2 Ozone Depletion

The ozone layer is a layer in the earth's atmosphere located 15–50 km above the earth containing a relatively high concentration of ozone. This ozone-rich layer is known as the ozone layer. Solar radiation in the stratosphere contains UV radiation of three wavelengths. The shortest of these, UV-C (<280 nm), is completely filtered before reaching the earth by oxygen and ozone. UV-B (280–320 nm), the middle range UV radiation, is only partially absorbed by ozone. The stratospheric ozone layer plays a beneficial role by absorbing most of the biological damaging UV-B radiation, allowing only a small portion to reach the earth. The higher wavelengths of UV radiation, UV-A (320–400 nm), are minimally absorbed before reaching the earth. Therefore, the UV radiation reaching the earth's surface is largely composed of UV-A with a small proportion of UV-B. The ozone layer was discovered by two French scientists, Charles Fabry and Henri Buisson, in 1913. Later, a British meteorologist, G.M.B. Dobson, studied its properties in detail and established the Dobson unit (D.U.), which is used to measure the amount of ozone in the atmosphere. He was a pioneer in the field, and between 1928 and 1958, he set up a worldwide network of ozone monitoring stations (Sivasakthivel & Siva Kumar Reddy, 2011).

The term "ozone hole" is loosely applied, and it refers to regions where the ozone concentration is less than 200 D.U. A normal level of ozone in the layer is about 300–350 D.U. During spring time in Antarctica, and to a lesser extent in the Artic, special meteorological conditions and very low temperatures accelerate and enhance ozone depletion by man-made ODS.

It is now known that the depletion of the ozone layer is due to the release of pollutants containing chemicals, chlorine and bromine. CFCs in spray cans, which have been widely used in industrial countries, are mainly responsible for ozone depletion. When CFCs reach the upper atmosphere, the UV radiation breaks down CFCs, releasing chlorine. Released chlorine, in turn, breaks down the ozone molecule. The use of CFCs was banned by 1996 and the amount of chlorine is now falling. There is evidence that the ozone layer is slowly recovering (Nilsson et al., 2007).

12.6.1.3 Greenhouse Effect

The greenhouse effect is a natural process that maintains the earth's temperature in balance. When the sun's energy reaches the atmosphere, some of it is radiated back to space allowing some to be absorbed and re-radiated by GHGs, which include water vapour, CO_2, methane, nitrous oxide and ozone. The absorbed energy warms the atmosphere and the earth and maintains the temperature in the region of 33°C. However, an increase in some human activities such as burning fossil fuels, agriculture and land clearings raises the levels of GHGs. This enhanced greenhouse effect contributes to the rise in global temperature.

An extra UV-B radiation reaching the earth has harmful effects on the ecosystem. It inhibits the reproductive cycle of single-celled phytoplankton algae which are at the bottom of the food chain. The reduction of phytoplanktons affects the survival of other organisms in the food chain. The reproductive rates of young fish, shrimp, crabs, frogs and salamanders have also been affected as a result of exposure to UV-B radiation (National Geographic, 2018).

12.6.2 Water Pollution

There are many sources of effluent-treated or untreated water discharged into surface waters. Effluent can originate from industries, treatment plants and sewers. Industrial waste dumped into rivers and lakes cause an imbalance in the water. Insecticides and pesticides used in agriculture ultimately find its way into ground water. Oil spills from tankers are another source of contamination causing enormous harm to marine life. Untreated water contaminates ground water reservoirs and damages water treatment systems. Sources of pollution of water are presented in Table 12.7 (Rinkesh, 2016a).

Table 12.7   Sources of Water Pollution

Pollutant	Details
Industrial waste	Lead, mercury, asbestos, sulphur, nitrates and other toxic chemicals
Sewage and waste water	Treated or untreated water from households containing pathogens and chemicals
Mining operations	In contact with water, extracted ore may contaminate water with harmful and toxic chemicals
Marine waste	Garbage produced by households in the form of paper, aluminium, rubber, glass, plastics and food waste dumped into the sea and rivers
Oil spillages	Accidental damage of tankers carrying oil may release tonnes of oil into the sea
Agricultural chemicals	Chemicals used as fertilizers and pesticides can contaminate water sources
Fossil fuel	Combustion of fossil fuel releases particles containing gases. When mixed with water during rain produces acid rain harmful to organisms. Also carbon dioxide is released contributing to global warming
Radioactive waste	Wrong disposal of nuclear waste
Urban development	Increase in construction activities, inadequate sewage collection and treatment, landfills. Noise pollution. Leaking landfills pollute underground water sources with a variety of contaminants
Animal waste	Animal waste gets washed into rivers and water streams polluting the water with pathogenic organisms
Underground storage leaking	Pipes carrying petroleum products may burst releasing harmful material to the soil and water

Some of the effects of water pollution (Nilsson et al., 2007; Ahmad et al., 2016) are summarised here:

1. Oxygen starvation: Decomposing organic waste competes for oxygen and much waste water leads to oxygen starvation, threatening the life of aquatic animals and plants.
2. Polluted water carries pathogenic organisms spreading infectious diseases.
3. Aquatic animals consuming polluted water pass on the toxic materials down the food chain.
4. Ecosystems are destroyed by rising temperatures.
5. Human produced litter such as plastic bags, nets and strings in the water trap aquatic species that die of suffocation.
6. The accumulation of solid waste and soil erosion in streams and rivers causes flooding.
7. Oil spillages cause the death of aquatic animals.
8. Enrichment of water with nutrients containing nitrogen or phosphorus or both cases eutrophication which encourages the growth of algae (algae bloom) and other aquatic plants. They compete for sunlight, oxygen and space with disastrous effects.
9. Acid deposition is caused by mining operations.

12.6.3 Soil Pollution

A wide variety of sources contribute to soil pollution, and they may arise from discrete point sources or diffuse sources. Pollution may be deliberate (man-made) or a result of an accident such as a nuclear radiation leak or oil spillage from a tanker. Land pollutants originate from agrochemical, urban, industrial, atmospheric and incidental sources. Soil contamination occurs by direct exposure to the pollutant and leakage into buildings and ground water. Such contaminants remain in the soil for a long time. Fertilisers, manures, pesticides used in agriculture, and fuel spillages from heavy machinery are agrochemical sources of soil contamination. Urban sources such as electric power stations, ash, fall-outs of wind transported pollutants, gas works, tars and heavy metals also pollute the soil. Mining and smelting industries, heavy metals from metallurgical industries, and chemicals from the chemical and electronic industries, contribute a fair share to soil contamination. Oil refineries, pipelines that transport oil, gas stations, garages, metal treatment and coating plants, chemical factories, dry cleaning and printing businesses, the textile industry, and sites where hazardous materials are stored are potential sources of land contamination. In addition, wind-blown pollutants and acid deposits in the atmosphere can contaminate the soil. Explosives and poisonous gases released to the atmosphere deliberately or as a result of an accident pollute the soil. Toxic materials released to the soil as a result of industrial accidents can contaminate a large area of land (Mirsal, 2008).

Soil pollution damages the upper layer of the soil due to overuse of fertilisers and by soil erosion caused by running water and other pest control measures. Soil pollution leads to the loss of fertile land for agriculture, forest cover and fodder patches for grazing. The climate pattern is also directly or indirectly affected. Loss of tree cover during deforestation leads to an imbalance of the rain cycle causing irregular rain patterns and flash floods. Toxic chemicals in the polluted land reach the human body through the consumption of produce grown in contaminated soils. Landfills become homes for rodents that carry diseases. Wildlife is seriously affected by the loss of habitat and the natural environment. They are forced to move to new habitat where they find it difficult to adjust. Ultimately, they are faced with the possibility of extinction (Rinkesh, 2016b; Ahmad et al., 2016; Israel Ministry of Environmental Protection (IMEP), 2012).

12.6.4 Noise Pollution

Noise pollution occurs when there is either an excessive level of noise or an unpleasant or irritating sound which disrupts the natural balance. There are several sources of noise pollution (Rinkesh, 2016c):

1. Industrial activities: Industries utilise machines, some of which generate loud noise when they are being used. Equipment such as compressors, exhaust fans and grinding mills also produce a loud noise. Regulatory requirements define standards that should be followed by industries that generate excessive noise.
2. Poor urban planning: Congested houses, overcrowded houses, lack of adequate parking facilities in the community, and frequent conflicts over sharing basic amenities lead to noisy arguments.
3. Social events and open markets: Social events that go on after midnight violate noise restrictions disrupting the lives of people in the neighbourhood. In open markets, it is not unusual for the seller to promote their products to attract customers by shouting at the top of their voice.
4. Transportation: Traffic on the roads, aircraft flying over houses, and underground and surface trains produce heavy noise which regularly disrupts daily activities.
5. Construction work: Housing projects, the construction of bridges, dams and flyovers, and clearing land for mining and other explorations uses heavy equipment which generates a loud noise.
6. Domestic chores: TVs, conversations using mobile phones, pressure cookers, vacuum cleaners, lawn movers, washing machines, dryers and air-conditioning equipment that we use generate noise, although they make a minor contribution to noise pollution. But it affects the quality of life of the people in the neighbourhood.

A noisy environment impacts on humans and wildlife. Those who are exposed to excessive noise regularly are prone to hearing loss. In a social environment, noise disrupts communication and often the misinterpretation of the intended message may lead to poor decision-making. Excessive noise prevents wild animals from hearing the approach of predators. They also suffer from hearing loss, and when they do they are easy targets and this leads to their dwindling population. The hunting abilities of animals are affected, disrupting the balance of the ecosystem (Rinkesh, 2016c).

12.6.5 Marine and Coastal Pollution

Marine and coastal pollution is the introduction of substances to the marine environment by humans directly or indirectly, causing harm to the marine environment and hazards to human health and lowering the quality of sea water (Bharucha, 2005). There are some specific causes that pollute marine waters:

- Municipal waste and sewage discharged into the sea.
- Pesticides and fertilisers from agricultural activities are washed off the land by rain and eventually reach the sea.
- Storm water overflows carry petroleum and oil washed off from roads.
- Leakage of oil from tankers.

- Offshore exploration and extraction can also pollute sea water.
- Litter dumped by humans.

Toxic waste in the sea is harmful to marine animals. Oil spills obstruct the gills of fish and stick to their features and also prevent marine birds from flying. Oil floats on the surface and blocks sunlight from reaching marine plants, which affects the photosynthesis process. Debris in the ocean degrades very slowly and uses oxygen during the degradation process, thus reducing the oxygen level. Therefore, the survival of marine animals such as whales, turtles, sharks, dolphins and penguins is seriously threatened. In addition to eutrophication, organic waste can create the development of red tiles, which are phytoplankton blooms, causing a red colouration. Drill cuttings deposited on the seabed create anaerobic conditions, producing toxic sulphides threatening marine species. Chemicals from pesticide residues reaching the sea accumulate in the fatty tissue of marine animals, which affects their reproductive cycle. Toxic chemicals ingested by marine animals go down the food chain and cause health hazards in humans (Rinkesh, 2016d; Bharucha, 2005).

12.6.6 Solid Waste and Hazardous Material

Solid waste constitutes a wide variety of items. Solid waste pollution occurs when the environment is dumped with non-biodegradable and non-compostable biodegradable material, which is capable of producing GHGs, toxic fumes and particulate matter as they accumulate in open landfills. This type of waste can leach organic and chemical compounds to the ground, contaminating the surrounding environment. Debris from construction sites and demolition sites, agricultural waste, waste from industrial processes and hazardous waste also contribute to solid waste (Hill, 2004).

When natural resources are used in industrial processes, the material actually used is only a tiny fraction of the resource. Others go to waste, e.g. the metal recovered from ore is only a small portion and most of the mined ore becomes waste. Similarly, during paper production, waste is produced when harvesting forests, converting wood into paper and during the printing process. Eventually, the product itself becomes waste at the end of its life cycle. It is difficult to determine accurately the amount of waste generated globally, but it is estimated that 1.3 billion tonnes of municipal waste are generated each year and this is expected to grow to 2.2 billion tonnes by 2025. Electronic waste is also expected to increase, even with recycling efforts, and currently, about 40 million tonnes are produced (Open University, 2016). Table 12.8 shows the waste and recycling figures in the United Kingdom.

Taiwan textile firm, Super Textile Corporation, has used an innovating approach to convert recyclable plastic (PET) bottles to high-quality fabrics, handbags, blankets and sports jerseys. Fibres are extracted from recycled PET bottles. According to the Industrial Development Bureau of Taiwan, over 13 million recycled PET bottles were used to produce 2010 FIFA World Cup jerseys for teams and retailers. Their innovation has been certified by the Rheinland Group in Germany (Taiwan Today, 2010).

Municipal waste is only one type of waste. Hazardous materials are widely used in a variety of industries and in agriculture. Hazardous wastes are toxic by-products of manufacturing and farming operations, city septic systems, construction projects, automotive garages, laboratories, hospitals and other industries. The waste may contain solids, liquids or sludge contaminated with chemicals, heavy metals, radioactive substances, pathogens and other toxins. They are not only toxic but also ignitable, corrosive and reactive. Even households generate hazardous waste from items such as batteries, computer parts, left-over paints and pesticides. Regulations dictate how these materials have to be correctly stored. The improper storage, handling and dealing with such substances is a potential cause of contamination (Hill, 2004).

Table 12.8 Waste and Recycling in the United Kingdom

	Type of Waste
1	Out of 600 million tonnes of products entering the UK market, only 115 million tonnes were recycled in 2011
2	In 2010–2011, 50% of local authority waste was diverted to landfill
3	8.3 million tonnes of food and drink waste were produced in the United Kingdom in 2009 out of which 7 tonnes were uneaten food
4	52% of commercial and industrial waste was recycled or reused in 2009
5	Between 2012 and 2020, the United Kingdom is expected to generate more than 12 million tonnes of electronic waste out of which 3.3 million tonnes will be IT equipment, consumer electronics and display screens. Electronic waste will include precious metals estimated to worth £7 billion
6	Nearly 25% of electronics and electronic equipment dumped into household recycling centres could be reused with a gross value of £ 200 million

Solid waste and hazardous waste both damage the environment and cause health effects either directly or indirectly (Gour, 2016; El-Fadel et al., 1997).

1. Due to the improper disposal of waste, biodegradable materials undergo decomposition, producing foul smell and become ideal breeding grounds for disease-carrying organisms such as rodents and pathogens.
2. Hazardous waste spills from drums, tankers or when dumped evaporate into the air, run-off into surface water, percolate down to ground water or are absorbed by the soil. Health hazards occur when polluted water is consumed or eating grain and produce, or animal food is contaminated with pollutants deposited from the air or taken up from soil or water.
3. Toxic material and hazardous waste affect the soil characteristics and productivity when they are dumped in the soil.
4. The combustion of industrial or solid waste such as cans, pesticides, plates, radioactive material and batteries produces toxic fumes, dioxins and polychlorinated biphenyl that are harmful to humans.
5. Fire and explosion hazards are known to occur in landfills where garbage accumulates, polluting the air.
6. Landfill waste undergoes a short initial aerobic decomposition phase followed by a longer anaerobic decomposition phase. During decomposition phases, many types of gases (e.g. methane, CO_2, hydrogen sulphide and other gases in varying amounts) are produced.
7. The polluted environment adversely affects the ecosystem, and it becomes inhabitable by plants and animals.

12.6.7 Radioactive Waste

Radioactive material consists of disposable materials that are either contaminated by radionuclides or contain them. They are unstable and undergo spontaneous decay or disintegration, emitting radiation. Radioactive waste can originate from many sources. For example:

- Military weapons production and testing.
- Mining operations.
- Power generation facilities.
- Medical diagnosis and treatment.
- Some consumer product development, manufacturing and testing.
- Chemical and biomedical laboratories.
- Hospitals.

The duration of radioactivity is measured in terms of half-life: The time taken for the material to reduce its radiation to half its initial value and this can vary from fractions of seconds to millions of years. Radioactive waste may primarily be items such as water, soil, paper, plastic, metal, ash, glass, ceramic or a mixture of widely different physical forms. Their physical form can be liquid, solid, gas or sludge, and its chemical form may vary as well (Pollution Issues, 2016).

12.6.7.1 Chernobyl Nuclear Explosion

The Chernobyl Nuclear Power Plant is located in Ukraine, 20 km south of the border with Belarus. At the time of the accident, there were four nuclear reactors. On April 26, 1986, the world's worst nuclear disaster happened in at this plant. A cascade of events triggered a massive, explosion releasing a large amount of radioactive material into the environment (Cartwright, 2018). It blew apart the reactor's enormous steel and concrete containment structure. The radioactive cloud spread across much of Europe and in Ukraine and Belarus and consequent fires lasted for 10 days.

Two workers died on the day of the accident, and within a few weeks, 28 more people died as a result of radiation. Over the following years, a large number of cases of cancer and leukaemia were detected. Areas and air near the reactors were heavily contaminated. During the early months of the accident, agriculture products were also contaminated with short-lived radioactive material. But long-lived radioactive caesium will be a major concern for years to come. As a result of radiation, the ecosystem was also polluted. Water and fish were found to be contaminated with radioactive material. Contamination levels were seen to decrease over the years due to dilution and decay of radioactivity. The accident also affected many plants and animals within a 3 km radius. Mortality rates increased and reproduction was also affected. Genetic abnormalities in animals and plants will prevail for several years (Chernobyl Forum, 2006).

12.6.8 Thermal Pollution

Thermal pollution is defined as a sudden rise in temperature of air and/or water in oceans, river, lakes, etc., by humans and other organisms. This usually occurs when a plant or a factory takes in water from a natural resource and releases it back into the environment with an altered temperature. Water is used as a coolant in factories. Forest fires also cause a rise in temperature in the environment. Sources of thermal pollution are:

- Thermal power stations.
- Nuclear power stations.
- Petroleum refineries.
- Domestic sewage.
- Industrial effluent.
- Soil erosion: Raises the water table making it more exposed to sunlight.

- Deforestation: Forest clearing destroys the leaf cover and water resources are directly exposed to sunlight.
- Run-off from pavements during the hot season.
- Natural causes.

Thermal pollution causes a change in the ecosystem. The species that cannot tolerate warm temperatures are replaced with those that can tolerate warm temperatures. This transition is often accompanied by a change in species balance and an overall reduction in species richness. The growth of algae in heated effluent increases the biomass but decreases the number of species. Fish are particularly susceptible to changes in temperature, and with a rise in water temperature, metabolic activity increases, as does the demand for oxygen. However, the amount of dissolved oxygen is less in warm water and aquatic species that thrive in cold water suffocate and die. Thermal pollution causes the water properties to change. The solubility of toxic compounds increases with a rise in temperature, and this leads to water pollution. It has been observed that thermal pollution disrupts the reproductive cycle of aquatic animals due to the premature hatching of eggs (Bagad, 2009; Rinkesh, 2016e).

12.7 Sustainable Development

The origin of sustainable development can be traced back to the Bruntland Report, also known as *Our Common Future*, which was commissioned in 1987 by the United Nation's World Commission on Environment and Development (WCED). In this report (Bruntland, 1987), sustainable development is defined as "the development that meets the needs of the present without compromising the ability of future generations to meet their own needs". Essentially, it means development without exhausting resources beyond future requirements. It involves the control and decision-making of inter-related areas such as the environment, the social community and the economy (Bagad, 2009).

12.7.1 Objectives of Sustainable Development

- Social objectives:
  - Promote equity and fairness.
  - Enhance quality of life.
  - Uphold economic objectives.
  - Consider economic and environmental decisions.
  - Consider the system as a whole.
  - Long-term planning and implementation.
- Environmental objectives are sustaining the resources, protecting the ecosystem and fulfilment of international obligations

Following the "Earth Summit" in Rio in 1972, there were additional treaties not only on maintaining biodiversity and protecting the forests but also on protecting the human environment and cultural heritage of communities (Bagad, 2009; Farmer, 1997).

Sustainable development cannot be achieved without economic growth. But economic growth in both developed and developing countries has to be achieved following the principles of sustainable development. Environmental pollution is a key element in the assessment of the impact of development on the environment, and managing the issue becomes an essential prerequisite for achieving sustainable growth.

12.7.2 Factors Affecting Sustainable Development

Several factors affect sustainable development (Bagad, 2009):

■ Availability of renewable and non-renewable resources.
■ Population growth and density.
■ Health of the economy: gross domestic product (GDP)
■ Consumption of energy and other resources required to deliver products and services.
■ Extent of pollution.
■ Conservation and land use.
■ Poverty index.
■ Awareness of environmental issues, education and literacy.

12.7.3 Carrying Capacity

Environmental resources of the ecosystem provide a wide variety of services for all the economic activities of the planet. The concept of carrying capacity implies that there is a limit for the environment to absorb some form of activity, e.g. pollution, resource extraction, land use, etc. The resource base of the planet is finite. Economic development and population growth can take place, at least for short period of time through resource system management and resource conserving efforts. Such efforts can only be successful if warnings are generated to detect the reducing levels of resources. Resource depletion is only one aspect of carrying capacity. There is also a limit for the environment to absorb pollution. The environment may accumulate pollution to a point where adverse effects are felt. For example, if an artificial wetland is created to absorb pollutants from contaminating water, over time accumulated pollutants may start leaching from the wetland. There is no fixed formula for determining the carrying capacity in nature. Some of the factors that contribute to the carrying capacity are technical performance, level of production and consumption of resources, and the changing state of interactions between the physical and biotic environment (Arrow et al., 1995; Farmer, 1997).

Economic development and population growth inevitably result in the use of nature's valuable resources and pollution due to industrial activities. Organisations and individuals both have a social and ethical obligation to protect the environment by managing resource systems, while re-conserving structural changes in the economy in order to make this planet a better place to live in for future generations.

References

Ahmad, S., Ali, A. and Ashfaq, A. (2016). Environment hazards through pollution. *International Journal of Current Research and Modern Education*, 1 (1), 289–300.

Arrow, K., Bolin, B., Costanza, R., Dasguptha, P., Folke, C., Holling, C.S., Jansson, B.O., Levin, S., Mäler, K.G., Perrings, C. and Pimentel, D. (1995). Economic growth, carrying capacity and the environment. *Ecological Economics*, 15, 91–95.

Bagad, A. (2009). *Environmental Studies*. Pune: Technical Publications.

Belcham, A. (2015). *Manual of Environmental Management*. New York: Routledge.

Bharucha, E. (2005). *Textbook for Environmental Studies for Undergraduate Courses for All Branches of Higher Education*: India: University Press.

Bruntland. (1987). *Report of the World Commission on Environment and Development: Our common future*. United Nations. UK: Oxford University Press

Cartwright, J. (2018). Mystery of crucial first moments of Chernobyl disaster solved. *Chemistry World*, 15 (1), 40.

Chen, F.F. (2011). *An indispensable Truth: How Fusion Power Can Save the Planet*. New York: Springer.

Chernobyl Forum. (2006). *Chernobyl Legacy: Health, Environment and Socio-Economic Impacts and Recommendation to the Governments of Belarus, Russian Federation and Ukraine. Chernobyl Forum 2003–2005*. Austria: International Atomic Energy Agency.

Citizen Group (2016). *Business activities and environmental impact*, Retrieved October 25, 2018 from http://www.citizen.co.jp/global/csr/environment/impact.html.

Cong, R.Y., Gielen, D., Jannuzzi, G., Marechal, F., McKane, A.T., Rosen, M.A., van Es, D. and Worrell, E. (2012). Energy end use: industry. In R. Banarjee (Ed.), *Global Energy Assessment – Towards a Sustainable Future*. UK: Cambridge University Press.

Cosgrove, W.J. (2001). Megacities: Water as a limit to development. In R. Ragaini (Ed.), *Water Pollution: Proceedings of the International Seminar on Nuclear War and Planetary Emergencies*, pp. 219–235. E. Majorana Centre for Scientific Culture, Erice, Italy, August 19–24, 2000. Singapore: World Scientific Publications.

Davis, E. (2016). Accident and emergency. *Chemistry World*, 13 (1), 20–21.

ELAW. (2010). *Guidebook for Evaluating Mining Projects EIAs* (1st ed.). Oregon: ELAW.

El-Fadel, M., Findikakis, A.N. and Lecke, J.O. (1997). Environmental impacts of solid waste landfills. *Journal of Environmental Management*, 50, 1–25.

Encyclopedia.com. (2003). Environmental movement. *Dictionary of American History*. Retrieved October 21, 2018 from http://www.encyclopedia.com/earth-and-environment/ecology-and-environmentalism/environmental-studies/environmental-movement.

European Commission. (2007). *The Montreal Protocol*. Luxembourg: Office for Official Publications of the European Communities.

European Commission. (2016). *Climate action: Paris agreement*. Retrieved October 24, 2018 from http://ec.europa.eu/clima/policies/international/negotiations/paris/index_en.htm.

Farmer, A. (1997). *Managing Environmental Pollution*. New York: Routledge.

FoEE. (2009). *Overconsumption: Our Use of the World's Natural Resources*. Austria: Friends of the Earth Europe.

Gour, M. (2016). *Solid waste management – Sources, effects and methods of disposal*. Retrieved November 21, 2018 from http://mjcetenvsci.blogspot.com/2013/11/thermal-pullution-source-effects-and.html.

Hill, M.K. (2004). *Understanding Environmental Pollution* (2nd ed.). UK: Cambridge University Press.

IEA. (2017). *Key World Energy Statistics*. France: International Energy Agency.

IMEP. (2012). *Impact of business and industry on the environment*. Retrieved November 20, 2016 from http://www.sviva.gov.il/English/env_topics/IndustryAndBusinessLicensing/Pages/EnvironmentalImpactOfBusiness.aspx.

Johnston, E. (n.d.). 20 Years after Kyoto Protocol, where does world stand on climate? *The Japan Times*. Retrieved June 14, 2018 from https://www.japantimes.co.jp/news/2017/12/04/reference/20-years-kyoto-protocol-world-stand-climate/#.WyTwvaczbIX.

Khopkar, S.M. (2004). *Environmental Pollution: Monitoring and Control*. India: New Age International.

McKinsey Germany. (2009). *Energy: A Key to Competitive Advantage*. Germany: McKinsey & Company Inc.

Mirsal, I.A. (2008). *Soil Pollution: Origin, Monitoring and Remediation*. Germany: Springer-Verlag Berlin Heidelberg.

Mussarani, L. (2016). Brazilian mine disaster pollutes river. *Chemistry World*, 13 (1), 13.

National Geographic. (2018). *Ozone depletion: How is Earth's atmosphere losing its most important layer?* Retrieved November 6, 2018 from http://environment.nationalgeographic.com/environment/global-warming/ozone-depletion-overview/.

Nibusinessinfor.co.uk. (n.d.) *Causes and effects of air pollution*. Retrieved November 6, 2016 from https://www.nibusinessinfo.co.uk/content/causes-and-effects-air-pollution.

Nilsson, L., Persson, P., Ryden, L., Darozhka, S. and Zaliauskiene, A. (2007). Industrial impacts on the environment. *Environmental Management*, Book 2: Chapter 1: Cleaner production – Technologies and tools for resource efficient production. Sweden: Baltic University Press.

Norman, N. (2016). Going for gold. *Chemistry World*, 13 (1), 53–57.

Open University. (2016). *Environmental Management and Organisations* (1st ed.). UK: Open University.

Ozone Secretarial. (2018). *Montreal Protocol on Substances That Deplete the Ozone Layer. Handbook for the Montreal protocol on Substances That Deplete the Ozone Layer* (12th ed.). Vienna: United Nations Environmental Programme.

Pollution Issues. (2016). *Radioactive waste*. Retrieved November 15, 2016 from http://www.pollutionissues.com/Pl-Re/Radioactive-Waste.html.

Rinkesh, K. (2016a). *What is water pollution?* Retrieved November 15, 2016 from http://www.conserve-energy-future.com/sources-and-causes-of-water-pollution.php.

Rinkesh, K. (2016b). *What is land pollution?* Retrieved November 13, 2016 from http://www.conserve-energy-future.com/causes-effects-solutions-of-land-pollution.php.

Rinkesh, K. (2016c). *Understanding noise pollution*. Retrieved November 14, 2016 from http://www.conserve-energy-future.com/causes-and-effects-of-noise-pollution.php.

Rinkesh, K. (2016d). *What is ocean pollution?* Retrieved November 14, 2016 from http://www.conserve-energy-future.com/causes-and-effects-of-ocean-pollution.php.

Rinkesh, K. (2016e). *What is thermal pollution?* Retrieved November 14, 2016 from http://www.conserve-energy-future.com/causes-and-effects-of-thermal-pollution.php.

Royal Swedish Academy of Science. (1995). *Press release: The Noble Prize in chemistry 1995*. Retrieved October 25, 2018 from https://www.nobelprize.org/nobel_prizes/chemistry/laureates/1995/press.html.

Sivasakthivel, T. and Siva Kumar Reddy, K.K. (2011). Ozone layer depletion and its effects. *International Journal of Environmental Science and Development*, 2 (1), 30–37.

Stanko, N. (2011). *Environmental movement*. Retrieved February 12, 2018 from http://www.greeniacs.com/GreeniacsArticles/Environmental-News/Environmental-Movement.html.

Taiwan Today. (2010). *Recycled fabric is fantastic for Taiwan industrial firm*. Retrieved June 17, 2019 from https://taiwantoday.tw/news.php?unit=6&post=9678.

Uni-Consultancy Services. (2019). *Final Report: Environmental Impact Assessment (EIA) for the Proposed Extension of Pipe-Borne Sewerage Coverage for Dehiwala-Mt.Lavinia Municipal Council Area*. Sri Lanka: University of Moratuwa.

United Nations. (2014). *A summary of Kyoto Protocol*. Retrieved October 24, 2016 from http://unfccc.int/kyoto_protocol/background/items/2879.php.

United Nations. (2018). UN documentation: Environment. *Dag Hammarskjold Library*. Retrieved October 23, 2016 https://research.un.org/en/docs/environment.

United Nations. (2019). *What is Kyoto Protocol?* Retrieved January 20, 2019 from https://unfccc.int/process-and-meetings/the-kyoto-protocol/what-is-the-kyoto-protocol/what-is-the-kyoto-protocol.

UN World Water Association Programme. (2017). *The United Nations World Water Development Report 2017: Facts and Figures* (Vol. 7). Italy: Programme Office for Global Water Assessment.

Vault. (2019). *Environmental science and conservation*. Retrieved April 20, 2019 from https://www.vault.com/industries-professions/industries/environmental-science-and-conservation?id=background.

Chapter 13

Environmental Aspects and Impacts

13.1 Introduction

All businesses have activities that provide services and products. The way these activities, services and products impact on the environment defines the environmental aspects of the organisation. Activities, services, aspects and impacts are closely related elements of an environmental review. An aspect is a constituent part of the organisation's business. In a manufacturing environment, the aspects are inputs to the manufacturing process: raw materials, chemicals and natural resources. However, not all aspects are inputs to manufacturing processes. Also, not all aspects create a significant impact on the environment, and the organisation should focus on aspects that do have. The relationship between activity, service, aspect and impact is shown in Table 13.1.

Table 13.1 Activity, Service, Aspect and Impact

Activity/Service	Aspect	Impact
Transport	Use of fuel	Depletion of non-renewal resources
	Emissions	Air pollution
Cleaning tanks	Use of water	Depletion of natural resources
	Use of chemicals	Water pollution
		Soil pollution
Storage of fuel	Potential for spill or leakage	Pollution of water and soil

13.2 Classification of Aspects

Aspects can be classified into three types: aspects related to company operations, services and products (Block, 1999).

1. Aspects related to company operations: These aspects are closely associated with the company's core processes, and they generally receive greater attention. Examples of core processes in this category are the production of an item, mining operations and car assembly.
2. Aspects related to company services used or offered by the company: These are generally processes that support core processes. Examples of such services are transportation, storage, the maintenance of equipment and facilities and cleaning.
3. Aspects related to products: These aspects are associated with finished products and packaging. However, the manufacturer has only limited control over this aspect. The company may use recyclable material such as glass or packaging with a view to minimising landfill waste, but it is the responsibility of the end user to decide on the manner of disposal.

Examples of categories of aspects associated with operations, services and products are shown in Table 13.2.

Aspects can also be divided into direct and indirect aspects. Direct aspects are concerned with operations, services and products over which the organisation has direct control. For example, the noise in the production environment or the manner of disposal of waste can be controlled and managed by the organisation itself. However, the company has no control over indirect aspects such as how subcontractors manage waste or how consumers dispose of items at the end of their life cycle. All parts of the company's operations should be included in the scope when identifying environmental aspects. They include not only core manufacturing or service activities but also activities such as catering, parking, ground maintenance, etc. Generally, the organisation considers environmental aspects such as emissions to air, disposal of waste, release to soil and water, use of renewable and non-renewable resources, impact on biodiversity, noise creation, etc. (Verbanac, 2016).

Table 13.2   Examples of Categories of Aspects Associated with Operations, Services and Products

Operations	Services	Products
Energy	Cleaning	Power sources
Materials	Maintenance of equipment	Types of packaging
Natural resources	Transport and delivery	Transport and delivery
Methods of packaging	Food service	Communication aids
Chemicals	Pest management	Use and disposal
Facilities and equipment	Fire prevention	Waste
Office activities	Facility maintenance	
Emissions	Ground maintenance	
Noise		

13.3 Methods of Identifying Environmental Aspects

The starting point of identifying environmental aspects is the creation of an inventory of processes, products and services offered by the organisation. Several methods have been used for the identification of environmental aspects with varying degrees of success (Block, 1999).

13.3.1 Value Chain Method

The scope of this method includes the entire value chain of a company from suppliers through to manufacturing and distribution to the disposal of products. Life-cycle analysis (LCA) is employed in this method with an emphasis on mass and energy balance.

13.3.2 Materials Identification Method

This method considers all the materials and constituent parts used in production and captures information on the chemicals and hazardous substances used in processing, but it tends to ignore aspects such as energy and water use.

13.3.3 Regulatory Compliance Method

In this method, only the materials controlled by federal, state or local government environmental agencies are considered in the analysis, and therefore, non-regulated items are not included.

13.3.4 Eco-Mapping

Eco-mapping is a simple tool that can be used when implementing environmental management systems (EMSs). Essentially, it is an inventory of practices and problems and is a systematic method of conducting an on-site environmental review. It includes a collection of information that shows current information. Eco-maps create an awareness of environmental issues while promoting involvement and participation (Weiß & Bentlage, 2006; Ligus, 2013). Development of eco-mapping on water, soil, air, waste management, etc. is not a goal in itself, but it is a review of environmental performance for continual improvement. An eco-map checklist is a useful tool for preparing eco-maps (Engel, 1998).

13.3.4.1 Uses of Eco-Maps

- Can be used to conduct an environmental review.
- Provides knowledge about environmental issues.
- Can be used for training and communication.
- Is a basis for developing environmental documentation.
- Promotes participation of staff in the absence of written procedures and instructions.
- Helps define and prioritise problems and is useful for all stakeholders.

13.3.4.2 Eco-Map Checklist

An eco-map checklist includes the following information:

1. Information about the organisation and quantification of energy and material flows.
2. General data: Historical development, size of the organisation, location and thematic eco-maps.

3. Organisation's operations: Production processes and use of raw materials.
4. Data on waste: Origin, storage, elimination and its disposal.
5. Waste water: Quality and quantity of waste water and its treatment, sewage systems, penalties for waste water discharges.
6. Soil and ground water contamination: Storage of chemicals, permeability of soil, risk of leakage and soil analysis.
7. Noise and vibration: Sources of noise and its measurement, site and edge of site.
8. Emissions to air: Gaseous emissions and odours, points of emissions and current controls to reduce emissions.
9. Impact on the surrounding environment: The organisation's immediate environment, type of ground on which it is located, drainage and water collection.
10. Environmental costs: Penalties, taxes, charges and insurance fees.
11. Permits and licences: Relationship with regulatory authorities and community and responsibilities.
12. Environmental action plan.

13.3.4.3 Eco-Maps

Eco-mapping involves the generation of eight eco-maps (Engel, 1998):

1. Eco-map of urban situation: It describes the location of the facility in an urban context.
2. Eco-map of nuisances: This map is the overview of the facility created using the eco-map checklist. It includes an input–output analysis of the material and energy flows in the facility on physical terms. Input elements include consumption figures of raw materials, energy, transport and packaging, while the output elements are the amounts of solid and liquid waste, air pollution, nuisances, noise, odours generated and land use.
3. Eco-map of water: This map includes the consumption of water and the generation of waste water.
4. Eco-map of soil: This map describes the storage of inflammable, dangerous and hazardous materials in relation to ground water.
5. Eco-map of air odour, noise and dust: This map shows the points of emission of pollutants to air.
6. Eco-map of energy: This map presents the consumption of energy and its impact.
7. Eco-map of waste: The management and prevention of waste are included in this map.
8. Eco-map of risks: This map identifies the risks of accidents and pollution.

13.4 Selected Techniques for Identifying and Evaluating Environmental Aspects and Impacts

There are numerous techniques for identifying and evaluating environmental aspects and impacts (EPA, 2016; Morris & Therivel, 2009). Table 13.3 presents some of these techniques.

13.4.1 Identification of Activities, Products and Services

Environmental aspects of an organisation are associated with its activities, products and services. Before identifying the activities, products and services, the boundary of the EMS should

Table 13.3 Techniques for Identifying and Evaluating Environmental Aspects and Impacts

Techniques and Data Sources	Application
• Emission inventories	Quantify emissions of air pollution
• Environmental compliance audits	Assessment of compliance to federal, state and local regulations. Not typically used to evaluate environmental impacts related to production
• Environmental cost accounting	Assessment of full environmental costs associated with activities, products and services
• Environmental impact assessment	Assessment of conformance to National Environmental Protection Act (NEPA) on evaluation of environmental impacts of proposed projects. Not typically employed to assess the environmental impact of existing operations
• Environmental property assessment	Assessment of environmental liabilities associated with the facility or business acquisition or divestitures. Does not assess impacts associated with production or services
• Failure Mode and Effects Analysis (FMEA)	Identification and prioritisation of equipment and process failures and potential corrective actions. Often used as a preliminary step to root cause analysis
• Life-cycle analysis (LCA)	Assessment of cradle to grave impacts of products and processes from raw material procurement through to final disposal. Methodologies can be intensive and subjective
• Pollution prevention or waste minimisation audits	Identification of opportunities to reduce or eliminate pollution at the source and the identification of recycling options. A comprehensive assessment of facility operations is required but does not examine off-site operations
• Process flow diagrams	Understand the activities associated with processes and improve work processes
• Process hazard analyses	Identification and assessment of impacts associated with unplanned release of hazardous materials
• Process safety/hazard reviews	Assessment and mitigation of potential safety hazards associated with new or modified projects. Does not include environmental issues
• Risk assessments	Assessment of potential health and/or environmental risks associated with the exposure to chemicals.

be defined. It relates to the physical border and the content-related border of the system (Ligus, 2013). There are two ways to identify activities, products and services:

1. According to this method, the main processes are divided into small areas of activities and assigned the maximum number of environmental aspects. This approach serves two purposes:

– It enables the organisation to identify aspects in small manageable chunks, minimising the likelihood of overlooking significant aspects.
– It enables the organisation to relate its aspects to specific operations and activities.
2. Environmental assignment method: This method involves the creation of a map of environmental components and connecting the activities, products and services with identified environmental aspects. For example:
– Impact on the air – mining operations.
– Impact on the water – waste water following cleaning of tanks.
– Impact on the soil – pesticide and fertiliser application.
– Impact on the landscape – deforestation.
– Waste generation – solid and liquid waste in chemical manufacture.
– Release of energy (vibration, noise, warmth, coldness, electromagnetic field) – land preparation prior to mining.

Using both methods is advantageous because it provides information on the impacts of the activities on the environment and on environmental components.

13.4.2 Preliminary Information

The following documents are helpful for identifying and evaluating environmental aspects and impacts (Ligus, 2013):

■ Technical and process documentation of the facility.
■ Materials and energy balances of processes used in the facility.
■ Opinions and comments from interested parties.
■ Industrial sector standards and guidelines.
■ Technical papers.
■ Eco-maps.

13.4.3 Identification Process

The identification process involves the following steps (EPA, 2016):

1. Sub-divide the facility into functional units.
2. Develop process flow diagrams including inputs and outputs.
3. Transfer information on inputs and outputs from process flow diagrams into aspect identification form.
4. Evaluate the identified environmental aspects.

13.4.3.1 Sub-Dividing the Facility

The facility is sub-divided into units that reflect staffing and supervision. Table 13.4 shows the common activities and functional areas of a winery. In this table, 19 common activities across seven functional units have been identified, and some activities such as cellar activities can be further subdivided. For example, harvesting grapes, crushing grapes, fermentation, filtration, etc. are some cellar activities. Activities and processes also include services, products, spills and activities

Table 13.4   List of Common Activities with Functional Areas

Activity	Functional Area
Growing grapes	Vineyard
Application of pesticides	
Application of fertilisers	
Harvesting grapes	
Receiving inward goods	Inward goods
Issue of inward goods	
Cellar activities	Cellar
Purchasing	Production
Production, assembly	
Quality control	
Cleaning	
Laboratory testing	
Maintenance and repair	Engineering
Facility maintenance	
Pest management	
Storage of finished goods	Warehouse
Picking and packing orders	
Delivery of orders	
Maintenance of forklifts	
Storage of bottles and pallets	Yard
Marketing and sales activities	Administration
Administration	
Disposal of waste	

done off-site for the company. Environmental aspects of products, vendors and contractors used by the organisation may also be appropriate.

13.4.3.2 Developing Process Flow Diagrams

a. Process flow method: This method is the most common and easiest method to identify the environmental aspects associated with the organisation's processes. The process flow method identifies the individual activities of the processes. The following steps are involved in the process flow method.

i. Step one: Establish a cross-functional team: A team approach is necessary to collect the necessary information from all functions such as sales, marketing, purchasing, production, storage, distribution, environmental, quality and food safety functions. Although the cross-functional team is responsible for identifying the aspects associated with individual processes, employees under each function will contribute their knowledge when aspects are identified. The identification of environmental aspects associated with the receiving department will involve staff from the inward goods section, because they monitor what is received, and the staff from the warehouse where storage and distribution take place. Similarly, the identification of aspects associated with warehousing function will involve those from the receiving department, employees in the warehouse, and customers who obtain items from the warehouse.

ii. Step two: Generate the flow diagram: The flow diagram is constructed by identifying each step in the process using standard flow diagram symbols. A generic manufacturing process involves the following stages:

1. Select supplier.
2. Place order.
3. Receive and check raw materials.
4. Manufacture the item.
5. Quality assurance.
6. Packaging.
7. Distribution.

The cross-functional team should review the flow diagram when all operational and supporting activities are inserted into the master flow diagram. Using the flow diagram, inputs and outputs associated with each step are identified, and these provide the basis for identifying environmental aspects.

iii. Step 3: Input, output analysis: The flow diagram shows an overview of the organisation's operations. Each process is subjected to an input/output analysis. When identifying inputs and outputs, all modes of operation are considered because set-up, shutdown or emergency operations might introduce extra items or activities (EPA, 2016). Inputs include raw materials (major non-chemical supplies used in the process), chemicals (chemicals used in the process), energy consumption (energy type and use), water consumption (water type – city, well, treated, chilled, etc., and use) and other inputs (those included in the above categories).

Outputs: Depending on the nature of the organisation and its activities, outputs might include some or all of the following:

• Emissions to air.
• Emissions to water.
• Energy use.
• Raw material and resource usage including water.
• Solid waste including hazardous waste generation.
• Liquid waste.
• Spills.
• Storm water discharges.
• Habitat and land pollution.
• Noise.
• Traffic and transport.
• Recycling and recovery operations.

Figure 13.1 shows the input/output diagram of a generic organisation. Figure 13.2 presents an input/output analysis of the winery operations.

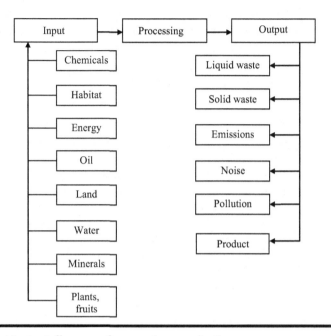

Figure 13.1   Input/output diagram of a generic organisation.

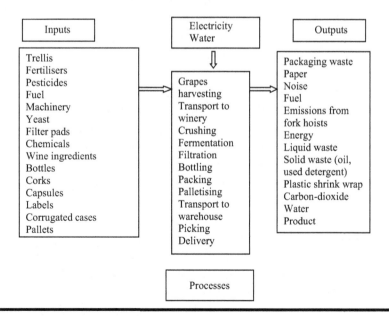

Figure 13.2   Input/output analysis of winery operations.

13.4.3.3 Environmental Aspects Outside the Organisation

The environmental aspects outside the organisation are associated with the contractors and purchased products and services. An organisation can exercise its influence by monitoring the performance of the contractors who provide products and services. Environmental aspects that can be influenced are emissions from vehicles and cleaning companies' products (SCCM, 2014).

For each process, input sub-categories (such as supplies, energy and water use and chemical use) and output categories (such as noise, liquid and waste water discharges, air emissions, storm water discharges and spillages) are identified.

13.4.3.4 Environmental Risk and Environmental Impact

The terms "environmental risk" and "environmental impact" are sometimes used interchangeably. The results of environmental risk assessment provide essential input information for the identification of environmental aspects and impacts. Environmental risk deals with uncertainty, whereas environmental impact considers both planned and unplanned events. As far as activities are concerned, there is a clear demarcation between environmental risk and environmental impact. Consider, e.g. a wine production facility. During the processing operation, wine is pumped from one tank to another, but this involves several risks. The receiving tank can overflow and cause spillage. In the winery in New Zealand where I was in charge of quality assurance, the winery operator pumped wine from one tank to another, keeping the top vent completely closed in the first tank and leaving no room for air to enter the tank when wine was pumped out. When the operation was finished, the empty tank collapsed! Returning to the example, the environmental risk and environmental impact of pumping wine and the use of chemicals can be shown as follows:

1. Activity: pumping wine	Aspect: pumping wine
Risks: tank spillage, tank collapsing	Impact: contamination of ground water and soil
2. Product: hazardous chemicals	Aspect: hazardous chemicals
Risks: fire, explosion	Impact: atmospheric pollution
	Release of toxic fumes
	Destruction of infrastructure
	Adverse effects on the eco-system

13.5 Environmental Impact of Food and Food Production

The production, processing, transport and consumption of food generate a significant impact on the environment. In a study involving 12 areas of consumption, the environmental impacts were assessed under a range of themes used in the LCA, e.g. resource depletion, global warming potential (GWP), ozone layer depletion, human toxicity, eco toxicity, photochemical oxidation, acidification and eutrophication (Foster et al., 2006).

Food, drink, tobacco and narcotic areas of consumption account for at least 20%–30% for most impacts. Meat and meat products have the greatest impact of 4%–12% for GWP and 14%–23% for the eutrophication for all products. Milk cheese and butter contribute 2%–4% to GWP and 10%–15% for eutrophication. Cereals, soft drinks, sweets and alcoholic drinks contribute considerably lower levels of impact. Generally, organic produce and farming require more land than non-organic produce and farming (Table 13.5).

Table 13.5   Environmental Impact of Food and Food Production

Aspect	*Impact*
Water and eutrophication impact	Carbohydrates: Major contributors are bread and potato. Organic wheat has higher impact than non-organic Fruits and vegetables: Water use is significant in tomato production Dairy products: Eutrophication is significant in agriculture phase Meat products: Major contributor is livestock farming Fish and other protein food: Nutrient release from fish farms is significant locally Drinks: Significant water use
Energy use: global warming potential (GWP) and acidification	Carbohydrates: Energy use evenly spread across life cycles. Energy use is very significant in consumer stage for potato and pasta. Organic wheat consumes less energy than non-organic. Consumption by wheat is similar to non-organic Fruits and vegetables: Energy use depends on growing methods and location Dairy products: Agriculture phase contributes to 90% of GWP of dairy life. Organic milk requires less energy but more land and has higher GWP per unit of milk produced Meat products: High energy use for all meat products. Production of feed is a major contributor Fish and other protein food: Most significant source of GWP. Different impacts for different farming methods Drinks: Production phase has GWP equivalent to hop, barley growing. Bottled water contribution to GWP is higher than for tap water
Non CO_2 global warming impact	Carbohydrates: 80% of total GWP is due to N_2O emissions from soil from primary production of arable food commodities Fruits and vegetables: N_2O emission is very significant Dairy products: Same as for meat products Meat products: Animal methane and N_2O emissions from soil used for feed and forage production
Processing impacts	Carbohydrates: Potato processing has high energy requirements Fruits and vegetables: Impacts can be considerable for major processing Dairy products: Processing has high energy demands. High water and energy use due to product diversity Meat products: Energy and water impact high for chicken processing Fish and other protein food: High water use in fish processing

(Continued)

Table 13.5 (*Continued*)   Environmental Impact of Food and Food Production

Aspect	Impact
Refrigeration and packaging impacts	Carbohydrates: Refrigeration phase of post-harvest is very significant Fruits and vegetables: Depends on processing and end use recycling Dairy products: Refrigeration impacts can be high; packaging methods vary Meat products: Additional impacts associated with frozen meat Fish and other protein food: Consumers' role is significant Drinks: Refrigeration on hospitality sector may have a major impact
Other impacts	Carbohydrates: Land use is high for organic produce, but low pesticide use Fruits and vegetables: Organic produce use more land, but lower pesticide use Dairy products: Organic produce use more land, but lower pesticide use Meat products: N_2O emissions Fish and other protein food: Legumes are a good source of proteins than red meat

13.6 Evaluation of the Significance of Environmental Aspects

In EMS planning, the most crucial step is the assessment of the significance of environmental aspects. Decisions taken at this stage will have a strong impact on many other system elements such as setting objectives and goals, developing operational controls and defining monitoring requirements. The identification of significant environmental aspects involves some subjective decisions and it is therefore essential that the evaluation team is comprised of a cross-section of functions (EPA, 2016). The objective of assigning significance to environmental aspects is to set priorities and establish criteria in order to implement continuous improvements. Two commonly used methods are (SCCM, 2014) (a) the qualitative method and (b) the quantitative method.

13.6.1 Qualitative Method

The environmental management team must carefully define the criteria that will be used to determine the significance of environmental aspects. This qualitative method is suitable for organisations with relatively few environmental aspects. The following are the criteria used for qualitative assessment:

1. Legal requirements, voluntary commitments, company policy: An initial criterion is to check if the aspect is subject to legislative regulations and whether it is included in the environmental policy, goals or voluntary commitments of the company, such as targets for water and energy consumption and waste production. Aspects associated with processes and activities are considered significant if (a) environmental regulations specify controls and conditions; (b) information on particular aspects has to be submitted to regulatory bodies; or (c) if there are periodic inspections or enforcement actions taken by the authorities.
2. Community concern: The environmental policy of the organisation includes a commitment to its stakeholders and their views are important environmental aspects for the company.

They may include issues other than pollution such as noise levels, contamination of air, etc. The complaints lodged by community groups should also be considered as significant in the aspect identification.

3. Resource use: Also significant are aspects that are related to high use of renewable or non-renewable resources. However, the significance depends on the value of the community and the facility. For example, a high rate of water use in a dry area is more significant than in an area where the water source is not a problem.

4. Potential impact on the environment: The activity would create a high impact on the environment due to (a) toxicity; (b) large amounts of emissions, waste or releases; (c) the consumption of large amounts of non-renewable resources; and (d) the frequency and severity of impacts and may require a local emergency service.

Table 13.6 shows an example of evaluating the significance of environmental aspects of grape growing and harvesting using the qualitative method.

In the evaluation process, normal, abnormal and emergency situations under which activities are conducted are considered. Examples of these situations are as follows:

Normal: Normal daily use of vehicles for delivery.
Abnormal: Deliveries during adverse weather conditions.
Emergency: Major spillage in the cellar.

13.6.2 Quantitative Method

The quantitative method of evaluating the significance of environmental aspects depends on a formula based on the Karnataka State Police Housing and Infrastructure Development Corporation Limited (KSPH & IDCL, 2015) method. According to this method, the risk score is calculated by adding the probability, severity, scale and duration of the impact. Severity represents the level of exposure of the environment to the particular impact on air, water, soil, natural resources, etc. It takes into consideration the quality of released items such as hazardous materials and the quantity of material released or used. Probability is the indicator of how often some impact could occur. When environmental aspects and impacts are evaluated, organisations should not ignore positive aspects which are triggers for continuous improvement. Some examples of positive environmental aspects are (a) improvement of environmental education and awareness among employees, suppliers and customers; (b) use of "green" products; (c) recycling bottles and using recycled packaging; and (d) communicating the importance of sustainability to the community, co-workers, sports groups, etc.

In the proposed method, the following categories are used in the assessment of significance of environmental aspects:

1. Probability.
2. Severity.
3. Scale.
4. Duration.

1. **Probability**
    4 – Very often – daily. Continuous for about 15 times or more per month.
    3 – Regular/repeated – happens 1–15 times per month.

Table 13.6 Qualitative Assessment of the Significance of Environmental Impact

Activity	Aspect	Legal requirement, Voluntary Commitment, Company Policy	Community Concern	Potential Impact on the Environment	Resource Use	Significant (S) Not Significant (N)	Reason for Significance	Target
Grape growing	Use of trellis	No	No	Low	Low	N	Does not meet significant criteria	
	Use of fertilizers	Yes	No	Yes	Yes	S	Water and/or soil contamination	
	Use of pesticides	Yes	No	Yes	Yes	S	Water and/or soil contamination	
	Water usage	No	No	No	High	S	High volume of water usage	
Grapes harvesting	Fuel for equipment	No	No	Yes	Yes	S	Use of non-renewable resources, soil contamination	
	Water usage	No	No	Low	Low	N	Does not meet significant criteria	
	Plastic buckets	No	No	Low	Low	N	Does not meet significant criteria	

2 – Rare – occurs 1–2 times per year.

1 – Seldom – but possible.

2. **Severity**

The impact on the environment can be either detrimental or beneficial.

4 – Severe/catastrophic – very harmful. Significant impact, damages the environment, produces hazardous waste, likely interruptions of normal operations.

3 – Serious – harmful but not potentially fatal to plants and living organisms. Localised, containable, likely interruptions of normal operations but operation can be resumed without adverse effects.

2 – Moderate – slightly harmful. Temporary and operation can be resumed without adverse effects.

1 – Harmless/ mild impact – little or no potential harm. Interruptions of normal operations are unlikely or consequences are minor and can be easily remedied.

3. **Scale**

4 – Global – significant disturbance to particular environmental components and ecosystems. Some environmental components lose the ability to recover.

3 – Regional – environmental changes exceed limits of natural variation and cause damage to separate environmental components. Natural environment is self-recoverable.

2 – Confined – environmental changes exceed limits of natural variation – Natural environment is completely self-recoverable.

1 – Isolated – environmental changes do not exceed existing limits of natural variation.

4. **Duration**

4 – Multi-year and permanent – impact observed for more than three years. Controllable but not correctable.

3 – Long term – impact observed for one to three years.

2 – Medium term – impact correctable within 3–12 months.

1 – Short term – impact can be corrected within one day or one week.

13.6.2.1 Assessment of Significance

The following situations are considered significant and do not require further assessment:

  i. Environmental regulations specify controls and conditions.
 ii. Information on particular aspects has to be submitted to regulatory bodies.
iii. If there are periodic inspections or enforcement actions taken by the authorities.
 iv. Community concern: Includes noise, air pollution, complaints from the public, and awards from environmental agencies.
  v. Resource use: High levels of renewable or non-renewable resource use.
 vi. Potential impact on the environment: Impact on the environment due to (a) toxicity; (b) large amounts of emissions, waste or releases; or (c) consumption of large amounts of materials with significant potential to reduce, reuse, and recycle.

For other aspects not listed above:

$$Significance\ score = Probability \times Severity \times Scale \times Duration$$

A total score of ≥ 18 is considered significant. An average score can also be used to identify significant aspects.

Table 13.7 presents an aspect and impact evaluation of some winery operations. In this example, aspects with an **average** of 2.8 and above have been taken to be significant. In general, winery operations have major interactions with the environment. The following aspects are significant:

- Chemicals used in fertilisers and pesticides and during crushing are regulated.
- A considerable amount of water is used during crushing in order to wash the trailer.
- Noise from machinery.
- Packaging items: bottles, corks, capsules, cardboard cases.
- Solid waste.
- Fuel used in fork hoists, vehicles and other machinery.
- Warehouse waste.
- Plastic wrapping.
- Wooden pallets.

13.6.3 Evaluation of Positive Environmental Aspects

Numerous matrices are employed to identify and evaluate environmental aspects and impacts. Such evaluations have been based on the frequency, severity and duration of categories such as legal exposure, community concern, pollution potential, resource use, etc. However, such matrices often fail to capture positive environmental aspects such as the use of environmentally friendly material, recycling, limits on source use, etc. A table such as Table 13.8 can be used to evaluate positive aspects on the basis of (1) benefits to the environment; (2) benefits to the organisation; and (3) cost of implementation. The following criteria may be applied:

3 – Benefits highly likely.
2 – Benefits likely.
1 – Minimal benefits are possible.

Organisations should set their own criteria for the evaluation of the significance of environmental aspects.

13.6.4 Addressing the Significant Aspects: Issues to be Considered

After the identification of significant environmental aspects, organisations must consider ways and means of addressing the issues. The following are some general considerations (Sheldon, & Yoxon, 2006):

a. **Resource usage: electricity**
   - Efficiency of heating, lighting and wastage.
   - Use of the power management feature on appliances.
   - Avoiding unnecessary usage and use of efficient equipment.
   - Reuse waste heat where possible and co-generation opportunities.
b. **Resource usage: water**
   - Efficient use of water.
   - Maintain equipment, vats and tanks to minimise leakage.

Activity	Aspect	Impact	Frequency	Impact to the Environment	Legal Controls Applicable	Community Concern	Use Resources	Total Added Score Average	Total Multiplied Score	Significance Y/N
Grape growing	Wood for trellis	Depletion of natural resources	4	1	No	1	1	7 / 1.8	4	N
	Chemicals in fertilizers	Water quality and soil contamination	–	–	Yes	–	–	–	–	Y
	Chemicals in pesticides	Water quality and soil contamination	–	–	Yes	–	–	–	–	Y
	Fuel for machinery	Depletion of natural resources	4	2	No	1	2	9 / 2.3	16	N
	Water use	Depletion of natural resources	4	3	No	1	3	11 / 2.8	36	Y
Grapes harvesting	Fuel for machinery	Depletion of natural resources	4	2	No	1	1	8 / 2.0	8	N
	Water use	Depletion of natural resources	4	1	No	1	1	7 / 1.8	4	N
	Plastic buckets	Depletion of natural resources	4	1	No	1	2	8 / 2.0	8	N
Crushing grapes	Fuel for machinery	Depletion of natural resources	4	2	No	1	1	8 / 2.0	8	N

(Continued)

Table 13.7 (Continued)   Quantitative Assessment of Environmental Impact

Activity	Aspect	Impact	Frequency	Impact to the Environment	Legal Controls Applicable	Community Concern	Use Resources	Total Added Score Average	Total Multiplied Score	Significance Y/N
	Water use	Depletion of natural resources	5	3	No	1	3	12 3.0	45	Y
	Chemicals	Depletion of natural resources	–	–	Yes	–	–	–	–	Y
	Marc	Soil pollution	4	3	No	2	1	10 2.5	24	N
	Noise from operating equipment	Noise	–	–	Yes	–	–	–	–	Y
Fermentation	Use of filter pads	Solid waste	4	3	No	1	2	10 2.5	24	N
	Use of yeast	Solid waste	4	2	No	1	1	8 2.0	8	N
	Use of electricity	Climate change, pollution of environment	4	2	No	1	3	10 2.5	24	N
Bottling	Use of bottles	Depletion of natural resources	5	3	No	1	3	12 3.0	45	Y
	Corks	Depletion of natural resources	5	3	No	1	2	11 2.8	30	Y

(Continued)

Table 13.7 (Continued)   Quantitative Assessment of Environmental Impact

Activity	Aspect	Impact	Frequency	Impact to the Environment	Legal Controls Applicable	Community Concern	Use Resources	Total Added Score Average	Total Multiplied Score	Significance Y/N
	Plastic capsules	Depletion of natural resources	5	3	No	1	2	11 / 2.8	30	Y
	Corrugated board	Depletion of natural resources	5	3	No	1	3	12 / 3.0	45	Y
	Paper for labels	Depletion of natural resources	4	2	No	1	2	9 / 2.3	16	N
	Solid waste	Contamination, landfill area enlargement	5	2	No	1	3	11 / 2.8	30	Y
	Adhesive	Contamination Depletion of natural resources	5	2	No	1	2	10 / 2.5	20	N
	Use of electricity	Climate change, pollution of environment	4	2	No	1	3	10 / 2.5	24	N
Storage and delivery	Fuel for forklifts, transport	Depletion of natural resources Contamination of air by fumes	4	3	No	1	2	9 / 2.3	36	N

(Continued)

Table 13.7 (Continued)   Quantitative Assessment of Environmental Impact

Activity	Aspect	Impact	Frequency	Impact to the Environment	Legal Controls Applicable	Community Concern	Use Resources	Total Added Score Average	Total Multiplied Score	Significance Y/N
	Electricity	Climate change, pollution of environment	4	2	No	1	2	9 2.3	16	N
	Paper	Depletion of natural resources	5	1	No	1	2	9 2.3	10	N
	Spills Abnormal	Liquid waste	3	3	No	1	3	10 2.5	27	N
	Plastic wrap	Depletion of natural resources Landfill area enlargement	5	3	No	1	3	12 3.0	45	Y
	Wooden pallets	Depletion of natural resources Landfill area enlargement	5	3	No	1	3	12 3.0	45	Y
	Warehouse waste	Contamination Landfill area enlargement	4	3	No	1	3	11 2.8	36	Y
	Ventilation emissions	Air pollution	4	3	No	2	1	10 2.5	24	N

Table 13.8 Evaluation of Positive Environmental Aspects

Aspect	Benefits		Cost Savings ($)
	Environmental	*Organisational*	
Recycling	3	2	
Purchasing environmentally friendly material	3	3	

- Efficient use of water use for gardening by selecting plants that need less water.
- Focus on appliances and equipment that consume most water.

c. **Resource usage: chemicals purchase and usage**
- Establish methods to minimise contamination.
- Purchase smaller pack sizes.
- Purchase "green" chemicals and safer alternatives.
- Use existing stock before the next purchase.
- Reuse or recycle waste.

d. **Resource usage: paper usage**
- Reduce paper use.
- Eliminate waste paper.
- Double-sided printing.
- Use recycled paper and cardboard where possible.

e. **Resource usage: packaging**
- Minimise the use of packaging.
- Reuse packaging.
- Use recycled materials.
- Use environmentally friendly material.

f. **Resource usage: fuel**
- Maintain equipment in good order.
- Eliminate fuel usage when equipment is running and not in use.
- Excessive fuel usage due to inefficient equipment operations.
- Use more efficient or cleaner fuel source.

g. **Storage issues**
- Use good storage practices to reduce the chance of spillages.
- Maintain good housekeeping in storage areas.
- Label and segregate chemical categories.
- Bunding of liquids to contain spills.
- Remove excess raw materials not in use.
- Availability of Material Safety Data Sheets (MSDS) in storage areas.
- Availability of spill kits.
- Training of staff to manage spills.

h. **Generation of waste**
- Segregate for maximum reuse or recycling opportunities.
- Minimise the amount of scrap and waste.
- Minimise the use of disposable materials such as cups, plates, etc.
- Use recycled paper.

13.7 Using the Information

All the identified environmental aspects and impacts are opportunities for continuous improvement. They are candidates for environmental objectives and targets and should become a part of the organisation's environmental management programme. The EMS team must lead, monitor, target and manage future improvements in this programme together with operational control improvements. Significant environmental aspects and impacts will also define training requirements to create an awareness of the environmental programme. Achievable targets such as a 10% reduction in electricity consumption or a 5% reduction of waste can also be established (Academy, n.d.). Improvement can be made both at the input and output stages:

Input – use of environmentally friendly raw materials.

Output – use of recycled cardboard, recycled bottles and minimising waste generation.

13.8 Legal and Statutory Requirements

All organisations must comply with environmental legislation and/or regulations. One important consideration is the requirement to have an inventory of environmental legislation and/or regulations that apply to the organisation's environmental aspects (SCCM, 2014). The following are the uses of this inventory:

- Legislation and/or regulations can be used as a checklist to ensure that all environmental aspects have been identified.
- Environmental aspects can be directly linked to legislative and/or regulatory requirements.
- The degree to which these requirements apply is considered in determining the significance of the environment to all aspects.
- In developing additional activities, measures can be taken to guarantee compliance to legislative and/or regulatory requirements.

An EMS provides a basis for addressing environmental issues and complying with all legal and statutory requirements. Lack of attention to these requirements can lead to the imposition of heavy penalties by regulatory authorities, as well as polluting the environment, causing harm to the community and the habitat. Therefore, the organisation must understand the details of activities, products and services affected by environmental regulations. In addition, the EMS team must understand how environmental laws are developed in order to monitor such developments on a monthly or weekly basis. The organisation needs to realise that environmental regulations are a changing entity in response to further scientific evidence, improvements in monitoring technology, and a general greater understanding of environmental issues (Sheldon & Yoxon, 2006).

Companies that meet all environmental legal requirements comply with all environmental legal requirements that are applicable to the organisation. However, non-compliance is permitted if it is accepted by a regulatory authority by way of a special provision, remediation order with a transition period or with a documented approval.

13.8.1 Legal Requirements

Legal requirements include the following (Weiß & Bentlage, 2006): national, regional and local requirements, standards applicable to the location of the organisation and its products and services, permit and licence requirements, and regulatory obligations. Other requirements are organisation-specific codes, industry codes of practices, International Chamber of Commerce Charter for Sustainable Development, and codes or standards of institutions to which the organisation voluntarily subscribes.

Most frequently applied regulations are related to the following activities (Edwards, 2004):

- Waste carrying and disposal.
- Release of substances to water and soil.
- General nuisance such as noise, odour and smoke.
- Storage, handling and disposal of hazardous material.
- Planning permits.
- Packaging and packaging waste.
- Prescribed processes such as the Environmental Protection (Prescribed Processes and Substances) Regulations 1991 and the Pollution Prevention and Control Act 1999.
- COSHH (Control of Substances Hazardous to Health Regulations) 2002.
- COMAH (Control of Major Hazard Regulations) 1999.

13.8.2 Resources Required

The identification of legal requirements requires specialist knowledge. Organisations may not have a legal expert within the organisation so, to start with, they need some important resources such as (a) internal expert(s) who are familiar with environmental operations; (b) written documentation of all operations and activities; and (c) contact with regulatory bodies. Usually, training organisations conduct workshops on environmental management, and by attending, these organisations can gain useful information. Contact with government organisations is the best way to become aware of environmental regulatory requirements. The appointed person (whether they are a lawyer or an internal expert) must have a sound understanding of the legislative system and/or environmental legislation in the particular country (Sheldon & Yoxon, 2006).

13.8.3 Process of Identifying Legal Requirements

The following steps are involved in identifying legal requirements:

1. Create an inventory of all activities, processes, products and services that either (a) have a significant environmental aspect or (b) are related to local, regional or national legislation.
2. Test for relevance: This is an extremely important test during the early stages of EMS development. There may be legislation that applies only under special circumstances such as during certain operating hours or to processes and activities that produce above a specified output. However, exclusion clauses are subject to change and it is the responsibility of the authorised person to maintain contact with regulatory authorities and monitor the operations.
3. Characterise: Organisations must identify regulatory requirements that apply to specific requirements of the organisation because regulations may specify special monitoring and sampling techniques in the licences, permits and consents issued by the regulatory body to the organisation. This will have an important bearing on the capability to monitor the impacts. The planning process and future projects must take into account applicable regulatory requirements.

4. Update: It is important to monitor legal developments closely to identify new relevant legislation that may have been introduced or changes to existing legislation. In addition, activities that may not have been covered by environment laws may come under the umbrella of new laws.

13.9 Checklist for Identifying Legal Requirements

Environmental legislation relevant to an organisation depends on the nature of the operations. Therefore, a close match between the scope of the EMS and the laws that apply to it has to be found. A survey of the operations will reveal legal issues affecting the site and the operations. Such a survey is presented in Table 13.9 as a checklist (Sheldon & Yoxon, 2006; Weiß, & Bentlage, 2006). Detailed information will make the scope of legal monitoring clearer.

Table 13.9   Checklist for Identifying Legal Requirements Applicable to Environmental Aspects

Item	Issues to be Considered
Planning permission and land issues	Boundaries of EMS compared with physical boundaries Owner of the site Plan showing installations, drainages and storage facilities Existing land use by the plant Construction of a new plant Modifications to existing plants
Site history	Previous ground/water surveys On-site waste deposits Soil contamination Water contamination Liability and penalties for past contamination
Operations	After hours operation permission Approval for shift work Permits for special operations
Incidents	Incidents that require reporting to regulatory authorities Reports of reported incidents Safety measures for storage and spillage Corrective measures
Hazardous substances	Hazardous substances or potentially hazardous substances used in the organisation Obligation to report on hazardous substances Information regarding the use, handling and storage of hazardous substances Inspection of underground storage tanks to check the integrity of pipe work Ozone-depleting substances used Sources of radioactivity

(Continued)

Table 13.9 (*Continued*)   Checklist for Identifying Legal Requirements Applicable to Environmental Aspects

Item	Issues to be Considered
Air	Processes, operations or substances that give emissions to air, including exhaust fumes from vehicles Plan showing air emission points Measuring emissions including greenhouse gases Use of technology to prevent or minimise air emissions Regulatory authority controlling emissions and obligation to report Past history of emissions and corrective measures Calibration of equipment used for measurement Obligation to report to authorities on the use of specific substances
Waste water	Processes, operations and substances that give rise to discharge to water Measurement of discharges Use of technology to prevent or minimise discharge to water Plan showing discharge points Water discharge regulations Past history of discharges and corrective measures Requirements to conserve water Conditions for drainage systems Water treatment facilities
Soil	Special conditions for land near protected land Measurement of soil contamination Previous history of soil contamination and corrective measures Limits of soil contamination levels Obligation to inform authorities Land usage for production, storage, parking and green areas
Odours	Restrictions on processes, substances that may cause unpleasant odours Complaints from the local community to regulatory bodies
Noise	Sources of noise including operations, vehicles, maintenance work, shift work Permits Measurement of noise levels Corrective measures Obligation to inform
Waste	Regulatory classification of waste Waste types produced in the plant Segregation of waste types Records of waste disposal Disposal or treatment of waste Waste storage points Permits for internal waste facilities, separation and collection of waste External waste disposal
Handling of environmentally harmful substances	Quotas Handling requirements and storage facilities Safety procedures Dealing with incidents Obligation to report

13.10 Ways to Ensure Legal Compliance

To ensure effective and efficient coverage of relevant legal requirements, the structure for monitoring and associated procedures has to be developed. The information gathered has to be monitored, evaluated and communicated to relevant parties. Responsibilities for identifying and monitoring legal compliance have to be clearly defined in the procedures. They should include, e.g., (a) the person assigned to monitor the legal requirements; (b) what should be monitored; (c) methods of evaluating the gathered information; (d) authority to sign off approvals; (e) parties that require the information and communication; and (f) method of communicating the information.

Legislation applicable to the organisation may be international, national or European. International agreements may also be relevant. The timeframe within which they come into force can vary. European directives can take up to five years before that are realised. On the other hand, the effect of local legislation will be felt much sooner. Therefore, the responsible person must keep in close communication with the regulators (Sheldon & Yoxon, 2006).

The following are some of the ways of ensuring legal compliance (Weiß, & Bentlage, 2006):

- Establish and communicate an environmental policy that defines commitment to compliance.
- Communicate regularly with regulatory bodies.
- Set objectives and targets in keeping with the environmental policy.
- Develop implementation programmes.
- Develop a procedure to identify and analyse relevant environmental laws and regulations and make them accessible to affected parties.
- Provide training and communicate relevant EMS requirements.
- Develop operational procedures.
- Audit compliance with legal requirements.
- Develop procedures to implement corrective measures when and where necessary.

Organisations that are conscious of environmental issues successfully manage the environmental impacts of their products, activities and services, move towards sustainable consumption and production, create and deliver biodiversity action plans, become aware of corporate responsibility, and operate within the framework of relevant laws and regulations.

References

Academy. (n.d.). *Environmental analysis*. Retrieved February 8, 2017 from http://ec.europa.eu/environment/life/project/Projects/index.cfm?fuseaction=home.showFile&rep=file&fil=ACADEMY_Analysis.pdf.

Block, M. (1999). *Identifying Environmental Aspects and Impacts*. Wisconsin: American Society for Quality.

Edwards, A.J. (2004). *ISO 14001 Environmental Certification Step by Step* (revised 1st ed.). UK: Elsevier Butterworth-Heinemann.

EPA. (2016). *Promoting EMS for the ship building and ship repair sector*. Retrieved January, 6, 2017 from https://archive.epa.gov/sectors/web/html/ems-5.html.

Engel, H.W. (1998). *Eco-mapping*. Retrieved January 6, 2017 from http://www.sba-int.ch/spec/sba/download/Tools/EcomapGuideEnglish.pdf.

Foster, C., Green, K., Bleda, M., Dewick, P., Evans, B., Flynn, A. and Mylan, J. (2006). Environmental impacts of food production and consumption. *A Report to the Department of Environment, Food and Rural Affairs (DEFRA), Manchester Business School*. UK: DEFRA.

KSPH & IDCL. (2015). *IMS procedure IMSP 19: Identification and evaluation of environmental aspects.* Retrieved September 15, 2017 from http://www.ksphc.org/pdfs/IMSP/IMSP%2019%20 Identification%20%20evaluation%20of%20Env%20aspects.pdf.

Ligus, G. (2013). Identification and assessment of the environmental aspects according to the ISO 14001 standard. *Chemik*, 67 (10), 874–880.

Morris, P. and Therivel, R. (2009). *Methods of Environmental Impact Assessment* (3rd ed.). UK: Routledge.

SCCM. (2014). *ISO 14001: Identifying and Evaluating Environmental Aspects. N13126 Version.* Holland: SCCM.

Sheldon, C. and Yoxon, M. (2006). *Environmental Management Systems* (3rd ed.). UK: Earthscan.

Verbanac, R. (2016). Four steps in the identification and evaluation of environmental aspects. *Advisera Expert Solutions Ltd.* Retrieved December 3, 2016 from http://advisera.com/14001academy/ knowledgebase/4-steps-in-identification-and-evaluation-of-environmental-aspects/.

Weiß, P. and Bentlage, J. (2006). *Environmental Management Systems and Certification. Book 4.* Sweden: Baltic University Press.

Chapter 14

Food Safety and Principles of Hazard Analysis and Critical Control Points (HACCPs)

14.1 History of Food Safety

Some 10,000–12,000 years ago, humans were experienced hunters and gatherers. Their survival depended on the availability of wild animals and plants and their ability to hunt and collect edible plants. Toxic plants were identified through experience. People lived a nomadic existence moving from place-to-place following the weather patterns. Then came the period of domestication of animals and plants, which reduced the need for a nomadic lifestyle. Gradually, communities of skilled craftsmen evolved, and it was possible to barter their services in exchange for basic necessities, principally food. As agriculture flourished, communities grew larger with an abundance of food supplies. Communities evolved into cities, adopted the need for government, and pursued art and technology for further advancement (Knechtges, 2012).

With the adoption of agricultural practices and the abundance of food supplies, the human race faced new challenges, particularly the spread of communicable diseases. Diseases were unknown at that time, and the transmission of diseases was facilitated by poor hygiene conditions, the consumption of adulterated food and water, the accumulation of human and animal waste, an increase in populations of rats and other disease-carrying animals, and overcrowded living conditions. Merchants who carried goods, travellers who explored and colonised new land, and military personnel who conducted exercises also contributed to the spread of communicable diseases (Knechtges, 2012).

14.1.1 Protecting the Consumer

During the medieval period, the marketplace was the centre for politics, commerce, religion and art. Social gatherings also took place in the marketplace. It offered a wide variety of goods such as food, clothing, shoes, pottery and leather goods. The marketplace was kept clean because of the widely held belief that food was responsible for the spread of diseases. Municipal authorities constantly policed the marketplace to protect the consumer. In Florence, e.g., every evening the market had to be thoroughly cleaned to remove bones and other refuse. On Thursdays and on the eve of holidays, tables, benches and booths had to be dismantled to facilitate cleaning. Disposal of refuse within the marketplace was forbidden and severe penalties were imposed on those who violated the regulations. In Augsburg in 1276, meat considered objectionable was ordered to be sold only at special booths where inferior quality food was sold, and that too was for strangers. In Zurich in 1345, fishmongers were ordered to dispose of fish that had not been sold by evening. Florentines forbade the sale on Monday of the meat that was leftover from the previous Saturday (Knechtges, 2012; Encyclopaedia Britannica, 1983).

Food safety hazards can originate on the farm and can continue to be introduced or exacerbated in the supply chain. Therefore, food safety authorities are now focusing on a farm-to-table approach to ensure food safety.

14.2 Foodborne Illnesses

Technological progress in food processing has created a greater awareness of problems associated with food safety. With the expansion of trade agreements and global food trade, food safety has become a worldwide issue. According to the World Health Organization (WHO), in 2010, 31 global food hazards caused 600 million foodborne illnesses and 420,000 deaths. Among children under five years of age, foodborne illness was 40% with 125,000 deaths each year (WHO, 2015; Forsythe, 2010).

International food trade contributes to the spread of foodborne illnesses in five ways: (a) Introduction of new pathogens and contamination from one country to another causes new threats; (b) pathogens which have been controlled in one country can be reintroduced by another country where it has not been controlled; (c) transportation over long distances and long periods of time provides plenty of opportunities for contamination and the growth of microorganisms; (d) contaminated food can reach many people resulting in major outbreaks of disease; and (e) the history of the food product may be unknown by the importing country when trans-shipping takes place among several countries. International and national organisations have enforced laws and regulations to achieve quality and safety in food preparation and preservation in order to protect the consumer from foodborne illnesses and intoxication (Glavin, 2003).

Most foodborne illnesses occur because of poor food handling at home. However, a proper understanding of the cause of foodborne diseases and with the adherence to a few simple rules, the introduction of hazards can be eliminated. Bacteria contribute to about 79% of all foodborne diseases. They survive between temperatures of 40°F–140°F and this doubles every 20–30 minutes. A single organism can multiply to become trillions of bacteria in just 24 hours! Their survival depends on the availability of proteins, and meat, milk, eggs and fish are good sources of proteins. The amount of bacteria present in food at the time of purchase is not sufficient to cause illness. Therefore, it is crucial to avoid exposure of animal proteins to the danger zone (40°F–140°F) for over four hours (Redman, 2007).

14.2.1 Types of Foodborne Illnesses

There are three types of foodborne illnesses (City of Houston, 2010):

1. Foodborne infection: Caused by consuming food contaminated with microorganisms as they multiply in the body causing diseases. Some of the diseases caused by microorganisms are salmonellosis and listeriosis. Viruses include Hepatitis A and the norovirus, and parasites include trichinella and anisakis.

2. Foodborne intoxication: Caused by consuming food containing toxic substances. Some bacteria may release toxic waste products that cause diseases. Foodborne illnesses caused by toxins are *Clostridium botulinum* or *Staphylococcus aureus*. Some plants such as mushrooms also contain toxins. Seafood toxins include scombroid and ciguatera. Chemicals and poisons included in products such as cleaning compounds, pesticides, sanitisers and metals cause chemical intoxication.
3. Toxin-mediated infections: Some microorganisms release toxins in the intestinal tract and cause severe illness. Parasites and viruses do not cause toxin-mediated infections. Bacteria such as shigella and shiga toxin-producing *Escherichia coli* cause toxin-mediated infections.

14.3 Principles of Food Control

A number of principles and values which are essential ingredients of food safety have to be considered when establishing, maintaining and updating food control systems (Food and Agriculture Organisation (FAO), 2003):

1. Maximise risk reduction throughout the food chain by applying the principles of prevention effectively. In this approach, the producer, processor, transporter, vendor and consumer play a vital role in assuring food safety. Instead of sampling and testing the final product, preventive measures have to be introduced throughout the supply chain. Food safety and quality have to be built into the product. Good agricultural practices, Good Manufacturing Practices (GMPs) and good hygiene practices are essential to ensure food safety. An important preventive approach is Hazard Analysis and Critical Control Point (HACCP).
2. Adopt a farm-to-fork approach.
3. Establish procedures to deal with emergencies such as recalls.
4. Develop food control strategies based on scientific principles.
5. Prioritise actions based on risk analysis and efficacy in risk management.
6. Adopt a holistic approach which targets risks and impacts on the organisation.
7. Recognise that food control is a shared responsibility among all stakeholders.

14.4 Food Safety Management System

A food safety management system (FSMS) consists of a set of interrelated components necessary to establish and achieve food safety policy and objectives which direct and control the organisation's food safety programme. The scope of the FSMS consists of products or product categories, processes and production locations. All outsourced processes must be managed and controlled by the organisation that outsources the processes. Commonly outsourced processes are:

■ Cold storage or freezing of raw materials and end products.
■ Transportation of food and food ingredients.
■ Irradiation of ingredients and other products.
■ Packaging.
■ Washing of tanks and transportation of equipment or facilities.
■ Grinding, mixing or weighing food ingredients.

The FSMS must be accurately documented, and at a minimum, it should include the food safety policy and objectives, and the documents required by the standard and those necessary to manage and control food safety (Salazar, 2013).

14.5 Definitions

Hazard: A biological, physical or chemical property that may cause a food to be unsafe for consumption.

Severity: The seriousness or consequences of exposure to the hazard.

Risk: Estimate of the probability of a risk happening.

Hazard analysis: The identification of biological, physical or chemical hazards associated with ingredients, production practices, processing, storage, distribution, retail and use.

HACCP: A scientific, rational and systemic approach to identify, assess and control hazards during production, processing, manufacturing, preparation and the use of food to ensure that it is safe for consumption. A HACCP system provides a preventive and a cost-effective approach to food safety.

HACCP plan: A document that sets out the procedures based on the principles of HACCP to be followed to assure food safety.

HACCP system: The organisational structure, procedures, processes and resources needed to implement the HACCP plan.

Sensitive ingredient: An ingredient known to have been associated with a hazard about which there is a concern.

14.6 Development of HACCP

HACCP is a simple approach to assure food safety. The principles of HACCP have been applied to the chemical processing industry more than 40 years ago, particularly in the United Kingdom (Snyder, 1992). The Pillsbury Company together with NASA and the US Army's Research, Development and Engineering Centre at Natick first developed this system to ensure the safety of food throughout the food chain and eventually that of astronauts' food during space missions (Motarjemi et al., 1996). Since then, this system has been universally recognised as an effective method to assure food safety. The WHO, which plays a key role in global health issues, has acknowledged the importance of the HACCP system for the prevention of foodborne diseases, and it has been instrumental in its promotion and development (FAO/WHO, 1993). One of the landmarks in the history of HACCP was the Codex Guidelines for the application of the HACCP system, which were adopted by the FAO/WHO Codex Alimentarius Commission in 1993, requiring them for international trade. In the United States, large chemical industries have adopted the principles of HACCP. The US Occupational Safety and Health Administration (OSHA) introduced the HACCP principles to reduce accidents.

14.7 Costs and Benefits of HACCP

Lack of food safety systems costs the food industry millions of dollars annually through waste, reworking, recalls and through loss of sales. Foodborne illnesses are no longer confined to developing countries. In the United States, according to the Centre for Disease Control and Prevention

(CDC), foodborne diseases account for 76 million illnesses, 325,000 hospitalisations and 5,000 deaths each year. Known pathogens alone account for an estimated 14 million illnesses, 60,000 hospitalisations and 1,500 deaths annually (Mead, et al., 1999). It has been estimated that medical costs and value of lives in England and Wales, due to just five foodborne diseases, amount to £300 million to £700 million per year (Mead et al., 1999).

Internationally, the application of HACCP principles has been recognised as the most cost-effective approach to ensure food safety. By implementing an effective FSMS based on HACCP principles, the food industry can minimise the potential for things to go wrong and ensure the safety of food products. HACCP adds value to existing processing systems such as GMP and the ISO 9000 standard. Retailers and consumers both can benefit from an effective HACCP pro-gramme. In general, organisations find it difficult to estimate the costs and benefits of HACCP implementation. A thorough knowledge of HACCP principles and how the plan works are required to separate production expenses from HACCP costs. Therefore, they are interpreted by the perception of individual managers (Cusato et al., 2012). The costs and benefits of the HACCP system are presented in Table 14.1.

Table 14.1   Costs and Benefits of HACCP Implementation

Costs	Initial Phase of the Plan	Cost of Employing External Consultants Cost of Using Employees in the HACCP Team
	Implementation phase	Cost of training employees Adjustment to Pre-requisite Programmes Cost of equipment Laboratory analyses Adjustment of processes
	Maintenance phase	Costs of monitoring CCPs Recruiting staff to monitor Time consumed in completing forms and records
Benefits	To the consumer	Ensure food safety Production of high quality food products
	To the public sector	Reduction of public health services costs Easier to monitor by regulatory agencies Cost savings of audits and analysis
	To the company	Compliance with regulations Fewer incidents of production of unsafe food More effective control of processes Less rework Decrease in raw material and finished product losses Decrease in microbial counts and consequent increase in shelf life Gain in production efficiency Decrease in sampling plans to control the processes Decrease in the number of non-compliant products Harmonisation with international trade requirements Improved hygienic environment Fewer customer complaints

14.8 Management Commitment

Although the HACCP team is responsible for the design and the implementation of the HACCP programme, the senior management must be aware of the fundamental requirements of the food safety programme so that they can allocate the necessary resources and have a positive approach to the project. Management commitment is the single most important factor when implementing a food safety programme. The role of the management team is to influence the project's success by creating a "buy-in" from every member of the organisation. Management commitment involves not only providing the necessary resources but also working closely with the HACCP team and listening to them in all phases of development and implementation. In the absence of total commitment from the management team, the project runs the risk of failure at critical points. The senior management must acknowledge that a HACCP programme is a comprehensive tool that helps everyone in the organisation to maintain a safe food production and serving environment. They play the role of a leader in the food safety programme, and in small- to medium-sized companies, they are role models. As with a quality management programme, a food safety programme involves several stakeholders: suppliers, employees and customers. The management team is also responsible for the appointment and assembly of the HACCP team who then take ownership of the programme. In addition, the organisation has to meet regulatory requirements. Therefore, support from the senior management team, regulatory agencies, training providers and the industry is essential for designing and implementing the programme. The suppliers' role is to support the organisation's commitment by recommending the necessary equipment and effective procedures that will assist the organisation to achieve its food safety goals (Nieto-Montenegro & Cason, 2010).

14.9 Pre-requisite Programmes

Pre-requisite programmes (PRPs) are procedures and practices are essential for food safety and necessary during the implementation of the HACCP programme. They provide the basic environment and operating conditions that ensure the production and delivery of safe food. The HACCP programme cannot be developed without the necessary PRPs. Several groups have published helpful material on PRPs, but the most widely used PRPs are drawn from the recommendations of the National Advisory Committee for the Microbiological Criteria for Foods (NACMCF, 1998). Pre-requisites should be used to control the hazards associated with the food service environment such as premises and structures, personnel and equipment, while the HACCP should be used to control the hazards directly associated with the food processes of storage and preparation. Table 14.2 shows the recommended PRPs (Wallace et al., 2011; Corlett Jr., 1998).

Other PRPs might include (a) quality assurance procedures; (b) standard operating procedures for sanitation, processes, product formulations and recipes; (c) glass contamination control procedures; (d) procedures for receiving, storage and shipping; (e) labelling; and (f) employee food and ingredients handling practices. The incorporation of PRPs into the HACCP programme ensures that the food is safe and wholesome. Just like any other management programme, PRPs have to be regularly audited and reviewed. While some of the PRPs can be managed as separate entities, some management programmes such as recall procedures, preventive maintenance, sanitation and hygiene can be easily incorporated into the HACCP plan (Corlett Jr., 1998; De Silva, 2007).

Table 14.2 Pre-requisite Programmes

Pre-requisite Programme	Scope
1. Facilities and premises	• Suitability of production environment, including buildings, pathways, drainage, waste management, etc. • Provision of sufficient space for production, storage, cooling and refrigeration • Provision of adequate ventilation, water supply and lighting facilities for the staff
2. Supplier control	• Procedure for the approval of suppliers • An effective GMP and food safety programme
3. Specifications	• Documented specifications for all ingredients, packaging and processes
4. Equipment	• Calibration procedures • Preventive maintenance schedule
5. Cleaning and sanitation	• Validation of sanitation methods • Documented procedures • Regular cleaning and sanitation of equipment
6. Personnel hygiene	• Establish a personnel hygiene policy • Monitoring the policy
7. Training	• Provision, management and keeping records of training in personnel hygiene, GMP, cleaning, sanitation, personal safety and their role in the HACCP programme
8. Management of chemicals	• Proper storage of chemicals and segregation of food and non-food items
9. Receiving, storage and transport	• Storage of all raw materials and products under safe and sanitary conditions • Maintaining appropriate environmental conditions for storage
10. Traceability and recall	• Batch coding of all raw materials and products to enable traceability • Establish an effective recall procedure
11. Pest control	• Establish and maintain an effective pest control programme

14.10 Scope of the HACCP Programme

In the early years of introduction of HACCP, interest was focused on microbiological integrity. The basic philosophy was to examine the food ingredients as they are received and processed, until consumption of the finished food product by the consumer. Market competition forced companies to look for ways to reduce costs while maintaining quality. With increasing consumer awareness and legal liability to produce and sell safe food, organisations adopted a broader view of the food safety programme. At the same time, other significant changes were taking place such as changes in process technology, enhanced automation, complex packaging solutions, new ingredients, improved formulations, greater emphasis on sensory evaluations and complex distribution networks, leading to reduced delivery times. These changes had a major impact on food safety requirements (De Silva, 2007).

Codex Alimentarius, a collection of food standards adopted by the Codex Alimentarius Commission, defined the general requirement for food safety (FAO/WHO, 2016). The HACCP programme includes general principles of food hygiene as well as appropriate commodity standards. Since 1998, the British Retail Consortium (BRC) has developed the BRC Global Standards, a set of four industry-leading technical standards that define production, packaging, storage and distribution requirements that assure safe food and consumer products (BRC, 2017). The four global standards are (a) standards for food safety; (b) standards for consumer products; (c) standards for packaging and packaging materials; and (d) standards for storage and distribution.

BRC standards incorporate the management system of ISO 9000, the principles of the Codex Alimentarius and GMPs. Thus, a complete HACCP programme includes (a) HACCP principles; (b) management principles; (c) plant environment standards; (d) process and product control; and (e) personnel hygiene.

In September 2005, the International Organization for Standardization (ISO) introduced the food safety standard ISO 22000. This standard is an FSMS that incorporates continuous improvement designed to prevent and eliminate food safety hazards or reduce them to acceptable levels (ISO, n.d.). It has been revised in 2018.

14.11 Seven Principles of HACCP

HACCP is a programme designed to identify, evaluate and control food safety hazards based on the following seven principles (NACMCF, 1998; Bryan, 1999):

Principle 1. Conduct a hazard analysis.
Principle 2. Determine the Critical Control Points (CCPs).
Principle 3. Establish critical limits.
Principle 4. Establish monitoring procedures.
Principle 5. Establish corrective actions.
Principle 6. Establish verification procedures.
Principle 7. Establish record-keeping and documentation procedures.

14.12 HACCP Development Plan

There are 12 steps in the development of the HACCP plan (Cumpanici, 2006). The activities at each stage are applicable to any food processing operation. The HACCP plan (Table 14.3) evolves as the HACCP team works through each stage. It has to be developed for each new product. Hazard analysis critically evaluates the quality of all ingredients, processing steps and the product itself. The programme is managed by monitoring and reviewing the system through the implementation of corrective actions when necessary (Norton, 2002).

Table 14.3 HACCP Planning Stages and Steps

Stage	Step	Key Activities	Principles
1	1	Assemble the HACCP team	
	2	Describe the product and its intended use	
2	3	Develop and verify the flow diagram for food production	
	4	Conduct the hazard analysis	1
	5	Establish CCPs	2
	6	Establish critical limits	3
	7	Establish the monitoring procedure	4
	8	Implement corrective action	5
3	9	Establish verification procedure	6
	10	Establish the record-keeping procedure	7
	11	Validate the HACCP plan	
4	12	Review and maintain the HACCP plan	

14.13 Assemble the HACCP Team

The success or failure of the HACCP programme depends on the constitution of the HACCP team. It consists of members drawn from various disciplines in the food processing operation. The HACCP team is not a management team and should represent key functions of the organisation. At the very least, the team should comprise of a project leader, production specialist, food technology specialist, process engineer, other specialists when required and a secretary (Kirby, 1994). The roles of the team members are shown in Table 14.4. The HACCP team may need further training on HACCP principles, and they should be provided with the necessary tools to accomplish the tasks.

The main objectives of the team are to (a) define the type of food produced by the organisation; (b) specify how ingredients are received; (c) define the processes and their controls; (d) specify the storage and delivery conditions; and (e) identify the hazards and CCPs (Norton, 2002). If expertise is not available within the organisation, it may be necessary to seek the services of a specialist. The project leader has a significant impact on the outcome of the programme and will assign responsibilities to each team member.

14.13.1 HACCP Training

HACCP training has been recognised as the most cost-effective way to control the hazards associated with the microbiological, chemical and physical contamination of foods. The HACCP programme is a team exercise, and training and education are essential to reap the full benefits of the programme. Food producers have the responsibility to produce safe and healthy food products, and the regulatory agencies must be competent to monitor the food safety programme. The

Table 14.4   Responsibilities of HACCP Team Members

Team Member	Key Responsibilities
Project Leader	• Convenes and chairs meetings • Assigns roles and responsibilities
Production Specialist	• Constructs flow charts • Advises on production issues and process capability
Food Technology Specialist	• Advises on technical issues • Identifies hazards, CCPs and recommends solutions
Process Engineer	• Supplies information on the performance of equipment and machinery • Recommends new machinery, equipment or processes as and when required
Secretary	• Keeps records and distributes proceedings of meetings
Other(s)	• Provides information on specialist areas

purpose of the training is to provide (a) knowledge of the concepts; the principles and benefits of the HACCP programme; (b) the practical skills and competency required to implement the programme; and (c) the skills necessary to improve the HACCP programme.

The HACCP training programme should target the needs of food producers as well as regulatory authorities. Regulatory authorities need to learn the concepts, principles and benefits of the food safety programme while food producers need to have practical skills. Wherever possible, scientific data should be used to support the training material (Mayes, 1994).

14.14 Description of the Product, Intended Use and the Process

The first task of the HACCP team is to define the variety of food products that they produce or intend to produce. Each food product is different in terms of the process and associated hazards. Therefore, they should be defined through biological, physical and chemical characteristics. If a product requires an additional device or a component for processing, the hazards associated with the device or component should be defined (FAO, 1998). The following information should be provided in the product description:

1. Product name or name of the product group.
2. Product features such as water activity, pH and preservatives.
3. How the product is to be used: ready to eat, further processing required, heated prior to consumption.
4. Packaging: packaging material and packaging conditions.
5. Shelf life including storage conditions.
6. Distribution outlets including distribution method.
7. Labelling instructions: handling and usage instructions.
8. Shipping conditions.
9. Target consumer group including sensitive groups such as the elderly, immune-suppressed, pregnant population, infants as applicable.

The intended use of the product specifies the normal use by end users or consumers. Table 14.5 shows the product description of orange juice (Ausgrown, n.d.). Table 14.6 presents the raw materials used in the production of orange juice.

At this stage, it is helpful to group products by their characteristics or intended use. For example, all products that require baking could be grouped together. Similarly, all products intended to be used as beverages could be classified together. The processes associated with each product should be defined in sufficient detail to highlight hazards and control points (Product Quality Research Institute (PQRI), 2011). The details of processes include (a) process steps, equipment and whether manual or automated; (b) direct process control elements: online instrumentation, logic, manufacturing procedures, testing and inspection methods; (c) indirect process control: operator competence, maintenance, cleaning and storage; and (d) quality control of raw materials, finished products and their release.

The process of producing pasteurised orange juice (UNIDO, 2004) is shown in Figure 14.1

14.15 Types of Hazards

The three types of potential food safety hazards are biological, physical and chemical hazards.

Table 14.5   Product Description of Orange Juice

Product Features	Description
Product name	Pasteurised orange juice
Product features	Fat: nil; pH 2.8–3.8
How the product is to be used	Once opened consume within five days
Packaging	Clear bottle with metal cap
Shelf life	28 days; Store below 5°C
Distribution outlets	Retail outlets; refrigerated transport
Labelling instructions	None required for product safety Contains no added substances or genetically modified products
Shipping conditions	In cardboard boxes bottles separated by dividers No physical damage or extremes of temperature
Target consumer group	Suitable for all except those sensitive to acidic products

Table 14.6   List of Raw Materials Used in the Production of Pasteurised Orange Juice

Primary Ingredient	Chemicals	Packaging Material	Non-contact Packaging
Fresh oranges	None	New glass bottles Metal cap	Corrugated board cases Labels Corrugated board sections

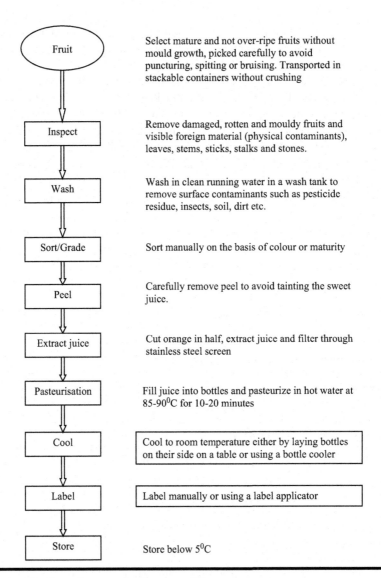

Figure 14.1   Production of pasteurised orange juice.

14.15.1 Biological Hazards

Foodborne biological hazards are microorganisms such as bacteria, viruses, fungi and parasites. Most foodborne illnesses are caused by pathogenic bacteria, and microorganisms are commonly associated with humans and with raw products entering the food establishment. Many of them occur in the environment where food is grown. Viruses can be foodborne/waterborne or transmitted by human, animal or other contact. They survive on living cells and cannot replicate in food but can be carried by it. Parasites are host-specific and can include humans in their life cycle. They are present in under-cooked meat products or contaminated ready-to-eat food. Fungi include moulds and yeasts, and some of them are beneficial. Some produce mycotoxins which are toxic to humans and animals (FAO, 1998). The factors that affect the microbial growth in foods are summarised in Table 14.7 (Hamad, 2012).

Table 14.7   Factors that Affect the Growth of Microorganisms in Food

Factors	Details
Intrinsic (related to food itself)	Nutrient content, water activity, pH, redox potential, presence of antimicrobial substances and mechanical barriers
Extrinsic (related to the environment where food is stored)	Temperature of storage, composition of gases and relative humidity in the atmosphere surrounding the food
Implicit (related to the microorganisms themselves)	Interactions between microorganisms contaminating the food, and between microorganisms and food
Processing	Treatments such as heating, cooling and drying that affect the composition of food also affect the types and the number of microorganisms that remain in food after the treatment
Combined	Interactions between the above factors causing additive or synergistic effects

14.15.2 Chemical Hazards

Chemical contaminants may occur naturally in food or may be added during processing. For example, pesticides are applied in agriculture and food additives are added during the formulation and processing stages of food production. The types and concentrations of chemicals used are important for safety aspects. Naturally occurring chemicals include allergens, mycotoxins, scrombrotoxin, ciguatoxin, mushroom toxins and shellfish toxins. Added chemical contaminants include but are not limited to polychlorinated biphenyls, agricultural chemicals, prohibited substances, toxic elements such as lead, arsenic, cyanide, food additives, vitamins and mineral contaminants, and packaging materials (FAO, 1998).

14.15.3 Physical Hazards

Physical hazards are caused by the entry of any foreign matter into the food at any stage from the processing of raw materials to the consumption of finished product. They may be visible to the naked eye or dissolved or dispersed in the food product. Their physical form can vary from powder to particulate matter depending on the type and origin. The detection of foreign matter in food is not easy because of the variability and infrequent occurrence. Some of the physical hazards associated with food products are hair, glass or metal fragments, pests such as rodents and cockroaches, jewellery, dirt, insects and fingernails (De Silva, 2007).

14.16 Routes of Contamination

Raw materials, processing steps, machinery, handling and environmental conditions are some routes through which food contamination can occur.

14.16.1 Raw Materials

Raw materials entering the food supply chain are the primary source of contamination. The raw materials that are most likely to cause microbial contamination are meat, poultry, fish and dairy products. The level of contamination depends on (a) source; (b) refining and handling practices; (c) packaging material; and (d) storage conditions (Underwood, 1995). Table 14.8 shows the hazards due to some raw materials (Early, 1995; Bauman, 1990).

14.16.2 Processing Steps

Contaminants can also be introduced during the processing steps of a food product. Uncontrolled processing operations contribute to hazardous situations. Failure to effectively maintain processing steps such as temperature/time delay in processing, using wrong formulations and procedures, and following unauthorised processing steps may all result in contamination or microbial growth. Mercury thermometers used in the production area are a potential hazard, and now most organisations prohibit their use. Ineffective cleaning practices may leave chemical residues on plant and equipment.

14.16.3 Machinery

Equipment and utensils provide ample opportunities for contamination or they become contaminated. They become contaminated from humans, rodents and insects, sewage escaping from faulty pipes and drains, unpotable water, condensation due to faulty ventilation and contaminated food. Proper setting up of equipment and an effective preventive maintenance programme are important aspects of a safety management programme. If glass bottle filling machines have not been properly set up, bottles can get chipped at the filler or capping machine. Imperfectly made containers can also contaminate the food with the material of the container. Metal pieces from wire meshes, machine parts and nuts and bolts from poorly maintained machines are potential hazards. Badly designed or modified plant and equipment can promote the growth of microorganisms in the dead ends of pipework or dirt traps (De Silva, 2007).

Table 14.8 Hazards Associated with Some Raw Materials

- Traces of chemicals and foreign matter
- Heavy metals such as lead, arsenic, mercury, tin and cadmium (may occur in vegetables grown in contaminated soil)
- Lead capsules in wine bottles
- Solder from side seams of cans
- Adhesives, coatings and resins in packages
- Cleaning chemical residues, solvents, lubricants and dirty or incompletely washed bottles
- Excessive amount of sulphur dioxide used in sterilising bottles prior to filling
- Additives such as preservatives colourings, flavours and food conditioners
- Pesticide residues, foreign objects such as stones and insect parts present in fruits and vegetables
- Rodent bait, insecticides and insects in an uncontrolled and unhygienic environment
- Glass fragments from broken bottles, fittings and thermometers
- Stones and particles of wood in sun-dried fruits, herbs and spices
- Accidental contamination with cleaning chemicals and other toxic non-food substances

14.16.4 Handling of Food

Highly automated and high-speed machinery is capable of processing vast amounts of food products, which are then stored and transported to distribution centres and retail outlets. Therefore, food safety depends on processing characteristics as well as handling during transport, storage and customer use. Hazards can develop due to inadequate temperature control during storage, transportation, handling in retail outlets and during consumer storage. Products such as chilled/frozen entrees and meal components are preserved by refrigeration. These products may prove hazardous if they are not stored above recommended temperatures or beyond their shelf life.

Failure to rotate stocks by the distributor may result in outdated products reaching retail shops and the consumer. An absence of clear storage or preparation instructions, and a lack of knowledge about handling, cooking and storage of food products, increases the risk of hazard occurrence. Personal hygiene is a critical factor for food safety in food-serving establishments. If adequate precautions are not taken, food handlers can transmit pathogenic bacteria (De Silva, 2007).

14.16.5 Environmental Conditions

Hazards due to adverse environmental conditions may affect raw materials, processing and equipment. Water and soil pollution can have alarming results through the food chain. Regulatory bodies monitor and control the disposal of domestic and industrial waste to prevent the entry of hazardous material and rodents into the food processing environment. Environmental contamination can also occur through foreign matter, chemicals in sprays and contaminants in water.

14.17 Some Measures to Control Hazards

14.17.1 Raw Materials and Packaging

Raw materials and packaging constitute one of the major areas that must be effectively controlled. Some raw materials such as eggs, fish, milk, cheese and shellfish can harbour microorganisms, and the processes used to remove or destroy microorganisms (Underwood, 1995) are shown in Table 14.9. In addition, quality assurance procedures (Table 14.10) can be established to ensure that incoming raw materials do not cause a health hazard (De Silva, 2007).

Other measures include using the recommended type of packaging, ensuring that bulk containers have an effective cleaning programme, and that only permissible products are transported in bulk containers, using tamper-proof seals, inspection of samples on delivery and the maintenance of appropriate storage conditions.

Table 14.9   Processing Methods to Control Microorganisms in Raw Material and Packaging

Method	Control Procedure
Heat treatment	Time, temperature and humidity
Filtration	Pore size and filter integrity
Irradiation	Dosage and density of load
Chemical	Concentration, pH and temperature

Table 14.10   Quality Assurance Methods to Control Incoming Raw Materials

1. Establish an effective approved supplier policy
2. Establish specifications taking into consideration those features that are critical to quality and food safety
3. Avoid using the cheapest price as the sole criterion for selection. Relate the price to risk assessment
4. Review any new ingredients introduced into the system. Instruct the supplier to inform you of all changes in the characteristics of the raw material, as even minor changes may have a major impact.
5. Monitor the performance of the supplier
6. Instruct the supplier to develop and implement a HACCP programme and a quality management system
7. Inform the supplier to label all raw materials accurately to avoid errors
8. Carry out random checks on raw materials on delivery
9. Monitor the storage conditions at supplier's and producer's premises
10. Encourage the supplier to develop safe and environmental-friendly packaging

14.17.2 Processing Steps

Control measures that can be applied at processing steps depend largely on the processing method. The following are some control measures that can be applied at the processing steps (De Silva, 2007): (a) monitor process control parameters; (b) ensure that all products have traceability information; (c) ensure that products under quarantine are not despatched; (d) take measures to prevent cross-contamination; and (e) ensure that all changes come under a change control procedure.

14.17.3 Plant and Equipment

Hazards due to plant and machinery can be controlled by the development and maintenance of equipment and accessories used to manufacture a food product:

■ Establish and implement a preventive maintenance programme.
■ Clean/sterilise all equipment and utensils before and after use.
■ Reassess hazards whenever changes are made.
■ Calibrate equipment according to the calibration procedure.
■ Use generally recognised as safe lubricants and grease purchased from approved suppliers.
■ Train operators to recognise hazards during production.

14.17.4 Storage and Distribution

Food safety hazards due to storage and distribution are associated with storage conditions, stock rotation and physical locations. The following are some control measures:

■ Store products in a manner that ensures protection, preservation and freedom from contamination, pests, etc.
■ Monitor storage conditions regularly.
■ Ensure that all storage areas are kept in a clean and hygienic condition.

- All products must bear a status sticker: PASSED, RELEASED, QUARANTINE, REJECT, etc.
- Ensure that only products that bear a RELEASED sticker are despatched.
- Train operators in the safe handling of food products.
- Monitor temperature/time records in refrigerated trucks.
- Use correct delivery procedures.
- Carry out regular inspections.

14.17.5 Premises

Control measures that can be implemented to prevent contamination within the premises depend on the proper design and the layout of processing areas. Several control measures can be employed to prevent the occurrence of hazards: (a) implement a pest control programme; (b) schedule a maintenance programme; (c) inspect vents and overhead pipes; (d) use guarded light fittings; (e) filter air supply within process areas; (f) install temperature/time record in manufacturing and storage areas; (g) clean walls, floors and ceiling regularly; (h) monitor the quality of water supply and its temperature when used for sterilising, sanitising or cleaning; and (i) implement an effective waste disposal programme.

14.17.6 Personnel

An effective HACCP programme includes hazards due to poor handling in the production facility and at food-serving stations. A major risk in catering facilities and in chilled and frozen food premises is poor physical health and a lack of personal hygiene. The accidental inclusion of items such as pens, paper, jewellery, metal items, cigarette butts and chewing gum in food products is not uncommon. Some common controls to prevent such incidents are:

- The introduction of a policy prohibiting smoking, using chewing gum and wearing jewellery.
- Monitoring illnesses and the provision of health care.
- Maintaining personal hygiene.
- Wearing clean and soil-free garments.
- Wearing head covers.
- Avoiding touching food with bare hands.
- Providing suitable hand-washing and drying facilities.
- Carrying out regular audits.

14.17.7 Measures at Post-processing and Packaging Stages

14.17.7.1 Retail Premises

a. Store the food at recommended storage conditions.
b. Take care in handling food.
c. Monitor temperature/time records during storage.
d. Inspect equipment and facilities.
e. Conduct audits.
f. Train staff.
g. Use tamper-proof or tamper-evident packaging.

14.17.7.2 Food Service

Hazards due to food service are associated with several factors: composition of menus and individual food items, storage, preparation, handling and holding procedures (Munce, 1984). Control measures are:

- a. Selection of suppliers.
- b. Inspection of raw materials on receipt.
- c. Temperature/time control in storage and food handling areas.
- d. Monitoring personal hygiene and food handling practices.
- e. Sanitation of utensils and food handling equipment.
- f. Provision of adequate covers to protect the entry of insects.
- g. Preventing the entry of insects.

14.17.8 Consumer

Food preparation: The consumer is the last link in the food chain, and hazards can occur due to poor handling and during preparation in the home. Consumer awareness of potential hazards in handling food in the household is essential to ensure the safety of food prepared at home. Control measures such checking the containers prior to purchase, handling the product correctly during transport, storing the ingredients and food as recommended, keeping the kitchen equipment clean, preparing the food correctly, and managing the pantry appropriately will minimise the chances of contamination (Beard, 1991).

Food usage: At this stage, hazards arise owing to consumer abuse. The label should clearly indicate the manner of reconstitution of the food. Food specially made for specific consumer groups such as diabetics should bear the details on the label. Controls can be exercised through the provision of consumer information as to how the food product should be handled, used and stored. Warning labels such as use-by dates and storage conditions, use of temperature/time indicators on high-risk and sensitive ingredients, and food items and packaging design that minimise abuse by the consumer are some approaches that can be adopted by the food processor in order to minimise the opportunities for abuse.

14.18 Allergen Control

An important aspect of food safety is allergen control by food producers. Food allergens are typically naturally occurring proteins in foods or their derivatives that cause abnormal immune responses. Eight foods have been identified as causing the majority of reactions (Food Allergy Research and Education (FARE), n.d.): peanuts, tree nuts, milk, eggs, wheat, soy, fish and shellfish. Food suppliers and food producers should have effective programmes to control the entry of allergens at each business location. They have an obligation to inform the consumer about the presence of regulated allergens present in food. The two main goals of any allergens control programme are the prevention of contact with allergens and proper labelling of food that contain allergens. A successful allergen management programme typically has four categories of controls: minimise the potential to cross-contact with allergens; managing work-in-progress; rework; and administration of management functions and label control programmes. These controls can be achieved through the development and implementation of standard operating procedures which address allergen control activities including the staging, warehousing and sealing of allergenic ingredients to prevent contact with non-allergenic ingredients (Grocery Manufacturers Association (GMA), 2008).

Food safety has evolved as a common concern worldwide, and public health agencies and governments are looking for more effective and efficient ways to monitor production chains. Food producers have an obligation to devise ways and means to ensure food safety so that the consumer is not put at risk.

References

Ausgrown. (n.d.). *Product specification: Orange juice*. Retrieved April 3, 2017 from http://www.ausgrown.com/assets/orange.pdf.

Bauman, H. (1990). HACCP: Concept, development and application. *Food Technology*, 44 (5), 156–159.

Beard, T.D. III. (1991). HACCP and the home: The need for consumer education. *Food Technology*, 46 (6), 123–124.

BRC. (2017). *BRC global standards*. Retrieved March 30, 2017 from https://www.brcglobalstandards.com/.

Bryan, F.L. (1999). Hazard Analysis Critical Control Point approach to food safety: Past, present, and future. *Journal of Environmental Health*, 61 (8), 9–15.

City of Houston. (2010). *Food service manager's certification manual*. Retrieved March 2010, from https://www.houstontx.gov/health/Food/FSMC%20Manual.pdf.

Corlett Jr. D.A. (1998). *HACCP Users' Manual, Appendix A*. Gaithersburg: Aspen Publishing.

Cumpanici, A. (2006). *ADP guide to hazard analysis and critical control point principles*. Retrieved March 30, 2017 from http://www.acsa.md/public/files/english/stand/HACCP_Guide_ENG.pdf.

Cusato, S., Tavolaro, P., Augusto, C. and de Oliveira, F. (2012). Implementation of hazard analysis and critical control point in the food industry: Impact on safety and the environment. In A. McElhatton and P.J.do A. Sobral (Eds.), *Novel Technologies in Food Science: Their Impact on Products, Consumer Trends and the Environment*, pp. 21–38. New York: Springer.

De Silva, T. (2007). Hazard analysis and critical control point (HACCP). In M. Shafiur Rahman (Ed.), *Handbook of Food Preservation* (2nd ed.), pp. 969–1010. Florida: CRC Press.

Early, R. (1995). *Guide to Quality Systems for the Food Industry*. UK: Blackie Academic and Professional.

Encyclopaedia Britannica. (1983). *Pure Food Laws in Middle Ages: Health and Safety Laws, 8, 695, The New Encyclopaedia Britannica*. Chicago: Encyclopaeda Britannica Inc.

FAO. (1993). Report of the twenty-fifth session of the Codex Committee on Food Hygiene. *Codex Alimentarius Commission, Session 20*. Geneva (Switzerland), 28 June – 7 July 1993. Italy: FAO.

FAO. (1998). *Section 3: Food Quality and Safety Systems – A Training Manual of Food Hygiene and the Hazard Analysis and Critical Control Point System*. Italy: FAO

FAO. (2003). Assuring food safety and quality. *FAO Food and Nutrition Paper 76*. Italy: FAO.

FAO/WHO. (2016). *Codex Alimentarius*. Retrieved March 30, 2017 from http://www.fao.org/fao-who-codexalimentarius/en/.

FARE. (n.d.). *Allergens*. Retrieved Aril 10, 2017 from https://www.foodallergy.org/allergens.

Forsythe, S.J. (2010). *The Microbiology of Safe Food* (2nd ed.). UK: Wiley-Blackwell.

Glavin, M. (2003). A single microbial sea: Food safety as a global concern. *SAIS Review*, 23 (1), 203–220.

GMA. (2008). *Food Supply Chain Handbook*. Washington: GMA.

Hamad, S.H. (2012). Factors affecting the growth of microorganisms in food. In R. Bhat, A. Karim Alias and Gopinathan Paliyath (Eds.), *Progress in Food Preservation*, pp. 405–425. UK: John Wiley & Sons.

ISO. (n.d.). *ISO 22000 family – Food safety management*. Retrieved March 30, 2017 from https://www.iso.org/iso-22000-food-safety-management.html.

Kirby, R. (1994). HACCP in practice. *Food Control*, 5 (4), 230–236.

Knechtges, P.L. (2012). *Food Safety: Theory and Practice*. Massachusetts: Johns & Bartlett Learning.

Mayes, T. (1994). HACCP training. *Food Control*, 5, 190–195.

Mead, P.S., Slutsker, L., Dietz, V., McCaig, L.F., Bresee, J.S., Shapiro, C., Griffin, P.M. and Tauxe, R.V. (1999). Food-related illnesses and deaths in the United States. *Emerging Infectious Diseases*, 5 (5), 607–625.

Motarjemi, Y., Kaferstein, J., Moy, G., Miyagawa, S. and Miyagishoma, K. (1996). Importance of HACCP for public health and development: The role of the World Health Organisation. *Food Control*, 7 (2), 77–85.

Munce, B.A. (1984). Hazard analysis critical control points and the food service industry. *Food Technology Australia*, 56 (5), 214–217.

NACMCF. (1998). Hazard analysis and critical control point principles and application Guidelines. *Journal of Food Protection*, 61 (9), 1246–1259.

Nieto-Montenegro, S. and Cason, K.L. (2010). Development and implementation of food safety programmes in the food industry. In *Enrique Ortega-Rivas, Processing Effects on Safety and Quality of Foods*, pp. 545–559. Florida: CRC Press.

Norton, C. (2002). Taking it step-by-step. *Food Management*, 37, 52–55.

PQRI. (2011). *Risk management case studies: HCCP training tool guidance*. Retrieved March 30, 2017 from http://pqri.org/wp-content/uploads/2015/08/pdf/HACCP_Training_Guide.pdf.

Redman, N. (2007). *Food Safety* (2nd ed.). California: ABC-CLIO Inc.

Salazar, E. (2013). *Understanding Food Safety Management Systems: A Practical Approach to the Application of ISO-22000: 2005*. Charleston: CreateSpace Independent Publishing Platform.

Snyder, O.P. (1992). HACCP – An industry food safety self-control programme – Part 1. *Dairy, Food and Environmental Sanitation*, 12, 26–27.

Underwood, E. (1995), Good manufacturing practices: A means of control biodeterioration. *International Biodeterioration and Biodegradation*, 36, 449–456.

UNIDO. (2004). *UNIDO Technology Manual: Production Methods, Equipment and Quality Assurance Practices*. Austria: UNIDO.

Wallace, C.A., Sperber W.H. and Mortimore, S.E. (2011). *Food Safety for the 21st Century: Managing HACCP and Food Safety throughout the Global Supply Chain*. UK: Wiley-Blackwell.

WHO. (2015). *The Estimates of the Global Burden of Foodborne Diseases*. Switzerland: WHO Press.

Chapter 15

Application of HACCP

15.1 Introduction

Principle 1 of Hazard Analysis and Critical Control Point (HACCP) is hazard identification and analysis, and it is the most important task of the whole process. An inaccurate hazard analysis can only produce an inadequate HACCP plan. It requires technical expertise as well as scientific background in various domains for a proper identification of all potential hazards. Therefore, knowledge of food science and HACCP is essential for the development of the HACCP plan. Hazard analysis needs to identify all hazards that are significant and must be eliminated or reduced to an acceptable level in order to produce safe food for consumption. The aims of hazard analysis are threefold: (a) to identify hazards of significant to food safety; (b) to select critical hazards on the basis of risk to the consumer; and (c) to identify specific hazards that warrant specific preventive measures (Norton, 2002). When the same food product is manufactured by different organisations, the hazards will vary depending on (a) the source of ingredients; (b) product formulations; (c) processing machinery and equipment; (d) processing and methods of preparation; (e) duration of processes; (f) storage conditions; and (g) experience, knowledge and attitudes of personnel (Food and Agriculture Organisation (FAO) Information Division, 1998a).

A comprehensive hazard analysis will identify the following (Product Quality Research Institute (PQRI), 2015):

- Actual and potential hazards associated with each step of the process.
- The potential sources of hazards.
- The possibility of introducing, controlling or enhancing the hazard by this step.
- The severity of adverse health effects associated with each hazard and its impact.
- The likelihood of occurrence of a hazard with suitable scientific control measures.
- The survival or multiplication of harmful organisms or the presence of toxins of concern and contributing conditions, if applicable.
- The introduction or creation of chemical impurities or degrading products and contributing conditions, if applicable.
- Reason(s) for identifying a hazard as significant to warrant its inclusion for further assessment.
- Control measures in place to eliminate or reduce the hazard to an acceptable level.

All existing and new products, changes in ingredients, product formulations, processing and preparation methods, packaging, storage and distribution and/or consumer use must be subjected to the analysis.

15.2 Information Sources

Specific information on particular food products and food processes should be gathered to assist the identification and assessment of hazards. The following are some of the commonly used sources: company complaints file, scientific research and review papers, epidemiological data on foodborne illnesses and diseases, and the World Wide Web (www).

15.3 Definitions

Hazard: Unacceptable biological (growth or survival of microorganisms), physical (glass fragments, metal pieces, hair, jewellery) or chemical (pesticide residues, cleaning chemicals, heavy metals) contamination that render the food unsafe and unfit for consumption.

Risk: Estimate of the probability of a hazard occurring.

Severity: Seriousness of consequence of exposure to the hazard.

Hazard analysis: Identification of biological, physical, chemical or other hazards associated with ingredients, production practices, processing, storage, distribution, retailing and end use.

Critical Control Point (CCP): A step at which a control can be applied and is essential to prevent or eliminate a food safety hazard or reduce it to an acceptable level.

Control point: An operational step in a manufacturing or distribution process that could be controlled to ensure quality and regulatory compliance.

HACCP: A scientific, rational and systemic approach to the identification, assessment and control of hazards throughout the food chain to ensure that food is safe for consumption.

HACCP plan: A document that defines the processes based on the principles of HACCP to be followed to assure food safety.

HACCP system: The organisational structure, procedures, processes and resources required to implement the HACCP plan.

Critical limit: One or more specified tolerances that must be met to ensure that controls at a CCP are effective in eliminating or reducing the hazard to an acceptable level.

Sensitive ingredient: An ingredient known to have been associated with a hazard and for which there is a concern.

Verification: Use of methods, procedures and tests to ensure that the requirements of the HACCP plan have been fulfilled.

Validation: A review of the HACCP plan to ensure that elements of the plan are accurate and correct.

Pre-requisite programme (PRP): Control measures applicable across the food chain aimed at maintaining a safe and hygienic environment supporting the HACCP plan.

Operational pre-requisite programme (oPRP): A form of PRP identified by the hazard analysis as essential in order to control the introduction food safety hazards and prevent the contamination or proliferation of food safety hazards in the products or in the processing environment.

15.4 How to Conduct a Hazard Analysis

Hazards identified under the HACCP system must be of such a nature that their prevention, elimination or reduction to acceptable levels is essential to the production of safe food. A systemic approach to hazard analysis involves the assessment of biological, chemical and physical hazards in all facets of the food production environment including delivery and consumer use. Biological hazards occur when there is a potential for pathogenic organisms to contaminate the food during all stages of processing. Chemical hazards exist when food is contaminated with substances such as pesticide residues, toxic metals, cleaning agents, and sometimes food additives and preservatives present in excessive amounts. Physical hazards are associated with particles such as glass fragments, metal pieces, wood, hair, jewellery or dirt contaminating the food (Rooney & Kilkelly, 2002). Table 15.1 shows a suitable form for hazard analysis.

15.4.1 Some Questions to Be Considered When Conducting a Hazard Analysis

Hazard analysis can be broken down into five major activities which must be conducted in a logical sequence to avoid any omissions. When completed, the hazard analysis team will have a comprehensive list of all potential hazards.

15.4.1.1 Receiving Incoming Materials

Subject all incoming materials including all ingredients and packaging to hazard analysis. It is important to interpret the results with reference to the finished product. For example, the presence of pathogenic organisms in ready-to-eat food is a potential hazard. On the other hand, if the end product is not a ready-to-eat product, further processing such as cooking will eliminate or reduce the level of pathogenic organisms to an acceptable level. The following questions may help in identifying potential hazards in incoming materials (FAO Information Division, 1998a; Corlett, Jr., 1998):

1. Does the food contain any sensitive ingredients that may contain microbiological hazards (e.g. *salmonella, staphylococcus aureus*), chemical hazards (e.g. aflatoxin, antibiotics or pesticide residues) or physical hazards (e.g. stones, metal pieces, glass)?
2. Are potable water, ice and steam used in formulating or handling the food?

Table 15.1 Hazard Analysis Form

Processing Step	Hazard Type	Significance (Yes/No)	Hazard Description	Control Measure

3. Are returned or reworked products that may present hazards used in the process?
4. Does the formulation contain additives or preservatives that inhibit or kill microorganisms or extend the shelf life of the product?
5. Are ingredients such as nitrites hazardous if used in excessive amounts?
6. Could any ingredients used in amounts lower than recommended or omitted altogether present a hazard because of microbial growth?
7. Do the amount, type of acid ingredient and the final pH of the product support the growth of microorganisms?
8. Do the moisture content and water activity (A_w) of the product affect microbial growth or the survival of parasites, bacteria and fungi?
9. Does the product require special storage conditions such as refrigeration during holding and transport?

15.4.1.2 Procedures Used for Processing

The objective of this step is to identify all realistic potential hazards at each process operation, the product flow and employee traffic pattern. In order to determine whether a hazard exists the following questions should be answered for each processing step:

1. Could contaminants reach the product during the operation through personal hygiene, contaminated equipment or material, cross-contamination from ingredients and raw materials, leaking valves or plates, dead ends splashing, etc.?
2. Could microorganisms multiply during this step to unacceptable levels?
3. Does the process include a step to destroy pathogens? If so, what pathogens? (Consider both vegetative cells and spores.)
4. Is there a possibility of recontamination with biological, chemical or physical hazards between processing (cooking and pasteurising) and packaging?

15.4.1.3 Observe Actual Operating Practices

The HACCP team must be familiar with details of operating practices. The team should observe the operations to ensure that correct practices are followed and determine if the product that is cross-contaminated could occur through handling or the equipment being used, employees not following hygiene practices, and whether there is a possibility of recontamination after this step if the processing step is designed to destroy microorganisms.

15.4.1.4 Take Measurements

It may be necessary to take some measurements of important processes with calibrated equipment in order to ensure that the operations are being performed as expected. Such measurements include:

1. Product temperature: Take the temperature at the coldest point of the product when the heating process is evaluated and at the warmest part of the product when chilling or cooling process is assessed.
2. Study the time/temperature of cooking, pasteurising, canning, storing, reconstituting, thawing, etc.

3. The dimension of the container that holds food for cooling and depth of the food mass.
4. Check the parameters important for correct process performance such as pressure, head space, venting procedure, closure integrity, initial temperature, etc.
5. Measure the pH at room temperature of the product during processing and that of the finished product.
6. Determine the A_w of the product in duplicate making appropriate corrections for ambient temperature.

For new products or when studying the shelf life, it may be necessary to conduct further studies such as inoculated pack studies and challenge studies.

15.4.1.5 Analyse the Measurements

The data obtained should be analysed by a food technologist or a person qualified in food science for interpretation:

1. Plot time/temperature measurements.
2. Interpret controlled data against optimal growth temperatures of microorganisms and temperature ranges at which they can multiply.
3. Estimate and evaluate probable cooling rates.
4. Compare A_w and pH values at which microorganisms multiply or eliminated.
5. Evaluate the shelf stability of the product.

15.5 Assessing the Hazard Potential

Hazard analysis involves knowledge of pathogenic organisms or any other agent capable of causing food spoilage of the product and poses a risk to the consumer. Complete assessment requires a broad understanding of how these hazards could arise. A detailed assessment requires a thorough examination of raw materials, processes, product and use by the consumer. Brooks and Reeves (as cited by De Silva, 2007) and Savage (1995) present some guidelines for assessment.

15.5.1 Assessment of Raw Materials

Hazards associated with raw materials can be grouped under microbial, foreign matter and those related to transportation and storage.

a. Biological hazards: Food products such as fish and meat are more prone to microbial contamination than fruits and vegetables. Chlorinated water and ingredients such as salt do not pose a microbiological risk. Factors necessary for microbiological growth must be considered when assessing biological hazards. It can also occur during uncontrolled transportation and storage. Ingredients such as salt and sugar do not require special storage conditions but chilled foods require appropriate time/temperature controls.
b. Physical hazards: Depending on the origin of raw materials, they can carry soil, metal parts, personal articles, etc. Some ingredients undergo deterioration or may be damaged during transport. The extent of damage and/or deterioration that can occur under uncontrolled conditions of transport and storage should be considered when raw materials are assessed.

c. Chemical hazards: Raw materials may be contaminated with chemicals and other pesticide residues and the possibility of such contamination should be considered in the assessment.

Assessing the risk: Cooked food items such as fish, meat and eggs have a low risk in contrast to uncooked food. Even if the hazard is eliminated at a later stage through control measures, any risk associated with raw materials should not be ignored.

15.5.2 Assessment of Processes

Each step of the process is analysed, and consideration is given to the possibility of contamination with biological, physical or chemical hazards.

a. Biological hazards: The destruction of pathogenic organisms is a critical factor in food processing operations, and if adequate controls are not in place, microbial contamination is a distinct possibility. Microbial contamination can also occur during the handling of food items. However, microbial growth will take place only if the food item is a suitable substrate for growth and storage conditions promote growth.

b. Physical hazards: Food processes are generally designed to remove or reduce foreign matter present in a food product through controls such as sieving, washing, inspection, metal detection, etc. The assessment is based on the efficacy of the process. During some stages of the process, foreign matter may be introduced. For example, plastic pieces can get embedded in the food product during a packaging operation and metal fragments or shavings can contaminate the product via faulty equipment.

c. Chemical hazards: Thorough cleaning of equipment is essential before food processing operations commence. Food that comes into direct contact with equipment is particularly vulnerable for contamination if it has not been cleaned properly. However, packaging equipment that does not come into direct contact with food products does not pose a hazard.

15.5.3 Assessment of the Product during Storage and Delivery

The storage and delivery conditions of food items depend on the characteristics of the food product. The product is evaluated on the basis of hazards associated with its stability. During the assessment storage conditions, packaging requirements and the delivery instructions necessary to prevent the product from undergoing deterioration or spoilage should be carefully considered.

a. Biological hazards: Some products such as bottled wine, canned foods and jam do not require special storage conditions, and hence there are no hazards associated with their storage. However, perishable products such as meat, fish and ice cream require critical storage conditions to prevent the growth of microorganisms. Vegetables need special storage conditions but if abused, the potential hazards are less critical. Transport plays a vital role in maintaining the food safety of chilled and frozen food items. Over long periods of transport, they may be subjected to unfavourable storage conditions (temperature/time) and hazards that can occur can be critical to food safety. Such products require special packaging to maintain the temperature/time profile.

b. Physical hazards: Food products that do not require special storage conditions or handling techniques do not pose a threat to food safety. Some food items packed in glass or plastic containers require special storage conditions during transport to prevent damage and deterioration and subsequent spoilage. Therefore, food producers should bear in mind that their products are subjected to a wide variety of storage conditions and handling techniques over long distances of transport.

c. Chemical hazards: During the storage and transport of food items, chemical hazards occur due to unclean containers. Food ingredients are also delivered to food producers and, in some instances, contaminated substances are also transported along with food products (Archer, 1990).

15.5.4 Assessment of End Use

During the last few years, consumer awareness of food safety has increased and food producers have been aware of the rise in cases of customer dissatisfaction and complaints about food products (Beard, 1991). Mishandling of food products that leads to food spoilage has been cited as one of the cases of customer dissatisfaction. Hazards can also occur during consumer use as a result of inappropriate usage and abuse by the consumer.

Inappropriate usage: Food products that can be safely consumed by the general population do not cause a threat. Some food products that can be safely consumed by a section of the population may not be tolerated by others. Consequences can be mild to severe. A classic example is peanut allergies. Symptoms can vary from skin reactions to a major reaction requiring medical emergency. Hazards that can develop as a result of incorrect labelling of food products made specifically for a certain group of people such as the elderly, diabetics, and children with allergies are significant.

Abuse by the consumer: Food products that do not require special storage conditions cause no hazards during use and handling. Some products have a low risk of being abused and require moderate care in handling. For example, bread stored outside exposed to air soon develops mould. Food items such as cooked meat require special care in handling by the consumer to prevent spoilage that may not be obvious to the consumer. Consumption of such food may cause serious illness (e.g. *salmonella* poisoning), and they have a high risk of being abused.

15.6 Critical Control Points

The second principle of HACCP is the identification of CCPs. This step follows hazard analysis, which detects potential hazards that can threaten food supply and food production. A CCP in a food processing system poses an unacceptable health risk and can be effectively controlled to prevent or eliminate hazards to an acceptable level of low risk.

15.6.1 Classification of CCPs

CCPs are generally classified as CCP1 and CCP2. CCP1 identifies a step or location in food processing that on its own effectively eliminates a food safety hazard. For example, metal detection and sterilisation steps are examples of CCP1. CCP2 is defined as a step or location in a food processing system that contributes to the control of a hazard but does not guarantee elimination (Forsythe, 2002), e.g. inspection and cold storage. Although the classification of CCPs into CCP1 and CCP2 is not recognised universally, it helps in identifying CCPs that are of crucial importance (Forsythe, 2002). Another reason is that CCP2s are generally included in PRPs (Surak, 2009).

It is important to understand the difference between CCPs and control points which are less critical in ensuring food safety. In determining the CCPs, several key points should be considered (Kirby, 1994):

1. CCPs should not be restricted to a minimum or a maximum number.
2. Each CCP is specific to a product and a process.
3. Avoid duplication of CCPs.
4. Controls should not be introduced to points where they are not necessary.
5. Consult an expert when there is doubt about a product or a process.
6. The development of CCPs requires common sense.

Some examples of control points are presented in Table 15.2.

Even though controls may be present downstream, the opportunity of introducing controls in preceding steps should not be ignored. For example, in a filing operation, bottles are inspected for breakages and the presence of foreign matter. Even then, the bottle manufacturer has the responsibility to ensure the quality of bottles delivered to the customer.

15.6.2 Location of CCPs

HACCP is a useful tool that a food processor can apply to identify food safety hazards and risks, focus on locations in the process where they pose a threat to food safety and develop plans to control them. The actual location of CCPs depends on the nature of the hazard, ingredients, packaging, processing methods, storage and handling. Emphasis should be placed on prevention of entry rather than detection after the hazard has been introduced. It is important to introduce CCPs as early as possible in the process close to the origin of the hazard. The introduction of new hazards should always be prevented (Brooks & Reeves as cited by De Silva, 2007). Raw materials constitute the first source of food safety hazards, and they should be controlled at the origin of raw materials, i.e. supplier. This minimises raw material-related food safety risks and avoids

Table 15.2 Some Examples of Control Points

Process	*Control Point*
Prevention of entry of metal fragments	Use of sieves, meshes and magnets
Fill volume 750 ml	Fill to between 750 and 755 ml
Receiving raw materials	Select suppliers with a certified food safety programme
Labelling	Ensure the absence of foreign labels before loading into the magazine Clear the magazine of all previous labels
Performance of equipment	Implement a preventive maintenance programme
Contamination during manual handling	Ensure personnel hygiene and protective gear

unnecessary inspections on receipt. Therefore, subsequent processing operations such as washing and sorting will be more effective in controlling hazards.

Food processing operations are often associated with multiple CCPs. For example, in the production of pastry products, the following have been identified as CCPs: screening/dosing flour (foreign body contamination), freezing (microbiological development), packaging, weighing and metal detection (foreign body contamination), cold storage (microbiological development), and unloading at the premises (microbiological development) (Panfiloiu et al., 2011). The inspection of the finished product usually verifies the effectiveness of the controls introduced so far.

15.6.3 Identification of CCPs

Realistic CCPs are often confused with control points, and as a result, food processors generate a large number of CCPs for the processes, making the HACCP system unworkable. Therefore, careful consideration must be given to the identification process of CCPs. For example, the commercial process of smoked fish involves 13 steps out of which three are identified as CCPs: brining, smoking and storage (Lee, 1977). Another hot smoked fish processing operation identifies five CCPs in their 13-step manufacturing process: brining, smoking, cooling, packaging and storage (Hilderbrand Jr., 1997). There are two approaches for identifying CCPs: (a) the decision tree developed by the Codex Alimentarius Committee of Food Hygiene and risk analysis (a modified form of the decision tree) (Mueller, 2014; FAO Information Division, 1998b), which is shown in Form 15.1) and (b) risk assessment.

15.6.3.1 Decision Tree

The decision tree approach is based on responses to a series of questions:

Q1: Do control measures exist at this step or subsequent steps for the identified hazard?
This question refers to control measures such as temperature control, visual inspection or use of metal detection technology at this step or subsequent steps in the food processing operation to control the hazard. If the response to this question is "No", **and** if control measures are not required, this step is not a CCP. However, if controls are necessary for food safety, the HACCP plan should indicate how the hazard is controlled before or after the production process (outside the control of the food processor). For example, pesticide residue in grapes is controlled by the grape grower. On the other hand, the operation, product or process could be modified to ensure that an effective control measure exists.
A response "Yes" leads to Question 1a.

Q1a: Are control measures exercised through preventive actions such as good hygiene practices, personal hygiene, training, pest control, allergen control, preventive maintenance, product specifications, waste disposal, handling hazardous material, inward goods inspection, recall procedure?
A response "Yes" is a PRP and a response "No" leads to Question 2.

Q2: Is this step specifically designed to eliminate or reduce the likely occurrence of the identified hazard to an acceptable level?
For each operation, the HACCP plan must define acceptable levels. Examples of procedures specifically designed to eliminate or reduce the likely occurrence of a hazard include pasteurisation, chlorination of water, use of metal detectors, cleaning procedures, etc. Note that this process

Form 15.1   The Decision Tree

Question (Q) No:	Question	Response		
		Yes	No	
1	Do control measures exist at this step or subsequent steps for the identified hazard?	Go to Q1a	Are control measures necessary?	
			Yes: Modify step, process or product	**No:** Not a CCP
1a	Are control measures covered by preventive actions?[a]	PRP	Go to Q2	
2	Is this step specifically designed to eliminate or reduce the likely occurrence of the identified hazard to an acceptable level?	oPRP with acceptable criteria or **CCP** with clear measurable limits	Go to Q3	
3	Could contamination with the identified hazard occur in excess of acceptable levels or increase to unacceptable levels?	Go to Q4	Not a CCP	
4	Will a subsequent step eliminate the identified hazard or reduce likely occurrence to an acceptable level?	Not a CCP	oPRP with acceptable criteria **CCP** with clear measurable limits	

[a] Examples of preventive actions: good hygiene practices, personal hygiene, training, pest control, allergen control, preventive maintenance, product specifications, waste disposal, handling hazardous material, inward goods inspection, recall procedure.

applies to process operations only, and for raw materials, the response is "No", which leads to Question 3. However, if this step is specifically designed, the step is a CCP if there are clear measurable limits, or an oPRP if acceptable criteria are established.

Q3: Could contamination with the identified hazard occur in excess of acceptable levels or increase to unacceptable levels?
This question refers to the likelihood of the hazard having an impact on the safety of the product. The response to this question is based on risks, the company's complaint reports and scientific data on the subject. If the contamination does not pose a threat to health or is not likely to occur, the response is "No" and this step is not a CCP. A response "Yes" leads to Question 4.

Q4: Will a subsequent step eliminate the identified hazard or reduce likely occurrence to an acceptable level?

The purpose of this question is to identify hazards that are known to pose a threat to human health or that will increase to an unacceptable level with controls at subsequent steps. If there are no further steps downstream to control this hazard, the response is "No" and the step is a CCP if there are clear measurable limits, or an oPRP if acceptable criteria are established. However, if there is a subsequent step designed to eliminate the hazard or reduce it to an acceptable level, the response is "Yes". These step(s) should be identified in the HACCP plan.

15.6.3.2 Risk Analysis

Food safety has become a global issue with major costs to the health authorities. Several factors contribute to the introduction of hazards and the failure to reduce the hazards related to food production, delivery and service such as the uncontrolled application of agricultural chemicals, environmental pollution, the use of non-permissible additives and other abuses of food along the food chain. Therefore, food safety programmes designed to protect the consumer from foodborne illnesses have to meet several challenges: (a) changes in food processing technology and supply including more imported foods; (b) environmental pollution leading to food contamination; (c) better detection of outbreaks across various countries; (d) new and emerging pathogenic bacteria, toxins and antibiotic resistance; (e) increase in food safety awareness among consumers; and (f) development of tests that diagnose foodborne illnesses (Centre for Disease Control and Prevention (CDC), 2015). In addition, three other challenges have come into focus (Whitworth, 2014):

■ Endocrine-disrupting chemicals (EDCs) pose challenges to food regulators, as the risk-based approaches used currently do not address potential hazards because the duration and time of exposures are more important than exposure levels.
■ Nanotechnologies can be applied to food packaging to improve functionality and are also used to improve taste, enhance the bioavailability of ingredients, reduce the levels of sugar and salt requirements and slow down microbiological activity.
■ Fraud: Expansion of globalisation and complex food chains are likely to lead to more incidents of food fraud and adulteration. Although the horse meat incident fraud was not a public health issue, it illustrates consumers' concern about food content.
■ Bioterrorism: In view of the current political conflicts in the world, bioterrorism throughout the food supply chain cannot be ruled out.

Consumers are becoming increasingly aware of the safety of food additives, agricultural and veterinary chemical residues, biological, physical and chemical contaminants, radionuclide contamination, unsafe food handling practices and processing which can contaminate the food at any stage along the food chain. The level of risk to the consumer depends on the control exercised by growers, suppliers, processors and regulatory authorities to eliminate or reduce the risk to an acceptable level.

Risk assessment involves four interrelated steps (FAO Information Division, 1998c):

1. Hazard identification: Identification of hazards and awareness of their impact on food safety.
2. Hazard characterisation: Qualitative and/or quantitative evaluation of the hazard on human health.
3. Exposure assessment: Qualitative and/or quantitative evaluation of the extent of consumption or intake of the hazard.
4. Risk characterisation: Integration of the first three components to arrive at an estimation of the likely adverse effects in the target population.

Risk assessment models are generally represented as a matrix of severity and likelihood. One such approach takes into consideration the severity of the illness as well as customer complaint reports and product recalls (Lozier, 2011). Table 15.3 presents the severity and likelihood rating system. Based on the ratings, significant factors are assigned to various combinations as shown in Table 15.4. A CCP is assigned a value between 1 and 10.

Here is an example of an assessment of significance (United States Department of Agriculture (USDA), 2004):

> Process step – Receiving raw meat/poultry for the production of heat-treated shelf-stable meat/poultry.
>
> Potential hazard – Pathogens: *Salmonella*, listeria, monocytogenes, *Escherichia coli*, O157:H7, *Trichinella spiralis*.
>
> Severity: Level 2 (serious illness).
>
> Likelihood: Level D (not expected to occur in finished product because of subsequent steps of heat treatment and drying).
>
> Significance: Level 12 (not a CCP).
>
> Control measures: Receiving frozen, supplier HACCP compliant with specifications, control heat treatment and drying.

Table 15.3 Severity and Likelihood of a Food Safety Risk

	Severity		*Likelihood*
1	Fatality	A	Common (repeating) occurrence
2	Serious illness	B	Known to occur or "it has happened" (own information)
3	Product recall	C	Could occur or "I have heard it happening" (published information)
4	Customer complaint	D	Not expected to occur
5	Insignificant	E	Practically impossible

Table 15.4 Matrix for the Assessment of the Significance of Risk and CCPs

Likelihood ⟶		A	B	C	D	E
Severity	1	1	2	4	7	11
	2	3	5	8	12	16
	3	6	9	13	17	20
	4	10	14	18	21	23
	5	15	19	22	24	25

Shaded areas CCP.

15.7 Risk Management

Risk management is the process of weighing policy alternatives that are compatible with the results of risk analysis and applying appropriate control options including regulatory measures to prevent, reduce or eliminate the risk (FAO, 1997). The aims of the risk management programme are to (a) establish the significance of the identified risk; (b) compare the costs of reducing the risk with the benefits gained; (c) compare the estimated cost with the benefits to the consumer; and (d) promote regulatory and other changes to reduce the risk.

The outcome of the risk management programme is the development of standards, codes of practice, and other guidelines to ensure food safety. The outcome of the risk assessment process, food processing, quality and food safety requirements, food handling and distribution requirements, and food quality and food safety standards, to control hazards in food production contributes to risk management decisions. These decisions are implemented and the effectiveness of control measures is monitored to ensure that the food safety objectives are met (FAO Information Division, 1998c).

15.8 Risk Communication

Risk communication is the final element of the risk analysis process. According to the United States Academy of Science, it is an interactive process of sharing information and opinion among individuals, groups or institutions about the nature of risk and related matters. The responsibility for quality and food safety depends on each person involved in all stages of the food chain including consumers. They require access to appropriate information on potential hazards and precautions to be taken to eliminate or reduce risks. In addition, consumers should be aware of the control measures exercised by regulatory authorities to ensure food safety.

The purpose of risk communication is to educate the general public and specific target groups such as immunodeficient, elderly, diabetic, etc., on food hazards and their risk to their general health and wellbeing. Communication provides the information necessary to prevent, minimise or reduce risks associated with food intake to acceptable levels through voluntary or regulatory control measures. This information enables consumers to exercise their own control measures to protect their health (FAO Information Division, 1998c).

15.9 Establishing Critical Limits for Each CCP

At each CCP, critical limits should be established and specified. Critical limits are criteria that separate acceptability from unacceptability. They define the boundaries that are used to determine whether an operation is yielding a safe product. Critical limits should be established for operations such as storage, thawing, hot holding, cooling, reheating, cold holding, etc. Measurable limits are often defined by time, temperature, physical attributes, acidity, pH, moisture content, water activity, salt concentration and chlorine levels. The limits may be derived through various sources: experiments through validation, regulatory requirements, codes of practice and other valid sources. If the information needed to set critical limits is not available, a conservative value or regulatory limit should be selected. The rationale for the selection should be included in the HACCP plan.

15.10 Establishing Operating Limits for Each CCP

An operating limit is a form of interference to adjust the deviation when there is a trend towards a lack of control at a CCP (FAO Information Division, 1998d). The operators can then take action to prevent the loss of control of the CCP before the critical limit is exceeded. Operating limits should not be confused with critical control limits. They are more restrictive and are set at a level that would be reached before the critical limit is violated. For example, the pasteuriser temperature control may establish 160°F and 165°F as the operating limit. When the temperature starts drifting downward, operators can adjust the process before the temperature reaches 160°F. However, if the adjustment is made after the temperature drops below 160°F, then corrective action is required to address the production during that timeframe. Operating limits may be established for various reasons:

1. Quality: Higher cooking temperature for enhancing the flavour or product texture.
2. Avoids exceeding the critical control limit (see example above).
3. Accounts for normal variability: Setting a cooker with a 2°F variability at least 2°F above the critical control limit to prevent violating the critical control limit.

Table 15.5 shows some examples of critical control limits.

Table 15.5   Examples of Critical Control Limits

Hazard	CCP	Critical Control Limit
Pathogenic bacteria (non-sporulating)	Pasteurisation	72°C for at least 15 seconds
Metal particles	Metal particles detection	Metal particles larger than 0.5 mm
Pathogenic bacteria	Oven drying Acidification step	A_w less than 0.85 for controlling growth in dry food products Maximum pH at 4.6 to control *Clostridium botulinum*
Excessive nitrite	Curing Brining	Maximum 200 ppm of sodium nitrite in finished product
Food allergens	Labelling	Declaration of all ingredients on the label
Histamine	Receiving fish	Maximum 25 ppm of histamine in evaluating tuna for histamine
Salmonella growth on chilled, ready-to-eat food if held above safe temperature	Receiving ready-to-eat food product	Check temperature on receipt • Reject if >5°C • If at or below 5°C place in the appropriate refrigerator awaiting inspection and further processing

15.11 Establishing Monitoring Systems for Each CCP

Monitoring is defined as planned measurement or observation to ensure that CCPs are under control. It is the fourth principle of HACCP. Monitoring should be carefully defined so that loss of control can be detected. The procedure must clearly specify the parameter to be monitored, the method of monitoring, the physical location of the process where monitoring should be performed and by whom. The purpose of monitoring includes (a) evaluation of the effectiveness of the system's operation at the CCP; (b) detection of deviation from critical control limit before it is violated; and (c) provision of evidence that the performance level of the operation meets the requirements of the HACCP plan (FAO Information Division, 1998e; Norton, 2003a).

Continuous monitoring is more effective in identifying drifts than non-continuous monitoring, allowing timely corrective action to be taken. When monitoring is performed at time intervals the frequency of monitoring should provide confidence that CCPs are under control. When monitoring systems are designed, it is necessary to consider the time lapse between the measurement and the results. The higher the frequency of monitoring the lesser the amount of product affected in case of a deviation from the critical limit. Online measurements provide rapid results but they are not always possible. Microbiological tests provide results after a few days, and therefore, finished products should be held under quarantine until the test results are known. Monitoring equipment used for measurements should be calibrated regularly.

There are two kinds of monitoring: measurement monitoring and observation monitoring (Norton, 2003a). The choice depends on the nature of the critical limit, practical issues of monitoring methods, the cost of measurement method compared to the cost of a potential settlement in case of a food safety incident and the time delays involved in specific techniques.

Observation monitoring involves the use of checklists customised to each operational area. They include sensory and visual checks (sight, smell and taste), visual observations for physical characteristics (presence of foreign objects and package integrity) and checks for hygiene and cleanliness. Observation monitoring is generally easy to implement but has some disadvantages. The results of observation monitoring often require interpretation, and therefore, the operators need to be trained to make judgement calls.

Measurement monitoring involves instrumentation and can be automated. The results are unambiguous and do not require subjective judgement. Measurement techniques can be designed for easy interpretation. The results will also demonstrate trends and highlight deviations.

15.12 Taking Corrective Action

HACCP Principle 5 requires corrective action to be taken when there is a deviation from the critical limit of a CCP. The main purpose of HACCP is to prevent the occurrence of problems, and therefore, food processors should build in preventive corrective action. Therefore, there are two levels of corrective actions: actions to prevent deviation from happening and actions to resolve the deviation and deal with potentially unsafe product. In the latter case, the root cause has to be identified to prevent it from happening again.

15.12.1 Adjusting the Process to Maintain Control and Prevent a Deviation

This is achieved through the operating limits discussed earlier. A continuous monitoring system will automatically adjust the system when a drift is detected. For example, in the milk pasteurising process, automatic divert valves open up, pumping the milk back to the unpasteurised section when the pasteurising temperature falls below the operating limit. Corrective action may also be performed manually by an operator when a deviation is detected. Parameters that are often adjusted to maintain control include temperature and/or time, pH/acidity, ingredient concentrations and flow rates (Mortimore & Wallace, 2013).

15.12.2 Action to Be Taken Following a Deviation at a Control Point

Following a deviation, quick action has to be taken to (a) bring the process under control and (b) deal with the potentially unsafe product. Potentially unsafe products should be placed on hold, the situation assessed and further investigations conducted.

15.13 Verification

Verification is the sixth principle of HACCP. It is the process of documenting that all the methods, procedures, tests and other evaluations in the HACCP plan are taking place as expected. This is usually accomplished through checklists to help determine if the HACCP programme is functioning according to the plan and whether correct procedures are being followed. Verification activities include (a) a total review of the HACCP plan and associated records; (b) a review of deviations; and (c) confirmation that all CPPs are under control. Although it is carried out at planned intervals on completion of the study, verification may also have to be performed when there is a change in ingredients, products or process, whenever a deviation occurs or a new hazard is identified (Norton, 2003b). Some of the verification activities are given below:

1. Audits covering all areas of the food process operation.
2. Review of menus and recipes and conformation that documented procedures are being followed.
3. Maintenance and calibration checks of equipment.
4. Verification and adherence to flowcharts.
5. Checking time/temperature records.
6. Cross-contamination possibilities.
7. All records including relevant training records.
8. Corrective action reports.
9. Compliance with regulatory requirements.

It shall be carried out at planned intervals on completion of the study.

15.14 Documenting and Record-Keeping

The last principle of HACCP is record-keeping, and it is an essential requirement of the HACCP programme. Record-keeping demonstrates the history of the process, its measurements, deviations at CCPs and the corrective actions taken. It is also an essential regulatory requirement. Regulations governing food processing dictate the type of records to be maintained by the food processor. For example, according to the FDA's HACCP regulations, seafood operators are expected to document and follow basic sanitation requirements apart from other requirements (Rooney & Kilkelly, 2002).

Four types of records should be maintained by the food processor: (a) support documentation for developing the HACCP programme; (b) records generated by the HACCP system; (c) methods and procedures used; and (d) training records. Records may be in any form, e.g. charts, written procedures, electronic records, and they show the history of the processes, monitoring, deviations, corrective actions and disposal of unsafe products. Records should be regularly reviewed to ensure that the HACCP plan is effective, correct, and that relevant data are being recorded at specified intervals and operators are performing their tasks as instructed (FAO Information Division, 1998f). Records can be as simple as checklists or as complex as process control charts. The types of records to be maintained depend on the nature of the food processing operation. For example, temperature monitoring is essential for operations that use refrigerators, freezing cabinets, dishwashers, steam equipment, hot and cold cabinets and ovens. Some examples of records to be maintained are (a) pest control records; (b) premises inspection reports; (c) calibration records; (d) maintenance logs; (e) shipping records; (f) product release reports; (g) training records; (h) consumer complaints and corrective and preventive action reports; and (i) control charts as applicable (Norton, 2003c; Khanson, 2010).

A recommended HACCP manual contains the organisation's history, products produced and offered, PRPs referenced, flowcharts of processes, hazard analysis summary, HACCP master plan and forms to be used (Bennet & Steed, 1999).

15.15 Validation

While verification activity can be performed by audits and other methods at scheduled intervals, or as necessary, the effectiveness of operational processes and methods can only be ascertained by a proper validation exercise. Validation is the process of evaluating whether the HACCP plan for the product and process effectively identifies and controls all significant food safety hazards or reduces them to an acceptable level (FAO Information Division, 1998g). The HACCP plan validation includes a review of the hazard analysis, CCP determination, justification for critical limits based on scientific evidence and regulatory requirements, and determining the appropriateness of monitoring activities, corrective actions, record-keeping methods and verification activities.

A process may be verified as correct but may not be valid to produce the desired result. For example, cooling a stockpot of soup in a refrigerator may comply with documented verification procedures, but the long time required for the temperature to drop in the centre of a large container can permit the growth of bacteria resulting in the growth of foodborne pathogens and food spoilage (validation). Hence, the validity of the cooling process in the refrigerator in contrast to a blast chiller is doubtful (Norton, 2003b). Often, the equipment and procedures used are unique to the organisation and its processes, and therefore, the operating characteristics of the process will become important in the validation of a critical limit (Norton, 2003d).

15.16 Product Recall

All food processors must have a reliable and well-tested procedure to deal with a food item that has been known to be contaminated with a food safety hazard and poses a threat to the health and safety of consumers. Regulatory authorities place the responsibility on food producers to notify recalls in writing of such food products within a specified period of initiating a recall. Traceability information enables the food producer to isolate and recall affected products from warehouses, retail outlets and consumers. Recall refers to the removal of unsafe products from the distribution chain that extends to consumers. Withdrawal, on the other hand, is the removal of products from the distribution chain that does not extend to consumers. The product that is withdrawn does not pose a threat to human health. For example, a food product that has a quality defect such as wrong colour or texture or has labelling errors that is not a potential risk to public health and safety may be withdrawn from the market and is a voluntary process (Wilmcow, 2012; Ministry for Primary Industries, 2015).

There are seven steps in a food product recall procedure (Wilmcow, 2012):

1. Develop a product recall policy: A recall policy demonstrates the commitment to protect public health and provide the resources to ensure the successful removal of the product from the distribution chain extending to the consumer.
2. Develop a product recall plan: It is a documented procedure that enables the professional, efficient and effective removal of the product. The following elements may be included in the recall plan:
   - Recall policy.
   - Recall team members and their roles and responsibilities.
   - All contact details including a toll-free number (e.g. 0800).
   - Definitions of recall and withdrawal.
   - Product recall flowchart.
   - Notification list including regulatory authorities.
   - Traceability procedure reference.
   - Media contact guidelines.
   - Press releases and recall notices.
   - Product recall review procedure.
3. Test the product recall plan: A mock recall tests the food producer's ability to remove the product without actually recalling it and should be performed regularly. The objective of a recall is to evaluate the ability to track every affected product and identify the locations and contact details of the person/organisation holding the stock. Surprises may emerge that make it necessary to review the recall plan.
4. Communicate and initiate the recall: Four levels of notification are required in case of a recall: (a) within the organisation; (b) distribution chain: distributors, wholesalers, retailers and caterers; (c) regulatory authorities; and (d) consumers.
5. Manage the product recall: In order to manage the product recall successfully, the recall plan should include sources of information, risk assessment, product recall procedure, manner of disposal of affected stock and the closure of the recall.
6. Close the recall: When all the activities have been performed effectively, the recall should be formally closed so that all the interested parties know that it has ended. Food processors should also notify regulatory authorities when the recall process has ended.
7. Review the plan: This is a continuous improvement exercise to learn from the experience and apply the opportunities for improvement.

15.16.1 Recall Classification

Recalls fall into three categories according to the type of hazard involved (FDA, 2015):

Class 1: A dangerous or defective product that has the potential to cause serious harm, injury or death, e.g. food containing the *botulinum* toxin.

Class 11: A product that may cause temporary health problems or pose only a slight threat of a serious nature, e.g. a drug that is under-strength but not used to treat life-threatening situations.

Class III: A product that may not cause a health problem but violates regulatory standards, e.g. a minor container defect.

15.16.2 Media Release

The text for the advertisement placed in the daily media should comply with regulatory requirements and includes:

i. Names of the recalled products and producer.
ii. Pack size and description of packaging.
iii. Other details necessary for identification.
iv. Reason(s) for the recall.
v. The necessity to identify and quarantine the stock.
vi. The manner of disposal.
vii. Whether the hazard to the consumer is serious and, if so, indication of clinical symptoms, advice to consult a medical practitioner.
viii. A toll-free number to provide support to consumers.

15.17 HACCP and the Environment

Increasing awareness of environmental issues demands a proactive environmental approach from the food sector and a re-evaluation of competitive strategies. Sustainable development calls for a review of traditional standards of waste production, manufacturing practices, environmental management systems (EMSs) and the efficient use of non-renewable resources. The use of technologies that employ fewer natural resources such as water, energy and raw materials, a reduction in waste production and environmental impact, good operational practices, the efficient disposal of residues and the redesign of products and production methods are basic tenets of clean production.

The principles of HACCP enable food producers to identify problems early, thus preventing losses and errors and reducing waste products. In the absence of controls, unsafe finished products are produced which often cannot be reprocessed. The treatment of residues involves the use of large amounts of water, generating large amounts of effluent. A huge amount of environmental pollution is caused by discarded packaging material. Although materials such as plastic, cardboard and cans can be recycled and reused, they are not always recycled, increasing landfill use. Many of the raw materials come directly from primary producers, i.e. farms where the level of chemical contamination may pose a threat to human health. Quality raw materials sourced from reliable supplies are indispensable requisites for the quality and safety of finished products. This is achieved through the design and implementation of a good HACCP plan. Therefore, food producers and suppliers should demonstrate a greater awareness of environmental issues by means of the rational use of chemicals. Regular supplier audits are essential for maintaining an effective HACCP plan. The HACCP programme stimulates the responsibility of the food sector to achieve food safety, quality food safety and environmental protection (Cusato et al., 2014).

15.18 Case Study: Hot Smoked Salmon

1. Product description

Salmon is purchased from the salmon farms of primary processors. On delivery, they are packed in totes, iced and placed in a cooler until further processing. In the processing area, after heading and eviscerating the fish are filleted. They are brined for 24 hours under refrigeration to achieve the desired water-phase and salt content. Brined fillets are rinsed, surface-dried and hot smoked for about six hours. After smoking, they are transported to a cooler, packed in pre-labelled packaging, vacuum sealed and placed in boxes which are palletised and stored in a cooler until delivery (Seafood HACCP Alliance, 2017; Oregon Sea Grant, 1997). Product details are shown in Table 15.6.

Table 15.6   Product Description of Vacuum-Packed Hot Smoked Salmon

Product Features	Description
Product name	ABC Vacuum-Packed Hot Smoked Salmon
Product features	Hot smoked salmon containing natural flavours and omega-3
How the product is to be used	It may be eaten raw or cooked
Allergens	Not suitable for people with seafood (fish, crustaceans and shellfish) allergies
Preservatives/additives	None
Packaging	Frozen hot smoked salmon slices are packed in a vacuum bag and foil board. Each bag weighs 250 g. Ten 250 g bags are packed in a cardboard box
Storage	Stored in a fridge below 4°C Stored in a freezer below −18°C
Shelf life	From the date of packaging: 6 days if stored in the fridge below 4°C 18 months if stored frozen
Labelling	On individual vacuum packs and on the outer box: Product name, ingredients, net weight, allergens, nutritional data, storage and handling instructions, production date, batch number, best before /expiry date, production company and address
Shipping condition	No physical damage Delivered frozen at −18°C or below
Distribution outlets	Retail outlets
Target consumer group	General public, but not suitable for people with seafood (fish, crustaceans and shellfish) allergies

2. Flow diagram and its verification

The flow diagram breaks up the process into several sequential steps that assist with further evaluation. The process of producing vacuum-packed hot smoked salmon commences with the receipt of the frozen salmon. The steps include the entry of ingredients, all processing steps, packaging, storage, delivery and handling by the consumer. In a large food production organisation where they use many recipes, it is not possible to draw flow diagrams for each of the processes. Instead, they could be grouped together according to the method of processing, e.g. baking, cooking, chilling, steaming, cold preparations, etc. Another approach adopted by large food processors includes classifying according to the food category type, e.g. thin or thick cooking of sauces and brews, fruits and vegetables, starches, bread and bakery products, cold and hot combinations. In such instances, a single food diagram is adequate for each category (Taylor, 2003).

The accuracy and completeness of the flow diagram should be checked by the HACCP team during an on-site inspection. Its purpose is to ensure that all major process operations have been identified and the assumptions made about the movement of products and employees on the premises have been confirmed. During the inspection, the team should (a) verify the accuracy and completeness of the flow diagram; (b) detect any deficiencies; and (c) correct the flow diagram. The HACCP programme is a dynamic entity and the flow diagram should reflect any process or food safety consideration changes.

The symbols used in HACCP flow diagrams are shown in Table 15.7. The block diagram (Figure 15.1) is first prepared, and it is converted to a HACCP flow diagram (Figure 15.2) using the symbols.

Table 15.7   Symbols Used in HACCP Flow Diagrams

Activity	Symbol	Description
Operation	◯	Change in the physical (e.g., cutting of meat), chemical (e.g., pH) or microbiological (e.g. sterilisation) property of a material, mixing ingredients or separation of components (e.g. separation of bone from meat)
Inspection	▢	Control step to check product or process
Transportation	⟶	Change in the location without change in the product
Delay	D	Temporary stoppage of the process until the arrival of the next processing step. The delay associated with a process itself. Note: sterilisation is not represented by this symbol
Permanent storage	△	Keeping the product under conditions suited for the product in order to minimise deterioration (e.g. warehouse storage prior to dispatch
Combined operation	◁△▷	Combination of operation and inspection

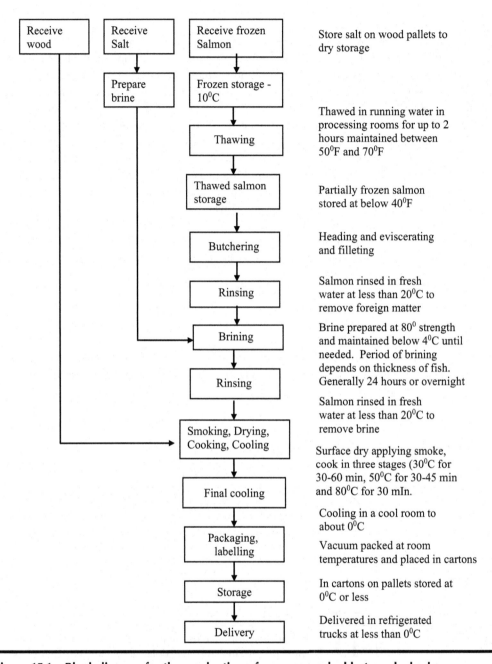

Figure 15.1   Block diagram for the production of vacuum-packed hot smoked salmon.

3. Assessment of the hazard potential

The hazards associated with raw materials, processing steps, finished product and end usage are analysed next. It will indicate the raw materials and the process steps that are critical for the operation of a safe product. The decision tree is used to identify the CCPs associated with process steps.

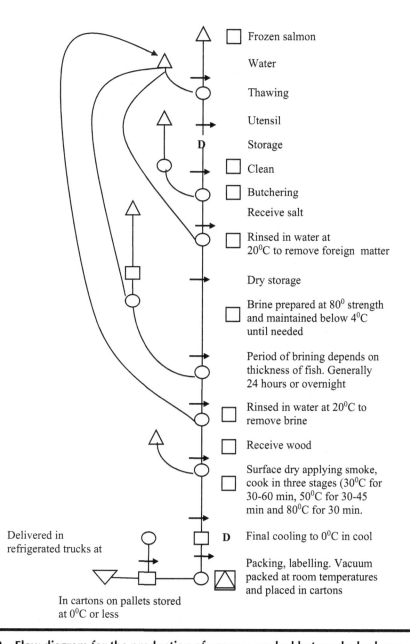

Frozen salmon

Water

Thawing

Utensil

Storage

Clean

Butchering

Receive salt

Rinsed in water at 20⁰C to remove foreign matter

Dry storage

Brine prepared at 80⁰ strength and maintained below 4⁰C until needed

Period of brining depends on thickness of fish. Generally 24 hours or overnight

Rinsed in water at 20⁰C to remove brine

Receive wood

Surface dry applying smoke, cook in three stages (30⁰C for 30-60 min, 50⁰C for 30-45 min and 80⁰C for 30 min.

Delivered in refrigerated trucks at

Final cooling to 0⁰C in cool

Packing, labelling. Vacuum packed at room temperatures and placed in cartons

In cartons on pallets stored at 0⁰C or less

Figure 15.2   Flow diagram for the production of vacuum-packed hot smoked salmon.

a. Raw materials

The assessment of hazard potential is shown in Tables 15.8–15.11.

Fish is an ideal breeding ground for pathogens such as *Clostridium botulinum*, *Listeria monocytogenes* and parasites. Throughout the handling process, adequate care has to be taken to prevent the growth of microorganisms. Fish should be packed in ice until delivered to the processing plant. Potential chemical contaminants may be due to allergens,

Table 15.8   Hazard Potential of Raw Materials

Raw Material/ Ingredient	Hazard Type	Significance (Yes/No)	Hazard Description	Control Measure
Receive salmon	Biological Physical Chemical	Y (High) Y (Moderate) Y (High)	Pathogenic bacteria survival growth unlikely. Parasites, *C. botulinum toxin*: not likely to occur in frozen state Foreign matter Allergens	Raw fish and end product frozen Supplier – primacy processor, HACCP compliant with controls and specifications Smoking /cooking step Butchering step Precautions on the label
Frozen storage	Biological Physical Chemical	Y (High) N N	Pathogenic bacteria survival. Growth unlikely Parasites, *C. botulinum toxin*: not likely to occur in frozen state	Frozen storage Hazard is controlled at brining, smoking, cooking step
Receive dry ingredients	Biological Physical Chemical	N N N	Foreign matter unlikely	Inspection on receipt
Food contact packaging	Biological Physical Chemical	N Y (Moderate) N	Pathogenic bacterial at supplier level unlikely Foreign matter at supplier level Sanitising chemicals at supplier level unlikely	Supplier HACCP compliant Inspection on receipt Supplier HACCP compliant
Dry storage of packaging	Biological Physical Chemical	N N N		None
Weighing salt and sugar	Biological Physical Chemical	Y (Low) N N	Microbial contamination from hands and equipment Cleaning chemicals from equipment unlikely	Personal hygiene Clean and disinfect equipment Cleaning procedure
Processing aid – water	Biological Physical Chemical	N Low N	Presence of water-borne pathogens unlikely in potable water Foreign matter such as sand, dirt Presence of chemical residues pathogens unlikely in potable water	Potable water from a reliable municipal system used for processing. Samples analysed

Production of hot smoked salmon.

environmental and chemical residues, and sanitation chemicals. Physical contaminants may be due to the presence of foreign materials such as nails, bits of wood, dust, etc. Packaging material that come into contact with fish may harbour microorganisms, and therefore, the packaging supplier should have a HACCP compliant programme to ensure that food contact materials are free from biological, chemical or physical hazards.

b. Process

Table 15.9 presents the hazards associated with processing steps.

Table 15.9 Hazard Potential of Processes

Processing Step	Hazard Type	Significance (Yes/No)	Hazard Description	Overall Risk
Thawing	Biological	Y (High)	Pathogenic bacteria survival but growth unlikely. *C. botulinum* toxin unlikely due to absence of low oxygen packaging	Monitor semi-defrosting
	Physical	N		
	Chemical	N		
Cooling	Biological	Y (High)	Growth of pathogenic bacteria on long term storage	Monitor temperature; Smoking step
	Physical	N		
	Chemical	N		
Butchering	Biological	Y (Moderate)	Contamination from hands. Pathogenic bacteria survival Foreign matter unlikely	Personal hygiene. Controlled at brining, smoking and cooking step Inspection. Brining and rinsing will remove any foreign matter. Possibility of introducing metal fragments unlikely. No historical problem.
	Physical	N		
	Chemical	N		
Rinsing	Biological	N		
	Physical	N		
	Chemical	N		
Brining	Biological	Y (Low)	*C. botulinum* growth and toxin production in finished product. Salt content in the fish is insufficient to inhibit growth	Proper brining. Hazard is controlled at the smoking/cooking step
	Physical	N		
	Chemical	N		
Rinsing	Biological	N	Microbial growth unlikely due to short time	
	Physical	N		
	Chemical	N		

(Continued)

Table 15.9 (*Continued*)   Hazard Potential of Processes

Processing Step	Hazard Type	Significance (Yes/No)	Hazard Description	Overall Risk
Drying	Biological	Y (Moderate)	Salt content in the fish is insufficient to inhibit growth	Hazard is controlled at the smoking/ cooking step
	Physical	N		
	Chemical	N		
Smoking/ cooking	Biological	Y (High)	Survival of bacterial pathogens; Growth of pathogenic bacteria if temperature/time is abused. *C. botulinum* toxin could form in the finished product	Adequate cooking is essential to inactivate the bacterial pathogens in raw materials and those introduced during processing. Controlled by proper smoking and cooking
	Physical	N		
	Chemical	N		
Cooling	Biological	Y (High)	Growth of pathogens	Controlled by operational procedures. Combination of salt and smoke inhibits pathogen growth. Reasonably unlikely due to the time of cooling
	Physical	N		
	Chemical	N		

The processing facility should maintain a hygienic environment and be clean with disinfected equipment and an employee personal hygiene programme to minimise or eliminate the chances of any contamination. The brining process has to be carried out under refrigeration because high temperatures can lead to pathogen growth. Immediately after brining, the product should be maintained below 4°C before further processing. The most critical step is the smoking step. It should be designed to eliminate *L. monocytogenes* by holding the product at a suitably high temperature for a sufficiently long period. The internal temperature should be continually monitored and recorded to ensure that an adequate temperature is reached. The smoking temperature of 80°C for 30 minutes is based on the coldest part of the fish in the oven. Uncontrolled temperature during packaging, storing and distribution can also allow pathogens to grow. It is important to specify the storage temperature of the product on the label so that consumers are aware of the danger of storing the product outside the stated limits.

c. **Packaging**

Packaging steps include vacuum packaging, labelling, boxing, cold storage until distribution and delivery. Hazard potentials are presented in Table 15.10

d. **Product**

It is important to have refrigerated trucks in good working condition to ensure that the finished product is maintained under controlled conditions. Microbial growth can

Table 15.10   Hazards Potential of Packing Hot Smoked Salmon

Processing Step	Hazard Type	Significance (Yes/No)	Hazard Description	Overall Risk
Vacuum packing/ weighing/ labelling	Biological	Y (High)	Introduction of bacteria during packing/labelling	Packing procedure Apply correct label Indicate storage conditions on the label (−18°C)
	Physical	N	Foreign matter	
	Chemical	N	Presence of allergens	
Boxing	Biological	N	Microbiological contamination unlikely	Packaging procedure
	Physical	N	Period of time at this step	
	Chemical	N	is short	
Cold storage	Biological	Y (High)	Growth of *C. botulinum*, if not refrigerated.	Correct storage temperature
	Physical	N	Pathogenic bacteria	
	Chemical	N	growth if re-contaminated	
Distribution	Biological	Y (High)	Potential contamination of pathogens; Growth of *C. botulinum*, if not refrigerated.	Transported in refrigerated trucks
	Physical	N		
	Chemical	N		

Production of hot smoked salmon.

occur if storage conditions are not adhered to at the food production plant as well as during transport and distribution.

e. **End use**

The product is intended for general use. The label must comply with regulatory requirements and should specify any colourants and additives added, storage conditions and the expiry date (Table 15.11).

Table 15.11   Hazard Potential of End Use

Processing Step	Hazard Type	Significance (Yes/No)	Hazard Description	Control Measures
Storage	Biological	Y (Moderate)	Growth of pathogenic bacteria, if not properly stored Seafood allergy	Correct labelling instructions Allergy warning on the label
	Physical	N		
	Chemical	Y (High)		
Consuming after shelf life	Biological	Y (Low)	Growth of pathogenic bacteria Possibility of chemical changes	Correct instructions on the label Correct instructions on the label
	Physical	N		
	Chemical	Y (Low)		

Production of hot smoked salmon.

4. Identification of CCPs

Form 15.1 and Table 15.12 show the decision tree and its application to the process. Raw fish may carry pathogenic bacteria and parasites. Risk assessment must take into account the severity of outcome and the likelihood of occurrence of the hazard. Throughout the process, the growth of pathogenic bacteria such as *Clostridium botulinum* and *Listeria. Monocytogenes* is a potential hazard that can lead to serious illness. The likelihood of triggering the event is extremely low (Huss, 1993). Pathogenic organisms grow at temperatures exceeding 1°C, and they compete with spoilage flora, which grows at temperatures below 1°C. Therefore, the fish is likely to be spoiled before the production of toxins or the development of a high number of pathogens. However, when products are cooked before consumption, the risk is totally eliminated. Thus, receiving fish is not a CCP.

Brining is an essential step in the production of hot smoked salmon because the salt content of the fish in combination with the smoke and heat treatment is necessary to control the growth of microorganisms. Cases of contamination of hot smoked salmon with *L. monocytogenes* have been reported (Flick, 2010). Because of the critical nature of brining, smoking and cool storage operations and known instances of contamination, they are classed as CCPs (Table 15.12).

5. Risk control and reduction

It is well established that fish is a main source of microbial contamination. On receipt, raw fish should be carefully examined for freshness and wholesomeness. All parts of the fish not being used should be kept below 1°C. Frozen fish should also be checked for wholesomeness. The food processor should ensure that cleanliness of the plant and equipment, a hygienic environment and personal hygiene are maintained to minimise food contamination risks. During frozen fish storage, the temperature of the storage facility can be monitored by continuous surveillance through security alarms. The smoking/cooking step is critical and the internal temperature of the fish can be monitored using thermocouple probes in the three thickest fish in the coldest part of the oven. A sample from each load should be tested for the water-phase salt level. The cooling step after smoking should be controlled because of the possibility of microbial growth if the cooling period is too long.

In order to prevent abuse by the consumer, integrated labels may be applied to the finished product to indicate any abuse of temperature. Tamper-evident packaging will provide further security against intended or unintended contamination. Automatic labelling systems with alarms will ensure the application of the correct label on every pack. A CCP control schedule is shown in Table 15.13.

15.19 Role of GMPs and ISO 22000

The GMP code of practice is complementary to any food safety programme. In a food processing operation, there are CCPs and control points. These control points can be effectively controlled by implementing GMPs. Some of the controls covered by the GMP code of practice include:

- Inspection and storage of raw materials.
- Cleaning of equipment.
- Use of food-grade detergents and disposable gloves.
- Training in personal hygiene.
- A preventive maintenance programme.
- Use of status labels.

Table 15.12   Critical Control Points (CCPs) for Vacuum-Packed Hot Smoked Salmon

Process Step	Significant Hazard	Q1	Q1a	Q2	Q3	Q4	CCP (Yes/No)
Receive salmon	Microbial contamination	Yes	Yes (PRP1 and PRP2)				No
Cool storage	Bacterial growth on long-term storage	Yes	Yes (PRP2)				No
Receive salt and sugar	Foreign matter	Yes	Yes (PRP2)				No
Weighing salt and sugar	Microbial contamination from hands and equipment	Yes	Yes (PRP3)				No
Mixing ingredients	Microbial contamination from hands and equipment	Yes	No	No	Yes	Yes	No
Cooling after thawing	Growth of pathogenic bacteria on long term storage	Yes	No	No	Yes	Yes	No
Butchering	Microbial contamination from hands and equipment	Yes	No	No	Yes	Yes	No
Brining	*C. botulinum* growth and toxin production in finished product	Yes	No	Yes			**Yes CCP**
Drying	Microbial growth	Yes	No	No	Yes	Yes	No
Smoking/Cooking	Survival of bacterial pathogens	Yes	No	Yes			**YES CCP**
Vacuum packing and labelling	Introduction of bacteria during packaging Application of wrong label or absence of label	Yes	No	No	Yes	No	**YES CCP (oPRP)**
Cold storage	*C. botulinum* growth	Yes	No	Yes			**Yes CCP**
Delivery	*C. botulinum* growth	Yes	No	Yes			**Yes CCP**

PRP1 Specifications.
PRP2 Receiving, storage and transport.
PRP3 Personal hygiene.

Table 15.13   Control Schedule for Vacuum-Packed Hot Smoked Salmon CCPs

Process Step	Potential Hazard	Critical Limit	Controlled Method	Responsible Person	Corrective Action	Verification	Records
Brining	*C. botulinum* production in finished product	1. Smoking time 24 hours minimum 2. Minimum salt content at 80° salometer at start 3. Minimum 2:1 W/W ratio of brine to fish	Check brining time, salt content of brine and weight of fish and brine	Supervisor	HOLD Adjust salt content Longer time in brine Investigate	Review the daily record Brining method provides at least 3.5% water phase salt Finished product analysis for water phase salt	Processing log
Smoking/cooking	Survival of pathogens	Minimum internal temperature of fish 30°C for 30–60 minutes 50°C for 30–45 minutes 80°C for 30 minutes (final cooking step)	Continuous check visually at the end of each batch Monitor fish internal temperature in three thickest parts in the coldest part of the oven using thermocouple probes	Smoker operator	Recook, destroy or HOLD product Investigate	Review the daily record Identify the coldest part in the smoker Calibrate the probe at the beginning and end of production each day Check water phase salt content quarterly	Temperature log

(Continued)

Table 15.13 (Continued) Control Schedule for Vacuum-Packed Hot Smoked Salmon CCPs

Process Step	Potential Hazard	Critical Limit	Controlled Method	Responsible Person	Corrective Action	Verification	Records
Vacuum packing	Growth of proteolytic *C. botulinum* Wrong label or no label	Presence of correct label statement	Visual check of the product label in-process Correct packing method	Packaging supervisor	Relabel Check label roll	Review the packaging log daily	Packaging log
Cold storage	*C. botulinum* growth during storage	Maximum storage temperature of 0°C	Continuous monitoring of cooler temperature	Supervisor	Readjust cooler temperature HOLD and evaluate on the basis of time and temperature of exposure	Daily record review Weekly calibration report	Cooler temperature log
Delivery	*C. botulinum* growth during transport	Maximum storage temperature of 0°C	Check the temperature log of delivery truck	Driver	Return the product to production facility HOLD Investigate	Review the temperature log of delivery truck before and after delivery	Delivery truck log

Regular audits provide a means of verifying the effectiveness of procedures. ISO 22000: 2015 defines the requirements for a food safety management programme which requires the organisation to demonstrate its ability to control food hygiene throughout the supply chain. The aim of the programme is to ensure that food is safe for consumption and the standard harmonises voluntary standards. With or without regulatory enforcement, all food processors have a moral obligation to ensure that all food products that they process are safe for consumption.

References

Archer, D.L. (1990). The need for flexibility in HACCP. *Food Technology*, 44, 174–178.

Beard, T.D. III. (1991). HACCP and the home: The need for consumer education. *Food Technology*, 46 (6), 123–124.

Bennet, W.L. and Steed, L.L. (1999). An integrated approach to food safety. *Quality Progress*, 32, 37–42.

CDC. (2015). *Challenges in food safety*. Retrieved April 28, 2017 from https://www.cdc.gov/foodsafety/challenges/index.html.

Corlett, Jr., D.A. (1998). *HACCP User's Manual*. Gaithersburg: Aspen Publishers.

Cusato, S., Tavolaro, P. and de Oilveira, A.F. (2014). Implementation of hazard analysis and critical control point system in the food industry: Impact on safety and the environment. In A. McElhatton and P.J.do A. Sobral (Eds.), *Novel Technologies on Food Science: The Impact on Product, Consumer Trends and the Environment*, pp. 21–38. New York: Springer-Verlag.

De Silva, T. (2007). Hazard analysis and critical control point. In M.S. Rahman (Ed.), *Handbook of Food Preservation* (2nd ed.), pp. 969–1010. Florida: CRC Press.

FAO. (1997). Risk management and food safety. *Food and Nutrition Paper 65*. Report of a Joint FAO/WHO consultation. Italy: FAO.

FAO Information Division. (1998a). Section 3 – The hazard analysis and critical control point system. *Food quality and safety systems – A training manual on food hygiene and the hazard analysis and critical control point (HACCP) system, Module 6: List all potential hazards associated with each step, conduct a hazard analysis*. Italy: FAO.

FAO Information Division. (1998b). Section 3 – The hazard analysis and critical control point system. *Food quality and safety systems – A training manual on food hygiene and the hazard analysis and critical control point (HACCP) system, Module 7: Determine critical control points – Task 7/Principle 2*. Italy: FAO.

FAO Information Division. (1998c). Annex 2 – The application of risk analysis to food safety control programmes. Food quality and safety systems – A training manual on food hygiene and the hazard analysis and critical control point (HACCP) system. Italy: FAO.

FAO Information Division. (1998d). Section 3 – The hazard analysis and critical control point system. Food quality and safety systems – A training manual on food hygiene and the hazard analysis and critical control point (HACCP) system, Module 8: Establish critical limits for each critical control point – Task 8/Principle 3. Italy: FAO.

FAO Information Division. (1998e). Section 3 – The hazard analysis and critical control point system. Food quality and safety systems – A training manual on food hygiene and the hazard analysis and critical control point (HACCP) system, Module 9: Establish a monitoring system for each critical control point – Task 9/Principle 4. Italy: FAO

FAO Information Division. (1998f). Section 3 – The hazard analysis and critical control point system. Food quality and safety systems – A training manual on food hygiene and the hazard analysis and critical control point (HACCP) system, Module 12: Establish documentation and record keeping – Task 12/Principle 7. Italy: FAO

FAO Information Division. (1998g). Section 3 – The hazard analysis and critical control point system. Food quality and safety systems – A training manual on food hygiene and the hazard analysis and critical control point (HACCP) system, Module 11 Establish verification procedures – Task 11/Principle 6. Italy: FAO.

FDA. (2015). *FDA 101– Product recalls*. Retrieved May 4, 2017 from https://www.fda.gov/ForConsumers/ConsumerUpdates/ucm049070.htm.

Flick, K.L. (2010). Smoked fish Part III: Smoking, storage, microbiology. *Global Aquaculture Advocate*, (Jul/Aug), 31–32.

Forsythe, S.J. (2002). *The Microbial Risk Assessment of Foods*. UK: Blackwell Publishing Co.

Hilderbrand Jr., K.S. (1997). *Hot Smoked Fish Company HACCP Plan. ORESU-I-97-001*. Oregon State University: Sea Grant College Programme.

Huss, H.H. (1993). Assurance of seafood quality. *FAO Fisheries Technical Paper 334*. Italy: FAO.

Khanson, Q.A. (2010). *An Introduction to HACCP*. Canada: Khanson.

Kirby, R. (1994). HACCP in practice. *Food Control*, 5 (4), 230–236.

Lee, S.J. (1977). *Hazard Analysis and Critical Control Point Application to the Seafood Industry. ORESU-H-77-001*. Oregon State University. Oregon: Sea Grant College Programme.

Lozier, T. (2011). *Quantitative risk assessment in HACCP plans – Decisions, decisions*. Retrieved April 28, 2017 from http://blog.etq.com/bid/57850/quantitative-risk-assessment-in-haccp-plans-decisions-decisions.

Ministry for Primary Industries (2015). *Recall Guidance Material*, Version 4, MPI Information Paper. New Zealand: Publications Logistics Office.

Mortimore, S. and Wallace, C. (2013). *HACCP: A Practical Approach* (3rd ed.). New York: Springer.

Mueller, B. (2014). HACCP: Identification of CCP, CP, PRP, oPRP in the standards IFS, BRC, ISO 22000 – Practical examples. *Safefood Online*. Retrieved April 26, 2017 from http://www.safefood-online.de/en/download.php?id=15.

Norton. C. (2002). Conducting a hazard analysis. *Restaurant Hospitality*, 86 (9), 82–84.

Norton, C. (2003a). You've got to measure to manage. *Food Management*, 38, 58–64.

Norton, C. (2003b). Don't trust verify. *Food Management*, 38, 68–74.

Norton, C. (2003c). Make food safety a matter of record, HACCP step-by-step – Part XI. *Food Management*, 38(3), 82–84.

Norton, C. (2003d). Validation: HACCP's final step. *Restaurant Hospitality*, 87(6), 110–112.

Oregon Sea Grant. (1997). Hot Smoked fish company. Retrieved October 17, 2019 from https://seagrant.oregonstate.edu/sites/seagrant.oregonstate.edu/files/sgpubs/onlinepubs/i97001.html.

Panfiloiu, M., Cara, M.C., Perju, D.M. and Dumitrel, G.A. (2011). Quality control of pastry products using the HACCP method. *Chemical Bulletin of Politehnica University Timisoara*, 56 (70), 47–51.

PQRI. (2015). *Risk management training guide: Hazard analysis and critical control point*. Retrieved April 17, 2017 from http://pqri.org/wp-content/uploads/2015/08/pdf/HACCP_Training_Guide.pdf.

Rooney, J.J. and Kilkelly, J. (2002). On today's menu. *Quality Progress*, 35, 25–32.

Savage, R.A. (1995). Hazard analysis critical control point: A review. *Food Reviews International*, 11 (4), 575–595.

Seafood HACCP Alliance (2017). Commercial processing example: Hot smoked salmon, reduced oxygen packed. Retrieved June 20, 2018 from https://www.flseagrant.org/wp-content/uploads/Hot-Smoked-Salmon-ROP-September_2017.pdf.

Surak, J.G. (2009). The evolution of HACCP. *Food Quality and Safety*. Retrieved April 25, 2017 from http://www.foodqualityandsafety.com/article/the-evolution-of-haccp/3/.

Taylor, E. (2003). HACCP and SMEs: Problems and opportunities. In T. Mayes and S. Mortimore (Eds.), *Making the Most of HACCP: Learning from Others' Experience*, pp. 13–31. UK: Woodhead Publishing Limited.

USDA. (2004). Generic HACCP model for heat treated, shelf stable meat and poultry products. *Guidebook for the preparation of HACCP plans and the generic HACCP models*. Washington: USDA.

Whitworth, J. (2014). EU food safety challenges revealed. *Food Quality News.com*. Retrieved April 28, 2017 from http://www.foodqualitynews.com/Regulation-and-safety/Report-outlines-food-safety-challenges.

Wilmcow, S. (2012). *HACCP Implementation in Food Manufacturing*. Florida: HACCP Europa Publications.

Appendix: Abbreviations and Acronyms

AFNOR	Association Francaise de Normalisation
ASQ	American Society for Quality
AT&T	American Telephone and Telegraph Company
BS	British Standards
CCP	Critical control point
CEO	Chief executive officer
CFC	Chlorofluorocarbon
CFR	Code of Federal Regulations
CIGNA	Connecticut General Life Insurance Company and Insurance Company of North America
EPA	Environmental Protection Agency
FDA	Food and Drug Administration
FIFA	Federation Internationale de Football Association
FSMS	Food safety management system
GE	General Electric Company
GHG	Greenhouse gas
GWP	Global warming potential
IDCL	Infrastructure Development Corporation Limited
ISO	International Organization for Standardization
IT	Information technology
JIT	Just in time
KSPH	Karnataka State Police Housing
LCD	Liquid Crystal Display
NBC	National Broadcasting Corporation
NEC	National Electric Company Limited
PET	Polyethylene terephthalate
RRC	Rapid Results College
SAANS	SysAdmin, Audit, Network, Security
SCCM	Stichting Coordinatie Certificatie ManagementSystemen
TQM	Total quality management
UNIDO	United Nations Industrial Development Organization
WHO	World Health Organization

Index

A

Airline catering company, 27–30
    certification, 29
    plan development, 28–29
Air pollution, 234–236
    greenhouse effect, 235–236
    ozone depletion, 235
    particulate matter, 234–235
Allergen control, 292–293
Automated teller machines (ATMs), 148
Automatic identification technologies (Auto ID), 188

B

Bacillus enteritidis, 8
Balanced score card (BSC), 49–52
    align the organisation to the strategy, 49
    demonstrate leadership to drive change
        customer perspective involves, 50, 51
        financial perspective deals, 50, 51
        learning and growth perspective, 50, 51
        process perspective, 50, 51
    makes strategy everyone's everyday job, 49
    make strategy a continual process, 49
    translate the strategy into operational terms, 49
Barcoding technology, 188
Basic cost of illnesses model (BCOI), 23
Basic financial planning, 41
Batch production, 127
BCOI, *see* Basic cost of illnesses model (BCOI)
Benchmarking model, Xerox, 22
Biological hazards, 286–287, 299, 300
Bioterrorism, 305
"Black Swan" events, 65, 71, 79
Botulinum toxin, 312, 318, 319, 320
British Retail Consortium (BRC), 184
Bruntland report, 242
Business continuity plan, 74–76
Business risks, 61–62
Buyer, definition, 103

C

Canning, 7
Carbon footprint, 13
Cathode ray tube (CRT), 146
CCPs, *see* Critical control points (CCPs)
Centralised purchasing
    advantages, 108
    disadvantages, 108
CFCs, *see* Chlorofluorocarbons (CFCs)
Chemical hazards, 287, 300, 301
Chief Risk Officer (CRO), 63
Chlorofluorocarbon (CFC)-free refrigeration
    system, 184
Chlorofluorocarbons (CFCs), 8, 227
Civil War, 8
Cleaning and sanitisation, 91–92
    Sanitising methods, 92
Cleaning-in-place (CIP), 92
Cleaning-out-of place (COP), 92
Clostridium botulinum, 277, 308, 317, 322
Competitive edge, 182
Computer-aided maintenance, 135
Conference of the Parties (COP), 13
Continuous production, 128
Continuous Quality Improvement (CQI), 17
Contract warehouses, 176
Control point, definition, 296
Core food business, 86
Cost of Quality (COQ) framework, 31
Critical control limits, examples, 308
Critical control points (CCPs), 296, 301
    classification, 301–302
    definitions, 296
    establishing monitoring systems, 309
    identification
        decision tree, 303–305
        location, 302–303
    establishing critical limits, 307
    establishing operating limits, 308
Critical limit, definition, 296

CRM, *see* Customer relationship management (CRM)
CRM programmes, 202
CRO, *see* Chief Risk Officer (CRO)
Cross-docking, definition, 172–173
Current Good Manufacturing Practices (cGMPs), 85
Customer relationship management (CRM), 196

D

Decentralised purchasing
    advantages, 109
    disadvantages, 109
The Decision tree, 304
Delphi method, 18
Deming Award (Japan), 23
Design, definition, 146
Despatch, 180
Distribution, 94–95, 181–183
    complexity of, 182
    golden rules, 183
    training, 183
Distribution requirements planning (DRP), 187
Distribution warehouses, 176–177
Document storage, 175
The Dream Speech, 47

E

"Earth Summit" conference, *see* World summits
Ebola epidemic, 60
"Eco-auditing" programmes, 12
Eco-design principles, 164
ECOI, *see* Enhanced cost of illnesses model (ECOI)
The Eco-Management and Audit Regulations
        (1836/93/EC), 12
Eco-Management and Audit Scheme (EMAS), 12, 31
Eco-mapping
    checklist, 249–250
    eight eco-maps, 250
    uses of, 249
eInforming, 118
Electronic data interchange (EDI), 187
Electrophotography, 22
Electrotechnical Commission, 12
eMarket sites, 118
eMRO, 118
Endocrine-disrupting chemicals (EDCs), 305
Enhanced cost of illnesses model (ECOI), 23
Enterprise asset management, 135
Enterprise resource planning (ERP), 118
Enterprise risk management (ERM)
    components
        governance activity, 67
        monitoring activity, 67
        strategic activity, 66
        Environmental aspects and impacts
    addressing significant aspects,

assessment of significance, 261–262
assessment of positive aspects, 262
classification of aspects, 248
evaluation of significance, 258
    abnormal situation, 259
    emergency, 258
    normal, 258
    qualitative method, 258–260
    quantitative method, 259–266
        duration, 261
        probability, 260–261
        scale, 261
        severity, 261
identification methods, 249
    eco-mapping, 249
    materials identification, 249
    regulatory compliance, 249
    sub-dividing the facility, 252
    value chain, 249
    process flow diagrams, developing, 253–254
outside the organisation, 256
selected techniques
    activities, products and services, 250–252
    identification process, 252–256
using the information, 268
Environmental Cost of Quality (ECOQ) framework,
        31, 32
Environmental damage, 231
Environmental management
    history, 12
    issues, 227
    timeline, 14
Environmental management systems (EMSs), 211
    benefits of adopting, 31–32
    impact, 30
        resource-based approach, 30
    implementation, 30
        Gastonia water treatment division, 30
            background, 32
            continual improvement programme, 33
            implementation, 32–33
        Novozymes North America Inc
            background, 34
            business practicability score, 34–35
            continual improvement, 36
            implementation, 34, 36
            planning, 32
            significance score, 34–35
Environmental events and disasters
    Amoco Cadiz, 11
    Bhopal plant, 11
    Chernobyl nuclear explosion, 223, 241
    public awareness, 11
    Seveso industrial disaster, 11
    Vietnam War, 11
Environmental impact
    food and food production, 256–258

Environmental movement, 224–225
    Development in United States, 225
    global concerns, 225
Envirinmental resources, 227–232
    adequate energy supply, 229–230
    depletion, 230–232
    global consumption, 229–230
    mineral use, 230–232
    water consumption, 228–229
Environmental risks, 62–63
Environmental risks and impacts, 256
e-Procurement, 116–119
    benefits of, 118–119
    challenges, 119–120
    eInforming, 118
    eMarket sites, 118
    e-procurement cycle, 118
    eReverse auctioning, 118
    eSourcing, 118
    eTendering, 118
    maintenance, repair, overhaul (eMRO), 118
    objectives of, 117
    web-based enterprise resource planning
        (ERP), 118
    web-based tools in, 119
eReverse auctioning, 118
Escherichia coli, 92, 277, 306
eSourcing, 118
eTendering, 118
European Foundation for Quality Management
    (EFQM) model, 18
European Quality Award, 23
Externally oriented planning, 41
External risks, 66

F

Factor-rating method, 188
Finished goods warehouses, 176
Flow line/mass production, 127
Food and agriculture organisation (FAO), 295
Food and drug administration (FDA), 85
Foodborne illnesses, 276–277
    types of, 276–277
Food contamination, 287–289
    environmental conditions, 289
    handling of food, 289
    machinery, 288
    processing steps, 288
    raw materials, 288
Food control principles, 277
Food products, information sources, 296
Food safety,
    history, 275
    protect the consumer, 275–276
    refrigerated storage, 184
    risk analysis, 305–306

    risk communication, 307
    risk management, 307
Food safety hazards, 64
Food safety issues
    handling food items, 209
    promotion, 209
    stock control, 208
    storage, 208
Food safety management
    HACCP era, 8–10
    pre-refrigeration era, 7–8
    refrigeration era, 8
Food safety management system (FSMS), 277–278
    benefits of, 25–26
    impact, 23, 27
Food safety risks, 63, 64, 306
Fraud, 305
Forecast based planning, 41
Forecasting sources, 206
Franklin Research and Development Corporation
    (FRDC), 31
Fukushima Daiichi nuclear reactors, 74
Fulfilment warehouses, 177

G

Gastonia Water Treatment Division, *see* EMS
    implemntatio
Global environment, 182
Global warming, 13, 229, 234, 236
Global warming potential (GWP), 257
Golden rules, warehousing, 183
Good design features, 161
Good hygiene practices (GHPs) requirements, 24
Good manufacturing practice
    activities of, 85–86
    benefits of, 96
    definition, 123
    food safety requirements, 97
    foundation
        food control, 87
        management controls, 87–88
        manufacturing operations, 87
    fundamental requirement, 88–95
        buildings, 91
        cleaning, 91–92
        defect action levels, 95
        distribution, 94–95
        equipment, 93
        facilities, 91
        for the organisation, 90
        personnel hygiene, 90–91process control, 93–94
        production control, 93–94
        sanitation, 91–92
        storage, 94–95
        training programme, 90–91
        warehousing, 94

Good manufacturing practice (*cont.*)
    philosophy, 86, 87
    preliminary process for, 88, 89
    regulations, 88
    role, 322
    ISO 9001 standard, 96
    ISO 22000 standard, 96
Greenhouse effect, 235–236
Greenhouse gas (GHG) emissions, 13, 226
Green procurement/sustainable procurement
    checklist for, 115–116
    green products, 115

H

Halocarbons, *see* Chlorofluorocarbons
Hazards
    biological hazards, 286–287
    chemical hazards, 287
    control measures
        consumer, 292
        packaging, 289
        packaging stages, 291–292
        personnel, 291
        plant and machinery, 290
        post-processing, 291–292
        premises, 291
        processing steps, 290
        product description, 284–285
        raw materials, 289
        storage and distribution, 290–291
    definitions, 278, 296
    physical hazards, 287
Hazard analysis
    definitions, 296
    during processing, 298
    form, 297
    measurements analyse, 299
    observe actual operating practices, 298
    receiving incoming materials, 297–298
    take measurements, 298–299
Hazard analysis and critical control point (HACCP)
    control points, 302–303
    critical control points
        corrective action, 309
        classification, 301–302
        definitions, 296
        deviations, 309
        establishing critical limits, 307
        establishing monitoring systems, 309
        establishing operating limits, 308
        identification, 303–306
        location, 302–303
        maintain control, 309–310
    Cost and benefits, 278–279
    management commitment, 280
    scope, 281–282

    seven principles, 282
    team members, 284
    training, 283–284
Hazard analysis and critical control point (HACCP)
        application
    hot smoked salmon, vacuum dried
        control schedule, 324
        flow diagram, 315–316
        hazard potential, 317–321
        identification of CCPs, 321–322
        product description, 314
Hazard analysis and critical control point (HACCP)
        implementation
    airline catering company, 27–30
        certification, 29
        plan development, 28–29
        plan implementation phase, 29
    benefits of, 25
    cost structures, 24
    maintenance costs, 25
    negative tax before profit, 26
    pasteurised milk plant, 29–30
Hazard analysis and critical control point (HACCP) and
        the environment, 313
Hazard analysis and critical control point
        (HACCP) plan
    definition, 278
    development, 282–282
    pre-requisite programmes, 280–281
    documenting and record keeping, 310–311
    validation, 311
    verification, 310
Hazard potential
    end use assessment, 301
    processes assessment, 300
    raw materials assessment, 299–300
    storage and delivery conditions, 300–301
Health and Safety Authority (HSE), 187

I

Ice boxes, 8
Ice man, 8
Initial environmental review (IER), 211
    communication, 220
    features, 212–213
    life-cycle management approach, 214
    outcome of, 212
    preparation, 213–214
    purpose for, 211
    site review
        air and noise levels, 219
        chemical and chemical products, 216, 217
        company description, 214–215
        company's products, 220
        consumptions and emission, 220, 221
        energy consumption, 217

energy use, 217
  history of accidents, 216
  impact on surroundings, 219
  indoor and outdoor emissions, 219
  legal and other requirements, 215–216
  organisation's operations and activities, 215
  raw materials and components, 216, 217
  site history, 214
  transportation, 220
  transport effects, 220
  waste and recycling, 218, 219
  team selection, 213
Innovations
  definitions, 146
  highly innovative products, 149
  low innovative products, 150
  moderately innovative products, 150
  Input/output analysis, 255
Inter Agency Procurement Working Group (IAPWG), 118
International Organization of Standardization (ISO) standards, 17
Interstate Commerce Act, 171
ISO 22000, 96
ISO adopters, 19
ISO 9000 standard, 96
ISO 14001 standard, 12

J

Job descriptions, 36, 90, 193, 208
Job shop production, 127
Just-in-time (JIT) delivery, 173

K

Kitting, 179
  definitions, 172
Kyoto Protocol, *see* World summits

L

Leadership Through Quality, 22
Lean maintenance, 135
Legal requirements, 268–269
  checklist for, 270–271
  ensure compliance, 272
  identifying legal requirements, 269–270
  resources required, 269
Listeria monocytogenes, 317, 320, 322
Local warehouses, 177
Logistics, 180–181
  definitions, 173
London Stock Exchange (FTSE), 31
Los Alamos National Laboratory (LANL), 58

M

Macroeconomic analysis, 43
Maintenance management programmes
  advantages, 134
  disadvantages, 134
  predictive maintenance, 134
  preventive maintenance, 134
  reactive/breakdown maintenance, 133
  scientific maintenance management programmes, 135
Maintenance, repair, overhaul (eMRO), *see* e-procurement
Malcolm Baldrige Quality Award, 21, 23
Management systems, history
  pre-refrigeration era, 7
  refrigeration era, 8
  HACCP era, 8
Manufacturing Resource Planning II (MRPII), 182
MAO, *see* Minimum acceptable outage (MAO)
Marshalling, 180
Materials identification method, 249
Materials management (material planning), definition, 103
Minimum acceptable outage (MAO), 75
Mining operations
  air quality, 232
  energy use, 232
  impact, 231
  mine dewatering, 232
  noise and vibration, 232
  release of cyanide, 232
  release of mercury, 232
  social effects, 232
  soil erosion, 231
  water consumption, 231
  wildlife and habitat, 232
Mission statement, 42
Montreal Protocol, *see* World summits
Motorola, *see* QMS implementation

N

Nano car, 164
Nanotechnologies, 305
National Aeronautics and Space Administration (NASA), 8
National Nuclear Safety Administration (NNSA), 58
Natural resources
  biotic resources, 231
  bulk materials, 230
  macronutrients, 230
  mineral compounds, 230–231
Network planning, 182

New food product development, 167
  product formulation, 167
  product testing, 165–167
  New products
  profile of, 147
  reasons, 146–147
New product development (NPD)
  activities, 145, 147
  addressing complexities, 162
  addressing environmental issues, 163–165
  approaches, 151
  case study, 148–149
  definitions, 145
  evaluation of, 162
  factors influence
    leadership influences, 162
    organisational structure affects, 161–162
    teamwork, 162
  failure of, 163
  functional design, 161
  innovations
    highly innovative products, 149
    low innovative products, 150
    moderately innovative products, 150
  linear model, 154–158
    business and financial analysis, 157
    commercialisation, 158
    concept development and testing, 157
    external sources, 156
    idea generation, 156
    idea screening, 156
    internal sources, 156
    marketing strategy development, 157
    product development phase, 157–158
    product testing, 158
  models
  Go/Kill decision, 158
  milestone process, 166
  Stage-Gate process, 158–159
  product service model
    design phase, 160
    organisational preparedness, 160
    planning stage, 160
    post-processing phase, 161
  product testing, 167
  strategy plan
    allocate funds, 153
    define focus arenas and R&D effort, 151–152
    develop an entry strategy, 153
    establish business goals and objectives, 150–151
    establish priorities and strategic buckets, 153
    evaluate arenas, 152–153
    implement decisions, 153
  success factors, 163
  uses of, 146–147
  various categories, 147–148
Noise pollution, 238

Norma Brasileira Regulamentadora (NBR) ISO 14001
  certification, 31
Novozymes North America Inc, *see*
  EMS implementation

O

Oil spill, 11, 57, 225, 236, 237, 239
Operational pre-requisite programme (oPRP),
  definition, 296
Organisation for Economic Cooperation and
  Development (OECD), 30
Outsourcing, 182
Ozone-depleting substances (ODS), 227
Ozone depletion, 235

P

Particulate matter, 234–235
Personal protective equipment (PPE), 73
Personal selling, definition, 191
Physical hazards, 287, 299–301
Picking, definition, *see* warehouse operations
Pollution, 233–242
  acute and chronic pollution impacts, 233
  air pollution, 234–236
    greenhouse effect, 235–236
    ozone depletion, 235
    particulate matter, 234–235
  hazardous waste, 239–240
  marine and coastal pollution, 238–239
  noise pollution, 238
  radioactive waste, 240–241
  soil pollution, 237
  solid waste pollution, 239–240
  source–pathway–receptor model, 233
  thermal pollution, 241–242
  water pollution, 236–237
    sources of, 236
Portfolio management, 153
PPE, *see* Personal protective equipment (PPE)
PQRI, *see* Product quality research institute (PQRI)
Preliminary stakeholder analysis, 42
Pre-requisite programmes (PRPs), 24, 280–281
  definitions, 296
Pre-shipping operations, *see* warehouse operations
Private warehouses, *see* warehouse classification
Process
  definitions, 123
  management, 133
Procurement
  e-Procurement, 116–119
    benefits of, 118–119
    challenges, 119–120
    eInforming, 118
    eMarket sites, 118
    e-procurement cycle, 118

eReverse auctioning, 118
eSourcing, 118
eTendering, 118
maintenance, repair, overhaul (eMRO), 118
objectives of, 117
web-based enterprise resource planning
(ERP), 118
web-based tools in, 119
food processing and, 116
green/sustainable
checklist for, 115–116
green products, 115
Procurement, definition, 102
Product-market mix, 152
Production
batch production, 127
concept, 123–124
continuous production, 128
effective planning, 131–132
limitations, 131–132
objectives of, 131
flow line/mass production, 127
food processing operations, 138
job shop production, 127
risk assessment, 138–139
sparkling wine production
bottling process, 141
control operations, 141
environmental issues of raw materials, 141
food safety issues of raw materials, 140
quality of raw materials, 140
records, 144
specifications management, 135–138
control of, 136–138
standards, 136
Product quality research institute (PQRI), 295
Product recall, 311–312
classification, 312
media release, 313
Product service model
design phase, 160
organisational preparedness, 160
planning stage, 160
post-processing phase, 161
Provision of service
production and service operations
differences, 124–125
similarities, 125–126
Public warehouses, *see* warehouse classification
Purchasing
centralised *versus* decentralised, 108
contracts offer, 113, 115
day-to-day operations, 110
definitions, 102
evolution of, 101–102
features of
assembly industry, 104–105

manufacturing industry, 105
mining industry, 105
multifunctional organisations, 106
processing industry, 105
public sector, 106
service industry, 105
small organisations, 104
wholesalers, 105
objectives
cost, 103–104
others, 104
product, 103
supplier, 104
strategy, 108, 110
supplier selection process
categorical plan, 113
develop a sourcing strategy, 112
find potential sources of supply, 112–113
identify main sourcing requirements, 111–112
recognise the need, 111
select a few suppliers, 113
supplier evaluation methods, 113
weighted point plan, 113
Purchases types
capital expenditure, 107
component parts, 106
finished products, 106–107
maintenance equipment, 107
outsourcing provides, 107–108
production support items, 107
raw material category, 106
repair equipment, 107
semi-finished items, 106
services, 107
transportation service, 107
Purchasing agent, definition, 103
Purchasing management, definition, 102
Pure risk exposure, 66

Q

Quality assurance, definition, 123
Quality control, definition, 123
Quality improvement tools, 18
Quality management
history, 1–7
timeline, 6–7
Quality management systems (QMSs)
impact of, 17–20
Delphi method, 18
impact on financial performance, 18
impact on business performance, 18
Quality management system (QMS) implementation,
17–20
Motorola, 20–21
achieve zero defects, 21
certified supplier programme, 21

Quality management system (QMS) implementation (*cont.*)
  global leadership, 21
  Malcolm Baldrige Quality Award, 21
  our quality stinks, 21
  training programmes, 21
  wireless communication products, 20
  Xerox, 22–23
    benchmarking model, 22–23
    decision-making process, 22
    leadership through quality, 22
    new controls and procedures, 22

R

R&D process, 156
Real, win, worth doing (R-W-W), 156
Receiving goods, *seen warehouse operations*
Refrigerated storage, 184, 186
Regulatory compliance method, 249
Reliability-focused maintenance, 135
Risk
  assessment
    descriptors, 70–72
    risk tolerance, 70
    likelihood and impact, 70
  aware culture, 64, 77–78
  categories
    external
    preventable, 65
    strategy, 66
  communication, 65
  control and treatment, 72–74
  exposure
    pure versus speculative, 66
  identification, 69–70
  learning and reporting, 77
  nature, 60
    business risks, 61–62
    environmental risks, 62–63
    food safety risks, 63
  preventable, 65
  reporting, 77
Risk management
  benefits, 59–60
  evolution, 58–59
  guidelines for success, 80–81
  planning for, 67–68
  principles of, 63–65
  terminology, 59
  treatment options, 73–74
Risk management plan (RMP), 68–69
  implementation, 77
  measure, monitor and control, 76
  overview, 68
  problems of, 78–80
Risk matrix, 72
Risk predicting models, 79

S

Sales activities
  Environmental impact, 208–209
Safety data sheets (SDSs), 186
Sales/distribution model, 198
Sales forecasting, 204–208
  developing, 207
  process, 205–206
  sources, 206
  techniques, 206
  measuring success, 207–208
Sales funnel, definition, 191
Sales management
  addressing the problems, 196
  assessment issues, 196
  common mistakes, 199
  definitions, 191
  elements, 192
  environmental impact, 208, 209
  food safety issues, 208–209
  forces impact
    behavioural forces, 194–195
    managerial forces, 195
    technological forces, 195
  implementation issues, 195–196
  issues relating to research, 196
  management activities
    operational level decisions, 193–194
    strategic-level decisions, 192–193
    tactical-level decisions, 193
  process/model, 192, 193
  sales plan elements
    execute and measure 202
    execution and measurement, 202
    funnel, 201
    goals, targets, challenges and investments, 200
    investments, 201
    revenue model, 201
    selling cultures, 201–202
  sales strategy development
    key elements, 197
    pricing strategy, 198
    prospect segmentation, 197
    sales channels, 198
    sales/distribution model, 198
    sales funnel calculation, 198
    target market, 197
    upselling strategy, 199
  skills, 208
Sales tools, 199
Sales training and customer support, 199
Salesmanship, definition, 191
Sales process, 203–204
Salmonella, 297, 301, 306, 308
Sanitation, 91–92
  methods, 92

Scheduling
  limitations, 132–133
  process of, 132
  types, 132
Scientific maintenance management programmes, 135
Services
  classification, 128–130
  challenges, 129–130
Seveso industrial disaster, *see* environmental events and disasters
Six Sigma maintenance, 135
Soil pollution, 237
Source–pathway–receptor model, 233
Sourcing
  definitions, 103
  eSourcing, 118
South-east Asian tsunami, 57
Spare parts storage, 175
Specific, Measureable, Achievable, Realistic and Time-bound (SMART), 197
  Specifications management, 135–138
  control of, 136–138
  standards, 136
Speculative risk exposure, 66
Staphylococcus aureus, 92, 277, 297
Stock-keeping units (SKUs), 179
Strategic issues Identifying
  direct approach, 43
  goals approach, 44
  indirect approach, 44
  issues tension approach, 44
  oval mapping approach, 44
  systems analysis approach, 44
  vision of success approach, 44
Strategic Advisory Group on the Environment (SAGE), 12
Strategic management, 41
Strategic planning
  aims, 39–40
  benefits
    focus improvement, 40
    teamwork to achieve goals, 40
  definition, 39
  failure of, 53–54
  phases of, 41
  planning processes
    action plan, 48
    balanced score card, 49–52
    business strategy, 46–47
    clarify organisation's mission and values, 42–43
    corporate strategy, 45–46
    developing strategies, 44–45
    external analysis assessment, 43
    final assessment, 52–53
    functional strategy, 47
    identify organisational mandates, 42
    initiate and agree on, 42
    internal analysis assessment, 43
    review and audit, 47
    strategic issues, 43–44
    vision of success, 47
    vision statement, 48
  progressive evolution, 40, 41
Strategy implementation plan
  the "big 8 components," 48
  four basic questions, 48
Strategy-focused organisation, 49–52
Strategy formulation, 44
  business strategy, 46–47
  corporate strategy, 45–46
  developing strategies, 44–45
  functional strategy, 47
Strategy risks, 66
Strengths, Weaknesses, Opportunities, Threats (SWOT) analysis
  external analysis, 43
  internal analysis focuses, 43
Supply chain
  definitions, 103, 173
  physical flow, 181
Supply chain management, definition, 103, 173
  Sustainable development
  carrying capacity, 243
  factors affecting, 243
  objectives of, 242–243

T

Teamwork, 162
Telrad Telecommunication Electronic Industries, 20
Terrorist attacks, 60, 73, 204
Thermal pollution, 241–242
Total primary energy supply (TPES), 229
Total Quality Environmental Management (TQEM), 111
Total Quality Management (TQM), 17
TQEM, *see* Total Quality Environmental Management (TQEM)
Training
  Competence GMP requirements, 90
  Good hygiene requirements, 90
  distribution team, 183
  HACCP, 283
  recruitment and induction, 90
  sales force, 199
  warehouse, 183
Transportation, 183–184
  communication advancement, 184
  distribution management, 184
  economic impact, 184
  government regulations, 183
  interchange points, 183
  logistics facilitators, 184
  modes of transport, 184, 185
  type of cargo, 183

Transport management system (TMS), 187
Trichinella spiralis, 306

U

United Nations Framework Convention on Climate
    Change, 13, 226
United Nation's World Commission on Environment
    and Development (WCED). 242
UN World Water Association Programme, 228
US Department of Labour's Occupational Safety and
    Health Administration, 58
US Environmental Protection Agency, 74

V

Vacuum-packed hot smoked salmon, *see* HACCP
    application
Validation
    definitions, 123, 296
    HACCP application, 311
Value-added service warehouses, 177
Value chain method, 249
Vendor, definition, 103
Verification
    definitions, 123, 296
    HACCP application, 310
Vietnam War, 11
Vision, establish, 47

W

Wall Street Journal Technology Innovation
    award, 153
Warehouse management systems (WMSs), 174
Warehousing, 94
    classification
        distribution warehouses, 176–177
        finished goods warehouses, 176
        fulfilment warehouses, 177
        local warehouses, 177
        raw materials and components, 176
        value-added service warehouses, 177
        WIP warehouses, 176
    contract warehouses, 176
    definitions, 172
    environmental impact, 186

    evolution of, 171–172
    factor-rating method, 188
    health and safety issues, 186–187
    information technology impact, 187–188
    holding inventory, 173
    operations
        consolidation centres, 180
        despatch, 180
        marshalling, 180
        order picking, 179
        pre-shipping operations, 180
        receiving goods, 177
        reasons, 173
        sortation, 180
        storage, 94–95, 177, 179
        storage policies, 179
    performance assessment, 188
    private warehouses, 175–176
    public warehouses, 175
    reasons for, 173–174
    real time communication, 172
    transportation, 183–184
        communication advancement, 184
        distribution management, 184
        economic impact, 184
        government regulations, 183
        interchange points, 183
        logistics facilitators, 184
        modes of transport, 184, 185
        type of cargo, 183
Water pollution, 236–237
    sources of, 236
Wave picking, 180
Work-in-progress (WIP), 132, 162, 175
    storage, 175
    warehouses, 176
World summits, 226
    earth summit conference, 12
    Kyoto protocol, 226
    Montreal protocol, 227
World War II, 4, 58, 223
World Wide Web (www), 296
Worst-case scenario, 75

X

Xerox, *see* QMS implementation

Printed in the United States
by Baker & Taylor Publisher Services